ALICE
and
EDITH

ALICE and EDITH

The Two Wives of Theodore Roosevelt

A Biographical Novel by
Dorothy Clarke Wilson

Doubleday
New York   London   Toronto   Sydney   Auckland

About the Author

Dorothy Clarke Wilson is a well-known author of historical fiction and biography with twenty-seven books to her credit. Her latest books, *Queen Dolley* and *Lady Washington,* were selections of Reader's Digest Condensed Books, as is *Alice and Edith.* In 1988, she was the recipient of an achievement citation from the Maine chapter of the American Association of University Women and the Maryann Hartman Award from the University of Maine. She lives in Orono, Maine, with her husband, a retired minister.

Published by Doubleday

A division of Bantam Doubleday Dell Publishing Group, Inc.
666 Fifth Avenue, New York, New York 10103

Doubleday and the portrayal of an anchor with a dolphin
are trademarks of Doubleday, a division of Bantam Doubleday
Dell Publishing Group, Inc.

Library of Congress Cataloging-in-Publication Data
Wilson, Dorothy Clarke.
  Alice and Edith: a biographical novel of the two
    wives of Theodore Roosevelt:
    by Dorothy Clarke Wilson. — 1st ed.
      p.   cm.
    ISBN 0-385-24349-9
  1. Roosevelt, Theodore, 1858–1919—Family.
  2. Presidents—United States—Wives—Biography.
  3. Roosevelt, Alice Lee, 1861–1884.
  4. Roosevelt, Edith Kermit Carow, 1861–1948.
  I. Title.
E756.3.W55   1989
973.91′1′0922—dc19   89-31152
[13]   CIP

Contents

7
Part One
EDIE

61
Part Two
ALICE

137
Part Three
EDITH

245
Part Four
FIRST LADY

321
Part Five
MISTRESS
OF
SAGAMORE

394
Bibliography

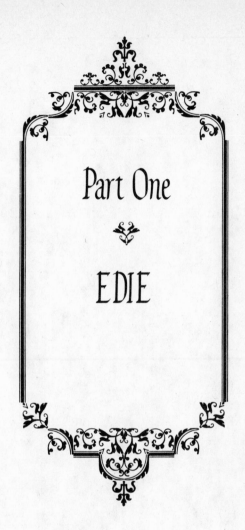

Part One

EDIE

1

"A parade?" The word conjured memories both attractive and repellent. Bright colors, lilt of fifes and bugles, rhythm of marching feet. But also the harsh blare of trumpets, the sharp glitter of sunlight on weapons, and, worst of all, the suffocating closeness of bodies.

"Och! No, colleen, not a parade. A procession, one of the biggest ye'll ever see! Somethin' ye'll niver fergit!"

The child's lips pursed. "I don't want to go," she said determinedly.

Patiently the woman continued to curl long strands of fair hair around her finger. "Sure, and of course ye do. Yer President's gone and got hisself killed, and the whole city's out to pay respect. Can't ye hear the noise in the streets outside already? There!" She gave a final pat to the bow of the child's blue sash. "Ye look rale fine, me darlin'. Now let's go and show yer marm."

Young Edith Carow was old for her not quite four years. Already she had learned to conceal her keenest emotions within a protective shell of reserve. Obediently, but with frowning brows and lips still pursed, she followed Mame, her Irish nurse, into her mother's bedroom. Here almost instantly the frown disappeared, and she was smiling delightedly over the cradle where her new sister Emily, just a week old, lay sleeping.

Gertrude Carow regarded her older daughter with obvious relief. No jealousy there of a rival for family affection! In fact, the new baby seemed to release emotions usually inhibited.

"You look lovely, dear," said Gertrude. "I'm so glad you can have this little outing with your friends. It will be an exciting day, even if not a happy occasion. I only wish I were well enough to go with you."

As the child turned from the cradle to the woman reclining on the chaise longue, her smile vanished. "Do I have to go, Mother?"

Gertrude's smile also disappeared. Her smooth white forehead between wings of beautifully coiffed dark hair furrowed. "Edie, the idea! After the Roosevelts were kind enough to invite you! And your friend Conie will be so looking forward to your coming! How could you even think of not going? Off with you now with Mame, and make sure you pay proper respect both to your hosts and to the poor martyred President." Not that I needed to tell her that, Gertrude reminded herself silently. The child was already more mature and proper at nearly four than most girls of her age —yes, and more self-assured and independent as well.

Brows still furrowed, from frustration more than displeasure, Gertrude watched the child dutifully accompany the nurse from the room. If one could only know what she was thinking and feeling! Why her reluctance today to go to the house of their neighbors, the Van Schaack Roosevelts, who had so kindly invited her to view the funeral procession with their grandchildren? Not just shyness, surely. She had gone there many times with her friend Corinne Roosevelt. She was too young to sense the tragedy of a funeral procession, this one of all others. Oh, dear, Gertrude wondered whether she would ever understand this child of hers!

"Hold to my hand tight," adjured Mame as they emerged from Livingston Place into Fourteenth Street. "Och, what a mob! Sure, and it's like tryin' to ford a river in spate!"

The distance from Livingston Place to the Roosevelt house on Broadway at the southwest corner of Union Square was short, but today it seemed interminable. Fourteenth Street was clogged with people, all pushing and jostling, trying to reach Broadway, where the procession was due to pass. It was just as the child had feared, only worse, the reason she had not wanted to come. The strings of her best bonnet came loose, the new pink one with roses under its brim. A careless hand swept it off, and though she tried to reach for it, it was trampled by someone's feet. Unprotected, her long fair hair, so carefully combed and curled, was soon disarranged and untidy. She felt soiled, mussed, her precious world of privacy invaded.

When they finally reached Broadway, the confusion was still worse. Crowds twelve- to fifteen-deep lined the sidewalks, spilling over into the streets, defying the efficient policemen to push them back. Steps, windows, eaves and roofs, even branches of trees in Union Square were filled with onlookers. One small boy was perched on a lamppost. In spite of the brilliant April sunshine there was little color. Out of respect for the occasion people had dressed soberly. The drab brownstone houses were made even more somber by long black drapings.

Mame was persistent, the child's small hand firm within her stout callused fingers. At last they reached the impressive four-story mansion belonging to Cornelius Van Schaack Roosevelt and climbed through the motley crowd, which had boldly appropriated the steps. When a servant opened the door, there was little Corinne Roosevelt waiting.

"Edie! You did come! I was so afraid you wouldn't."

"Ay, and we near didn't." It was Mame, long since graduated from the subservience expected of a servant, who made cheerful response. "And jist look at the poor colleen! Lost her pretty bonnet, she did, got knocked off and stepped on. But not to worry. We'll soon have ye as illigant as iver, me darlin'."

Competently she removed the child's coat, wiped some imaginary smudges from her face, and straightened her blue ribbon sash. Then she smoothed the untidy hair and reshaped the loosened curls. "There! Now ye've naught to be ashamed of."

"We're going upstairs," said Corinne. "We can see better from there." While Mame departed to join some of her cronies in the servants' quarters, the two girls, hand in hand, climbed the long imposing staircase. They had been friends from babyhood, Edith Carow and Corinne Roosevelt. Born within a few weeks of each other, they had been wheeled as infants in their prams side by side in Union Square Park and along Broadway between Fourteenth and East Twentieth Street, where Cornelius Van Schaack Roosevelt had built another respectable brownstone for his son Theodore.

"Teedie and Ellie are up here," said Conie as they entered a big room at the left of the stairs. "Grandpa said we could all watch from here."

The two Roosevelt boys, Theodore, nicknamed Teedie, aged six, and Elliott, called Ellie, a year and a half younger, were standing by an open window overlooking the street. "Come on, you two," urged the older boy. "You're just in time. It's starting! Hear the drums?"

The younger boy looked less agreeable. "Girls!" he muttered.

His brother pushed him summarily aside to make room for the newcomers between them. "It's one o'clock, and they're moving, just as they said they would! See those lines of soldiers? They're like that all the way down Broadway to the City Hall, sections, regiments, and brigades. They're going up to Ninth Avenue to the Hudson River railroad depot. Near a hundred thousand of 'em, they say."

The other three were suitably impressed by this glib display of knowledge. Someone more perceptive—his older sister Anna, for instance—might have suspected that his generous reception of the girls was due less to gallantry than to appreciation of a larger audience.

"How d'you know all that?" demanded Ellie enviously.

"It's easy, silly. You'd know too if you'd listen harder to Father and Grandpa. And it's all in the newspapers."

"Look!" marveled Conie, leaning so far out of the window that Teedie seized the ruffles of her full skirt and pulled her back. "It's a big parade, the biggest ever!"

"Not a parade," corrected Edie, already a stickler for accuracy. "It's a pro— a pro—"

"A procession," agreed Teedie, regarding her approvingly, and she flushed with pleasure. "It's the funeral procession of our President Abraham Lincoln," he elaborated, "who got himself killed saving our nation. Somebody shot him in a theater down in Washington. And Father says we must watch it with great sol-solemnity and respect and always remember that we saw it." The words, spoken in a rather high, thin voice, lost some of their impressiveness by ending in an asthmatic wheeze.

Poor Teedie, thought Edith Carow. As if it weren't enough for him to have such a thin, gangling body without his being cursed with that terrible asthma! Conie suffered from it, too, but not as badly as Teedie. Edie had heard that sometimes when it was impossible for him to sleep at night his father wrapped him in a blanket and walked with him in his arms, or even harnessed his horses to the family carriage and drove with him long distances at a furious pace so that the cold air would clear his lungs. Perhaps it was partly this weakness that made Teedie her favorite over Ellie, who, in spite of his propensity for headaches, seemed far stronger and healthier and was certainly better looking. Already she was developing an instinct for maternal protectiveness. But Teedie's superior attraction lay also in his ability to relay stories he had heard or read and to dispense information he had picked up. To Edie's admiration and envy, he was already at the age of six a voracious reader.

Voracious? Yes. He devoured every book he could lay his hands on. Once, Edie had heard, when he was only a very small boy in petticoats with his hair in a curl on top of his head, he had dragged down from the library shelf a huge book about David Livingstone's adventures in Africa and had been able to follow most of it through the words and pictures. But one word had baffled him. Hugging the big book in his thin arms, he went from one to another in the family asking what it meant.

"What are *foraging* ants?" he demanded.

No one could answer him, until finally someone discovered that the puzzling word was "foregoing," not "foraging."

That he applied his avid hunger for information to newspapers as well as books was now apparent.

"Twenty sections there are to a full regiment," the boy announced, "and it takes a lot of regiments to make a brigade. Look at those men with red trimmings on their uniforms. They're Colonel Le Gal's French regiment. And those regiments of horse, see them? Their uniforms have orange-yellow trimmings."

Dutifully, taking her turn at the window, Edie stared at the interminable flowing tide, for the most part a dull monotonous blue color except for the bright sunlight glinting on swords and shields and bayonets, stared until her eyes watered and her head swam. Was there no end to it? An hour passed—or was it two—or three?

"The head of the procession must have got to the station by now," Teedie went on. "It was s'posed to get there about two. The last of it might not get even here till about five. But we'll be seeing the funeral car long before that. And what a sight that'll be! I read all about it in the *Times*. It's a big thing, fourteen feet by eight, with a stage on top and the coffin on top of that. They call it a cat

—cata— something, I don't remember the word. And on top of the whole thing is something like a temple with lots of waving black plumes."

Edith's head ached. Her eyes smarted, and her feet hurt. She wished she and Conie could go somewhere and sit down, but of course it wouldn't be showing proper respect to the President. Anyway, Conie seemed as eager to watch as the boys. She would probably stay and watch all night if she knew it would please Teedie, whom she adored.

"Look! It must be getting closer, because there's the invalid corps, those who got wounded in battle. See how weather-beaten their uniforms look? They're still wearing the ones they wore in the war. How proud they must be to have done so much for their country!"

Edie looked. Some of the men were limping. Others were on crutches. There were those with only one leg or one arm. Her eyes widened in horror. She felt sick to her stomach. So that was what war did to people, besides killing them!

"There! It's coming at last. See, there's the Seventh Regiment, the guard of honor. And that platoon of policemen, they're sweeping the street clear of people from curb to curb, making sure there's plenty of room. And—yes, we can see it now, the funeral car! Move over, Ellie, so the girls can both see!"

It was huge. It towered in the air. It was black. It came nearer and nearer. *Death.* So that was what it was like: big, black, frightening. Oh, dear! Edie couldn't help it, she was going to cry. And cry she did, not just gentle, quiet tears, overflowing the eyes and running down the cheeks, but noisy, gasping sobs.

"Girls!" exclaimed Elliott in a tone of disgust. "You might know it. Always blubbering, spoiling everything."

"What's the matter?" demanded Teedie. "Scared? Well, you'd better not watch. We'll put you where you won't have to see what's going on."

Edie felt herself seized by the shoulders, propelled across the floor, and thrust into an adjoining room. "There! Cry away. We thought you were a sensible girl like Conie, not a sniveling baby!"

The door closed. A key turned in the lock.

Edie kept on crying, now from neither fright nor morbid horror but from anger and, far worse, humiliation. Ellie's disapproval mattered little. He was only about a year older than she and Conie, and they were always bickering. But Teedie! To incur the contempt of one so superior in age, in knowledge, in ability to tell stories so excitingly that it was almost like being able to read them!

It was a tearful and contrite Conie who finally released her. The boys had disappeared. "Are you all right, Edie? I didn't dare to come before. Oh, those horrid, horrid boys! And I don't wonder you cried. I almost did. That horrible big black thing—with the poor dead President inside!"

"Course I'm all right," said Edie stoically. Not even to Conie, her best friend, would she have revealed how she really felt. Fortunately the bedroom where she had been locked had contained a washstand with bowl and pitcher, and she had tried to remove all ravages of tears.

The crowds were just as distressingly rampant when she and Mame made their way home, for, though the procession had passed, a memorial service was being held in Union Square for the martyred President. A sonorous voice could be heard reciting in suitably lugubrious tones the words of Lincoln's Second Inaugural Address.

"Did you have a good time, dear?" asked Gertrude Carow anxiously. She smiled with relief when the child nodded. "There! I knew you would. It's something for you always to remember."

Remember, yes. For years the thought of it would rankle. Even the intense admiration she would come to feel for the martyred Abraham Lincoln could not quite efface it. But when more than sixty years later she would be reminded again of that day, the memory would by then cease to arouse any emotion but amusement.

"Did you ever hear that your husband saw President Lincoln's funeral?" The man asking the question was a historian writing a biography of another President.

She looked at the picture he held out, a large house with a huge mass of people gathered in the street outside, all seemingly enveloped in an aura of blackness.

"Oh, yes!" Her thin aging face lit up with tender memory. "I am sure that is my husband, and next to him is his brother." She chuckled. "That horrible man! I was a little girl then, and my nurse took me to Grandfather Roosevelt's house on Broadway so I could watch the funeral procession. But as I looked down from the window and saw all the black drapings I became frightened and started to cry. Theodore and Elliott were both there. They didn't like my crying. They took me and locked me in a back room. I never did see Lincoln's funeral."

But this was far into the future. Now, on that April 25, 1865, she was far from being amused. Small, hurt, vulnerable, she made specific if unconscious commitment to a rule of conduct which heretofore had been only instinctive: *Never reveal to others, by word or act, your deepest, most personal emotions.*

2

"Surprise!" Gertrude Carow entered the nursery, smiling brightly. "You are going to have company, darling."

Edie looked up briefly, then lowered her eyes to her book. "I know. Conie is coming."

"Not just Conie, dear. I invited all the young Roosevelt children to come and spend the day. That's the surprise. And this note just came. They'll be here right away." Noting the expression on her daughter's face, Gertrude frowned. "What's the matter, child? Don't you want them to come? I thought you'd be delighted."

"Yes. Oh, yes, of course. I—I am."

Dutifully Edie managed a smile, but she was not delighted. Teedie and Ellie coming! She had not seen them since that devastating experience of the procession a few months ago. *We thought you were a sensible girl—not a sniveling baby!* When her mother had gone, she began to work feverishly.

"Och! And what is it ye think yer doin', colleen?" demanded Mame.

"Putting away my old toys, especially the b—the broken ones." The "baby ones," she had almost said. But that would have meant more explanations. Mame would understand her desire to have everything neat and tidy for company, not her fear of revealing further proofs of her immaturity.

"Now, now," said Mame with a wisdom born of a poor immigrant's experience, "it mought be the ouldest and shabbiest they'd like the best. I 'member a tater doll I brung from the ould country with its head all wizened up and its clo'es all tatters. And it was that one I loved, not the new one wid a china face."

They came, the three youngest of the Roosevelt children, Teedie, Ellie, and Conie. Not the oldest one, Anna, usually called "Bamie" or "Bye." Edie was relieved. At the age of ten or thereabout Bamie felt herself almost grown up and superior to the childish activities of her siblings. Her presence would have inhibited Edie's confidence even further.

Besides, she had another small grievance against Bamie. It was because of her that her hero Teedie had received the first, and up to now, the only spanking of his life. She had to admit, however, that it had not really been Bamie's fault, but the monkey's. The Roosevelt children had an Aunt Lizzie, their Uncle Robert Roosevelt's wife, who lived next door on Twentieth Street. She had a monkey named Topsy, that she liked to dress in little boy's clothes, including shirt with studs and trousers. One day Topsy bit Bamie and, running off, tore all his garments in a rage and threw them on the floor, all except his trousers. The children had laughed and laughed at his antics as he danced up and down trying to get his tail out of his trousers, finally angrily tearing them off.

Teedie, in emulation of Topsy, had in a similar fit of mischief bitten Bamie on the arm, actually drawing blood; then, sensing that he had committed a crime, he had run off and taken refuge under the kitchen table, grabbing a handful of wet dough from the top before his disappearance. His father had followed him and, finding his whereabouts, had dropped down on all fours and reached for him. Teedie had thrown the dough straight into his father's face, then escaped on the other side of the table and run upstairs. His father had caught him and delivered thorough chastisement.

No, fortunately Bamie had not come. But to Edie's surprise the children were accompanied, not by their nurse Dora, but by their aunt, Miss Anna Bulloch, "Auntie Annie."

When Mother brought Miss Bullock into the nursery, Edie anxiously scanned her face. Her parents did not approve of the wife and sister-in-law of Conie's father, the older Theodore Roosevelt. She had often heard them talking. Martha Roosevelt and her sister were Southerners, from a place called Georgia. In the war their sympathies had been all with the South. Their brothers had been fighting, yes, even trying to kill Roosevelt men who were risking their lives to save the country. Probably they had been happy, not sad, that awful day of the funeral procession.

"That poor Mr. Roosevelt!" she had heard her mother say. "Torn between devotion to his wife and loyalty to his country."

"Yes," Charles Carow had agreed. "I know it made him heartsick, feeling that he had to hire someone to go as a soldier in his place. But he managed to make his contribution to the Union cause all the same, and a bigger one than if he had actually fought."

"I don't understand. Just what did he do?"

"Hearing how the families of Union soldiers were suffering for lack of funds, he got legislation passed in Congress to establish a fund for family support to which soldiers could contribute from their pay. Then he traveled tirelessly, for long months, through the camps, riding on horseback through mud and cold day after day, persuading the men to contribute to the fund and helping to provide millions of dollars to homes where it was desperately needed."

"Well—good for him." Gertrude Carow had sounded only mildly approving. "And of course the children are properly patriotic. But don't expect me to be more than decently courteous to those Roosevelt women. Why, it's said that Martha even dared to hang a Confederate flag out the window after a Southern victory!"

Edie could have told them of another pertinent incident related to her by a gleeful Conie. One night Teedie had been saying his prayers at his mother's knee. Peeved by what he considered unjust discipline during the day and knowing that she would not dare to interrupt his petitions, he had wheezily but furiously called down the wrath of the Almighty to "grind the Southern troops to powder." Fortunately Mittie Roosevelt had a sense of humor. Not so Auntie Annie, when he had tried the same trick on her. She had not been amused.

Though too young to fully understand the situation, Edie had astutely absorbed its essentials. A war was being fought. Mother and Father and almost everybody else, including most of the Roosevelts, were on one side, the right one. This aunt of Conie's was on the other, the wrong one. Now here they were together like armies on a battlefield. What would happen? She waited with baited breath. But Mother was smiling, greeting the guest cordially, inviting her to come with her to inspect the roses in the garden. So the war was really over, in more ways than one. She drew a long breath of relief.

She was even more relieved because her humiliation at Lincoln's funeral procession had apparently been forgotten.

"What a jolly nursery!" Ellie exclaimed, making a hasty tour of the room and fingering one object after another. "O-oh! Just look at this!"

He pounced on the model of a ship, ancient and battered, which Edie had neglected to put away. "It's a clipper ship," she explained. "It's made like one my grandfather Isaac Carow used to sail in, all over the world, bringing back things to sell. That's what my father does, too, runs merchant ships. But it's just an old thing, one of its masts broken."

"It's—wonderful!" Ellie regarded her with almost as much admiration as the model. "Aren't you lucky! The Roosevelts have done nothing but farm and own land and sell things like hardware and glass. Sometime I'm going to travel on a ship, maybe as far as Europe." He settled himself on the floor with his dilapidated prize. "I could play with this thing all day."

So Mame was right. It was the old, sometimes broken things they liked best. Conie, as usual, was engrossed in the old dollhouse which Edie's mother had played with as a child up in Norwich, Connecticut. And Teedie. Yes, for once he was standing stock-still in front of probably the oldest and sorriest object in the room, a stuffed parrot which one of the Carow ancestors had brought back from some country, half its feathers gone, the rest limp and bedraggled. He looked like a child confronting his first dazzling Christmas tree.

But Teedie never stood still for long. Presently he was striding up and down the room, thin arms gesticulating, talking in his high wheezy voice. This time he was not telling a story, as he so often did, perhaps about Daniel Boone or Davy Crockett or some other hero about whom he had heard or read, but recounting one of his own recent adventures.

He had been walking up Broadway and was passing the market where he was sent sometimes to buy strawberries, and there he saw stretched out on a slab of wood a big dead seal. How romantic! he had thought. Where had it come from? He had to know everything he could about it. It had been killed in the harbor, he had been told.

"I kept going back," Teedie squeaked excitedly. "I tried to measure it, to see how big it was around, but I didn't have a tape measure. I had to do it with a little folding rule. I wrote it all down in a book, and you know what? I'm going to write a history, everything I can find out, about lots of animals."

His siblings were not impressed. They were used to his extravaganzas. "You and your old dead seal!" scoffed Ellie. Conie did not even turn from her preoccupation with the dollhouse.

But Edie was fascinated. "You mean you're really going to write a book?" Her blue eyes shone with excitement.

"Well—maybe, sometime." Teedie turned suitably modest. "Now I've just got to learn everything possible. And the seal is still there. I go to see it every day."

"We have a book about animals," Edie suggested helpfully.

"You have? Does it tell about seals? Let's see it."

Running downstairs to the library, she returned with a large volume. Presently, coming to tell them their lunch would soon be ready, Anna Bulloch found the two of them crouched on the floor over the open book, excitedly studying a picture.

"Look!" exclaimed Teedie. "That looks like it, but—no, it's got horns."

"See what it says." Edie pointed to the writing below. "It's a w-a-l-r-u-s."

"A walrus," pronounced Teedie. "I've heard of them. They're like seals."

"And down here," pointed Edie, "it calls it a—some kind of h-o-r a horse!"

"So it does. A whale horse."

Aunt Annie watched and listened, eyes widening. "Child," she said finally to Edie, "do you mean you can actually read? And you're not yet four?"

"Not m-much." Edie stammered in embarrassment. "Just—just a few words, when the letters are big."

Sensing the child's distress, Aunt Annie hastily sought diversion. "Come," she said, taking a chair. "Let me tell you all a story. We've got just time before lunch."

There was a delighted chorus. "Oh, yes, please!" Conie instantly deserted the dollhouse, and Ellie looked up expectantly. "Tell about Br'er Rabbit and the Fox, the one about Tar Baby!"

"These Br'er Rabbit stories," explained Auntie Annie to Edie, "were told in the Negro cabins on our plantation in Georgia. They are legends, handed down for years. It's even said that they were brought long ago from Africa." She settled herself comfortably and began. "Yo-all see, Br'er Fox was always a'tryin' to catch poor Br'er Rabbit. One day he fixed up a kind of doll made outer tar an' turpentine, set it in de big road, an' hid to see what would happen. He didn't hafta wait long, 'cause soon here come old Br'er Rabbit . . ."

Edie was enthralled, her embarrassment forgotten. The voice, low and melodious with its soft Southern drawl, lured one into a different world. No wonder Teedie could tell stories so excitingly, with Auntie Annie for his teacher. She agonized with poor Br'er Rabbit, getting both his hands and feet, even his head, stuck fast in the tar, while Br'er Fox "rolled on de groun' an' laughed an' laughed" at the thought of his coming dinner; sighed with relief when Judge Bear came along and set Br'er Rabbit free.

It was the happiest day she had ever spent. They had lunch in the garden with all her favorite food, even ice cream and cake. Auntie Annie told more stories. But it was over far too soon. Watching her friends prepare to leave, she felt bereft. When would she see them again? Conie, of course—their nurses would take them to the park. But the boys, especially Teedie? Would she ever hear what happened to the seal?

"Your little Edith is very bright," Anna Bulloch was saying to Gertrude. "I was surprised at how well she can read. She is ready for schooling."

"Yes. I know. We should be getting her a governess, but—perhaps a little later. It's impossible right now."

Gertrude's lips clamped tightly together, and there was a sudden narrowing of her huge dark eyes. She wished she dared tell this Southerner, this onetime slave owner, why the Carows could not afford a governess, that the war had almost ruined the Kermit-Carow Shipping Company, that its aftermath and soaring prices had wiped out their savings. And—but heaven forbid that she should even whisper this!—that Charles Carow's failure in business, plus a physical weakness following a disastrous fall on one of the company ships, had aggravated an unfortunate propensity to drown his frustrations in alcohol.

"I understand," said Anna Bulloch quietly.

It was soon afterward that a message came from Martha Roosevelt, Teedie's mother, to the house in Livingston Place. She begged a great favor of Mrs. Carow. She was delighted that there had been such a long and close friendship between Corinne and Edith. Her sister, Anna Bulloch, who was an excellent teacher, conducted a little school in the second-floor nursery of the Roosevelt house. The three youngest Roosevelt children were her pupils. But Corinne, being so much younger than the boys, needed both the stimulus and the companionship of someone her own age to share her lessons. Would Mrs. Carow be willing to permit Edith to attend this little school? If she would, Mrs. Roosevelt would be very grateful.

Charity? No. The tactful message had made such an interpretation impossible. Gertrude was asked to confer a favor on Mrs. Roosevelt. Gratefully she agreed.

3

Edie could hardly believe her good fortune. Each schoolday she walked with Mame—or if the weather was inclement they took the horsecar—up Broadway to the Theodore Roosevelt house at 28 East Twentieth Street. Here Mame left her and returned home for her other duties as nurse to the two Carow children.

The house was a sedate brownstone, three stories high including the basement, part of a row of buildings, two of which had been bought by Cornelius Van Schaack Roosevelt for his two sons, Robert and Theodore. The latter, younger of the two, had been given Number 28 on his marriage to the beautiful Martha Bulloch of Roswell, Georgia. Each day as Edie climbed the dozen steps to the imposing front door, she felt as if she were Ali Baba, hero of one of the stories Teedie liked to tell, standing in front of a treasure cave. Sometimes she even whispered, "Open sesame!" as she lifted the brass knocker and waited for the butler to open the door.

The first day Mrs. Roosevelt—"Mittie," as most adults called her—had come to the front hall to greet her, smilingly commenting that visitors, especially children, were always asked to remove their shoes and leave them in the hall. She liked to have everything in her home very clean, she explained, and there was so much mud or dust in those awful New York streets! Edie understood this desire perfectly, for cleanliness was one of her own aspirations in life. She gazed at her hostess with awe mingled with admiration. That lovely fine black silky hair, that white skin with just the faintest color of rose petals! And in her white muslin ruffled dress she looked as if no spot of dirt could possibly touch her. Mittie, Edie was to discover, always wore white muslin, summer and winter, and she always looked as if she had just stepped from a fragrant bath.

"No wonder!" Conie once remarked sagely. "For she takes two baths every day: one, she says, for cleaning, and one for rinsing."

The round table in the upstairs nursery was for Edie a magic carpet, transporting her into worlds of fascinating reality as well as of fantasy and imagination—the languorous, magnolia-scented life of Aunt Annie's Georgia plantation, with its long-tailed horses Boone and Crockett, its wild Negro dances and plaintive songs, its legends of Br'er Rabbit and Tar Baby with their faint undertones of African drum beats; the jungles and battlefields and hunting grounds with strange beasts of Teedie's compulsive storytelling; the ever-varying milieus of a fascinating magazine called *Our Young Folks,* and, as soon as she was able to read with some facility, the magical worlds of *McGuffey's Eclectic Readers* and such books as *Little Men* and *Little Women.*

It was Teedie more than the other two who shared her fascination with reading. In fact, in spite of the age difference between them and their totally divergent personalities, they soon developed a rapport which aroused secret envy and some animosity in Conie, who both adored her older brother and considered Edie her special property. It was she who was relegated to the role of child when they played "house," while Teedie and Edie were father and mother. Ellie, who derided the pursuit as "girls' stuff," was not permitted to play at all. Teedie was always above such inhibitions as sex distinction, being as catholic in his recreation as in his tastes for literature. He was as fond of stories like *Little Women* and *Pussy Willow* and *An Old-Fashioned Girl* as of *Mr. Midshipman Easy* and his favorite poem of Longfellow, "The Saga of King Olaf."

Edie was impressed when he proudly showed her a notebook containing one of his first attempts at literature, a work entitled *Natural History of Insects, by Theodore Roosevelt, Junior.* With dutiful appreciation she read his slightly misspelled treatise on ants, beginning, "Ants are difided into three sorts for every species. These kinds are officer, soilder, and work. There are about one officer to ten soilders and one soilder to two workers." It was a long opus, covering many kinds of insects, all of which, he assured the reader, "inhabit North America."

So fond was she of Teedie that Edie attempted to sympathize with his growing obsession with live and dead animals, preferably the latter, for since his fascination with the seal, of which he had finally obtained the skull, he was starting a "Roosevelt Museum of

Natural History"; its collections were first kept in his room until one of the maidservants rebelled and it was transferred to a back room on an upper floor.

Others of the servants were driven to occasional rebellion. "How can I do my laundry," queried the family washerwoman, "with a snapping turtle tied to the legs of the sink?" And the family cook, good-natured though she was, objected firmly when Teedie, having killed a beautiful specimen of woodchuck and wanting to preserve it for further study, ordered her to boil it for twenty-four hours. "Either I leave or the woodchuck does!" she announced in ultimatum, and she had protesting company among family members when a nauseating odor of boiling wood-chuck pervaded the whole house.

So delightfully informal was Aunt Annie's teaching and so fasci-nating the contents of the books she was learning to read that Edie slowly emerged from her habitual shell of shyness and re-serve and became an active participant in both reading and reci-tation. But not always. If she suddenly became the focus of atten-tion, she became painfully self-conscious and tongue-tied, as when the class recited in concert Longfellow's poem "The Chil-dren's Hour":

> Grave Alice and laughing Allegra,
> And Edith with golden hair . . .

As they intoned the words, all eyes were mischievously turned in her direction, Ellie, always a tease, reached across the table and gave one of her long yellow curls a wrenching tweak. She felt herself blushing and wished she could crawl under the table.

"Quit it, Ellie," admonished Teedie, who, though himself prone to mischief, was already, if infrequently, revealing the instincts of a gentleman. "Can't you see Edie doesn't like to be teased?"

"That's enough of Longfellow," Aunt Annie's soft voice inter-posed tactfully. "Did I ever tell you the story about how old Br'er Rabbit lost his long tail? Well, you see, it was this way. . . ." And Edie listened as avidly as the others.

As time went by and her skill in reading increased, her self-consciousness continued to decrease. She was able to read aloud from the *McGuffey's Readers,* so absorbed in their exciting stories that she forgot to be embarrassed.

"Please," Conie would beg when a new number of *Our Young Folks* arrived, "you read to me. You make it sound so real, as if the people were alive!"

Teedie seemed to enjoy having her read to him, too, and they often took turns. Long afterward it would be remembered that "she was sometimes seen reading to Teedie on the steps" of the Roosevelt house on East Twentieth Street, her white dress a vivid contrast to the background of somber brownstone.

When Aunt Annie married James K. Gracie, a real estate dealer, in 1866 and moved to rooms on Fourth Avenue, Edie was agonizingly afraid that the paradise of books and learning would come to an end. She felt like Eve facing expulsion from the Garden of Eden. But to her unbounded relief Aunt Annie continued her teaching, even invited the girls to come to her rooms to learn sewing, at which Edie was to become dutifully proficient. Only the summers were barren wastes separating the fertile oases of study and companionship.

With the hot weather all prosperous New Yorkers moved to the country, even those who, like Charles Carow's family, felt the strain of a plunging economy. The Roosevelts went for several years to Loantaka, a rural place in New Jersey near Madison. Charles, now reduced to virtual unemployment, took his family to the country estate of General Daniel Tyler, Gertrude's father, near Red Bank, New Jersey. Already they had been forced to economize by moving into the home of Aunt Ann Eliza, the widow of Charles's uncle, Robert Kermit, whose property backed onto that owned by the Van Schaack Roosevelts. For Edie the summer exodus was just a period of marking time when she could start really living again.

For her, life in its fullness was experienced in the house at 28 East Twentieth Street, and not only in the nursery, where she sat enthralled with the others around the table and hungrily absorbed knowledge. The whole house teemed with life, from the strenuous games in nursery and garden after lessons to the basement kitchen where Teedie, the budding naturalist, shocked the cook by storing his dead mice and lizards and other specimens in the refrigerator. And she was a part of it all.

"Aunt Annie, Edith and Ellie send their love," wrote Teedie to his mother when Mittie and Conie were visiting Mrs. Roosevelt's old home in Georgia in 1868. This made Edie seem a member of the family.

There were other activities beside those in the nursery and garden. Theodore Roosevelt Senior was as interested as Aunt Annie in the children's education. A prosperous businessman, importer of glass, and an eminent philanthropist, he was also founder of many of New York's charitable institutions, including the Children's Aid Society, the Newsboys' Lodging House, and the Young Men's Christian Association. Still, he found time to organize and direct plays for the children to act in, take them on nature trips or visits to the Museum of Natural History or the Museum of Art, both of which he had helped to establish, and to accompany them on rides in the swan boats in Central Park.

Theodore Roosevelt Senior belonged to a long line of civic benefactors, going back to the time when the first immigrant, Claes Martenszen van Rosenvelt, landed in New Amsterdam in 1640, bringing with him his coat of arms, a knight's silver shield with a trio of red roses growing out of greensward, and his family motto of *Qui Plantavit Curabit,* meaning "He who has planted will preserve." He had taken for himself a section of land which he called Rose Field, after his own name, which later became Roosevelt. His son Nicholas had sired two sons, Johannes and Jacobus, from whom two branches of Roosevelts had sprung, Johannes being progenitor of the two Theodores, Jacobus becoming the ancestor of the branch which would be called the Hyde Park Roosevelts.

Nicholas, Johannes's son, had run for office and distinguished himself in public service, as well as adding to the family's extensive landholdings. Perhaps it was from Nicholas's wife Heyltje that the boy Theodore had derived his spirit of bold adventure, for she had dared to flout precedent by wearing a flamboyant petticoat and revealing it to male gaze as she crossed a muddy street, exposing her ankles "in unseemly fashion, to the scandal of the community."

The family had included congressmen, members of the New York Board of Aldermen, a justice of the State Supreme Court, a judge of the State Court of Appeals, lawyers, a U. S. district attorney. Teedie's grandfather, Cornelius van Schaack, had found time to be a director of the Chemical National Bank.

Mittie came from a distinguished line of Georgians, her forebears including a speaker of the Royal Assembly of the state and a delegate to the Continental Congress. Her father was Deputy Collector of the Port of Savannah and president of a bank.

Though she seemed to Edie as vague and helpless as a beautiful little china doll, Mittie also contributed to the children's pleasure. She read stories to them in her soft Southern drawl and sang plantation songs, providing the most delightful prizes for the party games they played. Once Edie received a doll's china set with knives and forks having genuine ivory handles, a gift she would treasure all her life.

But it was Bamie, Conie's elder sister Anna, who often organized the games, directed them with an adult competence seemingly at odds with her eleven or twelve years, Bamie with her dark skin and stooping shoulders and awkward gait. Bamie had a spinal defect which dated from babyhood when, it was rumored, she had been dropped by a nurse. Others later believed she had suffered from polio. In spite of her handicaps, she possessed irrepressible gaiety and charm and the ability to make a person feel of the utmost importance. Edie had come to admire Bamie, and she marveled at her kindness and skill in making her a doll's bonnet. But she was also a little afraid of her. Her pale eyes, though sparkling with mischief and good humor, sometimes seemed to look straight through a person, invading one's privacy and detecting one's worst faults.

It was due to Bamie's handicaps that Theodore Senior initiated one of his most important philanthropic projects. There ought to be a hospital in New York to provide care for such children. But how could it be financed? Few people he talked with seemed interested. Then he had an idea. He would give a reception in his home and show people what some of the new modern treatments could do. He had some of the crippled children he had seen in the slums brought from their poverty-stricken homes, laid them on the dining room table fitted to some of the new steel appliances which had helped Bamie and might help them, too. The invited guests were given a demonstration. As Mrs. John Jacob Astor leaned over one of the stricken children, she turned to her host with brimming eyes.

"Theodore," she said, "you are right. These children must be helped."

That day enough money was raised to start the first Orthopedic Dispensary, on East Fifty-ninth Street.

No wonder Edie found the Roosevelts' a remarkable household! Her friend Fanny Smith, writing about the family years later in her book *Perchance Some Day,* would call them "a family touched with a flame of divine fire."

Fanny, about Edie's and Conie's age, had become one of their intimate group. She was a member of Auntie Annie's sewing class. She had first met Conie in their Sunday school class at the Madison Avenue Presbyterian Church and would describe her later as "a little girl in a black velvet coat with a shoulder cape and with ardent blue eyes." They had become friends. Edie met her when they were both invited to dinner at the Roosevelt house.

Dining at the Roosevelts' was a festive occasion. Edie reveled in the sumptuous dining room running the whole width of the rear of the house, decorated with its ceiling rosettes and molded cornices, its huge mirror over the fireplace, and its gas chandelier, which lighted the crystal and silver with winking sparkles. The beautiful hostess would sit at the head of the long table in her white muslin dress with pink shining through, her white throat rising from a frothy ruff of real lace. Fortunately Edie's own long dress protected her from the horsehair-upholstered chairs, which made Teedie and Ellie complain that they scratched their bare legs. Between her and their hostess was a little girl about her own age with whom Conie was chattering across the table as if they had known each other all their lives. Edie, always tongue-tied with strangers, could find nothing to say until suddenly she heard her neighbor gasp.

"Oh, dear!" Fanny whispered. "Look what I've done!" There on the spotless damask tablecloth beside her plate was a big blob of cranberry sauce. "What shall I do?"

"It's all right, don't worry," Edie whispered back with the competent assurance she would have shown in comforting her small sister Emily. "Just lay your handkerchief over it. No one will notice, and only the servants will know."

Fanny obeyed, and apparently no one did notice. She looked at Edie gratefully. "Oh, thank you! I never would have thought of that."

They smiled at each other. Edie marveled. In just seconds she had made a new friend, whereas it might have taken months. And, she would discover, it was a friendship that would last a lifetime.

It was early in the spring of 1869, when Edie was seven and a half, that her gateway to paradise threatened to slam shut.

"We're going to Europe," announced Conie lugubriously.

Theodore Roosevelt Senior, it seemed, had decided that his children needed the intellectual stimulus of travel and the cultural education that only the Old World could provide. Also the change might benefit their physical weaknesses. Mittie was overjoyed at the prospect of seeing her two brothers who, having been active members of the Confederate Navy, had fled to England. Only once since the war had she seen either of them. Then one of them had dared to slip into New York under an assumed name.

The family had been at their summer place at Loantaka, Conie had told Edie excitedly, when an odd-looking letter had arrived. Her mother had opened it, and, turning with glowing eyes to her sister, had exclaimed, "Oh, Anna, this must be from Irvine!" It was a strange note that she read aloud. "If Mrs. Theodore Roosevelt and Miss Anna Bulloch will walk in Central Park up the Mall, at 3 o'clock on Thursday afternoon of this week and notice a young man standing under the third tree on the left with a red handkerchief tied around his throat, it will be of interest to them."

They had gone to the park at the hour mentioned, and there under the tree had found their younger brother, thin and haggard, but alive and eager. From Liverpool he had worked his way over in a sailing vessel and, afraid of bringing trouble to the Roosevelt family, had taken this way to meet his sisters. Now Mittie would be able to visit him in his adopted country.

5 ok

Teedie was as disgusted over the projected trip as Conie. It meant the cessation of his experiments, which had become a real obsession. His treasures, both alive and dead, were legion. In addition to Topsy the monkey Aunt Lizzie kept a whole menagerie in her backyard—pheasants and peacocks, which strutted up and down, guinea pigs, chickens, pigeons, even a cow, which had had to be "persuaded" down the basement steps, through the hall, and out into the yard. The cow, however, had been removed after threats by the neighbors, an almost impossible act to accomplish, since the poor creature refused to enter the house again and had to have her legs bound together and her eyes blindfolded, and then be dragged out through the house.

There were also the white mice which Teedie had stored in the refrigerator and flown into a tantrum about when his mother had thrown them out ("Lost to science!"), and the toads which he and his cousin had carried under their caps until, meeting Mrs. Hamilton Fish on the street, they had lifted their hats politely and the captives had hopped away, to their chagrin and the great lady's shocked amazement. His collection had increased considerably after his announcement that he would pay ten cents for each mouse contributed, thirty-five for a family. Was it one of these that once jumped out of a Dutch cheese placed before Theodore Senior at dinner? The house had been swamped with mice. His "museum" was already a treasure-house of animals, insects, and reptiles, some of which he had boiled and tried inexpertly to stuff. But he dreaded even more to leave his friends, especially Edith, his favorite little companion.

Edie did not weep, but her morose silence attracted her mother's attention.

"It's those Rose-velts lavin'," explained Mame to Gertrude. "They're a-kitin' off to Europe come May."

Gertrude sympathized with her daughter, but she also felt frustrated and envious. It was unfair that the Roosevelt children should have such privileges while the Carows were suffering privations. She herself, a daughter of Daniel and Emily Lee Tyler, had gone to France in 1852, studying French, music, dancing, Italian, art, taking courses in piano and singing at the Paris Conservatoire, training her pure contralto voice under a skilled Italian teacher who had wanted to fit her for the stage. If she had not succumbed to the charms of handsome Charles Carow, with his dark waving hair and flowing mustache, his courtly manners and flattering speech, she might have been a concert singer or even an opera diva. But now, her own poor children! What future could there be for the daughters of Charles Carow (once spelled "Quereau," denoting a noble Huguenot heritage), while those Roosevelt children . . . !

The Roosevelts sailed for England on May 12, 1869. As usual, Edie kept her emotions locked inside her. But she sat all day in the nursery rereading the last issue of *Our Young Folks,* which she and Conie and Teedie had all read together. She might have felt less sad had she known that Teedie had shed tears all the way to the docks and that he wrote in his diary that night, "It was verry hard parting from our friend."

It was not an unhappy year, merely an uneventful one, like marking time between exciting races. The Carow family went to Grandfather Tyler's country place that summer, where Edie dutifully entertained four-year-old Emily with hours of storytelling, satisfied her yen for solitude by long walks in the woods and fields, and listened with polite attention to Grandfather's tales of his army exploits and his achievements as a mining engineer. He had restored life to broken-down railroads, defunct coal companies, collapsed iron works, and crumbling canals, actually creating a new town in Alabama. Gertrude also listened to these memoirs with satisfaction.

"Remember," she admonished Edie, "you have a heritage to be proud of. Your grandfather is the fourth Daniel Tyler to bring distinction to the family. And there were two others in America before him, the first one, Job, coming from England in the early sixteen-hundreds. And of course the Lees on my mother's side were eminent builders and shipowners. My grandfather Benjamin was commander of a ship at nineteen and one of the first to carry the American flag to the Far East. In fact, almost all your forebears on *my* side of the family were distinguished and *successful* people."

Sensitive beyond her years, Edie hoped her father, back from one of his frequent forays in search of profitable employment, was not listening. The emphasized words were all too sharp and personal.

Letters from the traveling Roosevelts livened the monotony like flashes of sunlight on a dull day.

"When we were riding from Glasgow to York," wrote Conie, "Teedie talked about how sad he had been to part with Edith, and his cousins Jimmie and Emlen." And, Edie consoled herself, he had mentioned her first.

She would have been even more contented could she have seen an entry in his diary one day that fall, although Teedie's literary acumen had never extended to excellence in spelling! "In the evening mamma showed me the portrait of Edieth Carow and her face stired up in me homesickness and longings for the past which will come again never, alack never."

She received letters from him as well as from Conie.

"My dear Eidie," he wrote early in January from Sorrento. "We came from Naples today. I have recieved your interesting letter and reply to it on paper recieved at Christmas. Yesterday we made the ascent of Mt. Vesuvius. It was snow covered which heightened our enjoyment. We went first in caraiges for a long while. We then got out and mounted ponies . . . At first we walked but after a while Papa, Ellie and I galloped along until we came to a gulley coated with ice on which the hourses walked with 2 legs on one side and 2 legs on the other side. . . . We then began the ascent of Mt. Vesuvius I went first with one guide with a strap in which I put my hands. One place where the side was steeper than any alp I have been on the guide and I fell. We recovered ourselves right away." The letter continued with vivid description and ended, "But now goodby, Evere your loving friend, T. Roosevelt."

Back in New York Edie felt her loneliness increase. Aunt Annie's classes at the Roosevelt house had of course ended. Even Edie's favorite pastime, reading, was curtailed.

"Mamma thinks my eyes are not very strong," she wrote Conie in February. "She and Mame whenever they see a book in my hands give me no peace till I lay it down."

She took vicarious pleasure in finding on the map places mentioned in Conie's and Teedie's letters and tracing their progress—

Edinburgh, Loch Lomond ("where the poem 'Lady of the lake' was lade"), York, Oxford, London, where the children had played in "hide park" and visited "Westnubster abby"; Antwerp, Amsterdam, Strasbourg, where Teedie had been "verry sick" from asthma; Geneva, Zermatt, where he had climbed an eight-thousand-foot mountain; Vienna with its opera; Berlin, Cologne, where on October 28 Teedie had celebrated his eleventh birthday; Paris, the Riviera, Rome in time for Christmas ("We saw the Pope and we walked along and he extended his hand to me and I kissed it!!! hem!!! hem!!!")

But the year was over at last. "New York!!! Hip! Hurrah!"

Edie would have heartily agreed with the sentiment Teedie expressed in his diary. But she was fearful. They had traveled so far, seen and learned so much, while she had been standing still. Would there still be room for her in their lives?

She need not have worried. So glad were they to be back that they did not even want to talk about their trip. Though Aunt Annie no longer held her kindergarten school in the nursery, Edie was soon as involved in the activities at Twentieth Street as before. Also the children were now old enough to participate in social events outside the home. The previous year Edie and her friend Fanny Smith had gone weekly to Mr. Dodsworth's school for dancing and deportment. Edie had found the classes dull, especially the tiresome bowing and shaking of hands, and the curtseying to the resplendent Mrs. Dodsworth, who sat at a Louis XV desk and marked their attendance. Now, however, with the young Roosevelts attending, the classes became more exciting, if a bit embarrassing when all four Roosevelt boys—Teedie, Ellie, Alfred, and Emlen—vied with each other to become Edie's partner in the polkas and waltzes. The only dance programs she saved, however, were those on which Teedie's name predominated.

Yet to her dismay Teedie, suddenly surprisingly tall, grotesquely like a stork with his long legs and skinny body, seemed to have grown away from her in other ways. He had a new obsession.

Out of a back bedroom next to the nursery Theodore Senior had created a sort of gymnasium for his children by turning it into a large piazza. Here, on seesaws, horizontal and vertical bars, swings, and other paraphernalia, the children were encouraged to develop their bodies and correct physical weaknesses. For they all had them, Bamie with her spinal trouble, Elliott with his severe headaches, Teedie and Conie with their asthma. The European trip had not, as hoped, lessened or mitigated Teedie's attacks, but had accentuated them if anything.

"My father says," he explained to Edie, "that I have brains, but brains are no good without a strong body. He says I have to *make* my body, and I can do it if I try."

And try he did, spending hours in strenuous exercise, attempting to swell the muscles in his puny arms, to broaden his narrow chest, to somehow inject vigor into the lungs suffering from the terrible asthmatic shortness of breath. Day after day he applied himself, approaching the task with the same power of concentration with which he had once buried his nose in one of the British novelist Mayne Reid's adventure stories. The other children followed his example with less vigor.

Not one of his diversions, however. One day Mittie was looking out of the window opening on the piazza and she saw two boys, one of whom was Teedie, carefully balancing a seesaw on the high rail which protected the children from the possibility of falling into the backyard two stories below. Then, not daring to breathe, she saw Teedie crawling over the railing and attempting to balance himself on the outer length of the seesaw while one of his cousins held the other end with both hands, undoubtedly preparing to climb up on it. With immense self-control she managed to reach the scene in time to help hold the board while her intrepid young son slid back down it and crawled over the railing to the piazza. Needless to say, that sport was never tried again.

Edie tried the less dangerous feats, though she was almost embarrassingly healthy in contrast to the others. Still, her attempts to master the formidable swings and bars were, as she was to remember, "painful and faltering." Even a successful descent of a wisteria vine leading to a pantry roof below the gymnasium she found unsettling, since it wreaked havoc with her neat white dress and tore her sash, reducing her to a state of dishevelment that upset her far more than the physical risk involved.

"Spotless Edie!" Conie liked to dub her, in mingled derision and admiration.

Yes, Teedie was growing away from her in more than a few inches of height.

"Why," Fanny Smith once asked her curiously, "do you like Teedie so much better than Ellie? It's so queer. Ellie is much handsomer and more popular. Everybody likes him. And Teedie is so skinny and gawky. Did you ever notice how he stands on one foot when he reads, with the book propped on his hip? He looks just like a long-legged bird. And he squeaks when he talks, and—oh, those awful smelly dead animals and even worse live ones! You and Teedie are certainly not much alike!"

Why? Edie was silent. She had no answer. Fanny was right. She and Teedie had little in common except their love of reading, their appreciation of the magic cadence of poetry, their ability to find in words the excitement of living adventure. And never again, she sensed, would they sit on the steps of the old brownstone and read to each other.

4

Edith Carow's world was changing. Sometimes, in the years of her growing up, it seemed to be falling apart.

One day in 1871 she looked out a back window of her family's house toward the rear of the Roosevelt mansion on Broadway and saw men pounding and tearing at the roof. "Oh!" she exclaimed in distress. "What are they doing?"

Aunt Ann Eliza Kermit came and looked over her shoulder. "Tearing the house down," she said grimly. "They could hardly wait till old Cornelius Van Schaack was safe in his grave before getting at the job. It's been sold, I hear, and the land's to be used to build a big warehouse."

Edie watched the process with horrified fascination, saw through the gaping holes the dismantled rooms where she and the other children had once played, and the wonderful circular staircase winding around from the entrance hall clear to the roof, where Teedie, dared by Ellie, had once slid on the banisters from top to bottom; even the black-and-white squares of the beautiful marble floor in the hall were being chopped up and carted off somewhere and forgotten.

But there was even worse to come. Presently she overheard Mamma and Aunt Kermit talking.

"We can't wait any longer, Gertrude. Charles must see that, in spite of his easygoing reluctance to face facts. The tide of filthy, poverty-stricken, vice-ridden sections of the city is moving farther and farther north each year. And those terrible riots of the Irish immigrants! If we stay here, we may easily be murdered in our beds. Many of the old families have already gone. The Astors, the Goelets, the Stevenses are all building up as far north as Fiftieth Street, where there was once nothing but cow pastures."

"Yes." Mamma sounded troubled. "But how can we afford it?"

"We can't," replied Aunt Kermit, "at least not as far north as we might like. I suppose we shouldn't blame your husband, my poor nephew Charles, for our straitened finances. We're fortunate that my husband Robert was provident when the shipping business was in its heyday. But if only Charles would spend more of his time hunting for a better job and less trying to drown his frustrations in the taverns!"

Edie's ears and cheeks burned. She hadn't wanted to listen. They didn't know she was curled up with her book in the high-backed chair, and when they had begun talking it was too late for her to escape. She felt miserable. Not that she minded the idea of moving so much, and she certainly wasn't afraid of being killed in her bed by the poor Irish immigrants who, her nurse Mame had explained, were "jist makin' a bit of a fuss 'cause they had naught to eat and were hungry." It was what was being said about her father that made her close her book and stuff her fingers into both ears so she could not hear the rest of Aunt Kermit's incriminations. Handsome, gay, gallant Papa who had held her on his knee and told her such rollicking stories, introduced her to the wonderful world of books, trained her in horsemanship on their summer vacations, and on their long rambles taught her the names of birds and flowers!

That August they went to Pennsylvania for a holiday, leaving

Charles to hunt for a house farther uptown. Edie took special pains to write him long letters, knowing he must be lonely and hoping her letters might keep him from what Aunt Kermit had called "drowning his frustrations in the taverns." She described the beautiful surroundings, the mountains, the Susquehanna River, which they could see from the hotel "like a silver thread," their rides through the country, picnics, her fun with a pony called Spency. And when Aunt Kermit and Papa decided to move from the house on Livingston Place to 200 West Forty-fourth Street, she wrote gaily, "Won't it be fun packing up to move?"

A new house, a brownstone not much different from the old, and a new life, for that fall she was enrolled in a private school only four blocks away, on West Fortieth, recommended by Fanny Smith's father. Fanny also was one of the pupils, to Edie's relief, for she was still intensely shy with strangers, and her one regret over the change of residence was its greater distance from Conie and the other young Roosevelts. At first she was afraid of the headmistress, Miss Louise Comstock, with her dark flashing eyes, her precise, clear-cut features, and what Fanny called her "terrifying charm," but Edie soon came to respect and even to love her.

Edie adapted herself to the rigid routine more easily than some of the other pupils. She did not mind that Miss Comstock did not approve of jewelry for schoolgirls, and that if one of them appeared with a bangle or a locket, she was invited to drop it in the bowl provided at the entrance. Mamma had seen to it that she knew some French, so she was glad that it was the only language permitted in the schoolroom. They could lapse into English only at recess time, when they played in Bryant Park across the way.

Suddenly the world was at her fingertips. No need of crossing the ocean, like Conie and Teedie, to glimpse the glories of the Old World! Thanks to her history and English literature teachers, the Wars of the Roses became as exciting as the American Revolution, the London of Dickens as real as the streets and alleys of New York. As time passed, she explored the world of ancient Rome through the eyes of Caesar and Virgil, though she could never enjoy her Latin class shared with Fanny and one other student the way they did, in spite of her father's attempt to coach her in his favorite classics. Though languages were not her best subjects, especially German, she became fairly fluent in French. To her further delight, her study of zoology made Teedie's world of insects and animals seem less distasteful, more intriguing. Even a slight knowledge of botany enhanced the joy of summer rambles with her father. She could almost forget that soon he would be gone again in another fruitless attempt to improve his fortunes.

But, being Edie, her greatest joy was literature. Graduating from the pious platitudes of *Our Young Folks* and *McGuffey's Readers,* she reveled in the delights of Dickens, Scott, and especially Shakespeare. Even trips to Steinway Hall for symphony concerts, where a performance of the youthful Heifetz once stirred her to the heights of emotion, were not as exciting as jaunts to the library with her friend Fanny Smith.

"Sometimes," Fanny was to write much later, "Edith and I would spend the afternoon together in the dim dusty precincts of the Society Library on University Place. There we would find the books not always accessible at home. Rhoda Broughton's *Red as a Rose Is She* and *Goodbye, Sweetheart* would have been considered dangerous fare by my father and mother, but in the remote security of the Society Library I was able utterly to lose myself in their deliriously romantic pages. Whether Edith also indulged in forbidden fruit I don't remember; but I know that usually her taste in reading was for the best."

Though Edie's world expanded to wider horizons than formerly, she continued to have few intimate friends. Conie and Fanny remained her best chums, but Teedie, now in his teens, was developing interests which she found hard to share. Still enamored with his live and dead fauna, he was taking lessons from a taxidermist, exuberantly practicing his new knowledge and exuding an unpleasant odor of formaldehyde and arsenic. The summer of 1872, just before he turned fourteen, he had been given a gun. But dutifully Edie accompanied him to his "museum" and admired his trophies. Once when she visited he looked so strange that she hardly knew him; he was wearing spectacles.

For thirteen years he had seen the world through a nearsighted haze. Getting his new gun, he had been surprised because he could not hit anything. Then one day, seeing some huge letters on a distant billboard and being unable to read them, he had realized something was the matter and had spoken to his father about it. Hence the spectacles.

"No wonder I've always been so clumsy and awkward! I had no idea how beautiful the world was until I got these spectacles."

Edie rejoiced with him. He sounded like the man healed by Jesus in the Bible story that Miss Comstock had given them for a lesson. "Whereas I was blind, Now I can see!"

Teedie was exercising even harder these days, another interest which Edie could not share. A trip alone to Moosehead Lake in Maine in an effort to curb his asthma had resulted in an unfortunate incident. Two mischievous boys on the stagecoach where he was riding decided he was a suitable victim of their ridicule, and they made life miserable for him with their taunts and jibes. Driven to desperation, he decided to fight them. He found that either one of them could not only handle him alone but do it with such easy contempt that, without being hurt overmuch, he was ignominiously worsted. With his father's approval he started taking boxing lessons in addition to all his other exercises.

Perhaps it was because of her own new interests and widened horizons that Edie felt far less bereaved when the Roosevelts departed for Europe again in October of 1872, this time to spend the winter in Egypt. Theodore Senior had been appointed American Commissioner to the Vienna Exposition of 1873, and he wanted his family to derive cultural advantages from the opportunity. Conie was more devastated at the thought of "another terrible trip." Teedie, while reluctant to leave his friends, including Edie, was anticipating a harvest of exotic specimens such as ibis, zebus, storks, and pelicans for his "Roosevelt Museum of Natural History." Armed with his new gun, his new spectacles, and his precious preservatives, he departed with exuberance.

Out came the maps again; and as the letters arrived Edie's pen scratched slowly from dot to dot, this time halting at unfamiliar names—Brindisi, Alexandria, Cairo, Luxor, Karnak, Aswan.

"The other day we arrived at Edfoo," Conie wrote, "and we all went to see the temple together. While we were there Teedie, Ellie, Iesi (one of our sailors) and I started to explore. We went into a little dark room and climbed in a hole which was in the middle of the wall. The boys had candles. It was dark, crawling along the passage doubled up. At last we came to a deep hole into which Teedie dropped but we found it was a mummy pit. . . ."

Edie shivered vicariously. She was much more pleased with a letter Conie wrote from Thebes on February 1. "My own darling Edie, don't you remember what fun we *used* to have out in the country, and don't you remember the day we got Pony Grant up in the Chauncey's summerhouse and couldn't get him down again, and how we always were losing Teedie's India rubber shoes? I remember it so perfectly, and what fun it was!"

Edie read everything she could find about Egypt, then followed their journey on horseback through Palestine to Athens and Constantinople, where Teedie was again "verry sick" but managed to write a letter to Edie which she would treasure all her life.

"I think I have enjoyed myself more this winter than I ever did before. . . . I think I enjoyed the time in Egypt most, and after that I had the most fun while camping out in Syria.

"While camping out we were on horseback for several hours each day. . . . While riding I bothered the family somewhat by carrying the gun over my shoulder, and on the journey to the Jordan, when I was on the most spirited horse I ever rode, I bothered the horse too, as was evidenced by his running away several times when the gun struck him too hard. Our tent life had a good many adventures in it. Once it rained very hard and the rain went into our open trunks. Another time our tents were almost blown away in a rough wind, and once I hunted a couple of jackals for two or three miles as fast as the horse could go. Yours truly, T Roosevelt, Jr."

Now, thought Edie, for whom the winter had held no excitement other than trips to the library, a few concerts, and a Shakespeare matinee at the new Edwin Booth Theater, they will be coming home. But no. After Theodore Senior's meeting in Vienna he was taking the three younger children to Dresden, where they would spend the summer studying German and French with a genteel family named Minkwitz, while Mittie, who was not well, and Bamie would take the cures at Carlsbad and then go on to Paris and London for shopping. He himself was returning home to superintend the building of a new house in what was becoming the more fashionable uptown area of New York, far from the encroaching foreign elements.

Through Conie's letters and details which Aunt Annie Gracie shared from hers, Edie eagerly followed the family's progress. All the children were performing well in their studies. Teedie was continuing his scientific experiments. He had managed to secure a dead mole and a German marmot and had found a man with white mice for sale. He had stripped the animals of their skins in the kitchen and prepared to boil them in one of Frau Minkwitz's saucepans, but the good Frau had interfered, so he had gone to the backyard, built a little oven of bricks, boiled the carcasses, and skillfully put together their skeletons. But his scientific pursuits were causing the family some consternation. His arsenic had been confiscated and his mice thrown (with tongs) out the window. His teacher, Fräulein Minkwitz, was much impressed by his proficiency in German. He was becoming a bookworm, hungrily absorbing the German classics, especially his beloved *Nibelungenlied*. He could read German and French almost as well as English. Edie despaired. While the Roosevelt children were making great strides in knowledge, it seemed that she was standing still.

It was November when they finally returned, moving into the new house, even though it was not yet completely finished. Soon afterward Edie paid her first visit to 6 East Fifty-seventh Street, awed both by the splendid new residence and by meeting again these peers who had climbed the pyramids, stood on the Acropolis, walked the streets of Nazareth and Bethlehem, actually bathed in the Jordan, and become glib in foreign languages, while she . . . There had been the same worry before, of course, but this time her friends had been gone much longer and had traveled much farther.

The house was indeed awe-inspiring. "So big!" Edie described it later at home. "With beautiful carved wood on the walls and soft thick rugs from Persia, they said. And lovely polished new furniture, even a hand-carved staircase!"

"No wonder," sighed Gertrude, the little lines deepening in her pretty white forehead. "The Roosevelts have always been fortunate. Buying all that land when the city was bound to grow! Theodore Roosevelt must be a millionaire twice over."

Conie, to Edie's relief, had not changed. She was just as gay, vivacious, and changeable as before, laughing one minute and almost in tears the next as she described her futile attempts to dive in the Dead Sea, which was about the most "alive thing she had ever seen," and her disappointment at finding that the Jordan, instead of being a broad river with great waves parting to let the Ark pass, was just a little stream. Bamie, too, was just as bright-eyed and competent and cheerful, in spite of her awkward, misshapen body and almost constant pain. Ellie too had changed little, being still, as Fanny Smith once described him, "quite irresistible." But Teedie . . .

It was not his further increased height or broader shoulders or the still unfamiliar owlish spectacles that made him different. And that faint aroma of arsenic was certainly nothing new. The change in him was not merely physical. He had become more serious, more self-assured, and, yes, more gentlemanly (Teedie!), with courtly manners like his father.

"How are you, little Edie? You look just the same. We must get together again one of these days. I've been reading some jolly new books. Do you know the *Nibelungenlied?* No, I suppose you don't read German much, but it's wonderful. And I must show you the specimens I brought back for the museum."

Little Edie. Her heart sank. This time he really had grown up. And he now eschewed the old nickname "Teedie." He didn't mind "Ted" and would answer to "Teddy," if unwillingly, though he preferred "Theodore." The three years between them had become suddenly the gap between childhood and maturity. Soon afterward, when she was invited to attend a coming-out party for Bamie, their difference in age was even more pronounced. Though he danced with her, as with his other favorite young female friends, she suspected his attention held a slight trace of duty and condescension. And when she and Conie were hustled off to bed long before the dancing was over, she knew the delightful intimacy of their childhood was over. She would have felt even more inferior and bereft if she had overheard a conversation which had taken place a few weeks before in Dresden.

"I wonder what is going to become of my Teddy," Mittie remarked almost despairingly when she was about to leave Dresden for home with the children. She knew what a trial the boy must have been to the Minkwitzes with his asthma attacks, his black eyes and bloody noses acquired in boxing, especially his unsavory experiments with mice and moles and marmots.

Fräulein Anna Minkwitz, who had been his teacher, smiled. "You need not be anxious about him," she had said consolingly. "He will surely be one day a great professor, or, who knows, he may become even president of the United States."

"Impossible!" Mittie had scoffed with unconcealed amusement. "How could you have imagined such an absurdity!"

Soon after their return Conie asked, "Remember that letter I wrote you from Germany, the one about our literary club?"

Edie's eyes sparkled. "Oh, yes! And it sounded so exciting!"

Five of the American children, the three Roosevelts and two cousins, had met every Sunday at the house of Mrs. Stuart Elliott, "Aunt Lucy," who was also living in Dresden. "We read the poetry and stories that we have written during the week," Conie had written, "and one of us writes them down in a book. When the book is all done, we will sell it either to Mother or Aunt Annie and divide the money. I am going to write poetry all the time." They had taken for their motto the cryptic W.A.N.A., which, Conie revealed in strict confidence, stood for "We Are No Asses."

Edie had read some of the "book" resulting from the project, sighing over Conie's sentimental poems and chuckling over Teedie's humorous "Mrs. Field Mouse's Dinner Party." What fun they had had! If only . . .

"Why don't we form a club here?" suggested Conie. "We could get Fanny and our friend Grace Potter and perhaps another girl. I'm sure the boys wouldn't be interested, and Teddy is too busy with his tutoring for Harvard."

Edie agreed eagerly, though disappointed that Teedie would not be included. The group was formed, with Conie as president and herself as secretary, and it met each Saturday, calling itself P.O.R.E., which could be interpreted either as "Paradise of Ravenous Eaters" or "Party of Renowned Eligibles." Edie copied the resulting masterpieces in the swift-flowing script she had developed under Miss Comstock's rigid tutelage.

The club was one bright ray of sunlight in the clouded skies of her early adolescence. The economic depression that had followed the Panic of 1873 and which had further aggravated the decline in the Carows' financial fortunes was affecting her father's health as well as his bent toward dissipation. Her mother's lips narrowed with increasing tightness; the small lines of worry in her white forehead became deep furrows. Conversations overheard between her and Aunt Kermit were more and more sharply critical of Charles. Even the summers at Barbary Brae, Grandfather Tyler's house, seemed devoid of their former delights. Nature walks yielded fewer exciting discoveries, for Papa was away most of the time on fruitless business ventures, and when he was there to share them he was listless and indifferent. She would dutifully don her long pantaloons and skirted jacket and join the swimmers on the beach, for she always loved to swim, but it was a lonely pastime. Her sister Emily did not care for swimming, and she had never been interested in nature walks.

But each summer during Edith's adolescent years the dull skies brightened amazingly for a whole week or more. In 1874 Theodore Roosevelt Senior followed the lead of his father and brothers and established a country home at Oyster Bay on Long Island. He rented a house on the Sound, Southern style to please Mittie, with its high white columns and wide verandahs. The family named it Tranquillity, and it was to be their summer retreat for many years. To Edie's delight Conie was permitted to invite friends, and both she and Fanny Smith visited there for at least a week each summer.

Tranquillity! It should have been named Velocity, for every moment was packed with some thrilling activity. Only Mittie Roosevelt, gracing the porch in her immaculate white muslin after emerging from one of her frequent baths, could be said to typify the designation. And even she was not immune to the prevailing mood, as when Teddy once picked her up and set her on one of the high pillars at the entrance gate, where she was goodnaturedly but hopelessly stranded until he decided to take her down.

The house would burst into action at dawn with little cessation throughout the day except for early "Morning Prayers," announced by Theodore Senior just before breakfast. Even this period, as Conie described it, was entered into with the "same joyous zest" with which he had the power of imbuing every act of his life, making people feel it a privilege rather than a duty. Then there were long rides on horseback, vigorous swims, and boat rides to Yellow Banks on the other side of the bay, where they would picnic and climb Cooper's Bluff, then run down its terrifyingly steep slope. Even the games were vigorous, mentally if not physically. There were competitive essays, on Wordsworth, Washington Irving, or Plutarch's *Lives,* or amateur dramatics, like the play *To Oblige Benson,* coached by Theodore Senior, in which Teddy endeavored to play the part of a bad-tempered farmer and Cousin John Elliott that of an impassioned lover.

In 1874, Edie was at Tranquillity for the first time. She was thirteen and Teddy nearly sixteen and he seemed almost a stranger to her. Hoping to take his entrance examinations for Harvard the following summer, he was studying furiously under his tutor, Arthur Cutler, especially in his weakest subjects: mathematics, Greek, and Latin. The three years between them seemed to have stretched even further and although he entered into the more vigorous sports and games and pursued his experiments in taxidermy, he had little time for the literary activities he and Edie had once shared. Elliott also found him uncongenial, though not for the same reasons. Finding a snake under his bed in the room they shared, the fastidious Ellie had drawn a chalk line down the center of the room, vowing vengeance if it was crossed by any category of living things.

Of course Edie enjoyed herself. As her relationship with Teddy grew less intimate, that with Conie became even closer. Sometimes she wondered if Conie, whose devotion to her older brother was almost akin to worship, had not at times resented their mutual interests during childhood. But when the time came for her trip to Tranquillity the following summer, it was with less than excited anticipation that she started on the long and complicated journey. She had to travel from Grandfather's to New York by coach, train, carriage, across the Hudson by ferry, hansom to the pier, ferry to Long Island City, and finally train to Syosset, where someone would meet her with a buggy and take her to Oyster Bay.

But this year turned out to be different. She knew it was going to be when she looked out the train window and saw both Conie and Teddy waiting on the platform. As she descended the steps, she was glad that she had worn her new rose-sprigged muslin in spite of Mamma's warnings that dusty roads and train cinders would ruin its freshness ("Spotless Edie"?). She was also glad that the hair under her wide leghorn was piled high on her head, for Teddy's eyes widened in appreciation and surprise.

"Well, well!" he greeted her. "So our little Edie has grown up and become even prettier!"

"She's just fourteen, like me," Conie reminded him tartly.

"You'll never grow up, darling Pussie," teased Teddy, using his favorite pet name for Conie. "That is, I hope not. You'll always be my sweet little sister."

If there had been a hint of jealous pique in her reminder, it melted in her sunny smile.

So, thought Edie, he has acquired tact as well as the art of flattery. To say nothing of those broad shoulders and wiry muscles and—yes, those brand-new sideburns!

He was in high spirits during the six-mile ride to Tranquillity, partly because he had recently passed his Harvard entrance examinations. "Isn't it splendid?" he demanded with naive frankness. "I passed in all eight subjects I tried!"

There was the usual frenzy of activity, which Edie engaged in only partially. Most of the time she sat in Teddy's rowboat while with long strong strokes he propelled it for miles around the Sound. Unlike Elliott, he did not care for sailing, which involved too little action. In fact, his idea of rowing, as Conie described it, was to "row in the hottest sun, over the roughest water, in the smallest boat." Sometimes it took all of Edie's self-control to appear calm amid the onslaught of waves. Not for worlds would she have let Teddy know how she was quaking. While he rowed she would read to him some of their favorite poems of Browning and Owen Meredith, Swinburne, Shelley's "Prometheus Unbound" and "Ozymandias." It was almost like the old days, sitting on the steps of the brownstone and reading to him from *Our Young Folks* or *McGuffey's Readers*.

Edie suffered no illusions as to the uniqueness of being the recipient of Teddy's special attention. She knew that Annie Murray or some other girl would soon be taking her turn sitting in the same seat and being rowed by him with the same joyous gusto, that when fall came he would be dancing the waltzes and polkas and Germans at Mr. Dodsworth's dancing class as often with Fanny and Annie and Nellie Smith and Grace Potter as with her. And yet—would any of the others enjoy with him the cadences of Swinburne?

But, after all, what did it matter? She should be glad that he was showing more interest in people, becoming more social, like Ellie, enjoying the dancing, the skating parties, and spring picnics in Central Park instead of spending all his time reading or swinging on bars or stuffing mice and snakes and hedgehogs for his precious "museum." She certainly was not "in love" with Teddy Roosevelt, whatever that meant. Fourteen—fifteen—was too young to be "in love" with anybody—wasn't it?

5

Conie's fifteenth birthday party, held at Tranquillity on September 27, 1876, was spoiled for Edie because Teddy was leaving on the same day for Cambridge, Massachusetts, to enter Harvard College. If he shared her dejection at the thought of the impending separation, he gave no sign. Yet that summer there had seemed to be a deepening of their friendship, so much so that it aroused comment.

"Really, Edie," Fanny Smith had chided during one of their visits to Tranquillity, "it isn't fair, your keeping Teddy all to yourself. What do you do on all those boat trips he takes you on? Surely you can't be just reading, reciting poetry to each other, all the time!"

Edie had blushed, stammered. "Oh, but—but—really, that's all we do, read and—and talk—"

"Aha—talk! I thought so. And what about—or is it a secret? Plans, maybe? Plans for the future?"

"Well—yes. Sometimes."

But they had been Teddy's plans, she might have explained, not hers. He was confused about his future, his career. What kind of work should he be preparing for? Business? But his father had given up the family glassworks because of the recent financial panic. Should he become a naturalist? That seemed the best answer. But it might mean his father must continue to subsidize his work, at least for a while. What did Edie think? Yes, sometimes he had seemed to be including her in his plans.

Edie prepared for the Hallowe'en party she customarily gave on October 31, getting the tub ready for apple ducking in the kitchen, having the mirror hung in an adjoining room for squealing females hopefully to discover the faces of their future husbands reflected in it, and obtaining the ingredients for candy pulling. But she did this without her usual anticipation. Teddy would not be there. Without his contagious exuberance the party was bound to be dull. And yet Conie would be there, just back from Tranquillity, and she would have news of Teddy. Conie was eager to impart news, a bit relieved, perhaps, to discover that Edie, as well as herself, had received no letters from him.

He had written several times to Mittie, addressing her with his usual affectionate diminutives like "My Own Darling Little Motherling." He was well settled in Cambridge in his room in a private house, which had been arranged because of his asthma. Bamie, who had visited friends in Boston, had fixed up his room cozily, with fresh curtains, rugs, and pictures, and he didn't know what he would have done without his older sister's help. He was making new friends. He wanted his bookcase sent on, also his boxing gloves. He was attending Christ Church and was going to teach a Sunday school class of boys. He was sure there was not another fellow in college who was loved as much by his family as he was himself.

Time dragged that fall for Edie. Classes at Miss Comstock's, even those in her beloved English literature, became chores rather than exciting adventures. Visits with Fanny and Conie to the library, the museums, art galleries, and the National Academy of Design, where paintings of American artists were being displayed, failed to arouse her usual absorbed interest. And Mr. Dodsworth's dancing class seemed to lack zest, though there were usually youths eager to become her partners. Invariably she found herself looking in vain for a skinny, bespectacled absentee with rather ridiculous sideburns, who was by no means a graceful dancer like his brother Ellie but who executed the rondos and polkas and Germans with unrhythmic, slightly jerking exuberance.

He was coming for Christmas, Conie told her gleefully, showing her a letter beginning "Darling Pussie." He was bringing some of his friends with him, and he wanted a party for them, if it was "perfectly convenient." Of course it was, and Edie was invited. They danced a German, a sort of cotillion, together, then to her disappointment other people, including his college friends, appropriated her for the rest of the evening. Though they paired off later at a supper party given by Aunt Anna Gracie at her new house on East Thirty-fourth Street, she and Teddy had little opportunity for one of their old intimate chats. Then, before she knew it, the holiday season was over all too quickly.

"Teddy mentioned you in his last letter to me," remarked Bamie to Edith one day in February 1877, her dark face lighting with the usual concentrated interest she showed in every person. "He has been meeting some of the girls I know in Boston, a Miss Whitney, a Miss Revere, and a Miss Lindsey. He says of them, 'Some of the girls are very sweet and bright, and a few are very pretty. Still, oh Anneth, I remain faithful to Thee!' " Bamie chuckled. "I suppose that's a combination of you and Annie Murray. He has always thought you and she were unusually pretty girls."

Edith received other generous information a few days later. "You'll like this," Conie told her. "Teddy writes that he has been on a big sleighing party given by his friend Harry Jackson. He says, 'This was great fun for there were forty girls and fellows and two matrons in one big sleigh. We sang songs a great part of the time.' Now listen to this. 'One of the girls by name Miss Wheelwright looked quite like Edith only not nearly as pretty as her ladyship; who, when she dresses well and don't frizzle her hair is a very pretty girl.' "

It was early in May when the invitation came, fortunately not from Conie or Teddy, but in a formal note from Theodore Roosevelt Senior. He was taking his family to Cambridge to visit Teddy, and they were anxious to have some of his young friends go with them. He hoped Edith would like to go.

Would she! Conie also was bubbling with excitement. "You can go, can't you? Cousin Maud Elliott is going. Teddy asked for you especially. He says, 'We would have jolly fun. Be sure and come, and *make* Maud and Edith come.' He even underlined the 'make.' "

"Yes," agreed Gertrude. "Since it was Mr. Roosevelt himself who asked you, we think it would be proper."

Who when she dresses well and don't frizzle her hair is a very pretty girl.

Edie could think of nothing else. After packing her portmanteau with her best clothes (she could afford nothing new), Edie regarded herself in the looking glass with dispassionate candor. Pretty? She did not think so. True, her features were even but her nose rather too prominent, like her mother's; forehead broad and high (the kind people called intellectual?), lips full, complexion fair, hair still golden and falling in soft waves. (Never again would she put it in curlers, to "frizzle" it.) But it was a quiet face, not like Conie's, which seemed to glow and sparkle, revealing every passing thought and fancy. She could not know that its attractiveness lay in this very quality of restraint, suggesting hidden depths of emotion which only the favored few might explore. In fact, she had described it herself in a stanza of a long poem she had recently written for P.O.R.E. It was called "My Dream Castles."

> To my castles none may enter
>   But the few
> Holding to my inmost feelings
>   Love's own clue
> They may wander there at will
> Ever welcome, finding still
>   Warm and true.

They left by train for Boston on Thursday, May 24, Theodore Senior, Bamie, Conie, Ellie, Cousin Maud, and Edie. The following day they traveled to Cambridge by horsecar.

It was an exciting three-day visit, as they explored the Harvard yard with its historic brick buildings, some of them already two hundred years old; visited Teddy's homey bedroom on the second floor of a house on Winthrop Street; met his friends; drove over the cobblestone streets of Cambridge in two carriages; and enjoyed an evening at the theater. Best of all, Edie had a chance for an intimate chat with Teddy on Sunday, which almost restored the camaraderie of their early days. But it was over too quickly.

Over? Not quite. For the letter which "Dear Pussie" shared with Edith early in June gave a crowning touch to the adventure. "I enjoyed your visit so much," wrote Teddy, "and so did all my friends. I don't think I ever saw Edith looking prettier; everyone, and especially Harry Chapin and Minot Weld admired her little Ladyship intensely, and she behaved as sweetly as she looked. . . . Now good by, darling; I have enjoyed seeing sweet Pussie, darling energetic Bumble, and big, good-natured Father so much. Best love to Maud and when you write to Edith tell her I enjoyed *her* visit *very* much indeed."

It was Edie's grandfather, General Daniel Tyler, who, during one of the Carows' summer visits at his house in New Jersey, broached a subject that had long been a source of conjecture in the family. Big, bluff, heavily bearded, he was a man of great strength of will and determination, and wielded almost as iron a hand over the members of his immediate family as he did over his subordinates in the commercial world. Having once been caught in an error of judgment in marital matters, having sanctioned what he now considered his daughter Julia's unfortunate marriage, he did not intend to let such a mistake happen again.

"These young Roosevelts vacationing over at Oceanic," he began casually. "I see you're quite intimate with them, especially the older boy, the one that's at Harvard. Going rowing with him, taking long walks looking for bugs and animals for him to stuff."

Edie blushed. "Yes, Grandfather. He—he's a very good friend."

His old eyes, gimlet sharp, bored into hers. "No more than that?"

"I—I don't know what you mean."

"But I'm sure you do, child. Tell me now, do you and he have an understanding of any kind?"

Edie considered. What had they meant, those talks they had had about the future? "No, we haven't. I—I'm sure we haven't."

"Then don't," ordered Grandfather bluntly. "I've heard things about the Roosevelt family, and I don't want you getting mixed up with them. Not permanently."

Edie frowned. "What things, Grandfather?" Her gaze was suddenly as steady as his. "What have you heard?"

"Well . . ." His lips tightened. "You may as well know. I've heard that scrofula runs in the family."

"Scrofula?" Edie looked puzzled. "What's that?"

"It's a bad disease, like tuberculosis, only it affects the glands and bones, not the lungs. It's nothing for you to worry about as long as you remain just friends. But I'm warning you, child. Don't make any promises. I forbid it. Anyway, you are much too young to even think about marriage. Now you just remember what I've said."

Poor Grandfather, mused Edie, thinking he was still back in the Civil War commanding troops or building a railroad or a blast furnace down South, where he could tell people just what to do! He was doubtless mistaken. He had heard about so many of the Roosevelt family suffering from asthma and headaches and other ailments that he had confused them with something much worse. But one did not contradict Grandfather!

Anyway, he needn't worry about her. Teddy had so many girl-friends, all of them "so sweet," "so pretty," "so bright," that no one of them could really claim preferment. On New Year's Day of 1878 Edie knew he had called on twenty friends, herself but one of them. She would not have been at all surprised by the notation he made in his diary, that he had particularly enjoyed calling on "singularly sweet" Annie Murray, "pure religious" Fanny Smith, and Edith Carow. They were his trio of *"freundinnen."* Of course it was *something* to be one of three!

On February 9, 1878, Theodore Roosevelt Senior died of a

short sickness so torturing that it had turned his dark hair gray and was later diagnosed as malignancy of the bowels. So great had been his contribution to the city that the flags of New York were flown at half-mast. Newsboys he had befriended and little Italian girls from the Sunday school class that he had taught for many years had sat for hours on the steps of his house waiting for news of him. The whole city mourned.

Edie's heart ached for her young friends, especially Teddy, who had idolized his father. "He was the best man I ever knew," he would confess all his life and measure his every action by the rigid yardstick of his father's teachings. Encountering Teddy at the church after the funeral, she was shocked at the sight of the tortured young face, pale cheeks, lips clamped as in a vise, eyes empty and unseeing. Forty years would pass before she would see him looking like that again, and then, as now, there would be no penetrating the closed door of his grief. Conie was different. One could hold her in one's arms, murmur words of comfort, encourage the tears to flow. And there would soon be sunlight, the blessing of fond memories, shining through the tears.

Both Conie and Teddy remembered Edie's seventeenth birthday on August 6, 1878, Conie with a fond letter. "I often think of your future and wonder what it will be, and whether we will always be so placed as to see much of each other." Teddy sent greetings and a box of confections. But during her two-week visit to Tranquillity later that month their relationship seemed suddenly to become much more serious and intimate. He wanted her with him in all his activities, taking her sailing and rowing and on picnics, and driving her to Cold Spring to pick water lilies. Day after day they were constantly together. He shared with her memories of his father and seemed to find in her quiet, restrained, yet affectionately sympathetic understanding release for his own turbulence of emotion.

"I remember so well, years ago, when I was a weak, asthmatic child, he used to walk up and down with me in his arms for hours together, night after night, and, oh, how my heart pains me when I think that I never was able to do anything for him in his last illness!"

"But it wasn't your fault," Edie assured him gently. "You didn't know. You came as soon as you could."

Then again: "I often feel badly that such a wonderful man as Father should have had a son of so little worth as I am. How I wish I could sometime do something to keep up his name!"

"You will." Edie's voice was quietly confident. "Wait and see. I'm sure in time he would have been very proud of you."

Then, on August 22, after a sailing trip in the afternoon and a family party in the evening, Teddy took a lantern and the two of them went up to the little summerhouse where during the preceding days they had had many intimate conversations. All this, it seemed, was leading to a climax in their relationship. For this conversation proved to be a beginning—and an end.

At first they talked—or, rather, Teddy did—about various things, his Sunday school class in Cambridge and his attempt to follow his father's precept "Take care of your morals first, your health next, and finally your studies"; his father's promise to subsidize his career in natural history, if that was what he decided to follow ("I have about eight thousand dollars a year to live on, enough to be comfortable but not rich"); the good marks he had made in his examinations, except in French, perhaps because he had had to sit up all the night before with his asthma. Then suddenly, as if all this had been a carefully planned prelude, he leaned forward and placed his hand over hers.

"Isn't it about time we began to plan for the future, my dear Edie, *our* future, I mean? I think we both know how we feel. We've certainly known each other long enough to be sure."

Edie's heart hammered, but her voice remained calm. "Is—is this supposed to be a—a proposal?"

"Yes, of course. You know it is. Haven't I suggested something of the sort before?"

"Yes, you have. And I've told you more than once that we were too young to even consider—"

"But now you're seventeen," he countered, "and I'm nearly twenty. And, anyway, it would be at least two years, probably more, before we could begin to take it seriously."

Edie could not help it. In spite of the seriousness of the moment, some perverse impulse inspired a bit of teasing. "You're sure it's I, Teddy, that you're saying all these things to? You're not mistaking me for another of your female fancies, Annie Murray, for instance, or Fanny, or even that Miss Boden you rowed way over to Lloyd's Neck to see?"

"Ha! So you're jealous, are you?" He tried to match her unexpected mood of raillery, but the attempt was not a success. "I suppose I should consider that a good sign, but somehow I don't. After all this time you should know that you've always been tops in my affections."

"I'm sorry." She was instantly contrite. "I shouldn't have said that. But—" Withdrawing her hand from his, she got up from the bench where they were sitting and walked to the door of the summerhouse, breathing deeply the aromas of heliotrope and sweet alyssum tempered by the salt tang of the sea.

"Grandfather still thinks I'm too young," she said at last, but idly, without conviction.

"He's a stubborn dictator, and you know it" was the rather curt reply. "Since when did you cease to have a mind of your own?"

Edie knew that she had been looking forward to this welcome moment of decision for almost as long as she could remember. For years she had visioned no ultimate purpose in life apart from this not too prepossessing youth with the tightly clamped lips and slightly wheezing voice, spectacles gleaming owlishly in the dim lantern light, the faint but ever-present odor of arsenic vying with those of the sweet autumn night outside. Why, then, did she again yield to another perverse impulse which was bound to create argument, if not hostility? Was it only a further attempt at light teasing, a desire to postpone for a few moments longer a momentous decision? Or, more likely, was it a sudden reluctance to permit any penetration of the shell of privacy which had always been her precious protection, to keep inviolate that small inner sanctum in her "Dream Castles" which no other person had ever entered?

> Only one, one tiny room
>   Locked they find.
> One thin curtain that they ne'er
>   Gaze behind.

"Grandfather said something else," she confessed, only half seriously. "He actually forbade me to have any sort of understanding with you, because—" She hesitated, then plunged on— "because he heard that some bad disease runs in your family— 'scrofula,' he called it."

She was sorry the instant she had said it, for the color flared in his cheeks and his lips clamped. "And you believed it?" he snapped, "This crazy, unfounded rumor?"

"No," she returned quickly. "I really didn't. I was certain he was mistaken. And, anyway, I don't consider it important."

"As a matter of fact," he retorted, "some of my family have objected to my intimacy with you, because, they say, your father is a drunkard."

Edie's emotions, usually deeply hidden, erupted. "How—how dare anybody say that about my father!"

And suddenly they were quarreling, bitter words such as neither of them had ever thought of speaking, words that slashed at the delicate fabric of their longtime intimacy and almost tore it to pieces. Finally Teddy picked up the lantern.

"Well," he said, "I guess that settles things for us—at least for a while."

Silently they went down to the house, joined the family, and tried to act as if nothing had happened. Edie lay awake that night, dry-eyed but miserable, and wished she could find an excuse to go home long before the remaining days of her two-week visit had passed.

They did pass, but not without suffering and frustration for both of them. One day Theodore took such a wild ride on his horse Lightfoot that he feared he had done harm to the animal. At another time he shot and killed a neighbor's dog which had frightened his horse when he was riding, offering the weak excuse that the neighbor had been warned to keep the animal confined.

Edie spent most of her time with Conie, to the latter's delight. To her friend's curious query as to what had happened, if anything, in the summerhouse, she replied with a cryptic, "Nothing really. Teddy just wasn't very nice." That she succeeded in hiding her misery was evident from the first letter she received from

Conie after returning home, which stressed how much she was missed and what a pleasant two weeks they had enjoyed.

The misunderstanding would pass and be almost forgotten, of that Edie was sure. A friendship such as that between herself and Teddy could not be terminated by one silly quarrel. Of course she had news of him, as usual, through Conie. He was doing well at Harvard, where he had been admitted to the prestigious Porcellian Club. And he was making many new friends, among them several young women, doubtless very "sweet and pretty." At last, before Thanksgiving, he sent a message to her through Conie, but it did little to assuage her concern.

"Remember me to Annie and Fanny, and give my love to Edith —if she's in a good humour; otherwise my respectful regards. If she seems *particularly* good-tempered tell her that I hope that when I see her at Xmas it will not be on what you might call one of her off days. Good bye, sweet one."

Her "off days"! She couldn't decide whether to be hurt or angry. She saw him at Christmas, yes, but only with other members of his family. There was no chance for intimate conversation, and he did not seem anxious to create an opportunity. In April of 1879 she met him at Aunt Annie Gracie's, and again it was a friendly but impersonal confrontation. Later that month he sent her a message through Bamie. "I see Edith won a prize for answering the *World* questions; congratulate her for me."

Her hopes soared. The satisfaction of winning this honor for an intellectual achievement was made doubly gratifying because he was the one friend who could best appreciate it. But when she learned that Conie, Bamie, Ellie, Aunt Annie, and Teddy's mother had been invited to Cambridge to enjoy Class Day and meet some of his new friends, her disappointment was keen. This time his letter contained no invitation for her, certainly no *"make* Edith come." Fortunately, Conie did not share with her the most pertinent section of her letter.

"Darling Pussie. . . . I want you particularly to know some of my girl friends now. They are a very sweet set of girls; and I really now know them better than I do any New York girls. . . . Be sure and come on, Pussie. Your loving . . ."

Her whole life, it seemed to Edie, was falling apart. In June,

Great Aunt Kermit died while they were summering in Oceanic. So the Carows had to move again, this time to a house at 114 East Thirty-sixth Street. And when Edie made her usual visit to Conie at Oyster Bay, Teddy was off on a hunting trip to Maine, where he had previously made many friends. He did, however, remember to send her a present for her birthday in August, a copy of *Lucille* by Owen Meredith, one of their favorite authors, bearing the inscription, "To Edith K. Carow, on her eighteenth birthday, from her sincere friend Theodore Roosevelt."

Time! Now that she had graduated from Miss Comstock's, she had all too much of it. Most of it was spent in reading—Dickens, Blake, Thackeray, Swinburne, Henry James, dozens of biographies, the Greek and Latin classics. But the other girls, those in P.O.R.E., preferred lighter reading, and she missed the exciting dialogue she had enjoyed with Teddy. When he was in New York in November, during his senior year at Harvard, they had one of their old intimate chats, chiefly about the books they had been reading and his ambitious plan to write a naval history of the War of 1812. It was almost as if the debacle in the summerhouse had never been. She would have been even more relieved had she known that he recorded in his diary that Edith was the most cultivated, best-read girl that he knew.

He called on her again on Christmas Eve. Though it was a formal visit, customary among friends at that time, he complimented her with the joking remark that he had chosen her out of a list of ten pretty girls. And it presaged more meetings during the holiday season, for he was expecting some of his young friends from Boston, and he was anxious for her and others of his acquaintances in New York to see them. No, he replied to her question, they were not any of the fellows she had met that time in Cambridge. They were more recent additions to his circle of friends.

When Edie met them at a party at the Roosevelts', she was somewhat surprised to find that three of the four guests were girls. "One of my best friends, Dick Saltonstall, and his sister Rose," Teddy introduced them to her, "and their cousins Alice and Rosie Lee, who live next door to them."

Sweet and pretty, thought Edie with a good-humored lift of her eyebrows. The three girls certainly conformed to Teddy's norm of superficial attractiveness, especially Dick's cousin Alice, who was unusually tall and fair, with soft gray eyes and golden wavy hair. Beside this gracefully svelte, obviously athletic guest, also faultlessly and expensively gowned, Edie felt awkward and dowdy, slow and dull of speech. No wonder Teddy was attracted to such girls! But after talking with the three of them, learning what they were most interested in seeing in New York—shops of costumers and jewelers, the Astors' and Vanderbilts' mansions, the Crystal Palace on Murray Hill, and Booth's Theater (not libraries, museums, art centers, concert halls, the Academy of Music)—she wondered if the intellectual Teddy might not find their "sweetness and prettiness" a bit cloying. The guests stayed for a week, and doubtless Conie and her brothers satisfied all their whims.

It was about a month later that Theodore came to her door, eyes brighter even than his gleaming spectacles, lips parted over his big even white teeth in an engagingly youthful smile. No, he could not stop. He had come down from Cambridge on an errand. She was such an old and dear friend that he wanted to bring her his wonderful news in person, the first one to hear it except his family. He had fallen in love, he told her, with the most marvelous girl, surely the sweetest and prettiest in the world, and at last she had agreed to marry him. Edie was such an old, dear friend that he had wanted her to know, and of course she must come to his wedding.

Edie listened while the walls of her "Dream Castles" tumbled down about her ears. Thank heaven for the shell of reserve within which her deepest emotions lay hidden! She managed a smile.

"I appreciate your telling me," she said evenly. "And—I hope you will be very happy."

Part Two

ALICE

While the First Families of New York, including the Roosevelts, were moving north up Broadway and Fifth Avenue to escape the influx of alien multitudes, their counterparts in once-Puritan Boston were fleeing from a similar encroachment of immigrants in their inner city. Many were building new homes in the rapidly growing settlements outside the city boundaries—Brookline, Newton, Milton, Watertown, Chestnut Hill.

Two such families, the Lees and Saltonstalls, had built mansions at Chestnut Hill, though the Lees had retained their Beacon Hill house in the city for winter use. George Cabot Lee's three-storied, many-gabled edifice was only twenty yards from the big rambling house of Leverett Saltonstall. The two families were related by marriage, since Harriett Rose Lee, the sister of George Cabot, was the wife of Leverett.

Both families could boast of impressive forebears, and they belonged to the highest ranks of Boston society. George Lee was a banker, in the firm of Lee, Higginson, and Company, and he was especially proud of his Cabot connections. The Lees of New England were unrelated to the more famous Virginia Lees, and they would have scorned a relationship, since the latter were disdained by their Northern namesakes because they were Southerners. The Saltonstalls traced their roots back to and beyond Sir Richard Saltonstall, an early magistrate of the Massachusetts Bay Colony.

The children of the two families were as close as brothers and sisters. Names as well as relationships were sometimes confusing. There were three Roses—Harriett Rose Saltonstall, her daughter Rose, and Rose Lee, the younger daughter of George Cabot Lee and his wife Caroline. She was usually dubbed "Rosie" for identification. The Lees' older daughter Alice was almost the exact age of Rose Saltonstall, and the first cousins were closer than many sisters.

On a Friday afternoon, October 18, 1878, the two girls were together in an upstairs boudoir of the Lee mansion looking forward to what they hoped would be an exciting weekend. Rose, stretched out on a chaise longue, watched curiously while her cousin patiently wound a long strand of her golden hair around her finger and fastened it expertly to the row of similar curls crowning her head.

"Why do you take so much trouble, Alice Hathaway Lee? Why don't you let your maid do it for you?"

Alice turned with a sunny smile. "Because—"

"I know. Because she can't do it to suit you. And it will stay just like that, looking as if you've just stepped out of a bandbox, while you poke through bushes, walk bareheaded in the wind, rush about on the court playing tennis. You never have a hair out of place, while my untidy locks—" Rose sighed. "But, then, I can't expect to be beautiful like you."

"Nonsense. I'm not beautiful." Regarding herself critically in the mirror, Alice made a wry face. "How could I possibly be beautiful, even pretty, with a turned-up nose like this?"

"Silly, you know that's one of your most attractive features. Piquant, they call it. But don't worry. I'm not a bit jealous really, even though the Harvard friends my brother Dick brings home on weekends give one look at me, then swarm about you like bees around a honey pot." Rose leaned back, hands behind her head, and mused. "Who do you suppose Dick will bring this week? Don't you wish it could be that Bob Bacon again? He's so handsome, like a real Apollo, and Dick says they think he's the most likely man in their class to succeed."

Alice gave her cousin a roguish wink. "If you're hoping for an unattached man, Rose dear, don't set your little heart on him. I've heard he's already spoken for, by a charming girl named Martha."

"Oh, well," Rose sighed in mock resignation, "she can have him. I hope Dick doesn't bring him. He has lots of other good friends, Minot Weld, for instance. He's a lot of fun. Or Henry Chapin."

Alice gave a last lingering look at her hair, patting the curls and reshaping the sculptured waves with her fingers. "I really don't care which one he brings, provided it's somebody who can play a good hard game of tennis." She tugged impatiently at her long white muslin skirt bulging over its many stiff petticoats. "Isn't it ridiculous having to wear something like this on the tennis court just because you're a female and can't show your—yes, why not call them what they are?—*legs!* And these laces so tight you can hardly breathe! No wonder the men can usually beat us!"

"They don't always beat you," Rose reminded her sagely. "Look at all the tournaments you've won!"

"With other women," retorted Alice tartly. "While if I could only wear pants like a man, or even long pantaloons like that Bloomer woman—!"

"Ha! Don't let your mother hear you. Aunt Caroline would have another one of her 'turns' and take to her bed. She'd be sure all our precious ancestors, all the Cabots, Lees, and Higginsons—yes, and my father's Saltonstalls—would be turning in their graves. And you know you're no more like that Bloomer woman than—than a hothouse orchid is like a dandelion. And nobody likes stylish clothes better than you do—ruffles, bustles, trains, and all."

"I know." Alice sighed. "Sometimes I think I must be two people, the girl I am and the one—the one—"

"The one you might be if you weren't yourself," laughed Rose. "Well, who knows? If you live long enough, there's plenty of time. You're only seventeen." She swung herself off the chaise longue, her voluminous ruffled skirts swishing about the hidden extremities which were politely designated as "limbs." "Come on. If you've finished tinkering with those perfect curls and waves, let's go and see if Dick is home yet. He promised to come early if he could in time for tennis before tea."

The two girls descended the long curving staircase, passed through the imposing entrance hall, went out the front door, and started across the expansive lawn toward the Saltonstall mansion. Only a garden gate, surrounded in springtime by a profusion of purple wisteria, separated the two properties.

"They're coming!" exclaimed Rose just as they reached the

gate. "I can hear Dick's buggy coming up the lane. Let's hurry and see who—"

Presently two young men came toward them across the lawn. The one accompanying Dick was a stranger, certainly not the handsome Apollo-like Robert Bacon.

"Hello, girls," Dick greeted them. "I brought a new man with me this time, someone you've never met before. I'd like to introduce my classmate, Theodore Roosevelt. Teddy, this is my sister Rose. And this other young lady is our cousin, Alice Hathaway Lee, but after you've known her a while, you'll understand why we call her 'Sunshine.' "

While politely acknowledging the introduction, Alice bent a critical eye on the newcomer. She was not impressed. He was short, certainly not much more than her own five feet seven. His reddish side whiskers gave him a strange look, almost like an animal of some kind. His keen blue eyes seemed magnified into undue prominence behind a pair of glittering spectacles. When he smiled, his lips drew back over startlingly white and over-large teeth. When he spoke he almost stammered, perhaps because he tried to get his words out so fast, his voice sounding high and a bit wheezy. And there was something else. As they walked toward the house and he moved to her side, she caught a whiff of something, like—what was it like? A chemist's shop? Her nose wrinkled fastidiously.

"Good! There's time for some tennis before tea," announced Dick after the proper introductions to his family. "We four can have a set of doubles."

So he plays tennis, does he? thought Alice. That's one thing in his favor. But even that depends on how he can play.

They went down to the grass court at the foot of the lawn sloping to the southwest and tossed for partners. Alice was not displeased when she drew Teddy, as her cousin Dick called him. If he proved less than expert, perhaps she could make up for his deficiencies. Rose was never her equal at tennis, but she and Dick were well matched. Seeing the way her partner grasped his racket, clutching it more than halfway up the handle, she smiled grimly. Not just less than expert, a novice! But she soon changed her mind. Never had she seen such vigor, such constant restless motion. Teddy was all over the court, wielding his racket like a weapon—slamming, volleying, returning next to impossible backhands, leaping to intercept balls that seemed far out of a tall man's reach. His energy was a challenge to her own skill, and she managed a few clever shots which elicited from her partner a hearty "Bravo!" They won the match easily, 6–3, 6–2, 6–1.

"I say," marveled Teddy as he walked by her side to the house, the admiration in his voice slightly tinged with awe. "I've never seen a girl play tennis like that. My sister Conie is good, but even she . . . Somehow I wouldn't have thought, looking at you—"

Alice regarded him with cool amusement. "And just what would one think, Mr. Roosevelt, looking at me?"

He blushed and stammered. "Why, that—that—I don't know how to express it—that you were a—a lovely flower," he blurted, "A beautiful bloom to be carefully tended and—and cherished. And to think that you're also a good athlete!" It was almost as if he had said, "All this and heaven too!"

Alice was not pleased. It was the second time that day she had been called a flower, and a hothouse one, too, was implied. Moreover, the admiration she saw in the bespectacled eyes was no novelty. She was used to such looks in male eyes, and various poetic tributes from her admirers had come to her ears—"an enchanting creature," "unusual loveliness," "beautiful sunny temperament," "so gay and witty," "an exceptionally bright girl," "so lithe and athletic as well as lovely to look at." Yet Teddy's poor attempt at poetry did not negate the distaste aroused by his proximity.

But she was curious as well as repelled. "What is that—that peculiar odor?" she managed to query Dick when she caught him alone after tea. "That guest of yours, he—he smells. Like a chemist's shop."

Dick laughed. "Oh—that! No wonder you ask. It's probably arsenic you smell. We've all got used to it. He's a naturalist, my dear cousin. It's his hobby. He catches all kinds of birds and animals, skins them, and stuffs them. A real taxidermist. You should see his room at Winthrop Street. It's full of stuffed birds in glass cases and animal pictures and hunting trophies. He goes to Maine on hunting trips. And he's no amateur, either. He and Harry Minot made a trip to the Adirondacks one summer recently and together they wrote a very scholarly treatise on the birds they had catalogued."

Alice was only mildly impressed. Her slightly retroussé nose seemed to elevate a bit further. "Well—that explains *that.*"

Sensing her distaste, Dick hastened to bolster the reputation of his new friend. "Teddy's getting to be a very popular man on campus," he assured her. "This fall he was invited to join the two very select clubs, the A.D. and the Porcellian, which is the highest social honor a student can receive at Harvard. He's also in the Hasty Pudding Club, no mean honor. In fact, he's a member of thirteen of the forty societies on campus and active in all of them."

Somehow that weekend Alice continued to find the enigmatic guest frequently at her side. He was next to her that night as the four of them took a walk through the chestnut grove behind the two houses, golden and resplendent in its fall foliage; the next morning, first walking through the woods; then driving in the Saltonstall buggy to the home of a neighboring family, the Ellerton Whitneys, for noon dinner and afternoon tea and, later in the evening, singing and dancing. The latter, when Teddy managed to become her partner, proved to be a novel yet not unexciting experience. Again she could not help responding to the challenge of his vigorous mode of dancing, though, as her sister Rosie was to describe it later, "He danced just as you'd expect him to dance if you knew him—he hopped."

The next morning, Sunday, they all went to church at Chestnut Hill, Lees and Saltonstalls. Once again Alice found the guest at her side, both in the carriage and later in the pew. But now, it must be confessed, she was getting used to the slight redolence of arsenic; or perhaps the fact that it was in the interest of science made it more bearable. At least there was something intriguingly different about this new acquaintance.

That Sunday afternoon she found herself accompanying their guest to the chestnut grove. Expecting that they would all remain together, she had suggested impulsively, "Why don't we gather chestnuts? They're sure to be ripe and ready for picking. When we walked there Friday, they were all over the ground."

Dick, however, had begged off with the excuse that he had lessons to prepare. Rose had pleaded weariness, mischievously, Alice had suspected.

"I'll be glad to go with you, Miss Lee," Teddy had offered helpfully.

So here they were rambling through a golden paradise of chestnut trees in autumn—though it was more like a rampage than a ramble. For whatever this young Roosevelt person did, it seemed, he did with an almost fanatic zeal, whether playing tennis, dancing, or, as at the moment, chestnutting. He was rushing about, scrounging, scooping, stowing his trophies away by big handfuls, even shinnying up a tree trunk to shake the branches. Alice hardly knew whether to be amused, irritated, or—yes, as on the tennis court, challenged. Did he really think he would be the first to fill his basket? Instead of stooping in dignified fashion, as usual, carefully holding back her skirts, daintily picking up one after the other of the prickly balls with their clusters of dark brown, sweet-meated kernels showing through the split coverings, she was down on her knees, heedless of the earth staining her voluminous Sunday skirts and of the rough shells scratching her palms, grimly and doggedly competing with this human dynamo.

"I say!" he exclaimed, bared teeth vying in brightness with his gleaming spectacles. "Isn't this perfectly bully!"

When they had filled both baskets to overflowing, he took his big handkerchief and his neckpiece, while she took the silk scarf she was wearing, and they filled those, too. They returned to the house weighed down with nuts, and Alice was sure they looked like two ragamuffins. Even her perfect hairdo, she feared, was disarranged, for one of its carefully rolled curls had caught on a tree branch.

"Well!" Rose commented after the two men had left for Cambridge. "So you've made another conquest. And this time, I'll confess, I don't envy you."

"Nonsense!" Again the girls were in the boudoir, where Alice was attempting to repair her damaged hairdo. "He acted about as romantic as a bull in a china shop. And he certainly paid just as much attention to you."

"Ah, my dear, but not with the same look in his eyes. You're probably so used to it that you couldn't tell infatuation from simple courtesy. And, according to Dick, he was calling you such a 'sweet, pretty girl'!"

Alice tossed her head, now fully restored to sartorial perfection. "As if anything that queer person said could matter! Anyway, he probably says the same things about every new girl he meets."

She was both right and wrong. For on Saturday night Theodore had made the familiar hackneyed entry in his diary, that he had found Alice "a very sweet pretty girl." Yet later, much later he was to write, "I first saw her on October 18, 1878, and loved her as soon as I saw her sweet, fair young face."

Somehow the friendship between the two classmates, Dick and Theodore, grew, resulting in frequent invitations by Dick for his friend to spend weekends at Chestnut Hill. Teddy also managed trips with others of his classmates, once on November 10, writing to his sister Conie that he was spending Sunday with Minot Weld and that "we shall go out walking with Miss Rose Saltonstall and Miss Alice Lee and drive home by moonlight after tea." He added that for the second time that year he was "cutting Sunday School." Harry Chapin, he explained, was taking his class for him. The first time had doubtless been on October 18.

By Thanksgiving weekend, which he spent at Chestnut Hill, Alice was becoming reconciled to and sometimes even intrigued by Teddy's marked attention. Although he carefully treated her cousin Rose with equal deference and even included her younger sister Rosie in many activities, it was by now obvious that Alice was the focus of his interest. He fitted well into both families. Mother Caroline and Aunt Harriett Rose were charmed by his courtly manners and his rigid code of ethics, which prohibited smoking and strong drink. Alice's five-year-old brother George was an adoring slave when his idol threw himself into a chair and told enthralling yarns about wolves and bears and other denizens of his wilderness experiences both real and imaginary.

Father George Cabot Lee, familiar through his banking business with the sturdy Dutch Roosevelt reputation, almost as respectable as that of the Puritan Lees, Cabots, and Saltonstalls, also enjoyed discussions with him. At Harvard Teddy was studying political economy under the eminent Professor Dunbar and the instructor J. Laurence Laughlin, and he had organized a Finance Club at the professor's suggestion. Mr. Lee was especially interested in a paper on "Municipal Taxation" which Theodore had written with Robert Bacon and presented at the club's first meeting. Could he have foreseen the future, he would have been as amazed as Laughlin, who was to write many years later, "We little suspected that we were being addressed by a future President of the United States and his Secretary of State."

In fact, Alice herself was the only one who reserved judgment about the ubiquitous visitor, perhaps because she was the one most personally affected. Her emotions were ambivalent. She could not help being flattered by his obvious attention, and she often found his exuberant energy an exciting and stimulating challenge. But just as often she was repelled by the same oddities which at first had aroused her distaste.

Thanksgiving proved to be one of her lenient days. Theodore wrote in his diary that he and Alice and Rose had danced, walked, and played lawn tennis. "I have gotten very well acquainted with both of them," he added. "Rose is a very good pleasant girl, and as for pretty Alice, I think her one of the sweetest, most ladylike girls I have ever met. They all call me by my first name now."

After this entry history was cheated of what followed, for two pages of his diary were summarily torn out. But their content can be guessed at, for more than a year later he made another notation that on that Thanksgiving Day of 1878 he had vowed to win her hand if it were at all possible.

"I wonder," he dared to request during the Thanksgiving weekend, "if you would grant me a great favor. Would you—could you—" He was so embarrassed that he wheezed and stammered—"could we perhaps have a tintype taken of—of you and me together? And Rose too, of course," he added hastily. "I'd like to send it to my mother and sisters, just to show them what my new friends up here are like."

Alice was in a magnanimous mood and graciously agreed. Theodore beamed. He would make arrangements with a photographer and let them know the date. In December he sent them the information, which he followed up with a note written December 6 from the Porcellian Club.

"Dear Alice: I have been anxiously expecting a letter from you and Rose for the last two or three days, but none has come. You *must* not forget our tintype spree; I have been dextrously avoiding any engagements for Saturday. I send this by Minot Wood—who knows nothing of the contents, whatever he may say. Tell Rose that I never passed a pleasanter Thanksgiving than at her house. . . . Your fellow conspirator, Thee." The latter nickname was the one his father had adopted when courting his beloved Mittie.

The picture was taken, sent to his family, and preserved for future generations. It showed the two girls, hatted and festively clad, Alice with a long scarf cascading down her beruffled gown, her cameo features serene and lovely beneath the rigidly sculptured waves, leaning back pliantly against her seated cousin Rose, who looked a little too matronly in her heavy pleated skirt and ample overdress and appeared to be interposing her more substantial person between the youthful Alice and the militarily straight, bewhiskered but unspectacled figure standing at her side, hat and cane clutched tightly in his hands.

In fact, Rose continued to act as a kind of protective buffer between the two, as on the day when Theodore persuaded Alice to let him show her the Harvard campus. Dick was delighted to take the girls to Cambridge one morning in his buggy and turn them over to his eager classmate. Though she had visited the college many times for Class Day and other activities, Alice looked forward especially to the promised glimpse of Theodore's room. Was it really as gruesomely adorned with dead trophies as she had heard? She was happily surprised, finding it rather luxurious in its appointments, with tasteful rugs, curtains, and pictures. Even the few stuffed creatures, mostly colorful birds, were not offensive. And the antlers looked quite harmless. It was obviously the study of a gentleman. Only the pervasive and suggestive aromas of past experiments made her wrinkle her nose.

However, she was forced to acknowledge that Teddy's obsessive passion for animals was not wholly a liability, for it extended to the living as well as the dead. For instance, there was the episode of the horse which Dick had told them about.

Back of this house on Winthrop Street, it seemed, there was a stable. One night two other students who lived in the same house heard terrible noises coming apparently from the stable, neighs and screams. Should they investigate, they questioned sleepily. No, probably it was nothing. After the sounds continued for some minutes they rose reluctantly, donned some clothes, and went out of the house and across the alley to see what was the matter. The stable door was open. And there was their housemate Teddy trying to solve the poor horse's problem. The beast had put his leg through a hole in the side of his stall. Hearing the frantic sounds, Teddy had jumped from his bed, rushed down from his second-story room, and was rendering first aid. The other two were humbled and somewhat abashed. Teddy had not only showed concern for the poor horse, but, unlike them, he had not waited to take action.

Alice had to admit that there were admirable features to his obsession. She herself loved horses. And he obviously preferred to preserve some animals with kindness rather than with arsenic!

"Now," announced Theodore when they returned to the quadrangle at noon, "I am going to take you to lunch, at my club —the Porcellian."

Rose looked doubtful. "Oh, but—are you sure you're supposed to? Isn't it a men's club?"

"Sure, but I'm a member in good standing. I often eat lunch there. I'd like you to see the place." ("Also," he might have added, "have the fellows see what a—what attractive friends I have.")

He took them. If he noticed the shocked glances turned in their direction, or the raised eyebrows and audible mumbles of the assembled members, he gave no sign. Rose noticed and did not enjoy her lunch. Alice seemed happily oblivious of the strained atmosphere. Only when they met Rose's brother Dick at the end of the tour did Theodore discover that he had profaned one of Harvard's most sacred cows.

"Well!" Dick's eyes were twinkling. He could scarcely contain his merriment. "I hear you've made history, Ted. It's all over the campus. Taking a female into the Porcellian holy of holies!"

Theodore gulped. "You mean—what—"

"I mean no woman has ever entered the sacred doors of the Porcellian to eat there, at least not unless a member arranged for a special luncheon or dinner. You've shattered precedent!"

"I knew it," said Rose miserably. "I could tell by the way everyone looked at us."

But Alice's blue eyes sparkled. "Good!" she exclaimed. "What a silly rule! I'm glad Teddy had the gumption to break it. Men think they can keep women out of too many places, yes, and make too many laws treating them like slaves."

Theodore's relief was mingled with amazement. How could he have missed knowing about such a rule? Not for worlds would he have broken the traditions of the prestigious club had he known. However, now that he had, he was suddenly proud of his action. Alice was right. There was no reason why a woman shouldn't be allowed to eat in the Porcellian. But he was surprised. Somehow he had not realized that this "sweet, pretty" idol of his dreams, this lovely flower to be cherished and protected, could have a strong mind of her own. Yet any indication of her approval was cause for thanksgiving. There were few enough of them. He decided that he would have to consider his own traditional views of women's rights more carefully, perhaps bring up the question in his class on political economy. Just what were the laws pertaining to women in society?

The weekends at Chestnut Hill continued. Usually Theodore went by invitation in Dick's buggy or Minot's tilbury or his classmate Harry Shaw's cutter, but, since he felt bound to return to Cambridge on Saturday night for his Sunday school class at Christ Church, he was often obliged to make the return trip by horsecar, first to Boston, then to Cambridge, a long uncomfortable trip, for the cars were unheated and the straw on the floor did little to warm one's feet. A poor environment for his asthma! And occasionally the class itself was not devoid of crises.

One Sunday one of the little boys, Billy, came into class with a noticeable black eye. He was immediately the subject of curiosity and questions. How did he get it? Finally, to restore order, Teddy had to ask him about its origin.

"Well—" blurted Billy after some hesitation, "yer see, Sam—

that big feller Sam—he come along where I was playing marbles. And he swiped some of my marbles. And I told him to give'em back, and—well, that's how I come to get my eye blacked."

Teddy was for the moment stymied. He sympathized with the boy. What to say? "Bully for you!" was his first impulse. "Stand up for your property rights!" But—a Sunday school teacher?

"Of course you know, Billy, it's wrong to fight—that is, er— usually it is. I'm so sorry about your eye. Let's hope it doesn't happen again."

Later, surreptitiously, he slipped the boy a quarter.

Somehow this reward came to the ears of the extremely rigid rector. He shared it with other ecclesiastics, who were likewise shocked. But Theodore was so popular with the boys that he was only reprimanded, not relieved of his duties.

According to Dick Saltonstall, Theodore was no more popular with his professors than with the church elders. When they lectured, he often interrupted to ask questions or utter protests. Sometimes he would even dare to take issue with them, especially in his classes on natural history, a subject in which he was remarkably well versed.

Dick chuckled. "Listen to this. It happened in Professor Shaler's class. The professor had just got started lecturing. There he stood, pointer in hand, when Teddy asked a question. He started again, and was again interrupted. Shaler's bright eyes twinkled, but he was a bit irritated, too. 'Now look here, Roosevelt,' he said. 'Suppose you let me talk for a while. I'm running this course.' "

Dick came home with other stories, at least one of them highly personal.

"It seems our friend Teddy was in this class in rhetoric under Professor Sherwin Hill. One day the professor was reading his class a theme written by one of the students, criticizing it because it was too romantic. Right in the middle of his reading he stopped and asked Teddy, 'Mr. Roosevelt, what do you think of a young man falling in love?' They say Teddy blushed furiously and didn't reply." Dick looked significantly at Alice. "I wonder why. Do you suppose Teddy could possibly have written that theme?"

"I wouldn't know," Alice replied coolly. She shrugged indifferently. "Ask Rose. She would know as much about it as I. He certainly pays just as much attention to her."

"Aha! Don't tell me you're jealous?"

She tossed her bright curls. "Certainly *not.*"

It was true that Theodore attempted to be rigidly impartial in his attentions, as when he went on a hunting trip to Maine in March and brought back two beautiful lynx skins. He had them made into rugs, one for Alice and one for Rose, equal in size and quality.

Rose was also included in his invitation to attend the boxing match of the Harvard Athletic Association on March 22, in which he was entered in the semifinal bout of the lightweight championship at 135 pounds. In fact, many of his Boston friends were attending.

"Be sure and wear your furs," Dick told the girls. "The old gymnasium is freezing."

Alice and Rose went with him in the buggy, and they found excellent seats in the front row of the gallery. Alice had not been looking forward to the evening. She hated violence of any kind. Rose, on the other hand, became as excited as Dick once Teddy's first bout started. She applauded in the most unladylike fashion, even joined with Dick in shouting such encouragements as "Go to it, Ted!" and "Atta boy, Roosevelt!" Alice found it most distasteful and embarrassing. She huddled, shivering, in her furs. When Theodore won the match against a man named Coolidge, she did applaud—but delicately and without enthusiasm.

"Good for Teddy!" exulted Dick. "Those exercises he keeps taking are paying off. He's developed some powerful muscles, and all in spite of his short legs and arms. Once when he went to Dr. Sargent for a physical examination and the doctor commented on the slight development of his legs, Teddy asked him what he could do to strengthen them. 'Oh, you might take to skipping rope like the girls,' was the half-joking reply. And would you believe it? Teddy did just that. He got a skipping rope, and almost every afternoon we could see him out on the piazza at Winthrop Street vigorously jumping rope. How he was ribbed! But pretty soon a lot of his friends were following his example."

Victory in this first bout, however, did not mean that he had won the championship. A contender named Hanks, who had won his fight, was now paired with Roosevelt for the final bout. It was soon apparent that Teddy had met more than his match. It was a spirited battle, but Hanks had far greater quickness and power of endurance. He was taller, had a much longer reach, and another advantage: his eyesight was far better than that of his opponent, who had to fight without his spectacles.

"O-oh, poor Teddy!" moaned Rose. But Alice merely gritted her teeth. If people chose to indulge in such cruel and gory sports, they deserved to take the consequences.

Time was called, and Teddy dropped his arms, but his opponent immediately darted forward and landed a hard swift blow on the nose, which brought blood.

"Shame!" cried Dick, leaning over the balcony. He was joined by a chorus of hisses and other voices shouting, "Unfair!" "Foul!" "You rotten sport!"

But suddenly Teddy held up his hand for silence. "Hist! Quiet, please! It's all right," he gasped but in a voice loud enough to be heard. He pointed to the timekeeper. "Hanks didn't hear him call time." Then he stepped up to his opponent and shook his hand.

There was a burst of applause in which Alice joined, this time as heartily as Dick and Rose. Though her gloved hands made little sound, they beat hard against each other.

The bout continued, growing fiercer and bloodier by the minute. As one spectator was later reported to comment, "It was no fight at all. But you should have seen that little fellow staggering about, banging the air. Hanks couldn't put him out and Roosevelt wouldn't give up. It wasn't a fight, but, oh, he showed himself a fighter!"

"You sure gave him a good battle," praised Dick when they went to the floor to both congratulate and commiserate with Teddy. "You've nothing to be ashamed of." Rose, weeping over the blood and dishevelment, was equally complimentary. But Teddy was not looking at them. His eyes, fearful yet hopeful, were bent on the third member of the trio.

"You were wonderful!" said Alice, her blue eyes shining. "I was so proud of you."

His cheeks vied in hue with his bloody and swollen nose. "Well

—he certainly worsted me, and I deserved to be beaten. He's a much better boxer, and I still have a lot to learn. But at least—"

"Oh, I didn't mean the fight," Alice interposed quickly. "I meant the way you excused that—that horrible butcher for the mean advantage he took of you. That showed *real* courage, and"—she conferred the crowning accolade—"it was the act of a gentleman."

"Well—thanks," he returned lamely, gratified though obviously a bit disappointed. If he had hoped to impress her with his physical prowess, and he undoubtedly had, it was something to have won approbation from this unexpected source.

He basked in the euphoria of Alice's approval during the following weeks. She graciously accepted, along with Dick, Rose, and Mrs. Saltonstall as chaperone, an invitation to a little lunch party in his room at Harvard. Several other girls and young men of their acquaintance were invited. The lynx rugs, tanned and burnished to perfection, were presented in a formal ceremony to Alice and Rose after the daintily prepared and served luncheon. Alice was obviously delighted. The beautiful skin in its tawny, glossy final glory suggested little of its pristine savagery or of the gory violence the animal had experienced.

"I love it," she commended. And, she added, to show her gratitude she was going to make Teddy a lovely pair of warm wool slippers.

After the spring of 1879 arrived, the season seemed at last to color their relationship with at least a hint of romance. The pathway between the Saltonstall and Lee houses, blossoming with a riot of purple wisteria, was an invitation to leisurely strolls and intimate chats. It was also the perfect foil for sheer pastel gowns of silk and voile and dimity. One day in April Teddy made his appearance not in a buggy or a tilbury, but on horseback.

"Meet my own mount, Lightfoot," he announced to Alice triumphantly. "I had him sent on from our summer place at Oyster Bay."

Having his own horse would make his trips to and from Chestnut Hill much easier, especially for his return to Cambridge each week in time for his Sunday school class on Sundays. Also—and this he refrained from explaining—it would mean that he could come much more often. And he certainly did, not only on weekends but occasionally during the week. In fact, one letter to his mother, his "Darling Little Pet," chronicled almost daily visits.

"My horse is in beautiful trim, except that he is not filled out yet, and his winter coat makes him look shabby. I have ridden him every day last week, and of course my rides ended up quite often at Chestnut Hill."

And a week later, to Corinne, his "Darling Pussie," he wrote: "Saturday morning I rode over (very swell, with hunting crop and beaver hat) to Chestnut Hill, where I took lunch with the Lees. In the afternoon I drove Alice and Rose to Boston, to call on the Roches. . . ." On Sunday, he continued writing, "Immediately after midday dinner I rode back to Chestnut Hill. . . . We went out walking. Alice and I did not get back till nearly six o'clock. I took tea with the Lees and did not get back to Cambridge till about ten o'clock."

All this in spite of the fact that in addition to his required courses he was taking a stupendous number of electives—German literature, Italian, natural history, physical geography, structural geology, zoology, political economy—nine subjects in all, twenty hours a week. But by rising early enough, he managed to get in a couple of hours of study before breakfast, and by studying seven to ten hours a day he could get most evenings and every weekend free.

Poor Lightfoot suffered the brunt of this constant activity without his master's emotional stimulus. Once both came to grief. On May 13, Teddy's diary recorded, he started for Chestnut Hill in the late afternoon to reach the Lees' home in time for dinner. "I rode like Jehu, both coming and going, and as it was pitch dark when I returned (about 10.15) we fell, while galloping down hill— a misadventure which I thoroughly deserve for being a fool."

When Lightfoot became lame as a result of the mishap, Teddy was forced to walk the six miles each way for many of his visits until in June, he wrote "It makes me feel like a new man to have my horse well again; I had a most glorious ride. I spent the afternoon walking with Alice . . . the evening dancing . . . riding back at ten o'clock."

That his "Sunshine," as Alice was often called, had been bless-

ing him with more benign warmth since the episode of the boxing bout in March was evidenced by an exuberant entry in his
diary on May 8. "What a royally good time I am having. I can't
conceive of a fellow possibly enjoying himself more." At another
time he wrote, "Truly these are the golden years of my life."

Indeed Alice herself was enjoying the ceaseless round of activities as much as he. She thrived on excitement. With other young
people from both Harvard and surrounding towns they danced
the five-step waltz and the knickerbocker, played whist, read
ghost stories to each other. She reveled in their theater parties.
And now that she had become more used to the early noted
eccentricities—the tufts of reddish whiskers, prominent teeth,
wheezy voice, yes, even the slight unappealing aroma, which had
been growing fainter and fainter since Teddy had begun to question his decision to pursue a career as a naturalist—he was by no
means an escort to be ashamed of. He knew how to dress well
and did, with fastidious taste. The "hunting crop and beaver"
were supplemented by high collars, silk cravats, a blue diagonal
cutaway coat and vest on special occasions, yes, and even a silk
hat. Not, of course, that he occupied an exclusive place of favor
in Alice's affections—at least, not yet. She had many other admirers among her men friends, and she was not yet eighteen.

Alice knew she still had a long time in which to make up her
mind! However, sometimes it seemed as if others were trying to
decide for her.

"That young man of yours," Uncle Saltonstall once said,
"seems to be very up and coming, likely to succeed. Dick says he
does well in his classes. With his background and education he
should go far, especially if he goes into business like his father
and grandfather. They're considered to have been very wealthy
men."

That young man of yours . . . likely to succeed . . . It was *her*
life he was speculating about, not that of the son of one of his
financial peers.

"How lucky you are!" sighed Rose with more admiration than
envy. "That is, I suppose you are. I certainly never expect to have
a man look at me like that, as if I were a rare, tender flower to be
pampered and cherished. I can't help wondering, though." Rose's

sweetness often revealed tiny barbs. "A man might pamper and cherish a sweet flower just to pluck it and wear it in his button-hole."

Alice was startled. There it was again. It was Rose who had first compared her to a hothouse orchid as contrasted with a dande-lion. Was that one reason why she was so hesitant about taking Teddy's attentions too seriously? Did she feel instinctively that he wanted a woman to be just that—a lovely orchid to be pampered and cherished instead of a tough, persistent dandelion, defying convention, thrusting itself into all sorts of unexpected places? Was it her misfortune that she wanted to be both?

But no need to worry about that now. It was June, and when she and Teddy strolled through the chestnut grove the trees were in full glossy leaf, the catkins uncurling into long buff-colored streamers that tickled their faces when they brushed them and turned serious conversation into merriment. Teddy was on top of the world. After weeks of concentrated study and other demand-ing activities, nose to the academic grindstone, he had come through his finals with flying colors. It had been his best scholas-tic year yet. He had maintained an average of 86 and stood thir-teenth in his class of 246. Then suddenly it was Class Day with all its excitement. Alice, of course, was invited with Rose and all the other Lees and Saltonstalls.

Her first sight of Teddy when they met on campus was a shock. There was a bruise on his forehead, and his knuckles had appar-ently been bleeding.

"Sorry," he explained ruefully. "Last night I got into a fight with a mucker. Had to knock him down. Guess my fists got cut by his teeth. But his face looks even worse than mine."

He refused to say what "the mucker" had done. Knowing Teddy, it might have been any breach of gentlemanly conduct or even the use of improper language in some public place. Alice sighed but accepted the explanation with good grace. She was not going to let his impetuous heroics spoil her exciting day. He was a Junior usher, and at the Class Day exercises she saw him ushering in Saunders Hall. Regretfully he was separated from her at noon when he went to lunch at the Porcellian, then visited a party one of his classmates was tendering in the gymnasium, where, he later recorded, he "danced with twenty different girls from Boston and New York." Only after ushering again at the ceremonies attending Class Day Tree and a Hasty Pudding spread with one of his other girlfriends, Nina Botch, was he able to devote himself to his major interest, who, he was to record, "never looked sweeter or prettier."

Alice and Teddy attended two more teas given by some members of the graduating class. They then strolled across the campus, after which Teddy took her to Hollis Hall, one of the buildings on the grounds, where they found an unoccupied window seat looking out on the brilliantly lighted yard and listened to the Glee Club singing familiar nostalgic songs such as "In the Sunny Rhineland" and "Seeing Nellie Home."

It was a setting made for romance. The colored lamps swaying in the soft June air, the fragrance of honeysuckle outside the window, the enchanting music . . . When she felt her hand enfolded in a strong clasp, Alice was conscious of rushing waves of warmth coursing through her body. She knew suddenly that she must be in love with this unpredictable, impetuous, persistent, bewildering man who for eight months had both antagonized and attracted, repelled and excited her. Something told her that she was on the verge of a momentous, perhaps irrevocable choice between resistance and capitulation. He was leaning toward her.

"I've never seen you looking so sweet or so pretty," he murmured, his voice low and vibrant, for once free of its wheezy overtones. "Do you know what you've always reminded me of, since the very first time I saw you? I remember just how you looked, coming through the gate so straight and tall in your white dress, like—like a beautiful flower planted by loving hands and, oh, so carefully and lovingly tended! And I thought, No wonder they call you 'Sunshine'! I think I loved you from that first moment. And I wanted to be the one to take care of you, always, keep you beautiful and freshly blooming. I've waited all this time to tell you, to ask you, but we're going to be separated now, for long weeks during the summer, and I can't wait any longer. My dear, my sweet, will you promise that sometime you'll let me take care of you, that you'll become my wife?"

Her senses swam. The music . . . the fragrance . . . the unexpected proposal . . . the unfamiliar warmth of emotion . . . She felt as if she were drowning. Then her head cleared.

The flower again. He might as well have said the hothouse orchid. Something to be carefully tended, cherished. She withdrew her hand, gently but firmly.

"I—I'm very grateful. And—I'm sorry. I do like and admire you very much. You're a wonderful friend. But—I can't make any promises, not any at all." She groped for words. "I—I'm not sure yet about—about anything."

"I understand." He took her hand again, pressed it gently, and released it. "Don't worry. I can wait."

He talked then of other things, of wanting her to meet his family and his regret that they had been unable to come to Class Day, though he had invited them; of his plans for the summer; of the talks he had had with his professors about what kind of work he was best fitted for, because he was no longer sure that he wanted to be a naturalist. It would mean studying three years abroad, and it made Teddy blue to think of it. Professor Laughlin thought he should follow political science as his major interest.

They stayed listening to the Glee Club until about ten o'clock, then walked over to Memorial Hall and danced until half past eleven. It was time then for Alice to go home with Dick and Rose in the Saltonstall buggy.

She felt free, exhilarated, as if she were on the tennis court, unhampered, yes, even by the inhibition of a long white dress and voluminous petticoats. He had proposed and she had refused him. But he was still her friend. And she was mistress of her own life. Hothouse orchid or dandelion, she could choose whatever she was meant to be, and nobody could stop her.

She might have been a bit less confident could she have heard a conversation which was to take place in the not too distant future. It was at a function of the Hasty Pudding Club, which they both attended. During the evening, while she was dancing with another partner, Theodore happened to be standing next to Martha Waldron Cowdin, who was later to become the wife of his classmate Robert Bacon.

"See that girl?" he burst out suddenly, pointing. "The girl in the white brocade with the yellow hair, the one everybody calls 'Sunshine'? I am sure you know her. I am going to marry her. She won't have me, but I am going to have her."

2

Theodore visited his friends at Chestnut Hill only once that summer of 1879, arriving on August 20, when he was on his way to Maine. The ostensible reason was an invitation to attend a birthday party for Ellen Whitney, but of course it was really an excuse to see Alice. Although he was staying at the Saltonstalls' house, the families in the two adjoining houses were so intimately related that even guests were interchangeable. Again his attentions were so carefully balanced that a casual reader of his diary could not have spotted a preference among "dear, honest Rose, pretty little Rosie, and sweet Alice." And, as he wrote Conie, he had "brought Rose a little gold 'fichu' (don't know how to spell it) pin."

During the two months of Teddy's absence, while Alice's life had settled into its normal leisurely pace of social visits, picnics, dances, a few games, even the vigors of tennis moderated by summer heat, she had almost forgotten the impact of his contagious vitality. He burst into the quiet milieu with all the exuberance of a schoolboy just released from academic prison, energizing every activity like a charge of electricity. A beach party became a jamboree, a country barn dance a contest in endurance, a mere stroll in the woods a marathon.

He had been having a "perfectly bully summer" at Oyster Bay, he explained to Alice on one of their less vigorous strolls. It had been wonderful to be out of doors almost all the time, rowing, swimming, sailing, challenging his brother Elliott to physical contests, shooting. But always at inanimate targets, he hastened to assure her, knowing how she hated killing or bloodshed of any kind. And he had been rethinking his plans for the future. He had definitely decided against being a naturalist. All thought of that career was ended. And even though he had learned just that month that he had been at the top of his class in zoology as well as political economy, the latter would now become his major interest. His future would be in government, perhaps law, not science. There would be no more experimenting with animals, dabbling with those chemicals which, he implied, he knew she had hated.

But his big news was that he had acquired a tilbury, a dogcart, and had been training Lightfoot in the harness all summer. When he returned to Cambridge next month he would be free to come and go as he wished, to take her driving wherever she wanted to go. It was just big enough for the two of them. And he could hardly wait. Yes, and another exciting prospect! He had been planning with his sister Conie, and they both wanted Alice and Rose and several others of his female friends to come down and visit his family in New York at Christmas.

Alice's initial joy and enthusiasm in his presence began to wane. He was taking altogether too much for granted, seeming too sure of her acceding to his wishes, in both the immediate and the distant future. Perhaps she wouldn't want to go riding with him in his little dogcart every time he snapped his whip. She had other friends with better equipages than dogcarts. And how could she and the other girls tell yet what plans they might want to make for Christmas? He was such a self-confident and, yes, aggressive person that she must curb all such assumptions while there was still time. Didn't he realize that she had refused his proposal?

"We'll see what happens," she said coolly, "when the time comes."

When Dick insisted on Teddy's accompanying the two families on a holiday trip to the Glades, she was almost relieved when he said it was impossible. If there had been a telegraph line to Island Falls in Maine, he confessed, he would have broken his engagement with his friend Bill Sewall. As he recorded in diary and letters, he had found it "frightfully hard" to refuse the invitation, "Alice was so bewitchingly pretty and the Saltonstalls were so very cordial." He had to force himself to catch the train to Mattawamkeag.

He arrived at Chestnut Hill again on the weekend of September 27, feeling "strong as a bull" after his stay in Maine. He had climbed Mount Katahdin, taken a six-mile voyage up the Aroostook River in a pirogue, spending ten hours a day up to his hips in icy water, and feasting on salt pork, hardtack, and tea. His means of conveyance was the new dogcart, an equipage never before seen on campus, arousing much amusement and speculation among his college mates. However, as he wrote his older sister Bamie, he thought he had "as swell a turnout as any man." The stares of bypassers, he assumed, were indicative of admiration. He was proud of the cushioned seat, the gleaming side-lamps, the lacquered wood. Its deficiencies—very high wheels, a tendency to tip and wobble on cobblestones or even slightly uneven ground—seemed negligible, as well as his own failure to comply with the rigid rules of etiquette associated with such a stylish equipage.

"Some of us were surprised," wrote his classmate Richard Welling, "when we saw our serious friend Teddy driving a dogcart, and, between you and me, not a very stylish turnout. . . . In a horse show where the judges were passing upon fine points of equipment and etiquette, I fear Roosevelt would have been given the gate."

Owen Wister, who was a sophomore that year, was obviously poking fun at the turnout when he adapted an old song for a burlesque the dramatic club was producing, adding six lines to fit.

> *The cove who drove*
> *His doggy Tilbury cart . . .*
>
> *Awful tart,*
> *And awful smart*
> *With waxed mustache and hair in curls.*
> *Brand new hat,*
> *Also cravat,*
> *To call upon the dear little girls.*

Though Teddy was furious at the time, later he and Wister became lifelong friends.

That Alice was already applying a cooling restraint to their relationship was obvious in his record of this first weekend back at Chestnut Hill.

"Sun., Sept 28. I am having a wonderful time. Dear Mr. and Mrs.

Saltonstall are just too sweet for anything, and the girls are as lovely as ever. In the afternoon I took Rose out walking." Alice was not mentioned.

Nor did her name appear frequently, as formerly, during most of October and November. In fact, only once was she mentioned in connection with an opera party which he and Harry Shaw gave for "Mr. and Mrs. Saltonstall, Rose and Alice." Not that Alice excluded herself from activities in which they both would naturally be involved. She appeared pleased when her father and mother, on a visit to New York, were entertained at Teddy's suggestion by his mother, aunt, and other relatives. She attended parties given for Teddy's sisters, Bamie and Conie, when at Rose's invitation they came to visit the Saltonstalls. In fact, when Teddy gave a specially permitted luncheon for them at the Porcellian on November 22, she was there and sat on his left, and, as he recorded, the party was "the greatest success imaginable." But the absence of her name in his diary, as well as that of two pages which had been summarily torn out, gave proof that her decision to cool their relationship was being successfully implemented.

And that was what she wanted to do: cool it, not end it. For her own emotions were ambivalent. Was she in love with Teddy Roosevelt? Sometimes she was sure of it, as when he presided with such gentlemanly ease at his Porcellian luncheon. But not always. Not when she took her first jouncing ride, reluctantly, in the dogcart, conscious of curious and amused eyes swiveling in their direction. Not when he enthralled her young brother and the other children with tales of wolves and bears and serpents, or regaled the older Lee and Saltonstall males with accounts of his adventurous activities in the Northern wilderness.

"I'm worried about our friend Teddy," Dick said once. "He doesn't seem himself. I'm probably his best friend, and I ought to know. Oh, he's doing all right in his classes, as he has a pretty light schedule this year. But he seems to be driving himself furiously, into all kinds of activities—too many. He's serving as president, secretary, and treasurer of all sorts of clubs, giving parties, hiring a four-in-hand and driving a bunch of us fellows up to a former classmate's farm, where we shot glass balls and had a gay old time. But he's still not himself. One of the men who lives in his house says he goes out at night and when asked where, he just says he couldn't sleep. Sometimes he's out all night." Dick gave Alice a shrewd look. "Could it possibly be something you've said or done—or maybe not done?"

Alice tried to look indifferent. "Of—of course not. How could anything I've said or done have any effect on him? We—we're just friends."

"Maybe that's the trouble," returned Dick wisely.

Alice tossed her head. "Nonsense! How could it be?"

Nevertheless she was especially gracious when Teddy came to the Saltonstalls to spend the Thanksgiving weekend. She suggested that he be invited to eat Thanksgiving dinner at her house. The next day she even consented to go riding with him in the enforced intimacy of the dogcart, and she proved herself a good sport when they got caught in the rain and had to borrow an umbrella at a strange house. Later that afternoon she went with him and Rose for a long walk, when they all had great fun and she badgered him into finding a shop where he could buy them candy. But before he had gone, she was sorry she had so obviously let down her fences of reserve. For on a last stroll they took together he proposed again.

Alarmed and distressed, she made sure this time that she was more definite in her refusal. He was still taking too much for granted. She was much too young, she told him, to make any plans for the future. Why, just next week she was having her coming-out party where she would be introduced to society with all the new responsibilities which this entrance into womanhood involved. Yes, he interjected gloomily, and her debut would be the signal for half the hopeful young swains of Boston to come gathering like moths around a candle. How silly! she protested. But she made no effort to soften her refusal. She hoped she had made it plain that this time the decision was final—at least, almost.

Now, for the first time in months, she felt free. It was the same feeling she often had on the tennis court, with the balls flying and her only inhibition those long flounced skirts that so hampered her speed. Her coming-out party on December 1 was the symbol of her new freedom. It was a gala affair, with most of the young social elite of Boston and vicinity attending. Alice's new gown was of her favorite white brocade, long and tight in bodice, trimmed from the waist down with puffs, ruffles, overskirts, back draperies, and fringe. Attached to the bustle, which was long and flat, made of cotton and metal, was a heavy ruffled train. Her shoes were of white kid, cut out at the instep, laced with ribbon and trimmed with bows.

"Beautiful!" sighed her younger sister Rosie. "You look like—like—"

Like a flower, Alice finished for her silently. Probably that hothouse orchid. Certainly not a dandelion. And as for freedom! The corset of fancy-weave cotton with its stiff boning, steel-hooked front and back lacing, enclosed her torso in a rigid vise. As for trying to dance with that cumbering train—!

Teddy came to the party, but to her astonishment, he did not once dance with her. Nor did he come to Chestnut Hill on the next weekend—or the next. In fact, Alice did not see him at all during the two weeks before he went home to New York for the Christmas vacation. She should have been relieved, of course, yet she had meant to discourage only his suit, not his friendship.

"Where's Teddy?" demanded little George of Dick when the second weekend passed without his appearance. "He promised to bring his pet turtle to show me!"

"Busy," said Dick. "He's suddenly a big social lion. In these last two weeks, I hear, he's attended six formal dinners, gone to nine after-dinner parties, and paid I don't know how many calls and visits. Dances, whist at the Porcellian, champagne suppers. No wonder he has no time for us ordinary friends."

"He danced with me at the first Harvard Assembly," supplied Rosie, "Or, rather, I should say, he hopped."

For some reason Dick did not impart other reports he had heard, that Teddy had been spending sleepless nights wandering through the frozen woods around Cambridge, that night after night he had not gone to bed at all, that one of his housemates had become so worried about him that he had telegraphed to his family in New York and that one of his cousins, James West Roosevelt, had come on to try to rescue him from his frightful despondency.

Alice too was caught up in a social whirl, the predicted host of eligible suitors already captivated by her radiant charm. She was the most beautiful and popular debutante of the season and invitations abounded—to dances, teas, luncheons, and other holiday festivities. But somehow all these long-anticipated parties lacked verve and excitement. The young men, many of them scions of the Boston elite, though perfect in manners, looks, and dress, proved dull and uninteresting, their conversation mundane and flippant, their faultless social graces superficial. She found herself looking constantly, and in vain, for a slight figure with a toothy smile, flowing mustache, gleaming spectacles.

Dick and Rose, Alice and Rosie had been invited by the Roosevelts to visit them in New York during the Christmas holidays. Alice had almost decided to refuse the invitation.

"But you can't not go!" protested Rose, who had been planning an elaborate wardrobe for the visit. "If you don't go, then I shouldn't. You know you're the one he's most anxious to see."

"I'm not so sure of that," replied Alice noncommittally.

But as the time approached, she wavered. After all, Teddy's sisters were her friends. It would be impolite not to return their visit.

They arrived in New York the afternoon of the day after Christmas. Teddy met them at the station and drove them in the family coach and four-in-hand to 6 West 57th Street. Alice was relieved that he seemed his old genial self. Indeed, the very fact of her being willing to come had revived all his hopes and sublime self-confidence. The entries in his diary soared once more into the old superlatives.

"It is perfectly lovely having the dear, sweet Chestnut Hillers with us—and so natural." As the week of their visit proceeded, everyone seemed to be having "an uproariously jolly time." There were sightseeing trips, visits to museums, a drive to Jerome Park on New Year's Day for lunch, where they danced waltzes, polkas, and the Virginia Reel. No day passed without some party, festive meal, or expedition.

To her surprise Alice found that all four of her group were accepted joyously as a part of this huge and obviously remarkable Roosevelt family. There were aunts, uncles, cousins to an nth degree, in-laws, and friends who were as close as relatives, with the irrepressibly exuberant Teddy a sort of catalyst melding them all together. Outside the moil of activity, or perhaps at its center, as in the eye of a hurricane, was the serenely beautiful Mrs. Roosevelt, small, extremely feminine, just a little vague, but possessed of a sprightly wit and rare good humor.

She's like a beautiful gardenia, thought Alice, with that immaculate white muslin gown, that fine silky hair, and that creamy translucent complexion.

She felt almost instant rapport between them, perhaps because she sensed that they were much alike and had a great deal in common, both of them having been courted by strong-minded dynamos. Had Mittie ever yearned for something more in life than to be carefully tended and cherished? Probably not, for she seemed perfectly content to sit in her white muslin surrounded by adoring children who called her "darling little motherling."

In addition to the innumerable Roosevelt cousins, Alice met some of Teddy's New York "sweet, pretty" girlfriends. Of course there would be some here, like Nana Rotch, Bessie Whitney, Harriet Lawrence, in Boston. She was introduced to Fanny Smith, Annie Murray, Grace Potter, and Edith Carow, who had been his companion since early childhood. Alice was especially attracted to Edith. Though not a beautiful girl, she was certainly "sweet and pretty." And although she seemed quiet and withdrawn, she evidently had a fine mind and used it. At one party they attended she and Teddy paired off to discuss a book they had both read recently, resulting in a good-natured but heated argument in which they obviously challenged each other's intellectual skill. Why, wondered Alice, had he not chosen to court this old friend with whom he seemed to have so much in common? Perhaps he had known her so long that she seemed more like a sister than an object for romance.

Was it during the New York visit, surrounded by the provocative glamour of his family, that Alice made her decision? Or later that month when Teddy hopefully resumed his weekend, and even midweek visits to Chestnut Hill, Lightfoot patiently dragging the unsteady dogcart or sleigh, when snow was deep, over the six miles of rutted, frozen roads? Or was it when he accompanied her and her mother and Rose and Mrs. Saltonstall to Salem for a visit with some Lee and Saltonstall cousins? Teddy meanwhile was exercising doggedly in the gymnasium, "vaulting, sparring and running three or four miles a day," perhaps to bolster his hopes with sufficient courage to make a final desperate lunge after happiness.

Oddly enough, he chose Sunday, January 25, the day before semiannual examinations, to propose for the third time. Had she refused, despair might have jeopardized his whole semester of fairly creditable study. But to his unbounded joy she accepted. Why, after such long ambivalence? The answer was simple. She had discovered that she really loved him, that eccentricities like awkward dancing, a wheezy voice, yes, even the faint, disagreeable aroma of arsenic were unimportant. And if yielding meant relinquishing all aspirations of another self, freer, sturdier than a hothouse bloom, that dandelion Rose had suggested, well and good. She would be content, like Mittie, to remain a sheltered and cherished orchid, if that was what he wanted.

A pity she could not have read the entry in his diary that night.

"Sun., Jan 25. At last everything is settled; but it seems impossible to realize it. I am so happy that I dare not trust in my own happiness. I drove over to the Lees determined to make an end of things at last; it was nearly eight months since I had first proposed to her, and I had been nearly crazy during the past year; and after much pleading my own sweet, pretty darling consented to be my wife. Oh, how bewitchingly pretty she looked! If loving her with my whole heart and soul can make her happy, she shall be happy; a year ago last Thanksgiving I made a vow that win her I would if it was at all possible; and now that I have done so, the aim of my whole life shall be to make her happy, and to shield and guard her from every trial; and, oh, how I shall cherish my sweet queen! How she, so pure and sweet and beautiful can think of marrying me I cannot understand, but I praise and thank God it is so."

After this, action proceeded with typical Rooseveltian speed. Teddy rushed to New York to tell his family the glorious news, to buy a ring, to rush back to Cambridge, immediately jumping into his sleigh and driving to Chestnut Hill, poor Lightfoot ploughing through drifts of snow up to his belly.

"They were all perfectly delighted and too sweet for anything," he announced to Alice joyously, "though very much surprised."

"I know," she returned with a smile. "I got a lovely note from your mother yesterday, and I sent one back to her. She expressed her joy and welcomed me into the family. I was quite relieved." Her own parents had been reluctant to give their consent because of her youth, though she was already eighteen, agreeing only when Teddy promised to wait many months before the marriage.

"Feb. 3, 1880. My dear Mrs. Roosevelt," she had written, "I feel almost powerless to express my thanks and appreciation for your sweet note received this afternoon, full of such kind assurances of love and welcome. It is more than kind, and feeling unworthy of such a noble man's love makes me feel that I do not deserve it all. But I do love Theodore deeply and it will be my aim both to endear myself to those so dear to him and retain his love.

"How happy I am I can't begin to tell you, it seems almost like a dream. It is such pleasure to have known all his loved ones, and not to feel that I am going among perfect strangers. I just long for tomorrow to see Theodore and hear all about his journey home. I was so afraid you might be disappointed when you heard what he went for, and I assure you my heart is full of gratitude for your kindness. With a great deal of love, believe me. Ever yours devotedly, Alice Hathaway Lee."

On Wednesday, February 18, with the New York family in Boston, the engagement was announced and celebrated by three events, a dinner at the Lees', a luncheon at the Saltonstalls', and a party in Cambridge at the Hasty Pudding Club. So hectic was his schedule that Teddy went for forty-four hours without sleep. But nothing fazed him now. His heady exultation was more rejuvenating than sleep. Diary and letters continued to explode with superlatives.

"When we are alone I can hardly stay a moment without holding her in my arms or kissing her; she is such a laughing, pretty little witch, and yet with it all she is so true and tender." . . . "It is perfectly impossible to tell how much I love her; it is not merely thinking of her all the time, it is much more than that; she is *always* present in my mind." . . . "Sweet . . . pretty . . . my darling little Sunshine . . . a star of heaven . . . the purest, gentlest, and noblest of women . . ." and so on, ad infinitum.

For Alice one of the high points of that spring was an achievement of Teddy's last semester's work which he shared with her.

"Remember what you said once about men making laws that treat women like slaves?"

Alice did remember. It was the day he had shocked the campus by taking her to lunch at the Porcellian at a time when it was reserved for men only.

"Well, I've thought about it a lot and talked it over with my political economy professor. And I've chosen for my senior thesis the subject, 'Practicability of Giving Men and Women Equal Rights.' I'm sure some of the things I'm saying will raise a holy ruckus in certain quarters."

"What things?" she asked skeptically. After all, "practicability" could apply to many different points of view. And Teddy was a dominating male.

He pulled some scraps of paper from his pocket.

"Here's the first sentence of it," he said, reading. " 'In advocating any measure we must consider not only its justice but its practicability.' "

"Yes?" she prompted, not especially reassured. "What else?"

He kept on reading from one scrap after the other.

" 'A cripple or a consumptive in the eye of the law is equal to the strongest athlete or the deepest thinker, and the same justice should be shown to a woman whether she is or is not the equal of a man.' "

She frowned. "Good—I guess." But—classing women with cripples and consumptives!

"How about this? 'As regards the laws relating to marriage, there should be the most absolute equality preserved between the two sexes. I do not think the woman should assume the man's name.' That is, not necessarily," he amended hastily, no longer quoting. He consulted another scrap. "As for the question of suffrage," he went on, "I say during the thesis that it's unimportant. If women want to vote, they should be allowed to do so."

Alice regarded him with amazement. Such views would indeed raise a ruckus with certain people—her father, for instance. "It—it's wonderful," she said, unable to find words to indicate her approval. Even more satisfying than the surprising sentiments had been the suggestion that his interest in the subject had arisen because of something she had said. Was it possible that she had more to contribute to their partnership than sweetness and prettiness?

It was amazing that Teddy found time for theses or studies during his final months at Harvard. Not only did he spend five evenings a week at Chestnut Hill, but he took Alice for innumerable drives through all the regions around Boston, making calls, picnicking, attending parties, often just riding. Poor Lightfoot grew thin, and Teddy confessed that the dogcart was "a little the worse for wear." He still maintained, however, that "the turnout is really very stylish, and my love looks so bewitchingly sweet up on the high cart, while Lightfoot bowls along famously; and I feel very proud!"

In addition to weekdays he now had Sundays to spend at Chestnut Hill. Dick had arrived home one day, both amused and disgusted. "What do you think!" he burst out. "That rector at Christ Church found out that Ted belongs to the Dutch Reformed Church, not the Episcopalian, and he's ousted him as teacher of his Sunday school class. You should hear the furor. One instructor talked in class about religious intolerance by ministers, and the students cheered. One professor withdrew from the congregation."

Of course there was one advantage accruing from this development. Teddy could now attend church with the Lees and Saltonstalls at Chestnut Hill.

One happening during those months might well have marred the enchantment of those engagement days. In March during a physical examination by Dr. Dudley Sargeant, the college physician, Theodore was warned that his heart was weak. He must not take strenuous exercise, must even refrain from running upstairs. His reply to the doctor was blunt. He would keep on doing all the things forbidden, even if it meant dying young. While he was alive, he was going to *live,* and that was that. He told Alice nothing of the doctor's warning. That it did not cool his beatific ardor was obvious from one of his diary entries in April.

"In the morning Alice studied and practiced music a couple of hours, while I pumped the water and studied; then we played tennis; then she sewed while I read Prescott's *Conquest of Peru* alone. In the afternoon I took my sweet, sunny faced darling for a three hour ride in my dogcart, all round the country, way up to Dedham and the Blue Hills. After tea, I read aloud to Bella and George and romped with them, and told them stories—the other girls all coming in as auditors. Played whist till nine o'clock; then spent an hour with my sweet queen. This is a fair sample of my days; and no wonder I am supremely happy."

In spite of the surfeit of diversions that year, caused first by depression, later by elation, Teddy's last year at Harvard came to an end successfully. He was graduating on June 30, Phi Beta Kappa, magna cum laude, twenty-first in his class of 177.

Commencement saw a grand assemblage of guests— Roosevelts, Lees, Saltonstalls, and many of Teddy's friends from New York. Alice as much as Teddy was the center of admiration and attention. But the two still found time to be alone together. The evening of Class Day they went again to the room in Hollis Hall overlooking the illuminated Yard and listened to the Glee Club singing. There were both sadness and happiness. No more rides in the dogcart. Lightfoot would soon go from Pike's stable to the boat, where he would be shipped to Long Island. But Alice, Rose, and Rosie would be joining Theodore there the day after graduation. The summer would mean separations. After some weeks of vacation Teddy contemplated a Western hunting trip. But plans were already in motion for the fall wedding, even the bridesmaids and ushers considered and listed. Elliott, of course, would be best man, Rose the maid of honor.

The mood was well defined by Teddy as he wrote in his diary for the last time in his nearly denuded room at 16 Winthrop Street:

"I suppose under other circumstances I should feel melancholy, but who would feel blue with so pure and lovely and fond and beautiful a little bride elect? Only four months before we get married. My cup of happiness is almost too full."

3

In July of 1880, on one of their long hikes—no walk with Teddy could ever be called a stroll—he brought Alice to the top of a hill not far from Tranquillity. He made a wide sweeping gesture. "See? Isn't it magnificent? You can see way over the fields and woods to the Sound. I've come here every summer and spent hours studying the birds and flowers. This is called Sagamore Hill. The land once belonged to the Indian Mohannis, chief of the little Sagamore tribe. The white settlers made him sign away his rights two-and-a-half centuries ago, but the hill still bears the Indian name. Isn't it one of the most gorgeous places you've ever seen?"

"Y-yes." Alice was still breathless after the hard climb. "It's beautiful."

In his eagerness Teddy's eyes outgleamed his spectacles. "What would you say if I tried to buy some of this land? I could build a house here, a good big one, as similar to your house at Chestnut Hill as I could make it, with gables, wide verandahs, even one of those fancy little porchlike things over the front door. There'd be plenty of room for all the family and company you could ever want. Wouldn't it be absolutely bully?"

Alice caught her regained breath. "Why—" She looked around. There were only fields and woods as far as one could see. Not a sign of a house anywhere.

But Teddy was not waiting for her answer. "We'll do it, then. I'll try to get the land. And I've got another wonderful idea. We'll call the place Leeholm!"

Alice was uncertain whether to laugh or cry. These extravagant impulses of her unpredictable Teddy! She couldn't imagine spending the rest of her life in a remote place like this. But no need of quenching the fires of his enthusiasm at this point! It was a scheme no more likely to materialize than that other project he had undertaken, the writing of what he called a conclusive *Naval History of the War of 1812*. He had already finished two chapters of it. As if a brand-new graduate, even a brilliant one like Teddy, could compete with the expert historians of the last seventy-five years! She still had much to learn about her Teddy.

But she was learning fast. Two weeks of vacation in July at Tranquillity with the Roosevelt family were a compressed but thorough education. No leisurely rides here behind Lightfoot in the dogcart. Instead, cantering sidesaddle over pathless rough terrain on horseback, with Teddy fortunately refusing to let her risk her neck jumping fences and gullies. Instead of strolling through the woods with no special purpose, there were handicap races where she was supposed to follow the leader through or over every obstacle. Though she dutifully gritted her teeth and waded through bogs, climbed fences, and fought her way through brambles—scratching her hands and tearing her clothes—once more by Teddy's orders she was spared the final plunge down a steep sandy slope called Cooper's Bluff. Picnics were not the simple parties at a beach or under a shady tree that she was accustomed to. They were long rides in a small boat through pounding waves, arriving wet and shaken on a hot rocky shore, digging clams and steaming them over a smoky fire, smacking lips over their gritty succulence.

"Isn't this just bully?" was Teddy's gay appraisal of all these Rooseveltian amusements.

"Yes," Alice managed to reply gamely.

It was Teddy, she noticed, who was the dynamo energizing this whole sphere of almost perpetual motion. Not gay, bubbling Conie, his adoring sister, not Elliott, so handsome, so genial, so sensitive, who seemed always struggling valiantly to keep pace with his brother and the many visiting cousins.

"It was Ellie who used to be the strong one, not Teddy," Conie told Alice. "You'd never believe what a puny, delicate child Teedie used to be before he started 'making his body,' as he calls it. But in recent years Ellie has become almost an invalid, so Father insisted on his spending time out of doors instead of going to college. That's why he and Teddy are planning a long hunting trip to the Western wilderness in August."

"The Wild West . . . hunting . . . wilderness!" Alice did not realize she had spoken the words aloud until Mittie, rocking beside her on the wide pillared porch, smiled sympathetically.

"I know. It sounds awful, doesn't it? But you'll get used to it, dear, as I have. And after a while you'll learn not to worry. It reminds me of the time when Teedie was little more than a baby, and a neighbor ran to tell me he was hanging out of a second-story window. As I rushed off to catch him, I said to myself, 'If the Lord had not taken care of Teedie, he would have killed himself long ago.' I still say it. Sometimes I think he must lead a charmed life."

In spite of this assurance, Alice *was* worried. She envied Mittie her serenity. Only for her in this boisterous family was Tranquillity aptly named. Here on the porch, its high columns reminiscent of her Georgia plantation mansion, rocking gently back and forth in her immaculate white muslin, her slender fingers embroidering just such a sampler as she must have created in her childhood, she seemed more than ever the embodiment of that lovely but fragile Southern magnolia. How, Alice wondered, could she possibly have produced these four tireless, superactive, boldly audacious personalities? For even Bamie with her crippled back and the more delicate Ellie were never far behind Teddy and Conie in their intrepid pursuit of adventure. But they were Roosevelts, of course, not Bullochs, sired by that Theodore Senior who had driven his four-in-hand with such reckless speed through the streets of New York. Her children, too, if she had any, would be Roosevelts. Would they, Alice wondered, hang out of windows and rush off to wildernesses like Teddy?

The mad pace of activity continued when Alice and Teddy, together with Dick and Rose Saltonstall, journeyed to Mount Desert Island, Maine, where the Lees and Saltonstalls spent many summer vacations. During the first part of the holiday Teddy stayed with Dick and their friend Jack Tebbetts at Schooner Head, but he made two round trips each day the three miles to Bar Harbor, where Alice and Rose were staying with the Welds. To his disgust he succumbed to one of his old attacks of asthma and what they called *cholera morbus*.

"Very embarrassing for a lover, isn't it?" he wrote Conie. "So unromantic, you know." But with Jack and Dick taking care of him, he was soon back to normal.

The second week he moved to Bar Harbor, where he immediately organized the whole party. There were mountain climbing, tennis, bowling, and dancing, as well as long hikes to enjoy what he called the "perfectly magnificent scenery." These were activities that Alice reveled and excelled in, especially tennis. She even won the Mount Desert Ladies' Tournament, a feat that set Teddy almost bursting with pride.

The celebration of Alice's nineteenth birthday on July 29, 1880, in which he took a prominent part, raised him to further heights of elation. His pride soon suffered another blow, however, for he was again laid low with the old ailment. It was the first time Alice had seen him succumb to weakness, and in spite of her keen distress she took satisfaction in attending to his needs, feeding him strong coffee to ease his congestion, reading to him, and revealing unsuspected maternal skills. It was almost worth being sick, he confessed, to have such a beautiful and loving nurse.

But Teddy rebounded to strength like a rubber ball, and the dreaded parting soon came. He was off with Elliott on their Western adventure on August 16. For the next month and a half Alice endured a confused succession of emotions, all of them unpleasant. Only the knowledge that their wedding was but a few weeks away made the suspense of waiting bearable.

His letters, though overflowing with protestations of affection and loneliness, did little to relieve her. He and his brother were traveling through Illinois, Iowa, and Minnesota, hunting, roughing it with all sorts of rustic characters ("reformed desperadoes?"), reveling in the frontier life. He made light of numerous disasters, guns breaking, being bitten by a snake, thrown headlong out of a wagon, and soaked by rainstorms. But he was having a "bully" time. She would be surprised if she could see him, with his cropped head, unshaven face, dirty gray shirt, still dirtier yellow trousers, and cowhide boots. "Surprised?" No, decided Alice, wrinkling her nose. Disgusted was more like it. And all those 203 "items" he claimed to have shot! After they were married, she hoped, she could persuade him to forgo such hazardous and uncivilized activities.

But when he returned, arriving at Chestnut Hill the last of September, he had reverted to his usual role which some of his Harvard cronies termed "New York city dude," complete with afternoon suit, silk shirt, socks and cravat, patent-leather shoes, and beaver hat. And his bliss over his reunion with Alice was once more chronicled in superlatives. "She had a certain added charm that I do not know how to describe. I cannot take my eyes off her; she is so pure and holy that it seems almost a profanation to touch her, no matter how gently and tenderly; and yet when we are alone I cannot bear her to be a minute out of my arms."

"Frightful sentimentality!" the offshoot of this union was to remark years later about this and other such effusions in her father's diary.

The wedding was to take place on Teddy's twenty-second birthday, October 27. There was another Roosevelt wedding in that same month. At a dinner party given by Mittie in May a distant cousin, James, of the Hyde Park Roosevelts, had paid marked attention to another guest, Miss Sara Delano, a close friend of Bamie's, tall, dark-eyed, brown-haired, very dignified of mien. A widower, twenty-six years her senior, James had swiftly pursued his suit, and they were married on the seventh of October. It was an event destined to create interest far beyond that of family, for the first son of the union would be named Franklin Delano. Elliott, future father of a girl named Anna Eleanor, became the godfather of this young Roosevelt scion.

But Teddy saw little of importance in this family event. His eyes were focused on October twenty-seventh. Alice's parents had agreed to the date only reluctantly. George Cabot Lee had wanted the marriage delayed at least a year, until Theodore had established himself in a definite career. But his prospective son-in-law had no such intention, even though he knew that Lee was a formidable opponent. Bamie had helped solve the problem. Now the head of the Roosevelt household for all practical purposes, since Mittie was becoming more and more incapable, she had suggested that the couple spend their first winter at 6 West Fifty-seventh Street, having an apartment of their own on the third floor and sharing meals with the rest of the family. Alice would be freed from housekeeping duties and Theodore could pursue his law studies at Columbia University.

"After a long but very peaceable argument with Mr. and Mrs.

Lee," Teddy wrote jubilantly, "I finally carried the day and succeeded in getting their consent to my being married next fall."

Mr. and Mrs. George C. Lee
request the pleasure of your company
at the marriage of their daughter
Wednesday, October Twenty-seventh
at Twelve o'clock
Unitarian Church
Brookline.

Invitations descended like falling leaves on Boston and New York, arousing a variety of emotions. Fanny Smith shared hers with her friend Edith Carow.

"Don't you think it's funny, Edie, their not mentioning the names of the bride or groom? They have several daughters. How will people know which one it is? It might be Rosie."

"They'll know," replied the other briefly. "We all know."

"Will you go?" asked Fanny boldly, suspecting that her friend's apparent coolness concealed an inner turbulence.

"Of course," replied Edie calmly. "Teddy has always been one of my best friends. In fact, I believe I'll give him a dinner. Yes, I'll do just that. It's the least I can do for—for a lifelong friend. I'll have you and Conie and—why don't you help me make out a list?"

She did give the dinner, on October 13. It was a gala affair, as Fanny chronicled in her diary. "Theodore is in the city now and married in about ten days. He is as funny and delicious as ever and wild with happiness and excitement. I went with him to see the wedding presents he is going to give Alice. I hope she is very fond of him."

The presents were indeed sufficient to arouse fondness in any normal bride, for they included a diamond crescent, a ruby bracelet, and a sapphire ring, which kindled a kindred spark in Alice's blue eyes. But she dutifully demurred. "My dear! They're too much. Are you sure you can afford it?"

"Well, my sweet—" He was not sure, for the jewelry had cost him some $2,500, an extravagant amount of money to be spent on luxuries—"they're no more than you deserve." He would economize, he promised himself, after they were married.

It was Fanny, not Alice, who preserved memories of the wedding for future generations. She and Edith and Grace Potter left for Boston on October 26, with members of the Roosevelt family, and all were lodged at the Brunswick Hotel, where Theodore joined them.

"We arrived late at night and immediately went to bed," she wrote in her diary. . . . "The next day people called and we explored the city at intervals. Most of the party dined together at a big table and in the evening the ushers came—we had great fun. Theodore spent that night at the hotel. He gave me one of the little pearl usher-pins. What I do recall quite vividly," she remembered later, "were Theodore's wild spirits the eve of the wedding, as I was their victim: he indulged in one of his favorite pastimes, tipping back my chair so far that I was in terror of disgracing myself with a back somersault."

Her description of the actual wedding was brief. "The next morning we had to dress immediately after breakfast, and Edith, Grace and I in one carriage, drove out into the country to the church. It was the dearest little wedding. Alice looked perfectly lovely and Theodore so happy and responded in the most determined and Theodorelike tones. There were ten ushers, Emlen and West, two Lees, two Peabodys, etc." She did not mention the bridesmaids, who included Conie, Rosie Lee, Rose Saltonstall, and Fanny Peabody, nor did she describe the bridal finery. But many years later it would be noted that another Alice's wedding dress of white satin was trimmed with the rose-point lace which both Alice Lee and her mother had worn for their weddings.

Teddy's record of the event was devoid of details but eloquent. "At twelve o'clock on my twenty-second birthday, Alice and I were married. She made an ideally beautiful bride; and it was a lovely wedding. We came on for the night to Springfield where I had taken a suite of rooms. . . . Our intense happiness is too sacred to be written about."

On October 31 Teddy was writing from Tranquillity to his mother in an equally rapturous vein.

"Darling Little Muffie, I have been living in a perfect dream of delight. The house is just perfection. Kate cooks deliciously and Mary Ann is exactly the servant for us, and Davis does his part beautifully too, always sending in his respects to 'the good lady' as he styles Alice. We breakfast at ten, dine at two, and take tea at seven; thanks to Bysie's [Bamie's] thoughtfulness Alice does not have to order any meals. In the morning we go out driving in the buggy, behind Lightfoot, who is in splendid trim. In the afternoon we play tennis or walk in Fleets woods. In the evening I read aloud—*Pickwick Papers, Quentin Durward,* or Keats' poems. We are having an ideal honeymoon, and the dear little wife can rest all she wants to, and is the sweetest little dor-mouse that ever lived. The pretty darling sends her warmest love to you, Bysie, Pussie, and Nell. Ever your loving son."

For two weeks they lived in this paradise of autumn crimson and gold, inhabited only by themselves, the three servants, Teddy's horse Lightfoot, a collie dog named Dare, a little calf, and a "melancholy cat." Alice did not have the heart to protest when Theodore spent $10,000 to purchase land which included his favorite hilltop, the first step toward the realization of his dream house. After all, it was a beautiful spot, and perhaps he would be content to make it a summerhome. But—a year-round home in this remote place—! Though it was a delightful honeymoon retreat, she could not picture it as a permanent home.

They drove with Lightfoot to New York, where they set up housekeeping in their own rooms on the third floor in the West Fifty-seventh Street house. Alice fitted easily into the life of her new family. December was filled with parties in her honor, dinners, receptions, operas, balls. She joined the Fifth Avenue Presbyterian Church, which Teddy and the other Roosevelts attended. Teddy fervently asserted that "she is too sweet to me in *everything*" and that she behaved "like a queen" on every occasion.

Teddy had applied for admission to the Columbia Law School and had been accepted. Each morning he left the house for a three-mile vigorous walk down Broadway to the school at 8 Great Jones Street, where under the tutelage of the eminent jurist Professor T. W. Dwight he resumed his Harvard role of persistent and irrepressible questioner. Sometimes he chafed under the teaching.

"They don't seem to be talking about justice at all," he complained to Alice. "This *caveat emptor* in law repels me. It doesn't make for fair social dealing. It's like 'let the buyer beware' in business, which means the seller can make a profit at the expense of the buyer, whereas a bargain should benefit both sides."

Alice listened sympathetically without really understanding what he was talking about. Such things were men's problems, as remote from her affairs as had been her father's banking interests. She was immersed in far more interesting concerns, such as Conie's courtship by Douglas Robinson, a big, rather bluff-mannered Scotsman, heir to a large fortune; he certainly doted on her, but did she love him? Other concerns were the menu for the first "at home" she was arranging in return for their many invitations—on the evenings between January 3 and 15 they had attended eleven different parties; the wardrobe she must plan for the trip to Europe they were taking this spring and summer as a completion of their honeymoon; and Teddy's obsession with the writing of his *Naval History of the War of 1812,* which was taking up a great deal of time. Sometimes when they were due for an important engagement she would find him downstairs in the library by a bookcase, standing on one leg, the other crossed behind him, toe touching the floor, a half-dozen books piled in front of him, trying to figure out which way ships would be traveling in what winds.

"We're dining out in twenty minutes," someone heard her exclaim on one occasion, "and Teddy's drawing little ships!"

How he could thrive on such constant activity was beyond her comprehension. The operas they attended lasted until eleven-thirty, the balls often until dawn. A three-mile walk twice a day, law classes and study until afternoon, then bundling her into the sleigh and taking her for a ride through Central Park, or perhaps thirty miles around the city, writing in his spare time! In addition he was attempting to fill his father's shoes in many charity organizations, notably the Newsboys' Lodging House, the Orthopedic Dispensary, and the New York Infant Asylum. But he was never wanting in a new husband's courtly courtesies, and he participated with gusto in every family or social event.

In February 1881, Conie announced her engagement to Douglas Robinson, more, Alice suspected, in response to Mittie's urging than to an awakening of romantic sentiment, for tears rather than her usual quick laughter seemed nearer the surface. Financial security was for women of Mittie's world a necessity, romance a luxury. Of course there was a big engagement party, with all the Roosevelts and their friends attending. Alice felt almost as much at home with them now as with her intimate coterie in Boston, at least with Fanny Smith, Annie Murray, and Maud Elliott. Only with Conie's most intimate friend, Edith Carow, had she never been able to establish a feeling of rapport.

"Why is it?" she wondered aloud to Conie. "I've tried hard to be friendly with her, but there always seems to be something— like a wall between us. I know I'm not as intellectual as she is, but we should be able to find something in common. I too like poetry and reading, and, after all, I had a good education. Why should she be so—so standoffish?"

"Not standoffish," replied Conie. "She's just—well, just Edie. People find her hard to get acquainted with. I remember one of our schoolmates once said you could live in the same house with Edie for fifty years and never really know her." ("Perhaps," she might have added shrewdly, "you have too much in common, a romantic devotion to the same man.")

Spring came to Central Park with a burst of green and a riot of myriad-colored blossoms. Alice would have preferred that on their afternoon outings they should ride around and around in this paradise so close to the Roosevelt home, but instead Teddy chose to drive far and wide through the city streets, not just the respectable areas of the well-to-do on Fifth and Madison Avenues. North beyond Fifty-ninth Street, he drove through lanes choked with mud and refuse, lined with shanties made of packing boxes and odds and ends of lumber scrounged from building leftovers. Some had stovepipes for chimneys. Pigs, goats, chickens roamed at will! It was even worse when he drove south beyond Trinity Church, the domed Post Office, and Western Union Building to the section of downtown tenements where immigrants barely existed among beer dives and opium joints. In spite of the cologne-scented handkerchief held to her nose and eyes deliberately closed, Alice cringed with distaste. But Teddy apparently did not notice.

"See!" he would exclaim almost in triumph. "It's disgraceful, the condition of the streets in some parts, their cleanliness in others. It depends on whoever represents the particular district. That's why I'm pushing the movement to get a nonpartisan Street Cleaning Bill for the city into the State Assembly. I'm going to make a speech about it at Morton Hall."

It was all a part of his latest diversion. To the shock and dismay of his male relatives, he had joined the Twenty-first District Republican Association. "Politics are low," his uncles and cousins told him. "They're run by saloonkeepers, horsecar conductors, and people like that. They are brutal and unpleasant people to deal with. Gentlemen of our class should have nothing to do with them."

"All right" was his reply. "If that means that the people I know don't belong to the governing class and the other people do, then some of us should certainly join the governing class, and I intend to do so. If they're too tough for me I suppose I'll have to quit, but not before I try to hold my own in the rough and tumble."

After one of his rides with Alice, or even after a late social engagement, he would very likely go down to this strange outpost of culture called Morton Hall and return reeking of tobacco smoke and redolent of those indefinable odors one always associated with slums and poverty. Worse even than the old aroma of arsenic! But Alice made no protest. It was undoubtedly another passing fad, like his obsession with taxidermy. She was sure that once they returned from their trip to Europe and he became established in the respectable law profession, he would forget politics. And, if his excessive energy demanded another outlet, she would even encourage the planning and building of the home on his beloved remote hilltop—a *summer* home, she insisted to herself firmly.

Visiting her family at Chestnut Hill in April, Alice was careful not to divulge news of Teddy's most recent aberration. George Cabot Lee would have been as adamant as the Roosevelt uncles and cousins in opposing participation in "low" organizations not controlled by "gentlemen." And fortunately, when Teddy came to join her, their stay was so brief that there was little time for conversation.

They sailed for Europe on May 12 on the White Star steamer *Celtic,* guaranteed to carry "neither cattle, sheep or pigs." In spite of the ninety-degree temperature a big crowd of Roosevelts came to the wharf to see them off. Theodore was ebulliently happy, writing in his diary that night, "Hurrah! for a summer abroad with the darling little wife." But the sentiment was soon altered to read, "Confound a European trip, say I!" For Alice was desperately seasick all the way across the Atlantic. Only in a letter to her sister Rosie from Cork, Ireland, did he vent his frustrations.

"We had a beautiful passage; very nearly as gay as a funeral. . . . I fed her every blessed meal she ate; and held her head when, about 20 minutes later, the meal came galloping up into the outer world again. I only rebelled once; that was when she requested me to wear a mustard plaster *first,* to see if it hurt. . . . After each one of these internal convulsions Alice would conclude she was going to die, and we would have a mental circus for a few minutes. . . ."

But once arrived in Ireland she made full atonement, for after ten days of grueling travel he was writing that she was "the best traveling companion I have ever known." His diary abounded with "Hurrah's!" and "By Jove's!" She rode in ancient railroad cars, on shaggy ponies, in small rowboats, all with cheerful gaiety and appreciation of the scenery "lovely beyond description." They explored London and Paris, spent five days in a Venetian palace, and four days on Lake Como, then rode north in a rented carriage on a tour of the Alps, where Alice, on horseback, accompanied Theodore up a "fair-sized mountain." But in Austria and Switzerland, for the most part, she remained contentedly passive while he climbed mountain after mountain: Mount Pilatus, where he exhausted his guide; the Jungfrau, about which he remarked only that it was "great fun coming down" and that he was "rather tired." But when he insisted on climbing the Matterhorn, partly, as he confessed, "to show some English climbers staying at the same hotel that 'a Yankee could climb just as well as they could,' " she protested in alarm.

"No—please, Teddy! It's terribly dangerous. So many people

have fallen. It's fifteen thousand feet, and they say the high winds make breathing difficult. Please—!"

But it was a challenge, and, being Teddy, he had to face it head on. He was gone two days, while Alice walked the floor of their hotel room in Zermatt and pictured him falling and lying at the bottom of a four-thousand-foot precipice. It was indeed fortunate that she knew nothing of Dr. Sargeant's warning that because of his weak heart he should not even run upstairs!

He returned in one piece, although he did admit that the climb had been "very laborious and dangerous" and that he had been nearer to giving up than on the Jungfrau, but that he was not nearly as tired afterward.

Mountain climbing was not Teddy's only alternative to the usual tourist's program of sightseeing. Every spare moment he could find he was working on his manuscript of *The Naval History of the War of 1812,* materials for which formed a major part of his luggage. Arriving back in Liverpool on the way home, he picked the brains of his genial seafaring uncle, Irvine Bulloch, Mittie's exiled brother, who helped him solve some of his most perplexing nautical problems.

Fortunately Alice enjoyed the sea trip home on the *Britannic.* Though the crossing of the Channel in early September had been exceedingly rough and Theodore had written that "poor baby-wife was reduced to a condition of pink and round-eyed misery," either the Atlantic seas were calmer or the previous bouts had immunized her to *mal de mer.* They arrived in New York on October 2, welcomed by as exuberant a throng of family as had bidden them godspeed, and went straight to 6 West Fifty-seventh Street. Both were glad to be back home, though for different reasons.

For Theodore the trip had aroused a new appreciation of his own country and its democracy. "Though I have enjoyed it greatly," he wrote his Maine friend Bill Sewall, "yet the more I see, the better satisfied I am that I am an American; free born and free bred, where I acknowledge no man as my superior except for his own worth, or as my inferior, except for his own demerit."

Alice was delighted to be back in the social whirl, to be reunited with family, to prepare for the future as the wife of a successful lawyer. Theodore was back at Columbia studying, at the same time working furiously to finish his manuscript for submission to a publisher before Christmas. As she had hoped, the trip had apparently cured him of involvement with those low brutal elements that made up the world of politics. She could not have been more wrong.

4

When Theodore told her his latest news in October 1881, Alice was almost speechless.

"You—you don't mean—you can't—"

But he could and did. The Republicans of the Twenty-first District had nominated him as candidate to the New York State Assembly. It was the work of his new friend Joe Murray, an Irish immigrant of great energy and courage. At first Teddy had thought Joe was joking when he had suggested it. But no, Joe really thought this fellow from uptown whom they had laughed at because—Teddy winked, as his voice assumed a high-pitched drawl, "he looks like a dude, side whiskers an' all, y'know"— might be just the one to oust the Democratic cat's paw of the Tammany bosses. "So I said I would. I'd run."

The reaction to this news was varied. Predictably, the friends and relatives who had warned against mixing in "dirty politics" were shocked and revolted. But most of the immediate family approved. Bamie, who was very much her father's daughter, was delighted. Conie, always athirst for adventure, made plans to further the campaign. Mittie, reminded that one of her Bulloch ancestors had served in the South Carolina Colonial Assembly and that another had been a speaker of the Royal Assembly of Georgia, gave placid approval. But Uncle Rob, Theodore Senior's brother, Robert Barnwell Roosevelt, who had encouraged Teddy's study of law and given him tutelage in his own office, was the most enthusiastic.

"Your father would be proud of you, son. If ever there was a public servant, it was he. And he had occasion to suffer through the evils of corrupt politics when his appointment as Collector of Customs was stymied because of the political bosses. I think it was what helped kill him, the disillusionment. Perhaps you can help settle the score in his memory."

Alice was ambivalent in her reaction. The very thought of participation in what their social class considered the rowdy, unsavory world of the Joe Murrays was repellent to her. She admired Teddy's desire to improve conditions, of course. But why, she wondered, couldn't he do it like other gentlemen of his class, keeping his own hands clean and supporting charitable organizations which helped the poor? Or, if he felt impelled, he could write denunciations of political corruption. And suppose the unlikely happened, and he won. This would mean another change, just as she was getting accustomed to life in New York!

Yet she had always found it easy to adjust to fresh challenges. She had not been nicknamed "Sunshine" for nothing. Perhaps life as the wife of a respected legislator would present interesting social possibilities. And the excitement pervading the household was contagious. With Bamie and Conie she eagerly awaited news of Teddy's vigorous campaigning during the brief week or so before the election.

Reports were not always encouraging. One day Theodore had set off with Joe Murray to visit some of the local saloonkeepers in the district to urge their support. The first man they called on, a Carl Fischer, complained about the heavy taxes he had to pay. He hoped Roosevelt, if elected, would treat the liquor interests fairly. Of course, Roosevelt assured him, he would treat all interests fairly. "Why, I have to pay two hundred dollars for the privilege of operating!" the saloonkeeper protested.

"Oh, but that's not nearly enough!" Theodore replied. "I thought it would be twice as much." Joe Murray had hustled him out. Discovering that his candidate had an unfortunate tendency to speak his mind, he had advised him to confine his campaigning to his personal friends in what was called the "silk-stocking district," which included the fashionable brownstones off Fifth Avenue.

It was also the district of the Columbia University Law School, and some of the law professors, including the Warden, signed a manifesto supporting Teddy. Many of his father's old business friends, though unwilling themselves to engage in "dirty politics," out of respect for his father's memory helped defray his expenses. His college mates, as well as Columbia athletes, "worked like beavers" on his behalf. Never had the polls in the rough areas been so well manned. Boxers, wrestlers, football and baseball players came, all bent on preventing ballot cheating and roughhousing. Bamie and Conie folded ballots. Conie's fiancé, Douglas Robinson, paid two dollars to use a newsstand, where he spent all day giving out tickets. Theodore carried the district by fifteen hundred votes, nearly twice the usual margin.

Family and friends celebrated. Newspapers printed interviews. When groups gathered, Theodore gave assurances that he was "owned by no man," that in Albany he "would obey no boss and serve no clique." Even at informal parties he could not refrain from moralizing. One of the parties was given in December by Edith Carow in her home at 114 East Thirty-sixth Street. Of course Alice attended. It was a gala occasion, with Theodore resplendent in a new crimson satin waistcoat, outdoing himself in exuberance. Accustomed now to his queer bouncing awkwardness in dancing, Alice gaily joined him in leading the cotillion.

Though still perplexed by her inability to establish a friendly rapport with Edith, she no longer felt sensitive about the girl's apparent coolness, and the perplexity was joined now with a feeling of pity. She was sorry for this clever, attractive young person who seemed to hold herself aloof from intimacy, like a statue on a pedestal. And now that she had heard the whispers about the handsome, genial Charles Carow, his financial failures, his propensity for dissipation, she was even more understanding. A pity that, unlike herself, and, yes, even unlike Conie, poor Edith had no Theodore or Douglas to surround her with ardent devotion, to pull the statue off the pedestal and waken it to warm, responsive life!

There was sadness too about the gala parties, for they presaged separation. She would soon be moving with Theodore to Albany, perhaps never to return permanently. He was talking about buying a farm up in northern New York, like those Roosevelt cousins who had settled near a place called Hyde Park. Preferable, perhaps, to the remote hilltop on Long Island, but still much too far from pleasant, pulsing big city life! At least they would be coming home every weekend, Theodore promised that. His family, she knew, dreaded the separation as much as she did. It would have pleased her to read the contents of a letter Mittie wrote to Elliott.

"I do dread parting with Teddie and Alice. Alice has endeared herself to me and she is so companionable and always ready to do what I ask her and I do love her and I think she loves me."

Albany, 1882, "that dear, dull old Dutch city," as Theodore was later to describe it! He arrived there on January 2. Perhaps it was fortunate for Alice, who had gone for a visit at Chestnut Hill, that she did not join her husband for the first weeks of his initiation into the role of legislator. With her sensitivity to emotional turmoil she might have been painfully conscious of the reactions his entrance into the legislative arena aroused. Not Theodore. He barged into the new political milieu as confidently as he bounded up the hundred or more steps of the new Capitol, strode through the marble corridors and up another hundred steps, and made his way along the Golden Corridor and into the famous Assembly Chamber, which some called an architectural monstrosity, others the most magnificent legislative hall in the world. Being Teddy, he was completely oblivious to the fascinated stares, the amused asides, the sly innuendos that greeted his appearance.

The normal accessories of a gentleman of the "silk-stocking district"—pince-nez, cutaway coat, gold-headed cane, gold fob and chain, silk hat carried in one hand, tight trousers with bell-shaped bottoms—were all food for muttered expressions of wonder and jocular hilarity. "Who's the dude?" . . . "A foppish Oscar Wilde?" . . . "Look at the Jane-dandy!" . . . "Some punkin-lily?" . . . "Theodore Roosevelt, you say, from New York? Should have named him Percival!" . . . "What on earth will New York send us next?"

As days passed, Theodore recorded epithets for them also, some fully as uncomplimentary. "Some twenty-five Irish Democrats . . . a stupid, sodden, vicious lot, most of them being equally deficient in brains and virtue!" . . . "Over half the Democrats vicious, stupid-looking scoundrels!"

But slowly the sentiments mellowed a little on both sides. "Has a good honest laugh, hear him for miles" . . . "Good strong teeth, seem to be all over his face" . . . "Must have guts to go out in this weather without an overcoat!" . . . "Good natured, seems to mean well, but of course green as grass!" . . . "That queer accent! Suppose it's Haavard!"

Theodore, too, was slowly picking friends from among the motley group. One, a young lawyer from the country named Isaac Hunt, was to become his loyal ally through future months in efforts to curb corruption.

By his second weekend, when he went to Chestnut Hill to bring back his "baby wife," as he was wont to call her, he had reduced most of the ridicule to a milder consensus that he was surely "different." And soon after that he made his maiden speech, startling the room almost into convulsions with his piping, insistent "Mis-tar Spee-kar! Mis-tar Spee-kar!" He offered a simple and sensible solution to the impasse that was preventing the election of a Speaker. So sensible and simple was it, in fact, that he was applauded, and the New York *Evening Post* reported that he had "made a very favorable impression." Fortunately Alice did not see the less flattering appraisal by the *Sun,* which described him as "a blond young man with eyeglasses, English side-whiskers, and a Dundreary drawl."

They took rooms in a residential hotel at the corner of Eagle and State Streets not far from the Capitol. Alice was relieved, of course, that no housekeeping was expected of her, for she had grown up in a ménage with servants. But, unfortunately, nothing seemed to be expected of her. Few of the legislators had brought their wives to the capital, and, appraising the assemblymen she met, she was sure she would not have found their families congenial. She was soon longing desperately for the New York City social season, now at its height. She marked time between weekends—oases in the desert—when they boarded the train for New York, where she would spend three delightful days of concerts and theater parties, dancing until midnight on Saturdays, helping Conie shop for her trousseau, even finding the services at the Presbyterian Fifth Avenue Church a welcome compensation for the lonely hours in her hotel room reading or writing letters or embroidering.

She tried hard to become interested in the legislative problems which so concerned Theodore and listened to the heated discussions which took place night after night, especially when that queer fellow lodger, Isaac Hunt, came to their rooms. Sometimes they were joined by two Irishmen, Mike Costello and Billy O'Neill. All were heatedly opposed to the corruption they witnessed in the Assembly through bills passed and aimed at furthering crooked gains for big business. Especially were they shocked by the actions of a Judge Westbrook, who had seemed to use his official position to benefit Jay Gould and other financiers in connection with bankrupt insurance companies, the receivers of which had apparently taken an excessive part of the companies' remaining assets. Isaac Hunt, who had discovered the possible corruption, believed the judge's actions should be investigated. Theodore was hesitant. It was a grave matter to attempt the impeachment of a judge.

Alice tried to understand the problem, but she was not really interested. After all, politics were men's concern. True, she believed that women should have more freedom, that they should be able to play tennis without those long confining skirts, that there should be equality in laws relating to marriage. Wasn't it largely her influence that had inspired Teddy to write his senior thesis on women's rights? But—to go down into those dirty foreign slums the way Bamie and Conie had done during his campaign, to actually take part in an election by folding ballots! She was sure her father would not have approved.

Though she tried to be polite and hospitable to Teddy's guests, it was an effort to be agreeable. She thought the two Irish legislators crude and boorish, too hearty in speech and deficient in manners. They didn't even know enough to rise when a lady entered the room. Even Isaac Hunt, though more of a gentleman (he had tried to disguise his rural background by appearing in a custom-made Prince Albert) was almost ludicrous in his attempts to please.

"Hunt thinks you're a very charming woman," Teddy told her

proudly, "Tall and willowy-looking, he describes you. He's very much taken with you."

"How very—flattering!" she commented caustically.

If he noticed the sarcasm, he gave no sign. "Of course he's not the only one." He beamed. "Everywhere I go I hear compliments about my little pink wife."

Soon, when they went home for weekends, Theodore seemed to have little time for dancing and theater parties, or even for drives through Central Park. He was delving into city records, poring over past issues of the *Times,* interviewing all kinds of people. One night he brought the editor of the *Times* home with him and spent until the small hours of the morning questioning and cross-examining him about the facts behind an exposé he had written the previous December of the activities of a certain judge he suspected of illegal actions.

"I'm getting it!" he told Alice excitedly. "And it's even worse than we thought. The facts are all there. At first we only saw irregularities that made us suspect that the judge was in collusion with bankruptcy receivers. Now we know he conspired with a lot of big financiers led by Jay Gould to get control of the Manhattan Railway Company at a huge cost to New York taxpayers. Just wait till I spring some of this on the Assembly!"

Alice was alarmed. "Oh, but, Teddy—should you? Aren't they very powerful people? Won't it make you unpopular?"

He smiled, but with a clamping of his jaws. "Perhaps. But you wouldn't have me keep quiet, would you, pet?"

He did not keep quiet.

"Mis-tar Spee-kar!"

He did not mince words. In his high-pitched, rather squeaky but penetrating voice he called spades spades, in this case "thieves" and "swindlers." But there was no vote, for immediately a legislator leaped to his feet and filibustered until closing time, contemptuously denouncing the young upstart from New York.

Alice's worst fears were realized. He was unpopular, yes, and with important people. But to her surprise he was famous also. Though Tammany and its financial cronies had become his implacable enemies, the common people whose cause he was defending were aroused. Newspapers joined the fight. "In these days of judicial, ecclesiastical and journalistic subserviency to the robber barons of the Street," said the *Times,* "it needs some little courage in any public man to characterize them and their acts in fitting terms." But the adverse reaction was deadly. A prominent lawyer, one of his father's friends, took him to lunch and begged him to be "sensible," not to jeopardize his chances for advancement in law or business by antagonizing the right people.

"The right people!" Theodore echoed grimly when he reported the conversation to Alice. "I suppose he meant that Tammany ring that tries to control not only the city but the state!"

Alice was troubled. She was almost certain her father and Uncle Saltonstall would have given the same advice. She hoped that if New York newspapers reached their eyes, it would be the *Times* or the *Herald,* not the *World,* owned by Jay Gould, which was scurrilous in its contempt and ridicule. Fortunately there were less disturbing activities to demand her attention—Conie's wedding, for instance. She was almost relieved when the family urged her to spend the remaining weeks of April with them instead of returning to Albany with Teddy.

Along with Edith Carow and others of Conie's intimate friends, Alice was one of the eight bridesmaids who participated in the wedding of Corinne Roosevelt and Douglas Robinson on April 29 in the Fifth Avenue Presbyterian Church. She hoped that the decorations of smilax blossoms, with their glossy, bright green leaves, were symbolic of the occasion's happiness. Alice felt a surge of gratitude for her own good fortune. Whatever unexpected and disturbing crises she might experience with the unpredictable Teddy—and she knew now there would be many—she at least enjoyed the blessing of a fulfilled romantic love.

She almost wished she had not overheard the brief interchange between Teddy and his old friend Edith Carow at the reception following the wedding.

"I've been wanting to tell you," Edith's voice, usually suggestive of a cool reserve, was warmly resonant, "how much I commend your courage in the Assembly. I've been following it all in the papers. But, knowing you as well as I do, it's just what I would have expected. You always were a crusader, like your father. And fearless. How proud he would be of you!"

"You think so? Thank you, Edie." His reply was eager. "I certainly hope so. You know how I feel about my father. He was the best man I ever knew, or ever will know. And I'm glad you approve of my crusade, as you call it. I'd like to discuss the problem with you sometime. You always were one to understand."

"Oh, and I want you to know," continued Edith, "how happy I am for the success of your book. I've been reading it with the greatest interest. Remembering that first opus of yours, *Natural History of Insects,* which you wrote at about age nine, it was evident then that you could do a thorough job of research, and I knew you were capable of something really noteworthy like this *Naval History of the War of 1812.* I do want to congratulate you."

A perfectly normal and innocent interchange between two old friends, yet it had aroused in Alice an inexplicable emotion. Jealousy? No. She knew she possessed Teddy's complete, almost worshipful devotion. Certainly not envy. One could not be envious of "poor Edie," as Conie called her, with her aloof manner, her alcoholic father, her lack of matrimonial prospects. Was it frustration she felt, perhaps, or even just a hint of guilt? Why could *she* not have interested herself in Teddy's political affairs so that he could discuss them with her, not just attempt to explain them? And why couldn't *she* have had more faith in Teddy's potential as a researcher and writer, instead of resenting the time he spent on his literary sidelines, even smiling indulgently as at a child's hobby when he had proudly put a first copy of the book in her hands? Why, to her amazement, with its publication this spring, it was already being widely acclaimed, was in a second printing! She really must try to read it, though she had always found history boring.

Back in Albany Alice made an earnest effort to interest herself in Teddy's political concerns. She asked questions, listened intently to discussions among his guests, even though she could not approve of them, and even sat in the gallery during some legislative sessions. This was the greatest concession of all, for she hated the noise and confusion, especially the bickering and acrimonious debates between hotly differing factions. She was there on May 30 when the report of the committee on investigation into the Westbrook scandal came to the floor.

"We've taken a straw vote," Teddy told her excitedly, "and the majority report is almost certain to recommend impeachment of Westbrook."

He was wrong. The forces he had been fighting had been busy, using bribery, cajolery, and threats to persuade members of the committee to change their votes. The minority report recommending non-impeachment became the majority one. Westbrook and his associates were exonerated by a vote of 77 to 35.

Teddy was angry, frustrated, disillusioned. Many of his Republican supporters had deserted the band of reformers. "There seem to have been no *leaders,*" he commented bitterly. Even the newspaper publicity, much of it favorable, which made his name known in almost every household in the state, was small encouragement.

In spite of giving him appropriate sympathy, Alice was relieved. Perhaps he would be content now to follow the advice of those friends and relatives who urged him to leave dirty politics and identify with the right kinds of people. At least when the legislative session ended on June 2 life once more became normal. It meant a return to New York for a summer of joyous activity, with Teddy at his law study during the week and exciting excursions to Chestnut Hill or Oyster Bay on the weekends.

Over the Fourth of July, as Theodore wrote Mittie, he and his "blessed little pink wifie" were at Chestnut Hill, where he amused and deliciously terrified Alice's young brother and sister, Georgie and Bella, and their young friends by playing "bear," and also celebrated the day in his own way with ninety-one furious games of tennis.

In August, while Teddy studied law in the office of his cousin John Ellis Roosevelt, son of his Uncle Robert, Alice took tennis lessons, visited art galleries and museums, shopped with Conie, and settled contentedly into a life which, she hoped, would be far removed from politics.

Teddy was unsure about his future. Law? Business? Literature? The astounding success of his *Naval History of the War of 1812* (already enjoying more printings and receiving favorable reviews even in England) made the latter an attractive possibility. In September, with Doug, Conie, and Mittie, they were vacationing in the northern Catskills, where, as Teddy wrote Bamie, Alice was "just the same little darling as always" and seemed "enchanted with the country." Though he was attracted momentarily by the idea of buying a farm in the region, Alice was relieved that its distance from New York proved a decisive drawback. By now Teddy's preference seemed to be to either law or business.

She was even more reassured when he suggested that they secure a house of their own in the city. After some searching they found just what they wanted, a brownstone at 55 West Forty-fifth Street, next door to Conie's. They moved there in October of that year, 1882. "A small, pleasant house," Fanny Smith, who became a frequent visitor, described it. Alice was delighted. Her own home, to buy furniture for, a place to entertain her friends! But she knew nothing about running a household. Fortunately Aunt Annie Gracie came to the rescue, writing a detailed program for the two maids, including long lists of necessary cleaning as well as cooking utensils, the duties of each maid for each day and almost each hour. Theodore was much intrigued. He read it with respect, mixed with amusement.

"Hm! Very thorough, like Auntie. Sounds as if she's back in Georgia giving orders to slaves who had to stay put. Hope our maids don't both up and leave!" Suddenly he chortled. "What's this? 'Every morning the cook should meet the ashman with a pail of boiling water.' I say, what has the poor ashman done to deserve a daily scalding?"

5

Alice's contentment was short-lived. "I think I'll try to go back to the legislature," Theodore announced in the fall of 1882. "My work there has really only just begun."

She wisely did not try to dissuade him. In the thinking of her generation parity of the sexes in marriage did not extend to a wife's interference in masculine activities. Perhaps it would take another term to sate his appetite for politics. At least they were

firmly established in New York City. No more talk of a farm somewhere upstate!

Because of his record in the previous session Teddy won re-
election with 67 percent of the district's vote, a margin far greater
than that of Grover Cleveland, the Democratic candidate for governor. Alice went with him dutifully to Albany to look for rooms,
but after she expressed dissatisfaction with all possibilities, Theodore awoke belatedly to the truth.

"You didn't really want to come, did you, Pet?" He was full of
remorse. "I can see now. It must have been dull and boring for
you here last year, with me away at the Assembly all day. You
were a little darling not to complain."

She was relieved when he suggested that she stay in their new
home in New York. The family, especially Conie, would take good
care of her during the week, and he would be there every weekend. It was a happy arrangement. During the week Alice's days
were full—balls, concerts, plays, operas, dinner parties. She
shopped with Conie, who was excitedly purchasing small infant
accessories. She entertained friends like Fanny Smith and Annie
Murray, frequently persuading them to stay overnight. And Theodore managed to come home not only on weekends but on business at other times, for his chief concern was reform of New
York's city government.

"Back again in my own lovely little home," he wrote in his
diary one day in January 1883, "with the sweetest and prettiest of
all little wives—my own sunny darling. I can imagine nothing
happier in life than an evening spent in my cosy little sitting room
before a bright fire of soft coal, my books all around me, and
playing backgammon with my own dainty mistress."

But even such peaceful interludes were not always immune to
interruption by the unsavory world of politics. One day there
came a vigorous rat-a-tat of the brass knocker. Theodore rose
with a muttered exclamation of disgust and went to the front
door, returning with one of his lawyer friends, who barely acknowledged Alice's presence before bursting into an excited ti-
rade.

"What's this I hear, Theodore, about your making a speech in
Albany about that accursed bill?"

"Come. Sit down, friend." Teddy waited until the guest was comfortably seated near the fire before continuing. "I suppose you mean the bill prohibiting the manufacturing of cigars in tenement houses here in the city. Yes, I did speak in favor of the bill."

"Yes, of course that's what I mean. An atrocious bill, giving working people a right to tell their employers how to run their business! I'm surprised at you, Theodore. And you the son of a successful manufacturer!"

To Alice's surprise Teddy's voice when he replied was calm, positive, but with none of its usual high-pitched wheeze. "Tell me, friend, have you ever been in one of those tenements?"

"No, of course not." The guest was shocked. "I keep just as far away from them as possible."

"Well, I have. Three times, in fact. The first time with Samuel Gompers, you know, the—"

"Of course I know. The president of that confounded crowd that calls itself a union. He's a dangerous troublemaker, you should know that."

"That's what I thought," returned Teddy. "You know how I've voted up to now about bills relating to capital and labor, against setting a minimum wage or raising the salaries of firemen and policemen. And I voted against this bill when it came up last year. But after that trip to the slums I changed my mind about some things. Let me tell you what I found."

Alice listened in horrified amazement. Teddy had actually been in those awful places, where in one case two families lived, ate, slept, and worked in one room. Tobacco was often stowed everywhere, especially alongside the foul bedding, and in a corner where there were scraps of food. Men, women, and children worked all day and far into the night rolling the stuff into cigars. Usually only one child could speak a little English. She felt nauseated and had to excuse herself and leave the room.

When she returned the guest was just leaving, apparently unconvinced but sobered into silence. "You can see," Teddy was telling him calmly, "that as a matter of practical common sense, to say nothing of human decency, I could not vote for a continuation of the conditions which I saw."

"Did—did that bill pass?" she asked when Theodore returned the following weekend.

Yes, he told her, and Governor Grover Cleveland had signed it, largely—but he did not tell her this—because of his own speech in favor of the bill at a private hearing.

Resolutely Alice put the incident out of her mind. If Teddy had been in any more of such horrible places she did not want to know about it. She was glad she did not have to hear about his political maneuvers, as she would have were she living in Albany. When he returned for weekends he was happy to leave them all behind him.

Her days were filled with activities, some pleasanter than others. One of the less enjoyable occurred in March. "Edith Carow's father has died," Conie told her, "the result of his drinking problem, I suppose. He had been sick for only seven days, could not get his breath. The funeral is to be on Tuesday at St. Mark's-in-the-Bowery. Of course I can't go." Conie was eight months pregnant. "I wish you would go in my place. She's your friend too."

Reluctantly Alice went with Aunt Annie Gracie. True to her nickname of "Sunshine," she hated all things somber, especially funerals. At this one there were not even flowers to brighten the scene. A notice in the *Times* had asked that they be omitted. And Edith in her black mourning looked even more remote and unapproachable than usual.

A pity, Alice could not help thinking after the funeral, that Edie would be unable to accept the invitation given her to dance the quadrille at the Easter Monday "Ball of the Century," that most splendid event of the spring social season. Alice herself had a new rose-colored silk for the affair, made in the latest mode, bodice very tightly cut with many seams, back with long tabs, the cut known as the postilion. The skirt was built out very long in the back over a huge bustle, and was weighted with a pleated overskirt and every kind of pleat and ruffle. Of course it had a train, which she hated. A monstrous liability when it came to dancing, like long skirts on a tennis court! Teddy covered his eyes, pretending to be blinded by its magnificence.

"Such splendor!" he commented. "Is that my little pink wifie tucked away under all that folderol?"

But even the excitement of this festive event was outrivaled by another in April, the birth of Conie's son, Theodore Douglas Robinson. For the first time Alice felt that something was missing in her marriage. Was she failing in the chief function expected of a wife? More than two years, and still no sign—! Coincidence, or the creative urge inspired by contact with the squirming, squalling Theodore Douglas? The following month she discovered that she was pregnant.

Theodore greeted the welcome news with his characteristic explosion of speech and was "dee-lighted." If before he had been protective of his "sweet, pretty, sunny little darling," now he was doubly so. She felt more than ever like the hothouse orchid that Rose had once called her. That summer, energized by the prospect of fatherhood and all its attendant responsibilities, Theodore embarked furiously on his building program at Cove Neck, starting with stables and lodge and buying ninety-five more acres of land adjoining his original sixty. He would sell some of them to Bamie and some perhaps to Aunt Annie, he assured Alice in response to her mild protests. They would have a summer colony of Roosevelts.

The word "summer" allayed some of Alice's fears, although she was still startled by the size of the house he visualized. Three stories, twelve bedrooms! How big a family did he expect to have? She was certainly not looking beyond the present promise of progeny! But dutifully she pored over plans with him for what looked like a mansion. Though remote, the hilltop was an ideal vacation spot, and of course the house in New York would remain their real home, surely through the important social season.

Perhaps due to this excess of energy and worries of approaching fatherhood, Theodore succumbed again to severe attacks of his old enemy, asthma. No treatment seemed to help. Even a trip to the mineral waters of Richfield Springs in the Catskills did him no good. The drive up behind Lightfoot was beautiful but harrowing, for there were heaves for Lightfoot and unpalatable food for Alice in the apologies for hotels. As Theodore wrote Conie, she led "a starveling existence on crackers which I toasted for her in the greasy kitchens of grimy inns." The water, which tasted like "steeping a box of sulphur matches in dish water and drinking the delectable compound from an old kerosene can," set him "rapidly relapsing." If he could get doses of that pure air out West, he grumbled, and ride hard for days, he would soon get back his strength!

Well, why not? Alice encouraged him. She felt perfectly well, and in their New York home with the family near, she would be well taken care of. But inwardly she was quaking with fear. The awful wild West again, and this time not even Elliott to accompany him!

He left on September 3, and the effects of travel and anticipated wilderness excitement acted so swiftly that he wrote Mittie from Chicago that he was feeling "like a fighting cock!" He returned a few weeks later, hardened and rugged, bursting with tales of buffalo hunts with near escapes from death, cold nights lying in the rain in soaked blankets ("By Godfrey, but this is fun!"); richer by an impressive buffalo head and a bevy of frontier friends whose first impressions of the spectacled New York dude ("Two eyes") had been transformed into wonder and respect; richer also (or was it poorer?) by the investment of fourteen thousand dollars in a partnership with some of his new friends in a cattle ranch.

"It's a sure thing," he told Alice jubilantly. "The buffalo are vanishing, and the rich grass in those lands is free and nutritious for cattle. We're getting in at the beginning of a boom."

Alice listened indulgently, as to the amorphous imaginings of a child. The Badlands of Dakota seemed as far away and unreal as castles in the air. Of more immediate concern was his decision to campaign for a third term in the Assembly. But that also seemed unimportant beside the change soon to take place in her life.

Some changes were coming too fast. She had not realized she would become so big and ungainly—at least, so soon, with the birth presumably several months away. Even her cheeks were puffed and unnaturally pale. She was certainly nobody's "little pink darling" now! She was almost glad that Teddy was so immersed in politics that he seemed not to notice her unattractive condition.

His election had been assured, and the victory of his party in the Assembly put him in a position of genuine power, especially if he could realize his ambition of being elected Speaker, a fight which he had lost the preceding term. He began a vigorous campaign for the position at once, making it clear that if elected he would promote a thorough investigation of New York City government, whose corruption he was still determined to fight. He would have had no time for social events even if Alice had not been excluded by rigid custom from all such activities.

And she missed them. Especially frustrating was it to be left out of the biggest family occasion of the year, the wedding of Elliott to the beautiful and socially prominent Anna Rebecca Hall, who lived about twenty miles above the estate of Cousin James of the Hyde Park Roosevelts.

"I hope," said Conie, who had come to show Alice her new gown for the festivities, "that she will be the right influence for Ellie. He's certainly in need of a steadying hand." Alice knew well what she meant. Elliott's weakness for strong drink was an acknowledged concern of the whole family.

The marriage made one significant change in Alice's life. Theodore was worried about leaving her alone in the house except for weekends. He arranged to sublet their brownstone to Elliott and his bride and moved his wife back into the third-floor rooms at West Fifty-seventh Street. He also persuaded Conie to move into adjacent rooms temporarily. After the new baby arrived, the two would convert one of the third-floor rooms into a nursery. It seemed an ideal arrangement. With three doting women to attend to her needs—Mittie, Bamie, and Conie—he could remain in his hotel room in Albany during the week with a clear conscience.

Arrived there, he found his candidacy for the Speakership, which had seemed assured of success, in jeopardy. The New York City delegation had been bribed to vote against him. It was a severe blow, but he rallied, somewhat encouraged by his appointment as chairman of the powerful Cities Committee.

"I feel as though I had the reins in my hands," he wrote Alice on January 22. "Ever your Fond. P. S. How I long to get back to my own sweetest little wife."

But even when he did get back on weekends, she saw little of him. He was either working on the bills he planned to propose or entertaining political cronies. He had promised to break the power of machines in New York City, and he meant to do it. Returning on Thursday nights for his weekend hearings of the Investigating Committee he had formed, he always found Alice waiting for him. Slamming the door, he would take her in his arms, and the long days of his absence would fade into memory —for a little while. She would call gaily up the stairs, "Corinne, Teddy's here. Come and share him."

Uncomfortable though she was, already in her eighth month of pregnancy, and unhappily conscious of her painful bulk and un- naturally puffed cheeks, Alice was grateful when Teddy proudly insisted on presenting to her the members of the Investigating Committee when he brought them to the house. Teddy's letter from Albany after their visit was reassuring.

"Darling Wifie," he wrote on January 28, "all of the men were perfectly enchanted with their visit to our house. . . . Welch said that he had never seen anyone look so pretty as you did when you were asking me not to tell the 'shaved lion' story."

At least she was still beautiful in Teddy's eyes, though he was certainly prejudiced. She suspected that Mr. Welch had not used the word "pretty."

In spite of adoring relatives, she felt lonely and neglected. Shouldn't a husband be with his wife during such a critical time? Were his precious bills more important than his "darling wifie"? Sweet words were all well and good, but they could not atone for absence. And she felt so miserable! It was hard for her to get up and down two flights of stairs, her ankles were so painfully swol- len. It wasn't fair for a woman to have to suffer so, when her husband—!

The sweet assurances kept coming. On Wednesday, February 6, he wrote from Albany, "How I did hate to leave my bright, sunny little love yesterday afternoon! I love you and long for you all the time, and oh *so* tenderly, doubly tenderly now, my sweetest little wife. I just long for Friday evening when I shall be with you again."

He wrote another letter that same day telling of a speech he had made on one of the municipal reform bills he was sponsoring. He thought it was one of his best speeches, "though I do not know that that is saying much."

Alice hated to see Conie leave with Douglas on a trip to Baltimore that Friday, even though Theodore was supposedly returning home that evening.

"Promise not to have that baby until I get back," Conie admonished jokingly. "We could return Monday if there's any need of it. Otherwise we might stay until Wednesday. Bamie knows where to reach us."

"I promise," Alice returned in the same cheerful vein. "Teddy has it all arranged. The baby will come on the fourteenth, not only Valentine's Day but the anniversary of the day we got engaged four years ago."

But after they had gone the third floor seemed indescribably empty. Even the proximity of baby Theodore Douglas and his nurse did not compensate for Conie's bright vital presence. Bamie was occupied downstairs because Mittie was sick abed with what appeared to be a slight cold. Yet the day passed, and Teddy bounced in with his usual admixture of boisterous exuberance and excessive tenderness. And he was sorry that those confounded sessions of the Investigating Committee would keep him busy tomorrow and Monday, but at least they would have Sunday all to themselves. Unfortunately he had to be back in Albany on Tuesday. Would she believe it, he was going to report out of his Cities Committee a total of fourteen bills! A telegram would reach him any time.

They had their Sunday, an interlude that encompassed all the memories of the past and all the hopes and promises of the future. On Monday Theodore continued his committee sessions, and they spent the evening together. Since Alice seemed stable, Conie was wired that she and Douglas need not curtail their visit to friends in Baltimore.

Tuesday, February 12, 1884. New York was enveloped, as it had been for a week, in a cold, thick, drizzly fog, the worst it had experienced in twenty years. It filled the streets with mud, muffled the din of traffic, probed with clammy fingers through invisible cracks around doors and windows, turned dawn into murky twilight. But it did not dampen Theodore's high spirits as he hurried through the densely befogged streets hoping the early train to Albany was still running. He might have been walking on clouds instead of through them. He was about to reap the fruits of grueling months of research and investigation. In the coming hours he would introduce out of his Cities Committee that total of fourteen bills. By tomorrow one of the most important of them, his Aldermanic Bill, depriving the New York Board of Aldermen of their power to confirm the mayor's appointments, was scheduled to come up for a vote. It was the foundation of all his efforts, for it would deprive the city bosses of much of their control. But, most exciting of all, he was about to become a father.

He had no qualms about leaving home at this critical time. Bamie was capable of handling all emergencies. He had left his mother sleeping, he hoped, without saying good-by. Rest was the best antidote for a cold. Little Theodore Douglas's nurse was close by Alice on the third floor, ready to answer her every need. Alice's father and mother had arrived in New York and taken rooms at the Brunswick Hotel. Elliott was but a few blocks away. And surely nothing would happen until Thursday the fourteenth, St. Valentine's Day and the anniversary of their engagement. It was too much of a coincidence to fail. He would be home in time for the blessed event.

Other than the depressing fog, there was nothing to warn Bamie that the day would be the most torturing she had ever experienced. The first indication came when she rushed to her mother's room, summoned by the maid who had taken in her morning tea. "She don't look good, miss! Worse than yesterday, I'm afeared. Please come!"

Mittie was indeed worse. Her cheeks were flushed with fever, her breathing was hoarse, and she was babbling incoherently. This was no mere cold, even a severe one! Bamie sent a servant posthaste for the family doctor, then with characteristic efficiency tried to make her mother more comfortable, sponging her face with cool wet cloths, raising her head to ease the labored breathing, uttering words of comforting assurance.

"There, there, little Motherling, don't worry. The doctor is coming. We'll soon have you feeling better."

The doctor came, regarded the patient gravely, shook his head.

"Another case, I'm afraid. There are many in the city. Perhaps it's this foul weather."

In spite of her alarm Bamie's voice was steady. "You mean— it's—?"

"Probably typhoid," he said briefly.

He bled the patient, prescribed calomel and oil of cinnamon, recommended more cool bathing, and left, promising to return later. Bamie spent the next hours with her mother, continuing the treatment. She changed the bedding when necessary, trusting that others were caring for Alice's needs. She could not have said how much time had elapsed when the baby's nurse came running, her usually calm, capable manner charged with excitement.

"It—it's happening, Miss Bamie. The labor pains—they've started!"

Leaving a trusted maid with her mother, Bamie climbed the stairs to the third floor, her back seeming more humped than usual, her step almost as slow and painful as in the childhood days when for a while her crippled body had been encased in confining braces. But her eyes were as luminously bright, her manner as vivacious as always when she entered the bedroom where Alice lay.

"My dear, don't look so frightened. It's just what we've been expecting, waiting for. Shall I wire Teddy to come back immediately?"

"No—I—I don't want him—please—don't let him see me—like this!"

"Very well, dear. Don't worry. I'll manage everything."

She did. She sent messages to the doctor, to Elliott. No telegram to Teddy. She knew he would just be in the way. He was of far more use in Albany attending to important business. The doctor arrived, checked the patient, and promised to return later. He gave directions and left. It would be hours before the baby came, he assured Bamie. Elliott arrived next, prepared to stay as long as necessary. He took ten-month-old Theodore Douglas to Aunt Annie Gracie's, leaving the baby's nurse free to minister to Alice.

So dense was the fog that it was hard telling when day ended and night began. Light and darkness, thought Alice. A few moments of blessed relief, then once more the terrible searing agony of pain, clenching her teeth to keep from screaming and not succeeding. One seemed to merge into the other, two parts of the same whole. She knew it must be night when the lamps were lighted and the pains became nearer together and much worse.

Though the room seemed as blurred as the world outside, she was conscious of faces and voices. The doctor's, familiar, kindly. "Courage, my dear. You're doing fine. Just a little longer. Push now, again—push hard." Bamie's, smiling as always but with less of sparkle in her eyes. "Sorry I can't be with you all the time, dear, but the little motherling is sick and needs me. I'll come when I can." A woman's, less familiar. Of course. The baby's nurse. They had prepared a nursery for the two babies, she and Conie, here on the third floor. Her mother's. What was she doing here instead of in Boston? "I know what it's like, darling, but it will soon be over and then, the joy of it! How well I remember when I first held you in my arms!"

And then suddenly—an eternity later, or just hours?—one final burst of agony, and it *was* over. She heard a small but robust cry. "Good, my dear. You have a fine healthy little girl."

So—there was to be another Alice. Teddy had insisted on it if it turned out to be a girl, just as she had insisted on Theodore if a boy. Just as well. Two baby Theodores in the same nursery would have been too much, especially if they were both like their name-sake. She managed a feeble chuckle. Yes, her mother was right. In spite of all the distortion of body and the terrible pain—and how she did hate pain!—it had been worth it. Unfortunately the pain was not over yet. Her cheeks, still unnaturally swollen, throbbed. Heat seemed to be coursing in waves through her body.

Later—again time meant nothing—she heard the same small robust cry. This time it held a demanding note. "Here we are. How about it, little mother? Your daughter says she's hungry. Think you can manage, dear?"

Almost automatically Alice adjusted the tiny body into the crook of her arm. She felt a tugging at her breast as the crying ceased. It was not just a gentle, tentative tugging. It was a vigor-ous, assertive expression of a newly created personality that sensed exactly what it wanted and meant to get it. Alice could not help smiling to herself. She wished Rose were here to share her discovery. This new Alice, this extension of herself, was no hot-house orchid, as Rose had called her, no fragile Southern magnolia like Mittie. Rather, she would be the tough dandelion, or, if a rose, one with plenty of thorns. Another Alice, the one she herself had sometimes longed to be! Why—Alice almost laughed aloud—if this creature found long full skirts hampering her action on the tennis court, she might even be bold and rash enough to wear pantaloons like that Bloomer woman who had dared to defy the unhealthy, tightly-laced costumes worn by "ladies."

Wednesday, February 13. It was to be a big day for Theodore Roosevelt, Assemblyman, the "Cyclone Assemblyman," some people called him, a far cry from their earlier designations of "city Dude," "punkin-lily," "weakling." This morning he was to report his fourteen bills designed to fight city corruption. This afternoon his Aldermanic Bill would gain final passage. Then he must request leave of absence to be present at an even more important event. But as he made his usual headlong rush up the hundred and more steps of the Capitol Building, he was charged with an even greater excitement, for he had just received a telegram. As he entered the assembly room he couldn't help sharing his news with close friends.

"I have a daughter," he announced exuberantly. "Born late last night." And the mother, he assured the anxious questioners who knew and admired Alice, was doing at least fairly well, so the wire had stated. Apparently nothing to worry about.

Presently he was surrounded by colleagues, all congratulating him. "He was full of life and happiness," his friend Isaac Hunt would remark later.

That morning he reported out of his Cities Committee the fourteen bills, then asked for leave of absence. When his Aldermanic Bill came up that afternoon, it was moved that it be laid aside temporarily due to the absence of its sponsor. "Mr. Roosevelt has gone to New York," it was explained, "to receive a father's congratulations."

However, that was not the real reason for his leaving early. He had fully intended to see his bill through that afternoon. But meanwhile he had received another telegram. When he read it, it was said he looked "worn" and that he had immediately rushed off to catch the train.

While waiting he paced the platform. Of course the train was late. All of them had been since the terrible fog started. Many had not run at all. When it did come, it seemed to crawl. Already it was dusk, and as they traveled south into increasingly thickening fog, its speed kept decreasing. The usual five and a half hours between the cities lengthened into almost as much again. Unable to curb his impatience, he ground his teeth, every muscle in his body tensed like taut steel. *Why* hadn't he left Albany at once after receiving the first telegram?

But it had said Alice was doing fairly well, only natural after what she had been through. And what had the second wire meant? *Come home immediately. Both patients much worse.* What had happened? The murky gloom outside matched his mood. No wonder the New York *Times* that very morning had called it "suicidal weather," adding, "Life does not seem worth living to a sensitive person easily influenced by atmospheric conditions." Well, he was sensitive enough, every nerve tip on edge, he who prided himself on his toughness.

When the train finally crawled into Grand Central, it was close to midnight. So thick was the fog that Teddy almost had to grope his way along the streets from East Forty-second to West Fifty-seventh. Streetlamps were but pale yellow blurs shedding no guiding light. Arriving at the house at last, he noticed a faint glow of light in a third-story window. A good sign or a bad? He stumbled up the steps and rang the bell. It seemed an eternity before the door opened and Elliott was there, looking distraught and disheveled.

"Ah, it's you! At last! Well, at least you're in time." His voice was harsh. "As I told Conie about an hour ago, there is a curse on this house. Mother is dying, and, yes, you have to know, Alice is dying too."

Pushing past him, Theodore tore up the two flights of stairs, cast himself on his knees beside the bed, and took her in his arms. "My poor darling—forgive me—taking so long—"

Her eyes regarded him vacantly. *She doesn't know me!* he

thought in panic. "What is it?" he demanded of Elliott, who had followed close behind him.

"The doctor calls it Bright's disease, named after some English doctor. He says it sometimes happens in pregnancy. I—I'm so terribly sorry, Teddy."

Only once during the ensuing hours when he sat at the head of the bed cradling her in his arms was Theodore certain that Alice knew him and was aware of his presence.

"Our—baby—" she said faintly but clearly. "We—have a—daughter—"

"Yes, darling. I know."

Time meant nothing. Was it still night or morning when Elliott came again, saying, "You'd better come, Teddy. If you want to say good-by to our mother, you'd better do so now. Mother seems to have acute typhoid fever. I didn't tell you when you came. I thought one blow was enough."

His little motherling! Conscience-stricken, Theodore followed his brother downstairs. Like Alice, Mittie did not know him. An hour later he stood looking down at her still form, at rest after its short fevered agony, the hectic flush gone from her cheeks. She looked almost as young and beautiful as when he had toddled after her as a child, pulling at her immaculate white muslin skirts, the shining jet-black hair still untouched by gray, the white cheeks as smooth and translucent as fine porcelain.

"There *is* a curse on this house," he muttered unintelligibly.

He climbed slowly back upstairs, and more hours passed while he sat motionless, holding his beloved, his "Sunshine," in his arms. Others came into the room, but he was hardly aware of their presence—the doctor, the nurse, a servant who brought him food, Elliott who tried vainly to persuade him to eat something or at least take tea, and Conie came with a small blanketed bundle, calling his attention to his new daughter. He did not even look at the child.

The end came finally, just sudden stillness. It happened at about two o'clock on that afternoon of February 14, 1884, St. Valentine's Day.

Theodore drew a big black cross on the day in his diary, followed by one simple sentence. "The light has gone out of my life."

Only once after that was he to give vent in writing to his devastating loss. A year later he would compose a little tribute to Alice's memory, appended to a short outline of her life and a few statements of others, the whole constituting a brief memorial. It would be the only time he was known to mention her name.

"She was beautiful in face and form and lovelier still in spirit; as a flower she grew, and as a fair young flower she died. Her life had been always in the sunshine; there had never come to her a great sorrow; and none ever knew her who did not love and revere her for her bright, sunny temper and her saintly unselfishness. Fair, pure, and joyous as a maiden; loving, tender, and happy as a young wife; when she had just become a mother, when her life seemed to be but just begun, and when the years seemed so bright before her—then, by a strange and terrible fate, death came to her.

"And when my heart's dearest died, the light went from my life forever."

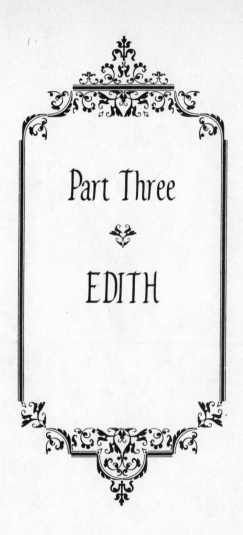

Part Three

❧

EDITH

1

The Fifth Avenue Presbyterian Church was crowded to the doors. The skies had cleared after the prolonged dense fog, to be followed by intense cold, and the chill, penetrating dampness seemed to linger in the poorly heated building like a brooding Nemesis, accentuating the somber mood set by the two coffins side by side beneath the altar.

It was a motley congregation. Perhaps never before had such a cross section of the city assembled in one place: members of society's upper echelons like the Astors and the Harrimans rubbing shoulders with immigrants from the Lower East Side; the mayor of Brooklyn and the chief justice of the Court of Common Appeals in close proximity to ill-clad newsboys and tough wardheelers; legislators who had been in deadly verbal combat the day before in Albany sitting amicably side by side, a hint of moisture in their eyes. In the front pews a host of descendants through six generations from Claes Martinszen van Rosenvelt, 1640 immigrant from Holland to New Amsterdam, were assembled to lend support to a bereaved member of the clan.

Edith was fortunate to secure a seat, though she had left home in what she considered plenty of time. The twenty blocks between Thirty-sixth and Fifty-fifth Streets had been clogged with other carriages and vehicles of every description. But she was not really late, for the service had not begun. She found herself wedged into the end of a pew beside a burly, clean, but casually dressed young man who could not possibly have qualified as a gentleman, that is, not the "silk-stocking district" definition of the word. Courteously he tried to move aside to give her more room, but the pew was filled to capacity.

"Sorry, ma'am. Begorra, I've niver seen sich a crowd, not aven at the biggest wake."

"It's all right," assured Edith quietly. "I was lucky to be shown to any kind of seat. I hope I'm not crowding you too much."

"Not at all, lydy, not at all. In fact, I'm the one out of place. I ought not to be here, but no priest could keep me away, no, not when my good friend is in throuble. Pore bloke," he continued, "what a turrible thing, losin' his darlin' wife and his mither, all in one day!"

A "friend" of Teddy, this crude Irishman? One of his charities, she surmised, like the newsboys. Fortunately he was enough of a gentleman to keep his voice low, unnoticeable amid the pre-service shufflings and rustlings, the vain searching for seats.

"Yes," she said, "a terrible thing indeed."

"Ye a friend of his mebbe, too?"

"His friend, yes." For some reason Edith did not resent the familiarity of this stranger from a different, alien stratum of society, his probing into the confusion of her emotions. His Irish accent, so like Mame's, was oddly comforting. "Yes," she repeated. "I have been his friend—for a very long time."

"Och, then ye know how I feel. Name's Joe, by the way. Him and me, we've done a lot togither, thryin' to get a little clean air into the dirty politics of this ould town. It was me got him to thry out for the Assembly."

Turning, Edith regarded the young man more intently, noting the rugged lines of his features, the squareness of chin, the keenness of the whimsical Irish blue eyes. No object of charity, this. Surely Teddy had mentioned his name, Joe Murray, the day he had taken her riding and shared with her some of his hopes and frustrations for reforming city government. "I know," she said. "He told me about you. You are indeed a good friend."

The church became suddenly quiet, for the service was about to begin. The pastor, Dr. Hall, gave an opening prayer, then the congregation, led by the choir, sang "Rock of Ages." Edith listened to the sermon that followed, but not too attentively, so confused were her emotions. Shock, grief, concern for the friends she had loved almost from birth . . . yes, and some other vaguer and even more profound emotion which she dared not acknowledge.

Dr. Hall's brief sermon was eloquent but simple. He spoke of

the two lives which had come so abruptly to an end, one whose
life work, though she was not old, might be considered done. She
had raised her children, seen them educated. But the other . . .
Here the pastor's voice became fraught with feeling. So young, so
hopeful of the future with the husband to whom she had been so
devoted—her going seemed both strange and terrible. He could
barely control his voice, and as he gave his final prayer, tears
flowed down his cheeks.

Many in the congregation were weeping. Not Edith. Her deepest emotions had never found release in tears. She sat rigidly,
motionless except for the curling and interlacing of her gloved
fingers inside the little muff that matched the fur of her small
sealskin hat. She scarcely noticed as the choir sang the hymn
"Angels of Jesus, Angels of Light" after the benediction.

But when the funeral cortege came down the aisle, she became
suddenly alert. At the end, after all the relatives, came the immediate family, Bamie, poised as usual and always thinking of others, holding the arm of a weeping Aunt Annie Gracie; Conie, managing a teary smile as her eyes met Edith's. And then—

"There he is," muttered Joe, his low rumble reaching her ears
alone. "Pore bloke. Look at him."

Edith was looking. Oh, my dear! Her lips shaped the words
silently, her confusion of emotions blending into a single outpouring of pity. Teddy? His familiar features, yes, but lifeless, like
—like a death mask, stonelike, as if he had been looking at some
Gorgon's head. As he passed, his eyes seemed to look straight
into hers, but with no sign of recognition. Only many years later,
when they were both long gone, would his features reveal such
stonelike rigidity, carved out of the rock of a Western mountain-
side called Rushmore.

As they stood to leave the pew, the young man spoke again.
"Since ye're his friend too, ma'am, sure and ye have my sympathy."

"Thank you, Joe," she returned gratefully. She had wanted to
be alone today, had discouraged her mother and sister Emily
from coming, fearful perhaps of betraying some secret of this
complexity of emotion. But the presence of this stranger, with his
bluff, crude acceptance of their common interest and concern,

had been oddly comforting. Though she could not be part of the bereaved family, close though she had been to them, he had somehow made her feel less excluded. She must tell Teddy when she saw him again that she had met his friend Joe, that she understood even better this alien world which had become so important to him, persuade him to share with her some of its problems.

She could not know that many months would pass before she would see him again.

She had news of him, of course, not through the family. Somehow she hesitated to resume the old intimacy with Conie and Bamie. It might seem like intrusion into the privacy of their grief, or—might they suspect that she had other motives? But the newspapers gave full accounts of his activities. He had returned to Albany three days after the funeral and been in his Assembly seat at ten on the following morning. She could imagine his reception, for the legislators had gone to unprecedented efforts to express their concern, making innumerable speeches of condolence on the day before the funeral and then adjourning the body. His political enemies had been some of the most voluble, one Tammany Democrat even quoting sentimental poetry.

During subsequent weeks, it was reported, he spent all his time shuttling back and forth between New York and Albany, meeting with his Investigating Committee, reporting his bills out of his Cities Committee for their consideration by the whole Assembly —bills involving benefits for colored orphans, for the better security of mechanics and laborers, for improved drainage in Brooklyn. During two days of March he reported a total of thirty-five bills out of committee, sitting up all one night to get one into proper shape.

He's trying to kill himself! thought Edith. But, no, she knew Teddy too well to believe that. He was merely indifferent to physical harm, as he had always been.

Never had Edith been so lonely—or so busy. She missed her father desperately. In spite of his weaknesses, his gay carefree spirit had been the transforming alchemy in the otherwise dull substance of her home life. He had encouraged her love of books, told her fascinating stories, introduced her to the miracles of nature, been her companion on horseback jaunts, visits to the

theater. Now, it seemed, she had no one to share her most intimate interests and activities. Gertrude, introspective, prone to
attacks of hypochondria, was bound up in herself. Emily, who
was inclined to be sickly, helpless in the face of difficulties, had
never been a compatible companion.

And the Carows were certainly facing difficulties, chiefly financial. Charles had left them with debts rather than assets. Gertrude's inheritance from her father yielded only a small income,
for wisely, knowing Charles, he had tied up the principal in a
trust. Aunt Ann Eliza Kermit, with whom they had made their
home for many years, had died in 1879, and, though Charles had
been her sole heir, whatever she left had vanished. Edith found
herself now the virtual head of the family, both mother and sister
incapable of either decisions or their implementation. She had to
let most of the servants go. Not Mame. Even though there were
no longer children for her to nurse, she had been more family
member than servant. She and Edith now assumed tasks for
which neither had been trained—purchasing groceries and other
household supplies, polishing silver, sorting laundry, even preparing meals when the cook had her day off.

More even than social diversions Edith missed her friends.
Fanny Smith, now married to Will Dana, was immersed in her
own affairs. Edith had not seen Conie or Bamie since the funeral
in February, and that only at a distance. She hesitated to renew
the old relationships. Surely they knew, or suspected, that her
friendship with Teddy had once come close to romance. Not for
worlds would she give them reason to think that, now he was
free, she hoped to revive whatever sentimental emotion he might
have felt toward her.

Then one day when the knocker sounded and she went to the
door, there was Conie, still in deep mourning, its somber aspect
belied by her sparkling blue eyes and warm, eager smile.

"Edie—darling! Where have you been? We've all missed you
so, waited for you to come as you always have. I just had to come
and find out *why.*"

"I've just been busy," faltered Edith. Then for once the shell of
her reserve dissolved, and she held out her arms.

After that she was no longer so lonely. She accepted their invitations as formerly, arranged little gatherings in her own home to which they were invited. She could not help noting, however, that their invitations never came when Teddy was in the city. She did not know, of course, that he had directed his sisters and aunt to tell him when she might be visiting so he could keep away. But there had been no prohibition on their dispensing news of him, and she was able to learn far more of his activities than newspapers could divulge.

"It's queer," Conie confided to her once. "Teddy never even mentions Alice's name. It's almost as if—as if he wanted to forget that she had ever existed. Yet—that couldn't be. No man was ever more deeply devoted to a woman than he was to her. You know that. He idolized her."

"Yes," said Edith. "I do know that."

"And he doesn't seem to pay much attention to Baby Alice," Conie continued. "He just turned her over to Bamie. And it's hard for her, too, with all she's having to do, selling the house, dividing up all its contents as well as those in the house Teddy and Alice lived in on West Forty-fifth. It would be easier if she only had a good trusted nurse for the baby, but as yet she hasn't found one."

"There's Mame," Edith suggested excitedly. "She's wonderful with children, and she misses them."

"She'd be perfect!" Conie's eyes shone. "But—could you spare her?"

No, thought Edith. Life without Mame? But—for Teddy's baby! "Yes," she said. "Mame is doing little for me now that any other servant couldn't do. And she belongs with children."

It was arranged, to Bamie's great relief. In May she moved into a home at 422 Madison Avenue, taking with her Baby Alice, Mame, and her share of the furniture and personal effects. "This year has been a perfect nightmare," she confessed, "parting with all the places we had cared for, dividing everything that had always meant home and deciding how to recommence life." But in spite of her dragging step and hunched shoulders she gave not the slightest impression of weakness, and her lively eyes and constant smile defied any inference of sadness.

Theodore was in Chicago that May of 1884 and the first week of June, a delegate to the Republican Convention, attempting vainly

to prevent the nomination of James G. Blaine, whose entangle-
ment in handling railroad stocks had aroused his moral indigna-
tion. From there he went on to the Badlands of South Dakota, a
wild, stark country that evidently suited his bleak mood of desolation, plunging into the life of the wilderness with a vigor which
savored of desperation.

"It looks as if he's decided to be a full-time ranchman," reported Bamie after receiving a letter dated June 19. "He's buying
a thousand more cattle, plans to go back this fall with some men
he met up in Maine, William Sewall and Wilmot Dow, and settle
them on a second ranch he's starting. He seems to be spending
all his time in the saddle, thirteen hours one day, either rounding
up cattle or hunting antelope. 'I got one the other day,' he says,
'another good head for our famous hall at Leeholm.' "

At least, thought Edith with a relief she refused to acknowledge,
he was not planning to spend all his time in the West. He was
continuing with his lavish building program at Oyster Bay, urging
Bamie to hasten on its construction. They would share the occu-
pancy of it together, it appeared, during the periods when he was
in the East. Meanwhile he would make his home with Bamie when
he came to New York.

It was obvious that all the members of the family did not approve of Teddy's obsession for Western speculation. His brother-
in-law, Douglas Robinson, who was in the brokerage business,
was especially critical.

"Douglas thinks he's being very reckless," worried Conie. "Two
ranches, and that huge house! With this latest investment in a
thousand new head of cattle, he's already spent about half his
inheritance."

Bamie, also skeptical, was less disapproving. "At least," she observed wisely, "he's finding an outlet for his grief and loneliness."

But she was wrong in assuming that furious activity, purchase
of cattle, a hunting safari into the Bighorns, replete with "fringed
and beaded buckskin shirt, horsehide riding trousers, cowhide
boots, braided bridle and silver spurs," even the acquisition of
six magnificent elk heads for the "house on the hill," were an
indication of waning grief or assuaged loneliness. Bill Sewall, installed that fall on the new ranch, named "Elkhorn" because of a

pair of interlocked elkhorns found on the site, could bear witness to that. Long afterward he would tell of a conversation he had had with Theodore when the latter had remarked that life had no meaning.

"Of course it has. You have your child to live for."

"Her aunt can take care of her a good deal better than I can," his friend had responded. And when Sewall, who had also lost his wife, offered words of comfort, Theodore had replied bitterly, "Don't talk to me about time will make a difference. Time can never change me in that respect."

It was one day in November 1884 that Edith received a note from Aunt Annie Gracie inviting her to dinner on the twentieth, adding that a certain guest would be there in whom she might be interested. Edith felt sudden excitement. Could it possibly be Teddy? Nine months had gone by since that glimpse of his stony face in the church. He had often been in and out of New York. Lately he had been in the East, giving his support to Blaine's candidacy and thereby incurring outraged denunciations from his reform group of Republicans. But he had decided that loyalty to the party was paramount in spite of his moral distaste for the candidate. Though she had been a frequent guest in Conie's and Bamie's homes, as well as Aunt Annie's, never once had her presence and Teddy's coincided. He had either just gone or was about to come. It was almost as if—

But no, they could not possibly think she expected to revive his romantic interest. If so, they did not know him as well as she did. His rigid moral code, dictated by the Victorian standards of the time, would preclude any possibility of a second marriage. But friendship—the give-and-take of two alert and questing minds, the affinity they had enjoyed since the days they had sat on the steps of the old brownstone and read to each other—surely they could not begrudge her that!

The "guest in whom she might be interested" was not Teddy. It was a Mr. Stratton, and instantly Edith knew why he was there. Another of Aunt Annie's attempts to secure for her the only life fulfillment considered appropriate for a woman! This candidate, though intelligent and obviously well able to support a wife, as well as her mother and sister if necessary, made no greater appeal than the others she had considered and rejected. She found his attempts at conversation boring.

It was a bleak winter. Unwittingly her appraisal of its cheerlessness coincided with that of Theodore, who, out in his frozen, snowbound wilderness, was writing, "When the days have dwindled to their shortest, and the nights seem never-ending, then all the great northern plains are changed into an abode of iron desolation."

Though he was back in New York just before Christmas, working furiously at a new book, to be called *Hunting Trips of a Ranchman,* as far as Edith was concerned he might still have been two thousand miles away hunting antelopes or, according to the story which had somehow come to her ears, proving his ability to cope with a bully who had made the mistake of dubbing him "Four-Eyes" and challenged him to "set up drinks" for all his cronies in a tavern where Teddy had taken shelter on a bitter cold night. But she had news of the family. Mame saw to that.

Sometimes on her day off Mame would come to the house alone. More often she would stop when taking her young charge for an afternoon stroll in her pram. She would bring the child in and exhibit her proudly for inspection. A little over a year old, Baby Alice was a plump, charming, crawling cherub, with small horns concealed, however, beneath the sprouting wings, as Edith discovered when she tried gently to remove her from contact with a priceless figurine which Gertrude had brought back from her student days in Paris. The angelic smile vanished, the small arms flailed. So—this replica of the beguiling Alice was even more obviously her father's child, endowed with all his stubborn will and self-assertion. She would go through life knowing and getting exactly what she wanted—at least trying to.

"He's a quare un," Mame remarked once. "Niver calls the bairn by her right name. It's either 'Baby Lee' or some foolish thing like 'Mousiekins.' "

So it was true, thought Edith, the report that Teddy refused to even mention Alice's name.

"Sometimes," continued Mame, her smooth brow puckering, "ye'd think he couldna bear the sight o' the sweet bairn, hates aven to look at 'er."

Edith was not surprised. Those yellow curls and blue eyes! No wonder he found them such a painful reminder. Words echoed in her mind, the final words of the memorial Teddy had written last fall just before leaving for the Bighorns. She had seen it on a table at Aunt Annie's, a little pamphlet which had been privately published. *And when my heart's dearest died, the light went from my life forever.*

Spring came, enticing Edith to the burgeoning florescence of Central Park, Theodore to his stark paradise in the West. Though he had delivered his manuscript in March, the effort of writing a hundred thousand words in nine weeks had brought on one of the old attacks of cholera morbus, and he did not depart until April. Once more the invitations came from Bamie and Aunt Annie. Conie was less available now, since she spent much of each year at Douglas's large place in Orange, New Jersey.

Edith was grateful when Aunt Annie invited her to spend some time in June at the new house she had built on land bought from Theodore's investment at Oyster Bay. Deciding she could afford to board her mother and sister in a country place they had sometimes visited, Edith installed them there and set off for Long Island, feeling more carefree than she had in years. Retracing the old familiar route—ferry from Thirty-fourth Street to Long Island City, train to Syosset, where Aunt Annie's coachman met her—was almost like reliving the happiest anticipations of youth, except that at the end there would be no Tranquillity, no Conie and Teddy.

But the latter was present in spirit if not in person. Conversation about his latest exploits abounded. Bamie, busy at completing the building of Leeholm, was in and out, sharing his letters, plus her own candid opinions of his actions.

"Hm! Looks as if he's really turning ranchman with a vengeance. He's bought another fifteen hundred head of cattle. Thirty-nine thousand more gone from his inheritance! And another forty-five thousand gone into Leeholm . . . !"

"What do you think of this! Not long out of bed from that asthma attack, and here he was falling with his horse into a swollen river, pushing iceblocks out of his way and barely making it to shore . . . Swimming again by choice with his horse Manitou, then traveling twenty miles before he could dry out, and listen to what he says about it! 'However, it all makes me feel very healthy and strong.' "

Presently there came an even more tangible token of his exploits, an advance copy of his new book to be published in July. Edith fingered the elegant object with the reverence she always accorded fine books. And it was *elegant,* bound in gray with gold lettering, with thick hand-woven paper and exquisite engravings. Since she could never afford one (fifteen dollars!), she read avidly, absorbing the fascinating tales of hunting trips, the amazingly detailed life histories of a dozen different animals. Yet not so strange, remembering the painstakingly accurate *Natural History of Insects* written by a boy of nine.

One day while visiting Aunt Annie, she walked alone along a path leading through the woods of Cove Neck, passing through a grove of locust trees and arriving at the foot of a high grassy hill surmounted by an imposing building. In past years she had climbed the hill many times, running to keep up with more hardy adventurers, plunging down the other side toward that horribly precipitous slope called Cooper's Bluff. Her pulses quickened and her throat tightened sickeningly as she recalled her first terrifying descent of that awful declivity. There had been no building on the hill then. Now the long grass had been cut. Its bareness was relieved by newly planted vines and shrubs. She climbed the hill slowly, eyes fixed on the huge, raw, rambling structure which, with its multiplicity of gables, dormers, verandahs, ells, projecting angles, looked as if, like Topsy, it had "just growed."

So this was Leeholm, the house Teddy had planned for his Alice. Certainly not beautiful! Its shingled walls, newly stained a mustard color, were a jarring contrast to the red bricks, the dark green trim. And the colored glass in some of the windows! It looked almost garish. Oh, well, Teddy had never been noted for his artistic acumen. He obviously had what he wanted, which was *size.* All that space, three stories, and there must be a couple of dozen rooms! He hadn't started to build until after losing Alice. All this for three people: himself, little Alice, and Bamie?

Edith did not try to go in, or even to look through the windows. She had chosen to come today because Bamie, who had been getting the house ready for Teddy's arrival, had gone to the city. After a long lingering look at the superb vistas, shimmering blue Oyster Bay and Cold Spring Harbor on either side, both merging into the dazzling expanse of the Sound, with a glimpse of the Connecticut shore in the distance, she turned and went back along the path.

"Conie seems very anxious for you to come," said Aunt Annie, looking up from a letter she had just received. "She suggests that you come earlier than you had planned. Though I would hate to see you go—"

Edith smiled grimly. Suddenly she felt like saying exactly what she thought—and did. "So Teddy is coming," she remarked coolly, "earlier than you expected, and I must be gotten out of the way."

Aunt Annie looked distressed. "Edie—my dear—"

"Oh, don't think I haven't noticed!" Now she had started she could not stop. "I suppose you think, you and Conie and Bamie, that I might have some idea of trying to—to—that is, now that Alice is gone—" She stopped, red with embarrassment. When had she ever so revealed her deepest emotions?

"Oh, no—my dear, no! It wasn't our idea—don't think that. It—it was Teddy's." Aunt Annie, betrayed into revealing a confidence, was equally embarrassed. But now she had started, she knew she must continue. "You see, dear, he told Bamie to let him know if you were planning to come at any time, so—so—"

"So he could stay away," Edith returned, her voice deadly calm. "I—see."

"No, dear, I don't think you do. I think he's afraid to see you, fearful that he might be tempted into more than just friendship. Of course it's just a suspicion on my part, but I'm almost sure I'm right. He's afraid of being untrue to the memory of Alice. I think he has very strict ideas about marriage, that it should be just once and for all time. Some men are like that. You see? You do understand?"

"Yes," said Edith. "I—see. And—I do understand."

Relief? Distress? Elation? Dismay? Edith felt all in succession; then they merged into a blur of confusion. So it was Teddy, not his sisters and aunt, who wanted to end their friendship, but not necessarily because it meant nothing to him, perhaps because it had meant too much. If she had unconsciously been nurturing some vague hope—and the bleakness of dismay was proof that she had—that hope was now dead. But at least there was one thing to be thankful for, her friendship with his aunt and sisters was relieved of all constraint and suspicion.

During the eight weeks which Theodore spent in the East that summer of 1885 the new house—mansion, some called it because of its size, not its beauty—teemed with life. When all the twenty-two rooms had been furnished and arranged to his satisfaction, his multiple elk, bear, moose, deer, antelope, and buffalo heads adorning a dozen walls, giving the place the aspect of a museum rather than a home, he could settle down to as near as he could ever come to leisure. He learned to romp with his young daughter, discovering that blue eyes and yellow curls were less painful reminders of his loss than accoutrements of a new and vivid personality. He even took pride in these features, especially when his brother Elliott's ten-month-old daughter Eleanor came to visit, her lanky little body, nondescript features, and shy, solemn manner so noticeably eclipsed by the attractions of his own chubby, cheerful cherub.

Guests flocked to the house that summer, for even grief could not long blunt Teddy's gregarious nature. There must be people, activity. Friends flocked as well as the numerous surrounding relatives. Fanny Smith Dana was one of those invited. Though just recovering from a miscarriage and unable to enter into the more violent pursuits, like catapulting down Cooper's Bluff into the sea, she found no lack of excitement. One person who had always been part of Fanny's Oyster Bay experience, however, was missing. Edith Carow.

For Edith it was a long, monotonous summer, but it finally passed, and the old intimacy with Bamie and Aunt Annie was revived. Theodore was again in the West, Bamie back in New York. With Conie in New Jersey, the home at 422 Madison Avenue became a haven from loneliness and frustration. Not only was the friendly and voluble Bamie a source of welcome news about Teddy, but her selfless concern for other people's problems made her an ideal confidante. And Edith had plenty of problems to confide. The Carow finances were becoming increasingly critical.

"Mother wants to take Emily and me to Europe," she told Bamie. "She thinks we could live more cheaply there."

"She's probably right," agreed Bamie. "And I can see Emily adjusting to a life like that, moving from place to place, perhaps finding a cozy refuge somewhere, surrounded by books and art and ancient culture. But—you, my dear—"

She regarded her friend appraisingly, with a sympathy born of long friendship. How sensitive she was, how afraid of penetration of that intense privacy! And yet, under all that aloofness, how soft and vulnerable! Edie had always been pretty, but now in maturity, at age twenty-four, she had really become beautiful—those wide-spaced eyes, the fine cheekbones, the beautiful classic nose, the porcelain complexion. And when she infrequently smiled, as she did now, sensing an unusual sympathy and understanding, it was as if a closed door suddenly opened, revealing depths of emotional potential which few, even among her most intimate friends, would ever know existed. A pity, Bamie may have thought, that more people—Teddy, for instance?—could not see this new more mature Edith, slowly emerging from the tight chrysalis of an inhibited girlhood!

And then suddenly it happened. Did Bamie purposely refrain from notifying her brother, as requested, when a certain person was likely to be visiting her? Or did he himself run the risk of appearing when he was not expected? Certainly Edith would never know.

It was a day in early October. She had been having an unusually satisfying teatime and tête-à-tête with Bamie in her upstairs sitting room and was coming down the stairs when the front door opened and with his usual precipitation he came barging in, stopping short in the hall when he looked up and saw her. She paused briefly, for little more than an arrested heartbeat, then calmly continued her descent, stopping just before she reached him in the center of the hall.

"Edie!" he muttered, almost inaudibly.

She regarded him steadily. "Hello, Teddy. It's good seeing you again. You're looking well."

And indeed he was. Gone were the narrow shoulders, the anemic pallor, the asthmatic slenderness of neck and flatness of chest. She was as much surprised as one of his friends, who that summer had been amazed "to find him with the neck of a Titan and with broad shoulders and stalwart chest." After all these years the tough life in the wilderness, together with his intrepid willpower and exertion, had enabled him to follow his father's injunction, to "make his body." His voice, too, when he spoke, had lost the affected Harvard drawl, had become clipped and energetic.

"So are you, Edie. I have never seen you looking better."

They exchanged a few more pleasantries, then Edith passed around him and, without looking back, crossed the hall and went out the door. It might have been any casual meeting between old friends. Nothing to show that it had changed the future not only for two lives, but for generations yet to come, possibly for a nation as well.

2

"Welcome, Edie dear." Bamie was, as always, the gracious hostess. "Welcome to Sagamore. Did you know the name has been changed? Theodore thought it more fitting for the place to bear the name of the old Sagamore chief Mohannis, who used to hold his war councils here on this very hill. He'll be pleased you were able to come. Theodore, I mean."

It was a weekend late in October 1885, a special occasion for him, for it was not only his twenty-seventh birthday but a meeting of the Meadowbrook and Essex hunts at Sagamore Hill. Edith had been invited, not to join the hunting parties, for it was a sport she did not enjoy, but as a member of the jolly party which he and Bamie liked to assemble for every possible occasion. To her surprise and delight the old friendly association with Teddy had been revived. Soon after their chance meeting in the hall he had invited her to go for a drive. Then he had dropped in for a call one evening, ostensibly to bring a new book he had found interesting. Then he had called again to discuss the book after she had had a chance to read it. There had been the same old challenge, disagreement, crossfire of ideas, and mental stimulus as formerly in their conversation, and, to the relief of both of them, not the slightest possible hint of emotional involvement.

Fanny Dana was one of the guests that weekend, also Conie with her husband Douglas and many of the cousins who had been part of the old youthful escapades. The Friday night after Edith's arrival all joined in rollicking games, familiar from childhood. There was dancing, which spread from the big parlor into the huge entrance hall and out onto the spacious west piazza. Big . . . huge . . . spacious. Seeing the inside of the house for the first time, Edith found even such adjectives inadequate. But, knowing Teddy, she could understand the insistent emphasis on *size*. He needed all this wall expanse for his multiplicity of animal heads. Already there were rooms full of them, and probably dozens more to come! And the twelve bedrooms were every one in use tonight.

The next day at noon, Saturday the twenty-sixth, the hunters began assembling, thirty-five horsemen in all, and after the traditional stirrup cup, they set off at about one o'clock over the hunting course, its already rough terrain made further perilous by high timber obstacles and stiff fences, being one of the most challenging on Long Island. Theodore, riding a spirited stallion named Frank, started off well in the lead and looked as if he planned to remain so.

"I hate these hunts," fretted Conie. "I always have. There's almost certain to be an accident."

Was her worry, Edith could not help wondering, for her husband Douglas or for Teddy? She wondered also if Conie was secretly as pleased as she seemed to be that the friendship, casual though it was, between her and Teddy had been revived. Conie's affection for her older brother had always revealed a trace of jealous possessiveness.

The day seemed to have lost some of its October golden glow after the huntsmen left. No Teddy to instigate frenzied activity! As soon as the horsemen were likely to return, many of the guests sauntered down to the stables, Edith, Conie, and Fanny among them. Presently Mame appeared with her twenty-month-old charge. "Look at the sweet colleen!" she greeted Edith. "Dancin' up an' down like the foolish little pixie she is! Caint wait for her da to come and mebbe give her a turn on his horse!"

The huntsmen began to straggle in, and it was obvious that there had been accidents. "I knew it!" mourned Conie when Douglas appeared, barely able to maintain his balance and looking as if half the skin on his face had been mangled. He had been thrown from his horse and knocked nearly unconscious. Another man had broken two ribs, and the master of the hunt had dislocated his knee. But Teddy, wondered Edith, becoming more and more alarmed, where was Teddy?

Suddenly Baby Lee began screaming, and no wonder! She saw a monster approaching, face battered and bleeding, pink coat covered with mud, left arm dangling, two rows of prominent teeth exposed in an expansive grin. When she fled in terror the apparition pursued her, laughing, caught up and swept her to him with his strong right arm. Even after discovering that the strange monster was "Da," she struggled to be free.

While a distraught Conie rushed back and forth between husband and brother, exclaiming, swabbing at bruises with a dainty handkerchief, Edith stood still, unable, it seemed, to move a muscle. She only half listened to the chorus of voices excitedly relaying the details of Teddy's accident.

"Led us all for three miles . . . Five miles out or so, his horse went lame, struck the rail of a five-foot fence . . . landed right on top of poor Roosevelt on a heap of stones . . . but he picked himself up, mounted again, took some twenty more fences, went on to the end . . . at least some of us, riding ahead, managed to take off the top rails . . . was there at the death . . . not a hundred yards behind the first riders!"

"Nonsense!" It was Theodore himself, decrying all suspicion of heroics. "What's all the fuss about? I took a tumble, got a few scratches, yes. So what? I'm always willing to pay the piper when I've had a good dance!" He shook off the supporting arms which tried to escort him to the house.

Scarcely was he out of sight when another horseman came charging up, horse in a lather, flung himself down, and looked about. Edith recognized him as a physician who had gone on the hunt.

"Where's Roosevelt?" he demanded. "Has he come back? How is he?"

Gone to the house, he was told. Seemed all right. Finished the hunt, was in on the kill. Why? What was he so concerned about?

The doctor snorted. "Don't you know?" he exclaimed. "Why, man, he broke his arm when his horse went down!"

Edith stood still, motionless, as she was likely to do when battling with intense emotions. Usually, if she just remained quiet, analyzing a situation calmly, turmoils would resolve themselves. Not this time. For, seeing that battered but indomitably cheerful figure, and watching Conie, who had a sister's right, mopping those bruises with her little handkerchief, she had made an alarming discovery. She was desperately, hopelessly, in love with a man who was desperately, hopelessly, in love with a memory. And she suspected that for this problem there was no solution.

The weekend continued, but for Edith all its delight had ended. Arm in splints, bruises plastered, Theodore was his usual boisterous self, entertaining guests at dinner with uproarious hunting yarns, presiding as host over the hunt ball held that evening at Sagamore, managing with one-armed deftness to twirl his partners, Edith included, in polkas, quadrilles, modern waltzes, even uninhibited by the vigors of the Highland *Schottische*. At midnight, with the advent of Sunday, October 27, though dancing ceased, there were lavish refreshments, toasts, speeches, presentation, all in honor of Teddy's twenty-seventh birthday.

Edith was glad when the weekend was over. Back in New York she could plunge into the multiplicity of mundane tasks in preparation for the coming exodus of the family to Europe. In addition to her mother, her sister Emily, and herself, Mame was going with them. Edith was delighted, for the Irish nurse had long seemed a member of the family. She had begged to accompany them, for she had never been really happy at Bamie's.

Edith almost wished she need not see Theodore again. But he continued to call on her, seeming to find her cozy living room at 114 East Thirty-sixth Street a haven from his political speeches and intensive research for his projected biography. She took little pleasure in his visits. His physical presence, the impersonal nature of their conversations, aroused more unrest than satisfaction. Still at every beating of the knocker her pulses quickened, and when the maid went to the door she held her breath listening for the high staccato voice demanding, "Miss Carow? Does she happen to be in?"

She was not expecting him when he came on the evening of Tuesday, November 17, for his calls were usually on a weekend. Gertrude and Emily had gone to a musicale, but she had remained at home to struggle with the discouraging household accounts. She hesitated about inviting him into the parlor as usual, with standards of propriety so rigid, but he charged in without waiting for an invitation, and, after all, the servants should qualify as chaperones (as if any were needed for a conversation about results of the recent state election or Wilmot Dow's latest figures on the beef roundup in October!). She laid aside her accounts, greeted him pleasantly, and took a chair by the little table where she always kept some sewing.

Tonight he seemed more restless than usual, for instead of sitting, even briefly (he never could sit still for long!), he walked back and forth, fingering gadgets, Gertrude's china tea set on the mantel, the figurine she had once rescued from Baby Lee's clutching fingers. He had some subject to discuss, that was clear. What was it this time? More ideas on his pet concern for civil service reform, or promotion of Negro suffrage in the South? Or, perhaps, a new story for his Western saga? She waited, fingers busy with a bit of embroidery, completely unaware of the picture of domestic felicity she created, the lamplight raising golden glints in her hair and highlighting the wide-spaced blue eyes and finely molded cheekbones.

"Why don't you read to me?" he suggested suddenly. "You haven't done that for a long time." Going to a bookcase, he picked out a book, seemingly at random, and brought it to her.

One of her rare transforming smiles curved her generous mouth. "Longfellow? A good choice, whether you meant it or not. It brings back old times, very old. Remember how you used to love 'King Olaf'?" She hunted for it in the index.

"Not that tonight," he retorted. "It—doesn't suit my mood. Maybe—yes, how about 'The Children's Hour'?"

She riffled the pages. "Just as you say. That *does* seem like old times."

She found the place and began reading, her voice low and musical, bearing little resemblance to the childish treble which had once intoned the words as they sat around Aunt Annie's study table.

> *Between the dark and the daylight*
> *When the light is beginning to lower . . .*

The familiar words flowed on.

> *From my study I see in the lamplight,*
> *Descending the broad hall stair,*
> *Grave Alice . . .*

Her voice trailed off into silence. *Alice.* Oh, dear! She had forgotten the name was there. But it was as if he had not heard the word. He went on to finish the couplet.

> *. . . and laughing Allegra,*
> *And Edith with golden hair.*

Emotion flooded her with sudden warmth as she felt his hand resting gently on the smooth waves and coils which had once been long curling tresses.

"You're looking very pretty tonight, Edie."

Then all at once he was on his knees beside her, his good right arm encircling her waist, his face buried in the folds of her full skirt. But his other arm, still rigid in the sling, hung like a hard barrier between them.

"Oh—I shouldn't be doing this!" he exclaimed. "It isn't right. Marriage is meant to be once for all—for life—and after—isn't it? But—we do belong together, Edie. Perhaps we always have."

"Yes," she said. Holding his head between her hands, she ran her long fingers through his thick waving hair, realizing that for years it was something she had yearned to do. It felt just as she had expected—resilient, vigorous, almost as if it had a life of its own.

They talked a long time, making plans. Finally it was decided. They would consider themselves pledged to one another, but the engagement would remain secret. Even their immediate families would not be told. They would wait at least a year for marriage. That would make it seem more proper to both relatives and friends. It would also give time for each of them to solve personal problems, Edith to establish her mother and sister in Europe, Theodore to determine what work and environment his future should encompass. Ranching? But he could not subject the city-bred Edith to the rigors of the Badlands, though she professed willingness to go. Even the Sewall and Dow wives, reared in Maine hardihood, were rebelling at the lonely austerity of the wilderness. Politics? Little prospect of opportunities in that field. Literature? Support a family on such meager royalties as his first book had yielded? Already he was feeling a financial pinch.

The following winter months were the happiest Edith had ever known. She and Theodore were soon being seen in many public places together. She accompanied him to plays, operas, dances, dinner parties. But since it had been the pattern of their lives before his marriage, their intimacy was viewed as merely friendly. Fanny Dana, seeing them together at many affairs, believed it to be only the old brother–sister relationship based largely on an intellectual affinity, and even his sisters, knowing his rigid ideas about marriage, suspected no romantic attachment. Theodore began writing in his diary again, and, though the date of February 14 was marked by a heart with an arrow thrust through it, many pages bore the significant letter "E." He had sealed their engagement by giving her several gifts—a ring, a watch, a pearl necklace—all of which she put aside for future display and use.

Edith knew that her fiancé was still tormented by guilt for his "unfaithfulness." Was his excessive interest in social activities, she wondered, an attempt to drown his self-doubting in action? Or was it perhaps an outlet for restlessness and futility because he was so uncertain about his purposes in life? In January and February he listed in his diary twenty-four dinner parties which he had attended! She was delighted when toward the end of January the man who seemed to have become his most intimate friend, Henry Cabot Lodge, came to New York to visit him. She recognized in this aristocratic, highly intellectual Bostonian, with his neatly trimmed beard, his keen hazel eyes, his confident, slightly rasping voice, the influence which Theodore so badly needed in charting his life's course.

"Our friend is one of the most lovable as well as one of the cleverest and most daring men I know," he remarked to Edith as he sat beside her at one dinner. "The more I see him, the more I love him."

But in February the frustration was at least temporarily assuaged. One day when Theodore came to visit he was afire with enthusiasm. "What do you think? I've been commissioned to write a biography of Thomas Hart Benton. I'm sure Lodge is responsible. He must have pulled strings with his Boston publisher. It's right up my alley, with its emphasis on frontier life." He plunged happily into the necessary research.

But it was not enough. The West was calling him. He would leave for his ranches, he decided, in the middle of March, before Edith and her family planned to start for Europe the last of April. Already he had collected enough material on the new book to take with him and start writing. Though he hated to leave her, of course, she must agree that these months of waiting before their marriage were frustrating. Surely she would understand.

She did. He had even left his precious Alice, she consoled herself, and answered the wilderness call, leaving her in the throes of pregnancy. She had no illusions. It would always be so. On March 15 she saw him off on the westbound express, noting that in spite of their tender and regretful farewells, the bespectacled eyes were agleam with excitement and anticipation. At least she could now give her full attention to the grueling task of selling the house, disposing of generations of family accumulations, ending a whole way of life.

Others also were finding the change wrenching. "The Carows have sold their house and are going abroad on the 24th of April," Conie wrote Theodore on March 29. "It makes me quite blue."

With pretended innocence he wrote back, "What day does Edith go abroad and how long does she intend staying? Could you not send her when she goes some flowers from me? I suppose fruit would be more useful, but I think flowers 'more tenderer,' as Mr. Weller would say."

Conie's grief at their parting was outspoken and intense. Would it be as sincere, wondered Edith, if she knew of the future relationship between her favorite friend and her favorite brother? It was one of the few flaws in her expectation of almost complete happiness. Another was the knowledge that Theodore still endured black moods of guilt. Fortunately she would not hear him, as some of his hosts would during his Western wanderings, pacing the floor and groaning over and over, "I have no constancy! I have no constancy!"

Edith was delighted that Mame wanted to go with them, and Bamie agreed that she could get along very well without her. In fact, Edith suspected, she coveted a closer relationship as surrogate mother to her young charge. Another flaw in Edith's happiness. What about Baby Lee? Would Bamie willingly give her up? To Edith any other outcome was unthinkable. A problem, but fortunately it need not be faced as yet.

The Carows sailed for Europe on April 24, as planned. During the following weeks and months, though the travel of which she had always dreamed was exciting and intellectually stimulating, Edith felt that she was just marking time. It was merely an interim between two lives. Events taking place in South Dakota were as vividly real as the changing of the guard at Buckingham Palace or a gondola ride in Venice or a visit to the fascinating cathedral in Prague with its mosaics and its bronze candelabra from Jerusalem. Letters crossed the ocean constantly, seventeen of them from Theodore in the first two months. She saw him "rising every day at dawn, standing for a moment on the piazza watching the sun rise through a filter of glossy cottonwood trees," then writing furiously, finishing most of his 83,000-word manuscript in just three weeks' time ("You must take me out West or I shall repent all my life not having seen the place my dearest is so fond of"); participated vicariously in the arduous, probably dangerous spring roundup ("Please try not to break your other arm until I can take care of you!"); agonized with him when the price of cattle fell so deplorably that his friends Sewall and Dow expressed a desire to return to their more predictable life in Maine.

"London is perfectly lovely now," she was writing him in June. "Last night we heard your cousin Mr. Scovell, poor Marcia Roosevelt's husband, sing in *Carmen* . . . His one idea of making love is to seize the prima donna's arm and shake her, violently. I am glad it is not your way. . . . Mame told me today I had never taken any care of my complexion, but she hoped I would now, but when I asked why, she could give no satisfactory answer. You should have seen her walking down Baker Street holding an umbrella over my head. She is always so pleased when she brings me a letter from you. . . . I have got the most entrancing hat, all tipped down over my nose and tipped up over one ear, with pale pinky-lilac flowers drooping around. It is almost too pretty to wear since you are not here to see it. . . . Mamma and Emily ask me to send you their love, and you know you have all of your—Edith.

"P. S. Do you think I wish you to hire Windsor or Buckingham for a honeymoon that you say that you can't give me such a one as you would wish?"

It was a long letter, the only one of this period to be preserved in its entirety. So strong was that innate compulsion for privacy that much of their most intimate correspondence would later be destroyed.

Given the omnipotence of gossip, it was not surprising that an announcement of the engagement appeared in the society columns of the New York *Times* in September, to be followed a week later by an apology, instigated, no doubt, by the vigorous disclaimer of Conie or Bamie, or both. "Savagely irritated," Theodore sent off a letter to Bamie denying all knowledge of the source of the rumor, yet having shamefacedly to confess that it was true. "I am engaged to Edith, and before Christmas I shall cross the ocean to marry her. You are the first person to whom I have breathed a word on the subject." He made all the excuses possible for not telling her, then heartily berated himself.

"I utterly disbelieve in second marriages. . . . You could not reproach me half as bitterly for my inconstancy and unfaithfulness as I reproach myself. . . . But I do very earnestly ask you not to visit my sins upon poor Edith. It's certainly not her fault; the entire blame rests on my shoulders. Eight years ago she and I had very intimate relations; one day there came a break, for we both of us had, and I suppose have, tempers that were far from being of the best. . . ."

Edith was not surprised to learn that in October Theodore was back in the East and had been persuaded to run for mayor of New York City. Good. His fascination for ranching would never have compensated for his urge to fight political corruption. His speech that Fourth of July out in Dakota had proved that.

"If you fail to work in public life as well as in private for honesty, and uprightness, and virtue . . . you are just so far corrupting and making less valuable the birth right of your children."

It was Bamie, apparently happy about the engagement, who kept her "Dearest Edith" informed of "the wonderful enthusiasm he inspires; never mind the results. . . . It is such happiness to see him at his very best once more; ever since he had been out of politics in an active form, it had been a real sorrow to me. . . . It is such a desperate feeling to realize that I cannot help him in the least except that he knows how interested I am. . . . It is very restful to feel how you care for him and how happy he is in his devotion to you. . . ."

He did not win the election, had not expected to. But he was satisfied. He had once more expressed himself boldly without compromise. "The true purpose of government is, among other things, to give everyone security that he shall enjoy the fruits of his labor, to prevent the strong from oppressing the weak, and the unscrupulous from robbing the honest." Too boldly, perhaps, if he wanted to win, with such statements as, "If I find a public servant who is dishonest, I will chop his head off if he is the highest Republican in this Municipality."

On November 6 he and Bamie sailed for England in preparation for the wedding. Conie had a good excuse for not going, having given birth that summer to a second child, a girl named Corinne Douglas. Theodore's "Sweet Pussie," unlike his "Darling Bysie," was not quite ready to acknowledge the superior claim on her brother's affections of "My Dearest Edie."

The long hiatus of separation was over. Edith felt like the sleeping beauty awakened suddenly to life. She and her mother and sister had rooms at Buckland's Hotel in Mayfair, while Theodore was close by at Brown's. Edith had pictured the three weeks before the wedding as an ideal interim of privacy, catching up on all the long months of absence, giving expression to the emotions which could not be shared in letters. And indeed they did have a few days of precious intimacy, usually in his hotel suite to escape the solicitous presence of Gertrude and Emily.

But she had failed to reckon with Theodore's reputation, as well as his gregarious nature. Though he and Bamie had tried to escape undue attention on the voyage by registering as Mr. and Miss Merrifield (the name of one of his ranching partners), at least one person on the *Etruria* had seen through their disguise. Edith soon met this new acquaintance, an aristocratic, esthetic young English diplomat named Cecil Spring-Rice. So friendly had they become on the ship that Theodore had asked him to be his best man. Edith liked "Springy" immediately, and he confessed to Theodore that he found her "charming."

But gone were all her hopes for privacy. Theodore's reputation as a rising young politician had preceded him, and Springy took full advantage of their new friendship to introduce him to London society. He was invited to join the most exclusive clubs, including the St. James and the Athenaeum. He dined with eminent statesmen, went into the country on shooting expeditions. As he wrote Conie on November 22, he had become "quite a lion." He had "three times as many invitations as I can accept to dine, hunt, and shoot, and go to country houses." But Edith's adjustment to this turbulent schedule, obviously a foretaste of her life to come, had evidently been satisfactory, for he added, "You have no idea how sweet Edith is about many different things, which Bamie will tell you. I don't think even I had known how wonderfully *good* and unselfish she was; she is naturally reserved and finds it especially hard to express herself on paper. Mrs. Carow and Emily have been marvelously sweet to me."

Fog. A dense, dank, yellow, pea-soupy fog such as only London was capable of producing—or New York on a February week nearly three years before. When Edith awoke on December 2, her wedding day, her heart sank. Would Theodore remember groping his way through just such a fog toward a house where the two women he had loved best were dying? An unpropitious day for their marriage? No! She would not let it be.

So thick was the fog that the hansom cabs carrying the wedding party to St. George's Church in Hanover Square had to be guided through the streets by link bearers. Edith could feel the lovely Italian lace of her wedding gown and her orange blossom veil wilting between the cab and the church doors. The narthex and nave were both wrapped in mist. When she started down the aisle in the wake of Emily, her sole attendant, the few guests in the front pews and the figures waiting at the chancel were almost invisible. But she proceeded, head held high, wondering if Teddy was comparing this dismal, befogged event to the colorful, crowded extravaganza of his first marriage.

As she approached the altar and the figures of the groom and his best man loomed out of the mist, her gaze encountered two bright orange blobs moving about like errant sunbeams. She stared at them, transfixed. Gloves! Teddy's! Springy, she was to discover later, noting his companion's bare hands, had interrupted their heated discussion on the population of a South Sea island to stop the cab, dash into a haberdashery shop, and come out with these incongruous appendages to the groom's sedate frock coat and silk ruffled shirt. Edith felt a wild desire to laugh. And suddenly the dismal fog became unimportant. She and Teddy—they were all that mattered. The blue eyes behind the gleaming spectacles were shining beacons, and the lips parted over the prominent white teeth almost mouthed the sentiment, *"Dee-*lighted." But, she noted, there was tenderness in the eyes as well as satisfaction. So—he was not remembering that other fog. And suddenly for both of them the sun might have been shining.

The precise British accents of His Eminence, Charles E. Camidge, Canon of York, began the brief ceremony.

"Dearly beloved, we are gathered together . . ."

3

"We are having the most absolutely ideal time imaginable," Theodore wrote Bamie from the first stop on their honeymoon trip. Not perhaps the ecstatic effusion of the young husband who had found the "intense happiness too sacred to be written about," but emotionally satisfactory to both parties concerned.

They had three weeks completely to themselves, traveling leisurely through France, from Paris to Lyons to Marseilles and on to Hyères in Provence, proceeding by carriage along the French and Italian Riviera to Pisa, exulting in roses and palms and orange blossoms after the chills and fogs of London, quoting poetry together as they watched glorious sunsets from their luxurious suite overlooking the bay at La Spezia. Theodore spared no expense on the trip. Edith, now inured to economy, made only mild protests. No worries must mar the idyllic happiness of these weeks of fulfillment.

But idyls have a way of ending. Arriving in Florence in January, they were joined by Gertrude and Emily, and, though Theodore wrote his "Darling Bysie" that "Mrs. Carow and Emily are really too sweet and good to me for anything," Edith was again burdened with the problems of a querulous mother and an unsympathetic sister who were flitting about discontentedly like pigeons looking for a place to roost. For Theodore also there came a rude awakening. Letters began reaching him from his ranches.

In November had come tremendous blizzards. It was being dubbed the "Winter of the Blue Snow," the worst in history. The Western country was buried in huge drifts, some a hundred feet deep. Then had come unbelievable cold. Cattle were freezing, starving. It was obvious that his investment in the Badlands was in jeopardy. And to Edith it was becoming increasingly apparent that her husband, though undoubtedly a literary genius and superior in some other areas, was a financial illiterate. She had been shocked when she insisted on discussing with him the state of their finances. Now she realized they were approaching a crisis.

"We could close Sagamore Hill," she suggested, adding tactfully, "just temporarily, of course, and go West for a couple of years."

"Yes," he admitted. Then his jaw set stubbornly. "Not unless we have to," he muttered. However, he did write Douglas Robinson, who managed his affairs, asking him to sell his favorite hunting horse Sagamore, an expensive thoroughbred, though soon he was regretting even that impulsive decision and hastening to negate it. Edith had to be content with bringing him face-to-face with the situation.

"I *must* live well within my income and begin paying off my debt this year," he was writing Bamie on January 3, "at no matter what cost, even to the shutting up or renting of Sagamore Hill, bitterly as I should hate such an alternative. Meanwhile at least 1886 has been as happy a year as any one could have."

Oh, yes, he must economize, would do so—but not yet. He continued to spend their honeymoon in luxurious quarters, even began purchasing expensive Florentine furniture for Sagamore Hill.

Edith suffered no illusions. It was an age and culture when woman's influence over man depended largely on subtlety, not domination. She had seen other techniques at work—querulousness, complaint, nagging—and they had soured a marriage, possibly hastened her father's downfall. She would not let that happen to hers. Anyway, both whining and nagging were foreign to her nature.

"It's a beautiful carved sideboard, and the dining table and chairs will be perfect at Sagamore," she said of his choices. "But —don't you think the elaborate bedroom set is a little—ornate for a country home? And they do make fine furniture in America."

And of the sumptuous suite which he rented in Rome: "You spoil me, dearest. I'm not used to all this grandeur. And it makes me feel a bit guilty knowing Mother and Emily have to climb all those stairs to get to the best rooms they could afford."

But there was one problem which could not be postponed or solved by subtleties. It must be approached with tact, yes, but also with forthright determination. It was the cause of their first argument, what some might have called quarrel.

"How fortunate it is that Mame and Baby Lee are so fond of each other!" she remarked casually one January day as they sat beside a cozy fire in their suite, she with her knitting, Theodore for once relaxed after a grueling tour of Rome's ancient glories, reminding him of his childish rhapsodies some seventeen years before.

"Eh? What's that you say?" Jolted out of his euphoric preoccupation with the past, he focused his eyes with difficulty on the present. "Mame—Baby Lee—what—?"

"It will make it so much easier," Edith explained, "for the child to adjust herself to a new household."

"But—I don't understand—"

"Yes, that's just what I mean. It will be such a change. She's become so accustomed to dear Bamie. At least she's used to Mame and, of course, to you, so she won't miss Bamie so much."

"But"—Theodore left his seat, catapulted out of it, in fact, and began pacing up and down—"you don't understand, Edie, dear. I have already assured Bamie, by letter in fact, that she could keep Baby Lee, I, of course, paying all her expenses. I'm sure she's counting on it, raising the child as her own."

"But you must see, dearest, that that is impossible." Though she spoke calmly, Edith's fingers were tense about her knitting needles. "You are her father. I am her logical mother. She will have brothers and sisters, our children. Of course her home must be with us, with her own family."

Theodore's pacing became even more furious. "I—I tell you I've already told her—promised her—"

"Then you'll just have to explain to her that circumstances have changed. Just think, dear. Running over to Madison Avenue every time you wanted to see your own daughter? What sort of life would that be for either of you? I'm sure Bamie will understand."

"But—"

The argument continued, calmly, reasonably, but unyielding on Edith's side, persistently but more and more helplessly on

Theodore's. Finally he threw up his hands. "Well—we don't have to decide now. We can wait until we all meet."

But, recognizing that they had reached an impasse, he reluctantly and with great embarrassment wrote Bamie explaining the situation. "Edith feels more strongly about her than I would have believed possible." At least the decision could be postponed until they were back home.

On February 5, after making trips with her mother and sister to Pompeii, Capri, and Sorrento, Edith felt compunction as well as relief to leave them in Rome, Gertrude was so unhappy and Emily so impatient with her mother's neuroses. It was heaven to be by themselves again.

Theodore too was in a honeymoon mood again. In Rome he had worked furiously on six articles for the *Century* magazine on ranch life and shipped them off, hoping they would be found acceptable. "I read them all over to Edith, and her corrections and help were most valuable," he wrote Conie from Sorrento on January 22. By the time they reached Venice in February his first copy of *Benton* had arrived ("good in places and rough in others" was his evaluation), and his brief bout of depression over finances and other problems had ended in a burst of optimism. His and Edith's tastes were similar, sightseeing as the spirit moved without the tourist's crutch of a Baedeker. But even this soon palled, and they were glad to be back in London at the end of February.

Here, once again, in spite of the absence of Spring-Rice, who was now secretary to the British legation in Washington, they were sumptuously entertained by Lord North and other titled dignitaries. They met Lord Shaftesbury, the eminent historians George Trevelyan and James Bryce, and, a crowning feature of the whole trip, their favorite poet, Browning. The fact that Edith, as Theodore wrote Conie, had "been feeling the reverse of brightly for some time" was no curb on their enjoyment, since it signified an expectation heartily welcome to both.

It had been an ideal honeymoon, but they were ready to end it. As Theodore had written Bamie, "I shall be glad to get home. I am an American through to my backbone." Europe, and especially England, with all their age-old culture, held no allure for him compared with his "beloved woods and mountains and great lonely plains." And "Edith, thank heaven," as he wrote Henry Cabot Lodge, "feels as I do and is even more intensely anti-anglomatic." They sailed from Liverpool on March 19, reaching New York on March 27.

Edith would never forget arriving at Bamie's new home at 689 Madison Avenue on that March day. There was little three-year-old Alice standing at the top of the stairs, a diminutive fashion plate in her best dress trimmed with Valenciennes lace, her curls, as Alice was to describe the meeting later, "licked and prodded into place." She descended the stairs and approached the new-comers, a large bunch of pink roses outstretched in her hands. Theodore picked her up and gave her a big hug. When he set her down, she extended her hand politely to Edith. She might have been greeting a stranger. Bamie, too, it seemed, was not quite so sincere in her protestations of welcome. Or did Edith imagine a slight undercurrent of coldness? But surely she had been right in her insistence that the child become a part of her father's household. Bamie must see that.

The homecoming was saved from what might have been early confrontation of the problem by the presence of Theodore's two close friends, Cecil Spring-Rice and Henry Cabot Lodge, whom Bamie had thoughtfully invited to celebrate the reunion. Edith felt remarkably at ease with both of them. Springy had shared the happiest event of her life. With Lodge, in spite of his perfunctory Boston manners, probing hazel eyes which seemed veiled in critical appraisal, and rasping voice, she found satisfying rapport in their mutual love of classical literature.

But the confrontation had to come, to Theodore's embarrassed reluctance, Edith's regretful insistence, and Bamie's tactfully concealed sorrow. Yes, the latter agreed, of course Edith was right. The child belonged with her father and—was there slight hesitation here?—with her logical mother. It was all arranged amicably. Baby Lee would remain with Bamie while Edith visited Tyler relatives in Philadelphia, and Theodore, almost intolerably impatient to be off, went west to check on his ranches. When they returned Bamie would go south for a vacation, later spending part of the summer with them at Sagamore Hill before ending permanently her role as surrogate mother.

Waiting. Edith seemed to do nothing else that spring. Waiting to hear Theodore's news from the West, which, when it came, was devastating. His losses had been crippling. He would lose at least half of his investment, perhaps much more. There were not even enough cattle left for a spring roundup. Waiting for the child within her—four months—five—to give signs of its presence. Waiting, with Bamie gone south and she and Theodore alone with Baby Lee, for her new daughter to respond to her anxious attempts to show affection.

But in May the waiting ended. Suddenly a world which had seemed crazily awry swung neatly into shape. Theodore took her to Sagamore Hill and in a burst of boyish zeal carried her over the threshold. They were together at last in their own home. And for the present they were alone. Little Alice—Edith was determined she was to be known by her real name, not Baby Lee!— was spending three weeks with her grandparents at Chestnut Hill. Bamie was still in the South. She would join them for a few weeks this summer to help adjust Alice to the transition.

Edith reveled in this new home, the first she had been able to call her own. She knew she would be content to live here to the end of her life. No matter that it had been planned for another woman, that still another had been its first mistress! It was Theodore who had done the planning, who had injected his vigorous personality into the multiplicity of rooms, the monstrous animal heads dominating the walls, the heavy masculine furniture, the huge porches designed to accommodate an overflow of invited and uninvited guests.

The few weeks alone together were a confusion of hectic but delightful activity—removing dust covers, cleaning, dusting until they resembled stevedores, unpacking hundreds of books and storing them on the library shelves; placing the heavy oak furniture purchased in Florence in the dining room off the hall (though it made the room look "full to bursting" Edith was properly admiring of Theodore's choice); mingling her own Kermit and Carow pieces with those which were Theodore's allotment of the Roosevelt furniture at Fifty-seventh Street.

Only two tasks they did not share—the hanging of more grisly specimens from the Western hunting trips, and the furnishing of the little parlor at the southwest corner of the hall, opposite the library. This was to be hers alone, a place of retreat. Let all the other rooms reflect Theodore's boisterous masculinity, with their heavy furniture, their game heads, their guns, their pictures and statues of men in action. This would be feminine, simple, dainty —floral-covered sofas and armchairs, a leather-covered table which was a family heirloom, a rosewood étagère, her wool-winder, the little rosewood desk which had belonged to Aunt Kermit.

"My life will be most uneventful this summer," Theodore wrote Lodge on June 11.

For him, perhaps, it was, spending much of his time at his desk writing a biography of Gouverneur Morris, American statesman who had been one of the drafters of the Constitution. For Edith it was a far more exciting and demanding time than any she had ever spent before. Merely running the household at a minimum of expense was a challenge. Theodore insisted on three servants beside Mame: a cook, a waitress, a chambermaid. She despaired of getting him really to economize, and his farm help cost as much as the servants, whose wages together amounted to sixty dollars a month. She entertained guests, the numerous Roosevelts who had summer homes nearby, Bamie, and Spring-Rice, thankful that her condition prevented the influx which Theodore probably would have liked. And she tried her best to win the affection of little Alice, while conscious that it was Bamie, outgoing, demonstrative, uninhibited, who still held, perhaps always would hold, the devotion accorded a first "Mother."

Theodore had no difficulty with this problem. The child idolized him, and he was her slave. He carried her downstairs pig-a-back each morning in obedience to her peremptory "Here, pig!" He cavorted and pranced about the porches with her so long and tirelessly that one Sunday morning he was afraid he would "incapicitate himself for church." He played with her on the floor, building blockhouses and telling fascinating stories about the people who lived in them. He's still something of a small boy himself, thought Edith, half in derision, half in envy.

For her, if not for Theodore, there was all the excitement desired in the hours they spent together that summer, riding in the buggy (until his horse Caution nearly upset them and Theodore in alarm forbade any further such hazards); sitting on the piazza watching flaming sunsets, swimming, walking in the woods, and especially going on long rides in what he called his "jolly" rowboat, often accompanied by his dog Peter.

"Last Saturday Edith and I spent the whole day in our boat," he wrote Lodge in June, "rowing over to a great marsh, filled with lagoons and curious winding channels through which the tide runs like a mill race; we took Browning and the Matthew Arnold you gave me along. . . ."

Books. Theodore. They were all the ingredients Edith needed for an "eventful" summer. But for both of them the greatest excitement was in the expectation fast approaching its climax.

On her twenty-sixth birthday, August 6, 1887, Edith was almost eight months pregnant. Plans must be made. She was almost glad when Gertrude wrote that she and Emily had decided they could not come for their proposed visit. But, Theodore insisted, she *must* have a woman with her. Bamie? No. Edith rejected the idea hastily, giving no apparent reason. Mame would be quite sufficient, she assured him. He was obliged to explain in some embarrassment to Bamie, "Mame is devoted; you know how much she is to Edith; I do not think there is need of anyone else."

Labor commenced early and suddenly at nine o'clock on the evening of September 12. Theodore was frantic. The hired nurse had not arrived. Fortunately Cousin West Roosevelt, their doctor, was nearby and was immediately summoned, also Aunt Annie, whose summer place was on adjoining property. While Theodore paced about distractedly, like one of his grim specimens come suddenly to life, family history was being made, for once without his assistance. In a calmer but exultant mood he wrote Bamie the next day about the night's developments.

"Things came with a rush even sooner than any one had expected. . . . The small son and heir was born at 2.15 this morning. Edith is getting along very well; she was extremely plucky all through. The boy is a fine little fellow about 8½ pounds. . . ."

Of course he was named Theodore Junior, to be called "Ted," a nickname distinct from the "Teddy" many people would always insist on ascribing to his father. Conie also, of course, had another "Teddy."

An uneventful summer? Hardly. Even Theodore, condemned to what he termed inactivity, could not call it that. His pride was commensurate with, or, rather, exceeded that in his usual grandiose exhibitions. And the family shared his delight in the birth of a Roosevelt heir. There had been too many girls of late.

For Edith one of the happiest by-products of Ted's birth was its effect on little Alice. The child set her small rocking chair beside the baby's cradle and refused to be moved from "my own little brother," though she added with less admiration, *"My* little brother's a howling polly parrot." Theodore wrote Conie, inviting her, at Edith's request, to come and see the "funny little fellow" and adding, "It is lovely to see Edie with him. Alice watches him, especially when she 'eats Mama,' as she calls it, with absorbed interest."

It had taken the baby, Edith decided with satisfaction, to join the four of them together as a family. Alice was even reluctant to go to Chestnut Hill for her usual fall visit unless she could take little Ted with her.

The new mother suffered the usual postnatal trials of that Victorian era, two weeks in bed incarcerated in wrappings like a mummy, then convalescence in confining corsets. She also suffered discomfiting hours of depression when she cried by the hour and for a time was unable to ride in the carriage without succumbing to fits of weeping. But such indulgences were foreign to her nature, and, while Theodore relieved his flagging energies in a five-week hunting trip beginning in November, ostensibly to check on his investments, she returned to her usual robust health and the happy responsibilities of a growing family. After Theodore returned, shocked both by the further ravages inflicted on his cattle and still further by the frightening scarcity of big game in the Badlands, they moved into the city in January and, with Bamie away, occupied her house at 689 Madison Avenue.

To Edith's relief, Theodore now had a new obsession to satisfy his thirst for action. Politics, with the Democrats in the saddle, were out of the question. His biography had gone to the printer's.

But out West he had seen the depredations of the "swinish big-game hunters," yes, himself included. Something must be done to save the great game animals from extinction. *Conservation.* He called together some influential animal lovers, among them George Bird Grinnell, editor of *Forest and Stream,* and together they formed a club which would "work for the preservation of the large game animals of the country, further legislation for that purpose, and assist in enforcing laws." They named it after Daniel Boone and Davy Crockett, two of Theodore's heroes. He was its first president. It was the beginning of a movement which would have a profound effect on the country's natural resources, not only its animals but its forests, its national parks, its whole ecology.

But of course, being Theodore, he must find another consuming interest, one, Edith hoped, that would be more lucrative. Her worry was as much for him as for the family, for she knew his frustration. Two of the three outlets for his energy had been closed, ranching and politics. Only literature remained, and, though it had been a critical success, his *Benton* had not sold well. His *Gouverneur Morris* would probably be similarly unprofitable. She was infinitely relieved when a new project burst forth full-blown, like Athena from the brow of Zeus. He would write a grand opus, the story of the march of the United States from east to west, from the Alleghenies to the Pacific. He would call it *The Winning of the West.* It would run to at least four volumes, perhaps eight.

He started research immediately, afire with enthusiasm. By March he had burrowed through thousands of letters, books, manuscripts, and obtained a contract with Putnam's to finish two volumes by the spring of 1889, a formidable but inspiriting challenge. But an unusually early and balmy spring was enticing him to Sagamore. Happily he remembered some books in his library there which he *must* have.

"I won't be gone long," he assured Edith, "just a few hours to pick up a few volumes." Yes, and to check on his beloved horse Sagamore, she thought indulgently, and commune with his precious animal heads.

He set off on Saturday, March 10, 1888, a day which saw crocuses blooming and the first robins appearing. Sunday turned cold, with a strong wind and freezing rain. And on Monday New York was visited by the worst blizzard of the century. Stores closed, the elevated trains were paralyzed, horse-drawn cars ran off their icy tracks. The streets were buried in snow to second-story windows. Fires blazed unchecked while the water from hoses turned to ice. Poles and wires were down, and that night the city was enveloped in Stygian darkness. The weight of snow, with winds up to eighty-four miles an hour, had caused the police to close the Brooklyn Bridge.

Edith was frantic with worry. Surely Theodore would not try to come home today, as he had planned! But, being Theodore, of course he did. It was early Tuesday morning when he arrived, looking like a huge snowman, eyes barely visible through ice-coated spectacles, white teeth gleaming in a broad smile. "Isn't this simply bully!" he exclaimed heartily.

"How—" Edith could barely mouth the word.

Easy, he explained. He had walked much of the way between stations, crossed the East River with hundreds of others on a huge ice floe which had wedged itself between Brooklyn and Manhattan. It was just now beginning to break up. Tugs had had to rescue some unlucky blokes. He had been worried about the family. Couldn't stay away and leave them alone.

Edith was silent, weak with relief and amazement. She felt like echoing Mittie's comment in his childhood. *"If the Lord had not taken care of Theodore, he would have been killed long ago."*

In May they were back at Sagamore Hill, all but little Alice, who had gone with Mame on her spring visit to Chestnut Hill, to be spoiled as usual by her grandparents. In spite of the storm's devastation the earth had come to life. Mayflowers had bloomed and passed. Violets and dogwood blossoms turned the grounds riotous with color. Noah Seaman, their farmer, had plowed and planted the fields. Little Ted, bursting with energy like the outside world, was crawling about, as active as his playmates, two dogs and a cat with newborn kittens.

It was a summer much like the previous one, with Theodore writing furiously each morning, not only on his opus, but hopefully turning out enough articles—at least one a month plus an occasional book—to provide the necessary four thousand dollars a year for household expenses. To Edith's dismay there were many more guests than last year, not only Spring-Rice and Cabot Lodge but Gertrude and Emily, Elliott and his family—a worry to Theodore because of his brother's weakness for strong drink—one of her own Tyler cousins, and numerous Roosevelt relatives. There were garden parties, yacht races, dinners, dances, polo games. Her tastes and Theodore's were sometimes in sharp opposition, she had to admit. A woman who cherished quiet and privacy and a man who thrived on crowds, excitement, conflict? Such differences could easily wreck a marriage, unless . . .

Perhaps it was that summer that she began consciously to make such self-adjustment that would enable her, twenty years or more later, to write to the child now crawling about with his father's exuberance: "One should not live to oneself. It was a temptation to me, only Father would not allow it. Since I have grown older and realize that it is a great opportunity when one has a house that one can make pleasant for younger—and also older—people to come to, I have done better."

Not that she would have to do all the adjusting! At about the same time Theodore also would confess to that same son on the eve of his engagement: "Greatly though I loved Mother, I was at times thoughtless and selfish, and if Mother had been a mere unhealthy Griselda I might have grown set in selfish and inconsiderate ways. Mother, always tender, gentle and considerate, and always loving, yet, when necessary, pointed out where I was thoughtless, instead of submitting to it. Had she not done this, it would in the end have made her life much harder, and mine very much less happy."

But the adjustment was painful, and at least once that summer her physical as well as her spiritual nature rebelled. Was it because of the Oyster Bay polo match in late July, when Theodore tried to outrun Elliott, was thrown from his horse, and lay like a dead man, then remained disoriented for several days, that soon afterward she suffered a miscarriage? So Ted would not be getting a little sibling next January, after all.

It was almost a relief when Theodore departed in August for his usual hunting trip in the West, even though she was left to face

alone the hypochondriac fancies of Gertrude and the gloomy dissatisfactions of Emily. Fortunately, surprisingly, little Alice took a
great fancy to Emily and followed her about like a shadow, accompanying her gladly to Gracewood, the Gracies' summer home
on the outskirts of Sagamore, where Aunt Annie was once more
plying her teaching skills for the younger generations of
Roosevelts. Edith almost envied her sister for this loyalty which
she coveted for herself.

That fall *The Winning of the West* gave priority to the "winning
of the presidential election" by Benjamin Harrison. Edith even
accompanied Theodore as far west as Michigan and Minnesota in
his campaigning. For the first time she saw him at the center of
political action, a dynamo of zestful challenge. "This is where he
belongs," she told herself shrewdly, not turning out page after
page, clever as they probably were, at a desk. But when the campaign ended triumphantly, he was back at Sagamore Hill again,
finishing his first volume before Christmas; after that in New York,
his family ensconced again at Bamie's, who was traveling in Europe, he set up his desk at Putnam's, laboring frantically to get
the second volume ready for publication in June. As soon as he
finished a chapter of the second volume, it would be rushed upstairs to the composing room.

He finished the last page of Volume Two on May 1, 1889. On
May 27 Cabot Lodge arrived at Sagamore Hill with a message
from the White House. President Harrison was willing to appoint
Theodore to the post of civil service commissioner. He did not
divulge the fact that both he and Spring-Rice had been pulling
strings in Washington to get their friend appointed to *some* position in the new Republican Administration because of his work in
the campaign, but heretofore without success. At last they had
succeeded, but the position offered was not an enviable one. Its
duties were highly controversial and the salary, $3,500 a year,
hardly sufficient to support two establishments and a growing
family. Growing, indeed, for they were expecting another child in
the fall!

"What do you think, Edie?" When they all retired that night, he
had not committed himself. He paced the floor of their bedroom,
stopping occasionally to grasp one of the carved footposts of the

huge bed, part of the impressive "modern gothic" set acquired by Theodore's father. Edith had never liked it, though it had been made by a distinguished cabinetmaker. It was too fussy, too ponderous, especially the gigantic wardrobe which stretched from floor to ceiling. Though it was late spring, the room felt cold—or was the coldness inside herself, created by the prospect of impending change? To move to a strange city, be in the public eye, her precious privacy invaded by curious, prying strangers, perhaps bear her child in a room far from this comfortable, familiar haven? Shivering, she stretched out her cold hands to the cheerfully glowing fireplace.

"It's no great plum," Theodore continued. "I'd be one of three, not even the head man in the office. And it certainly wouldn't make me popular. I've been critical already of the way civil service is abused, made people tired of hearing about it. But—somebody ought to do something—"

As he came closer in his aimless pacing, the glow of the fire seemed to strike answering sparks in his eyes. "You really want to do it, don't you?" Edith asked quietly.

"Well—it would be a challenge—an opportunity—to get back in the swim, where one could do things that really count."

It was decided. But at least she had a reprieve. Theodore insisted that at first he would go to Washington alone. Lodge was going on vacation, and he could use his house rent-free during the summer, then find cheap lodgings until after the new baby came, after which in due time the family would join him. He would of course come back in time for the new arrival, not expected until November. Meanwhile he would come home as often as possible and Edith would be secure with nearby relatives, especially her physician, Dr. West Roosevelt.

A reprieve, yes, but a lonely one. Theodore became so engrossed in his new duties that he returned home seldom, though when he did come he devoted himself completely to Edith and the children, even foregoing his usual polo games and other athletic activities. The absence of the usual influx of guests, in spite of its relief, only made the house seem more empty. And when in August he journeyed west on his annual hunting trip, she felt really bereft. Always, it seemed, she was left alone during the most difficult days of pregnancy. And he was not even there, as he had promised, when his proximity would have been most welcome. But that, she had to admit, was not his fault.

On October 10, 1889, Theodore received a telegram apprising him of the birth of his second son, several weeks before it was expected. He took the first train out of Washington for New York, arriving at the East Thirty-fourth Street ferry too late to catch the last train that night to Oyster Bay. With a reckless disregard for expense he crossed over to Long Island City and charted a special train, arriving at Sagamore at four-thirty in the morning. Though Edith was touched and humbled by his devotion, she was secretly infuriated. To spend that much money when they—*she* —struggled so hard to economize! At least, there was one hopeful prospect. His *Winning of the West,* published that fall, was already a success, winning favorable reviews. Perhaps the royalties would be more substantial than the pittances his other books had brought.

The two weeks following the birth almost atoned for all the preceding weeks of loneliness. Theodore sat by her bed during her convalescence and read to her from their favorite authors— Browning, Swinburne, Matthew Arnold, Thackeray. He shared with her, though reluctantly, for he did not want to worry her, some of his problems in the new position. He had aroused intense opposition by insisting not only that the civil service system be made to work in its present form but that it be reformed and expanded. Already he had made bitter enemies, among them John Wanamaker, the Postmaster General, who was a firm believer in the spoils system.

Edith was sympathetic, but, knowing his outspoken, often domineering methods, she could understand the situation. She counseled moderation. When gently prodded, he revealed other worries. How was he going to finance the coming move of his family to Washington? Prices there were exorbitant. Eight-room houses were selling for twice his meager salary. One the size of Sagamore Hill would cost four times that amount. And there would be food, servants, fuel, to say nothing of maintaining Sagamore. Why, he could spend every cent of his salary without buying a new suit!

Edith was relieved. At least he was beginning to consider finances seriously. They would manage, she assured him cheerfully. He would see. She had learned to practice economy since her father's death. They would get along in a small place, with a minimum of servants. Yes, they would manage. Meanwhile he must enjoy his family.

Alice was as entranced with the new baby, Kermit, as she had been with Ted, who, now a little over two, eyed the "little bruvver in a blanket" more warily. He nearly disrupted the gravity of the occasion when on November 3 the minister, the Reverend Mr. Washburn, arrived to conduct the baptismal service in Edith's parlor.

"What's that man wearing Mame's clothes for?" he inquired loudly, struck by the resemblance of the ecclesiastical surplice to his nurse's long enveloping apron. And when the recipient of the ceremony began to cry, he announced with audible glee, "Baby Bruvver Kermit miaous!" He was hustled off summarily to the library across the hall.

Returning from Washington before Christmas, Theodore was restored to a more cheerful, even more exuberant mood. His report had been approved by President Harrison and the civil service budget had been increased. After campaigning for Thomas B. Reed for the speakership of the House, he now had the support of that powerful leader of Congress. And he had secured a house, of a sort, nothing to brag about, only about a tenth as large as Sagamore Hill, but all he could afford. And at least it was in a good neighborhood, near the Cabot Lodges'.

Edith was ready to go. Even leaving the children temporarily with Bamie was not the wrenching chore she had expected. Theodore needed her. Compelling as were the joys and obligations of motherhood, for her those of wife would always be predominant, however much they might intrude on her innate compulsions for privacy. After Christmas she set off with Theodore for the new life which, had she but known it, was to become increasingly demanding and complex for the next twenty years.

4

Washington, 1890. Edith viewed the sprawling expanse of city with approving eyes. Not like other cities she had seen—London, Paris, Rome, even New York—which had grown up haphazardly, burdened with all the accumulations of centuries! This was young, barely a hundred years old, burgeoning, bursting with life. L'Enfante had planned it well, dreaming it out of the bogs and thickets and marshes, visioning, as the poet Thomas More had once described it,

> *This famed metropolis where fancy sees*
> *Squares in morasses, obelisks in trees,*
> *Which travelling fools and gazeteers adorn*
> *With shrines unbuilt and heroes yet unborn.*

The obelisk was already there, tall and white and slender, the Washington Monument, dedicated just five years before. The morasses had indeed turned into squares and some of them, like the one in front of the White House, into spacious parks. And there were certainly shrines—the ornate red sandstone "castle" of the Smithsonian, the National Museum, its dome resembling a "crystal palace" with its crown of electric lights, the Congressional Library, reminding one of the Renaissance architecture in Rome or Venice. Edith could not wait to explore all of them, especially the treasure-house of books.

There was space here, and cleanliness, not like the narrow, littered streets and alleys of downtown New York with their noisome drains and accumulating refuse. She gazed with delighted surprise at the horse-drawn devices of rotating twig brushes which swept the streets clean each day, so that, as one columnist had written, the "thousands of fine carriages and hundreds of bicycles, which go spinning along them, are kept shining like black enamel and polished silver." Even the makeshift shanties and tenements marking the presence of the poorer sector of blacks, who constituted a third of the city's 230,000 population, did not remind one too unhappily of New York slums. At least their occupants had room to breathe.

Space. Plenty of it in the city, yes, but not in the little house Theodore had rented at 1820 Jefferson Place, N.W.! Edith regarded its tiny facilities with dismay. Living room for a family of five with their necessary servants? Why, there was not even sleeping space for a guest except on a couch in Theodore's dressing room! But of course it was all they could afford and more, with rents in the city averaging two hundred dollars a month and running much higher. But there were advantages. No need to provide much furniture! With the addition of a few pieces left over from the East Thirty-sixth Street house, it was made fairly livable.

"The house is now getting to look very homelike and comfortable," Theodore was writing his "Darling Bye [Bamie]" on January 4, "such a contrast to when I was alone in it! I can hardly realize it is the same place; and I am thoroughly enjoying the change. I think the children will like it."

If Edith had been dreading the plunge into social life which their position must entail (and she had!), she was fast becoming inured to it. Already they had attended the President's New Year's Day reception on January 1, where she discovered that space was also at a premium in the White House, watching with some dismay her wrap being taken, rolled up, and thrust into a pigeon-hole. They had attended a dinner at the Cabot Lodges' and given a dinner themselves to some of Theodore's historical friends. They had seen a comic play, *The Senator,* at the theater, entertained at a few teas, and met a host of new friends.

On January 5, Theodore was again writing to Bamie: "Edith looked very pretty at the Blaines' and Mortons' receptions, and received much attention. . . . Last evening we had Rachel Sherman and Hattie Blaine to tea. . . . Our teas are so perfectly simple that I am a little inclined to wonder why people come to them; I suppose they do criticize them; but they always accept our invitations—and the company is generally good."

After Mame and the children arrived, making the house seem full to bursting, Edith felt like two people—three, in fact, mother, wife, and that curious anomaly of socialite-hostess-public servant which was the role demanded of many Washington women, even those whose husbands, like Theodore, were in the lower political echelons. That she slipped into this latter role with such apparent ease was a surprise even to herself. One reason, of course, was the overshadowing personality of Theodore. At their informal Sunday evening suppers, where, as their new friend Margaret Chanler was to describe it, "the food was of the plainest and the company of the best," he kept the guests spellbound with tales of his Western adventures.

"There was a vital radiance about the man," Mrs. Chanler was to write in her book *Roman Spring,* "a glowing, unfeigned cordiality towards those he liked that was irresistible. . . . One of his charms lay in a certain boyish zest with which he welcomes everything that happened to him. . . . Life was the unpacking of an endless Christmas stocking."

Of Edith she shrewdly commented: "She is more difficult of access; praise does not reach or define her. Just as the camera is focused, she steps aside to avoid the click of the shutter. . . . Her family was the all-important *continuum.* Apart from that she looked on the changing aspects of existence with a detached, intelligent curiosity; her warmth and passion lay far beneath the surface. One felt in her a great strength of character, and ineluctable will power. . . . A very long way after her husband and children came a small group of chosen friends to whom she was staunchly loyal."

Margaret herself was to become one of those friends, a coterie which was to make the enforced social melee of Washington not only bearable but rewarding. The wife of Winthrop Chanler and niece of Julia Ward Howe, she had lived many years in Italy, and the two shared a love of Italian art. Another intimate friend was Anna Cabot Lodge, "Nannie," one of the most beautiful women in Washington.

But of all Edith's new acquaintances she felt the greatest rapport with the crusty, brilliant, profoundly scholarly Henry Adams. Descendant of two presidents, professor, eminent historian, connoisseur of art, literature, and politics, he presided over a small coterie of like-minded Washingtonians. Edith became one of these chosen few. At his house on Lafayette Square, a veritable museum of rare books, treasures from the Far East, English and Italian paintings, she met such dignitaries as Augustus St. Gaudens, John Hay, John Singer Sargent, Rudyard Kipling. In spite of the rather uncomfortable low leather chairs in his drawing room, dubbed "nursery level" by one visitor, Edith reveled in the literary gatherings which the astute Alice was later to describe as "a host of adoring 'nieces' mouthing Dante and medieval Latin hymns and things like that." She would agree, however, with her stepdaughter's future appraisal of the "curious statue that he [Adams] had erected in Rock Creek cemetery in memory of his wife, who, it is said, committed suicide because he was in love with another woman. Ugh!"

Alice, now a lively six-year-old with wide, discerning blue eyes and yellow pigtails, was already revealing some of the qualities—insatiable curiosity, a slightly pert independence—which in time would make her a most conspicuous member of this same Washington society. The less admirable features of these qualities were enhanced by her semiannual visits to Chestnut Hill, where she was permitted without protest to jump up and down to her heart's content on her favorite sofa, sadly endangering the springs, or to climb into the pigpen and whack the squealing inmates. It was Edith, gentle but firm disciplinarian, who suffered the results of these visits. Theodore looked with a benign eye on all such excesses of energy, often participating in them with even more childish exuberance.

The children, Edith noted with relief, were the petcock releasing him from the tremendous pressures of his political problems. He played "bear" with them every night, often getting them so excited that they could not sleep. Already two-year-old Ted was being initiated into the disciplines and pleasures of the rugged life, being trained like his father before him to "make his body." Sometimes they all went together, Edith included, at the end of day to Rock Creek Park, where they climbed over the rocks, Theodore even letting the children down over the steep places with ropes. But he could be tender as a mother, too, as when little Ted was taken severely ill in April.

"It has been just heart-breaking to have the darling little fellow sick," he wrote Bamie, "and the first forty-eight hours I really look back to with a shudder. When he would rally at times and come out of his stupor, and begin to say the cunning things he always says, in his little changed sick voice, it was about as much as Edith and I could stand."

Theodore certainly needed a petcock. His attempts to combat the evils of the old spoils system had plunged him into a cauldron of hot water. As one of his biographers was to put it, he had "advanced on Washington like a combined Lochinvar and Galahad." He had told reporters, "You can guarantee that I intend to hew the line and let the chips fall where they will." And the chips were falling. His battle with the Postmaster General, Wanamaker, was involving him in bitter disputes climaxing in an investigation of his commission. Even though he considered Harrison a man with no backbone, the President was largely in support of his reforms. "The only trouble I ever had with him," Harrison noted later, "was that he wanted to put an end to all evil in the world between sunrise and sunset."

For Edith the high point of that first Washington year was the trip she took to Theodore's Western paradise that summer. It was a large and merry party that set out the last of August—Bamie, Conie, Douglas Robinson, Bamie's friend Robert Ferguson, a young Scot, and Lodge's sixteen-year-old son Bay.

They arrived in Medora at four o'clock in the morning on September 2, in a torrential rainstorm. As Conie described it later, "We had to get out on an embankment composed of such slippery mud that before we actually plodded to the station, our feet and legs were encased in glutinous slime; but the calls of the cowboys undauntedly rang out in the darkness, and the neighing of horses and prancing of hoofs made us realize that civilization as well as convention was a thing of the past."

At last Edith was able to meet the fabled companions of Theodore's early adventures, Merrifield and Ferris, his ranch foremen. Fortunately, she was not expected to ride a "bucking bronco" to Elkhorn Ranch forty miles away, but the springless wagon was hardly more comfortable. They forded the Little Missouri twenty-three times, always up and down steep banks, so that either coming or going they were in danger of immersion. It was torturing, exhausting, but as they approached the Badlands with their strange contours, their odd colors, their fantastic buttes, Edith felt strangely invigorated. At last she was entering that mysterious world so vital to Theodore, participating in the adventurous life that had so powerfully shaped his personality and career. Even the little two-story ranch house on the banks of the river, nestling under its fringe of cottonwoods, was no disappointment. For a wilderness cabin it was almost luxurious. Mrs. Merrifield, a refined, friendly Canadian woman, fed them a delicious lunch. Edith found herself in a comfortable bedroom complete with a rubber bathtub and shelves of books. The decor of guns, stuffed heads, bear rugs, was reminiscent of Sagamore. She felt instantly at home.

The days spent at the ranch were delightful—long hours on a little horse named Wire Fence, climbing the buttes, witnessing an exciting roundup, watching Conie's valiant attempt to "wrastle" a calf, from which she emerged bruised and encased in oozing dirt, to be carried triumphantly on the shoulders of the exultant cowboys; marveling at the relationship between Theodore, their "Boss," and the men of the ranch—one of honest comradeship but absolute respect. She was sorry to leave when they departed for the Yellowstone.

This trip, she knew, was a concession on Theodore's part to tourism and civilization. His idea of "roughing it" was not a guided tour, complete with guide, a Chinese cook, and a well-stocked larder, even though it dispensed little but ham, tomatoes, greasy cakes, and coffee. But it included more "roughing it" than he had planned—ice-cold nights shivering under as many as six blankets, long hazardous rides on horses unused to being ridden sidesaddle, and, for Edith, severe bruises when she was thrown from her horse, which was frightened by a sound of blasting. She narrowly escaped a broken back. But in spite of discomfort— even of suffering at times—she enjoyed every minute of the trip, reveling in the lavish scenery, the marvelous colors, the foaming falls, the fantastic rock formations.

Yes, this was Theodore's other world, and he dominated it. They saw its multiplicity of wild life through his eyes—bears, eagles, squirrels, elk, deer; heard through his ears the bird notes of sunbirds, longspur, grass finch, warblers, wrens, sparrows, and a hundred others. Far better than their guide, Ira Dodge, who proved incompetent, he kept them feeling safe and fully confident. For Edith it was a journey not only into another world but into a heretofore unexplored segment of her husband's multiplex personality.

"My dear Mrs. Carow," Theodore was writing Gertrude after the adventure was over, "I have rarely seen Edith enjoy anything more than she did the six days at my ranch and the trip through the Yellowstone Park; and she looks just as well and young and pretty and happy as she did four years ago when I married her— indeed I sometimes think she looks if possible ever sweeter and prettier, and she is as healthy as possible, and so young looking and slender to be the mother of those sturdy little scamps, Ted and Kermit . . ."

Of course he did not mention the many bruises and narrow escape from a broken back! Such risks were the natural and unimportant accompaniments of any jolly adventure.

Washington again, with another tireless social season, more civil service fights, with "the little grey man in the White House looking on with cold and hesitating disapproval, but not seeing how he can interfere." They enjoyed Christmas in the cramped quarters of Jefferson Place, when, as Theodore wrote Bamie, "Alice and Ted came near to realizing the feelings of those who enter Paradise as they ever will on earth." Then came the happy discovery that Edith was once again pregnant and the distressing news that Elliott, now in Europe, was actually endangering his pregnant wife Anna with his drunken rages; Bamie departed to act as the capable go-between, resulting in her brother's confinement in a sanitarium. But at last came springtime, with flowers in bloom, the trees bursting into feathery green, and Washington at its best. Still, Edith was not sorry to leave for Sagamore in the late spring, while Theodore remained in the city baching it with Cecil Spring-Rice, coming to Long Island whenever his work permitted.

"You look even sweeter and prettier than when we returned from the West," he greeted her appreciatively on one of these visits. "Having children certainly agrees with you."

It agreed with him, too, and his arrival after either brief or long absences was hailed with wild enthusiasm. He would enter the house with Kermit held high in his arms and Ted clinging so tightly to one of his legs that he could hardly walk. Their exuberance was due only partly to affection, he admitted, and partly to the large paper bundle of toys which Ted, dancing up and down ecstatically, would greet with the query, "Fats in de bag?" Every evening he would have a wild romp with them, usually assuming the role of "a very big bear" while they were either little bears or perhaps a raccoon and a badger. He would have spoiled all three of them shamefully without Edith's sterner insistence on discipline—did, in fact, in spite of it, as when at afternoon tea Alice and Ted would sidle up to his chair and, if he could find a minute when Edith was not looking, he would give them all the icing off his cake.

That summer of 1891 was not idyllic even when Theodore managed to visit, for Gertrude and Emily arrived in May for a visit which apparently had no end in sight. When they were finally to leave the last of October for more European wanderings, Edith would breathe a sigh of relief. It was easier by far to cope with their written rather than with their spoken dissatisfactions with life! Significantly she would write her mother in November promising that she would certainly join them when possible, paying them a visit "of a week or two."

This time her confinement in August was not devoid of womanly assistance, for in addition to Gertrude and Emily there was Bamie. After the birth of his third child, Hall, Elliott had sunk even more deeply into alcoholism and become so violent that Bamie had left him in an asylum in France. Edith was glad of her presence, a welcome antidote to the lugubrious atmosphere engendered by her other guests. Even Spring-Rice, who accompanied Theodore when he came in August, was not impressed with Emily, privately commenting that she was one of the most dismal persons he had ever met. With Bamie, Edith was now thoroughly at ease. Whatever constraint there had been between them over the problem of little Alice had completely vanished.

Perhaps it was the melee created by such diverse personalities that made this birth the hardest Edith had yet experienced. Her labor, beginning on August 13, was long and difficult. It was like being flung from that little Western horse, not once, but over and over, descending into fiery pits of excruciating pain, to emerge weak and exhausted, only to be thrust back and tortured again. Bamie was there, and Mame. She was vaguely conscious of their hands, their voices.

"Courage, dear. It can't be much longer . . ." "Och, me darlin'! Jist thry it agin—so. Ye'll forgit all about it afther . . ."

During one emergence she saw Dr. West Roosevelt standing at the foot of the bed, his kindly, concerned face attempting an encouraging smile. "Come, my dear," he admonished gently, "you're not responsible, you know, for an orphan asylum—only for one little baby."

It was over at last and, as always, the suffering seemed nothing beside the joy of its result, a sturdy, healthy little girl who, Theodore insisted joyously, was the picture of some of her Dutch ancestresses, Jannetje, for instance, wife of his first immigrant ancestor, Claes van Rosenvelt. Edith took a peculiar satisfaction in having given him another daughter. He was so fond of little Alice! Perhaps, much as she had grown to love the child, she had always been a little jealous of this visible reminder of his three years of bliss.

The arrival of baby Ethel, she knew, was for Theodore the one bright spot in an otherwise gloomy summer. His brother's delinquency—not only his alcoholism but also his involvement in an unsavory paternity suit—had both caused him distress and concern and shocked all his moral sensibilities. Edith could understand that well enough from her own experience. For once she was almost glad to see him leave for his annual Western foray. He needed all the cleansing and healing his beloved open spaces always gave him.

During Theodore's six years on the Civil Service Commission, life assumed a pattern, undulating like a rolling landscape of hills and valleys, with occasional peaks and deep depressions. Winters in Washington. Summers on Long Island. With increasing willingness—or was it resignation?—Edith adjusted herself to the changes in pace, the furious round of activities in the capital, the refreshing tranquillity of life at Sagamore Hill, if a household with four children, innumerable pets, constant guests, all infused with the energy of Theodore's erratic comings and goings, could be termed "tranquillity."

At least there was room to breathe now in Washington as well as Long Island. They had found a larger house at 1214 Nineteenth Street on the corner of Jefferson Place, fortunately not much higher in rent. For finances continued to be a grave concern. Prices in Washington were exorbitantly high. Rent, milk, meat, fuel, and doctors' bills consumed almost all of Theodore's $3,500 salary. Edith found it almost impossible to make ends meet. And it was her problem, for Theodore was notoriously impractical. He was delighted to turn over all the household accounts to her, even submitted cheerfully to being put on an allowance, treated it as a joke when once he attempted to pay his bill in a bookstore and found only twenty-five cents in his pocket.

He had graver worries than finances and the continuing frustrations of his job. They seemed nothing compared with his concern over the younger brother whom he had almost idolized from boyhood. Though Bamie returned with Anna and her new baby from Europe, news of Elliott's further dissipations, including his involvement with a woman of questionable reputation, took Theodore to Europe in January of 1892, where he succeeded in persuading a repentant Elliott to return to America, deed two thirds of his property to his wife, take a cure, and remain apart from his family for at least a year of probation.

An end to this problem—they hoped. Elliott returned, took the cure, and went to Virginia to manage Douglas Robinson's family estates. An end to other problems, too. Theodore was vindicated publicly by the investigating committee in his long battle with John Wanamaker and others opposed to his efforts to enforce the law. The death of Edith's uncle, John Carow, in England would bring to Emily and Edith about $35,000 apiece. Though the estate would not be settled for many months and then would provide only about $1,200 a year, it offered a hope for financial improvement. Life settled again into a normal routine.

Not to last, however, for 1893 was anything but normal! Harrison had been defeated, and Grover Cleveland, a Democrat, was again in the White House. Theodore, of course, submitted his resignation, waited in restless suspense, was delighted when in

April the new President asked him to remain in office. His friend Cabot Lodge had been elected again to Congress. Edith was an accepted member of Henry Adams's intellectual coterie. As she wrote Emily, she was enjoying "this pleasant life" and would have hated to relinquish it.

In May she went with Theodore to the Chicago World's Fair, meeting Bamie, who had official duties as a lady manager. It was a dazzling experience. She marveled at the huge white buildings in classical and Renaissance style, the statuary, the great terraces, the fountains, the bridges guarded by colossal animals. If only it were all permanent, instead of a temporary creation! Such a shame that it was all a glorious façade!

It was like their own false sense of well-being, she was soon to discover, for it proved to be a year of death and panic. The country was in economic turmoil. Businesses were failing. Theodore's own financial account showed a deficit of $2,500. Edith suspected it was nearer $3,000! He was talking again of selling Sagamore or at least part of his land there. And there were even graver portents. Last December Anna, Elliott's wife, had succumbed to diphtheria. Her death had blown to bits all of Elliott's good intentions, and the sudden death of his older son Ellie in May was an added incentive for dissipation. Still more devastating to all of them was the death of Aunt Annie Gracie in June, as shocking as it was unexpected. For Edith as well as for Theodore, this was a rending of a last precious link with childhood, for both of them like losing a second mother. Teddy had said his first prayers at her knee, Edith had opened the treasures of books at her study table. For Elliott, whom Aunt Annie had stoutly defended even in his weaknesses, it was loss of his last link with sanity. He gave up his job in Virginia and came to New York, sinking into fresh bouts of dissipation.

"It wears on Theodore dreadfully," Edith wrote Emily, "and if he gets thinking of it he can't sleep."

At least he had one source of relief from despondency, his "bunnies," as he liked to call his children. His brow cleared the moment he charged into the house, whether in Washington or at Sagamore. And they were always ready for him—Alice, blue eyes aglow and yellow hair flying, as straight and slim and self-confident at nine as she would be at seventy-nine; Ted, bursting with excitement and energy, like his father; Kermit, quieter and dreamy-eyed, very much his mother's boy; Ethel, chubby toddler, "Elephant Johnny," as her father dubbed her, so lively and vigorous and bent on having her own way that Edith confessed to fear that if she became any stronger, "she would kill us both."

They all adored their father, especially Ted, whose one ambition from babyhood was to be exactly like him. One day Mame had overhead him talking to himself in bed when Theodore was expected. "A little mufstache," he was saying, "and white teeth and black hair, very short." The description evidently aroused a sense of his own limitations, for presently she heard him wailing, "But Ted got no mufstache! Oh, Mame, Mame, Ted got nuffin' but a mouf!" Ted was delighted—not Edith!—when a weakness in his eyes developed into such a squint that he was obliged to wear glasses, another point of resemblance to his idol!

Five-year-old Ted exulted in his superiority over the three-year-old Kermit, not only in size and age but in wisdom and lustier, more masculine propensities. For Kermit, slight and rather pale in appearance, preferred his mother's company to his father's. Instead of joining in rough sports, he preferred to sit and dream. While Ted rushed around flourishing a tin sword or maneuvering the dozen little lead ships his father had given him, Kermit was enjoying his favorite toy, a "dushtpan" which he had requested for Christmas, so he could help the maids keep the house clean and tidy. Alice inspired in Ted no boy-girl superiority, for she was very much a tomboy at this stage, wishing repeatedly for trousers and short hair like her brothers, her chief acknowledgment of femininity being a yearning, loudly and embarrassingly expressed in public, to give birth, not, as formerly, to twins, but to a monkey.

That winter of 1891, to Edith's dismay, life in Washington was complicated by a visitation of measles. Since she was several months pregnant, she was alarmed over the possibility of contracting the disease herself, but she refused to let Mame assume all the duties of nursing. In spite of his problems both political and financial, and his dogged attempts to get the third and fourth volumes of his *Winning of the West* ready for publication, Theodore did all he could to help. During their recuperation he made Ted and Alice each a little battering ram and *Monitor* (small warship) out of cardboard and with the help of Ted's little lead ships acted out Farragut's naval victory at Mobile Bay during the Civil War. When he had to leave, they fought the battle all over again. Ted was not a good loser. When his *Monitor* was sunk, he determined that on a repetition of the game it should not happen again.

"Hah!" he exclaimed suddenly. "Bang! goes a torpedo, and Sisser's *Monitor* sinks!"

Alice would have none of it. "No, it did not!" she insisted. "My *Monitor* always goes to bed at seven, and now it's three minutes past!"

Pregnancy, Edith had long since discovered, was only a mild deterrent to normal activity. As Theodore wrote Bamie, who was in London acting as hostess for their cousin, James Roosevelt Roosevelt ("Rosy"), who was secretary of the American legation and had recently lost his wife, "We dine out three or four times a week and have people to dinner once or twice; so that we hail the two or three evenings when we are alone and can talk and read, or Edith sews while I make ineffective bolts at my third volume."

On February 1 they dined for the first time at the White House. Odd that it was Cleveland, a Democrat, who invited them instead of the Republican Harrison! Yet understandable, for Theodore had goaded Harrison beyond the latter's endurance, lamenting once in a letter to Cabot Lodge, "Oh, Heaven, if the President had a little backbone, and if the Senators did not have flannel legs!"

Edith was already a friend of Frances Cleveland, a great beauty and a startling contrast to her bullnecked three-hundred-pound husband, her senior by twenty-seven years. Both Edith and Frances were ardent supporters of the Needlework Guild of America, one of Washington's major welfare activities. She and Theodore were certainly honored that evening, for it became his duty to escort the First Lady to dinner, and Edith, escorted by her literary friend Richard Watson Gilder, found that her neighbor on the other side was the President himself. It could be considered a triumph for Theodore, whose work as commissioner was becoming more and more successful. Too much so, perhaps, for he was becoming a bit restless in the position.

As Cecil Spring-Rice once remarked shrewdly, "Teddy is consumed with energy as long as he's doing something and fighting somebody. . . . Poor Cabot *must* be successful; while Teddy is happiest when he conquers but quite happy if he only fights."

Edith was flattered but not too impressed by her first dinner in the White House. She much preferred simpler activities, meals with friends like the Winthrop Chanlers or the Cabot Lodges, or the intellectual stimulus of Henry Adams's little soirees. "I have been to more cheerful feasts but also more gloomy ones," she wrote Bamie.

She was glad, however, when advancing pregnancy brought an end to social engagements, for family was always her major concern and delight. Even in her ninth month, on the last day of March, she was still enjoying strenuous bouts of exercise. They all went for a long hike in Rock Creek Park. Never had she felt better or looked "sweeter and prettier," as Theodore commented in his hackneyed phrasing. Though she did not participate in their scramblings on the cliffs, she explored the woods with Kermit, who stayed close at her side, looking for signs of spring, which was coming late that year.

Just ten days later, on April 9, her fourth child was born, a boy named Archibald Bulloch, after Theodore's great-grandfather, a distinguished Georgian. It was the quickest and easiest birth she had yet experienced. Even Mame in her room upstairs heard nothing. When Theodore went up at one o'clock the next morning to tell her, Ted was roused and, wild with excitement, rushed to tell "Sisser." Edith seemed so well that Theodore let them come down and tiptoe into the room to see her in bed with the tiny blanketed bundle.

"Archie is a cunning little polyp," he wrote Bamie, "and the children adore him, except Kermit, who looks on him with some suspicion and yesterday announced that he cared less for his brother than for his 'dushtpan.' . . . Ted worships the baby and dances about him as if performing an incantation, taking every aimless movement of wee Archie as a return sign of recognition. He expressed an earnest desire to give, 'not lend,' his silver cup to Archie—a great proof of generosity. Even Ethel loves 'that Archibald baby.' . . ."

It was well that they had this high point in their life pattern, for it was the last one they would experience for many months.

It seemed like a normal summer, Sagamore Hill filled to bulging with children, guests, animals; with Theodore making flying visits, charging the atmosphere like a fresh battery. Besides their own children there were innumerable cousins from the surrounding Roosevelt enclave—Emlen's Christine, George, and John; West's Lorraine and Nicholas; and of course Elliott's Eleanor and Corinne's Theodore Douglas and little Corinne were frequent visitors.

All were grist for Theodore's constantly turning mills. He devised and led countless adventures—scrambles up and down Cooper's Bluff, a game called "point to point." They would select a landmark and go to it without turning aside for anything, haystacks, ponds, fences, gullies, thickets. He played hide-and-seek with them in the ancient, weather-beaten barn, where they tunneled the hay until it was like a rabbit warren. Another game he devised was called "obstacle race." They would travel from the front door of the barn, up and over the hay, back up a beam to the hay on the other side, out the window and around the barn to where they had started, each one timing his course. Clothes were expected casualties, their mutilation almost badges of honor. When Theodore brought back an assortment of muddy shirts and torn trousers, his own included, Edith's lips quirked in wry amusement.

"Do I have five children," she wondered, "or six?"

She took part in many of the milder activities, so heartily that one of her sons was heard to remark, "When Mother was a little girl, she must have been a boy." She rode with them, went on picnics and hikes, rowed, went swimming, action somewhat curtailed by her heavy bathing dress with skirt and pantelettes that came to her ankles. Theodore, clad in an odd bathing suit that buttoned down the front and had little half-sleeves coming just below the shoulders, like sprouting wings, had taught all the children to swim, his method being to toss them off the dock or force them to jump in by themselves. This elicited tears from Alice and muted terror from Eleanor, who, not daring to disobey, had come up coughing and spluttering in a frenzy of panic. But the method worked. They had all learned.

However, as Edith knew, this summer there was a fevered intensity about Theodore's activity which concealed a deep unrest. His work, it seemed, had reached an impasse. Though he continued to fight, fight, fight, and enjoyed the fighting, it was like knocking his head against a stone wall. True, he had accomplished much, yet he waged a losing battle against petty spoilsmongering, looting of federal offices, lack of necessary funds. But far more unsettling were his grief and frustration over Elliott's plight. And it was hopeless. He could do nothing. Edith understood—how well she understood! Just so had she agonized over her father.

On August 12 Theodore wrote Bamie from Washington, "Elliott is up and about again; and I hear is drinking heavily; if so, he must break down soon. It has been as hideous a tragedy all through as one often sees."

The break soon came. The following day Elliott went berserk, fell, was knocked unconscious, and died with no member of his family near him.

Never before had Edith seen Theodore weep. He cried shamelessly, like a child. But they were purging tears. Now he could remember his brother as "the gallant, generous, manly, loyal young man whom everyone loved."

Edith felt profound relief, but it was short-lived. For in that same month of August Theodore was approached with the proposition that he run as candidate for the mayoralty of New York City. She was surprised and dismayed that he seemed even to consider it. "What do you think?" he asked her.

She made no attempt to disguise her feelings. How could he possibly afford it, a campaign which would tax their finances so heavily? And how could he be sure of winning? He had run before and lost. Trust his whole future to a fickle electorate? His salary was small enough now, not enough to live on. And, besides, they were well established in Washington. He had proved himself successful with two Administrations, one Republican, one Democratic. Frankly, she was happy where they were and did not want to leave.

She was relieved when without protest he refused the proposition. Not until he had gone west on his hunting trip did she have the slightest inkling that he had deeply regretted the decision. It was Bamie, returned from England on September 12, who enlightened her. Soon after her arrival she came to Sagamore to visit.

"I wonder," she said as soon as she and Edith were alone together, the children having appropriated the full attention of their beloved "Auntie Bye" until they were finally hustled off to bed, "why Theodore decided to turn down the suggestion that he run for mayor if he was so terribly anxious to try for it again."

"Oh, but—" Edith stared at her sister-in-law in consternation. Bamie was, of course, mistaken. Theodore had shown no special interest in the proposal when he had asked for her advice. She started to protest, then stopped, for Bamie was continuing.

"His letter sounded so happy and excited, the one I got before leaving England. It was a real opportunity, he felt, a chance to redeem himself from his first failure and to be in a controlling position to fight city evils. Then this letter he just wrote me from Medora sounded so bitterly disappointed. He seemed to think he had made a grave mistake not to run. It was the one chance which would never return. Conie felt so too and tried to encourage him. I really can't understand it."

Edith could. And the knowledge was devastating. So Bamie had received a letter, when she herself had heard nothing except a brief note telling of his arrival! She felt no jealousy, only self-recrimination. What had she done! True, he had asked for her advice, and she had given it, but without finding out how he himself felt. It was *she* who had made the decision, not he. They had not quarreled. This was far worse than quarreling. This was separation.

Later, after Bamie had gone, she wrote her a letter confessing what she had done, making no excuses, expressing all her feelings of guilt.

"I never realized for a minute how he felt over this. . . . I am too thankful that he is away now for I am utterly unnerved and a prey to the deepest despair. . . . If I knew what I do now I should have thrown all my influence in the scale with Corinne's and helped instead of hindering him. . . . This is a lesson that will last my life. . . . I shall be myself again by Saturday when the darling gets back."

He came and seemed his usual self. He thought Edith looked tired and worn and insisted that she accept Bamie's invitation to take the "bunnies" and go on a trip to Vermont, while he returned to Washington. It was just what she needed to restore her self-confidence, to make decisions for the future—perhaps to save her marriage.

Even when the following spring the new mayor of New York offered Theodore the office of commissioner of street cleaning, Edith forbore to give advice, though the very idea of his occupying such a position shocked her. It was a relief when he refused, saying that the work was out of his line. And when another offer came, that of police commissioner, and he seemed to welcome the prospect of such a job which "he could perhaps afford to be identified with" and which certainly presented opportunities for reform, she encouraged him to follow his own best judgment. As she had written Bamie, she had learned a lesson "that would last my life."

Theodore's work as civil service commissioner, he felt, was finished. He had accomplished much. As many as twenty-six thousand jobs had been transferred from the status of political plums to that of successful competition in examinations. The principle of civil service had been brought to national attention. He had stepped on people's toes, rampaged through every sort of opposition, been ridiculed, scorned, vilified; but he had proved that "offices are not the property of the politicians, that they belong to the people, and should be filled only with regard to the public service." He accepted the position of police commissioner.

Edith had no time for regrets at leaving Washington. On April 27, two days after Theodore's resignation from the Civil Service Commission, she received a cable telling of her mother's death in Turin. She could not grieve overmuch, certainly not as she had mourned her father. Poor Gertrude had not been happy. She was freed at last from her ills, real and imaginary. Edith was most concerned about Emily, who would be more alone and helpless and more dissatisfied with life than ever. She hoped for yet dreaded the prospect of Emily's probable return to America.

Events moved with whirlwind speed. Edith and Teddy were honored at farewell parties, teas, dinners. On May 2 they had lunch with Henry Adams, whose enclave of intellectuals Edith hated most to leave. Not Theodore. He privately considered the crusty, cynical savant an insufferable prig. The friends he most regretted leaving were Spring-Rice, Cabot Lodge and his wife Nannie, and, to a lesser degree, John Hay, Winthrop Chanler, Thomas Reed, and his cronies in the Cosmos Club, a group of men of Washington's scientific community who met for discussions. Both he and Edith were loath to exchange clean, spacious, leisurely Washington, now lush with spring blooms, for the congested, bustling, brownstone-drab streets of New York.

As she looked back at the slender finger of the Washington Monument probing into storm clouds, Edith could not help wondering, "Will we ever return?"

5

Blessed ignorance of the future! If Edith could have foreseen the turbulent changes of the next six years, even her innate poise and self-command might have been sorely tested. But she settled the family that May of 1895 into Bamie's house at 689 Madison Avenue with her usual calm acceptance of disruption.

Theodore was of little help in making the move because already he had plunged with both feet into his crusade to clean up what he discovered "the most corrupt department in New York City." The police force, often with the connivance of city officials, had been accepting millions of dollars in bribes from prostitutes and brothels, gamblers, liquor sellers, and other suppliers of doubtful services. He was downtown in his office of police commissioner by nine in the morning, never leaving it before six or sometimes eight at night.

"I shall speedily assail some of the ablest, shrewdest men in this city, who will be fighting for their lives," he wrote Bamie on May 19, "and I know well how hard the task ahead of me is."

Bamie had returned to England, once more to act as hostess and housekeeper for her cousin Rosy. Meanwhile all of her own family were free to use her house in New York City as they found it convenient. Use of it was a welcome boon, and Edith, always conscious of expense, hoped it might continue indefinitely. However, there was soon a possibility of change.

Early that summer a surprising cable came from Bamie. She was engaged to be married! Yet why, wondered Edith, should it have been such a surprise? Because she was forty years old and crippled? But she was one of the most vivacious and attractive persons alive, and when even strangers were exposed to the magic of her brilliant eyes and warm, sympathetic voice, the warped shoulders and awkward gait were forgotten. Her fiancé was Lieutenant William Sheffield Cowles, an attaché to the United States legation in London. Edith and Theodore remembered meeting him in Washington, a dependable, respectable, if not brilliant officer, perhaps ten years older than Bamie.

"I don't believe she's in love with him," was Conie's comment.

"But he may make her very happy," Edith responded mildly, remembering similar comments when Conie's own marriage had been under discussion.

Edith was relieved when Theodore decided that because of his harassing problems as police commissioner they would be unable to attend the wedding. It would have been difficult to leave the children, and they could ill afford the trip. She almost begrudged the $500 that Theodore insisted on adding to Conie's similar gift in order to purchase the bride a wedding collar and jeweled tiara for her trousseau. But Conie and Douglas attended and gave them a graphic description of the service in St. Andrew's Church, Westminster. Rosy, in spite of his chagrin at losing his hostess-housekeeper, had given the bride away.

The wedding had one unfortunate corollary as far as Edith was concerned. Bamie explained apologetically that, though they would not be needing to occupy the New York house for a while, she and her husband felt that they could no longer make it available gratis to relatives. Though understandable, the arrangement caused a severe strain on Edith's already burdened finances. She agreed to pay Bamie $1,800 a year, $450 a month from January through April (more by half than her income from Uncle John's bequest). They would, as usual, spend the summer months at Sagamore.

She was almost sorry now when summer came, for it meant seeing Theodore even less than when they were in New York. Sometimes he could join the family only on weekends. Edith knew that the separation was even harder on him than on her, for he missed having time with the children. When commuting from Oyster Bay he had to leave at seven-thirty in the morning, cycle to the station, take the train to the city, work sometimes for forty hours at a stretch, often not returning for several days.

"In the morning I get little more than a glimpse of them," he wrote Bamie. "In the evening I always take a romp with Archie, who loves me with all his silly heart; the two little boys usually look over what they call my 'jewel box' while I am dressing; I then play with cunning Ethel in her crib; and Alice takes dinner with us."

In spite of his absences there was no dearth of teeming life. There was the usual array of some sixteen young cousins swarming about the place, ready to pounce on him when he did appear. He was especially elated when the horde was joined one weekend by Elliott's daughter Eleanor, for her grandmother with whom she lived, almost spartan in her restrictions, did not encourage her to visit her father's relatives. This daughter of his beloved younger brother was almost as dear to him as his own children.

"Eleanor, my darling Eleanor," he enthused, as he lifted her out of the carriage and crushed her in his arms, as Edith reported later, "pouncing on her with such vigor that he tore all the gathers out of her frock and both buttonholes out of her petticoat."

Poor child, she thought again and again that weekend, watching her struggle to keep up with her exuberant athletic cousins, gritting her teeth with desperation as she slid with them down the steep slope of Cooper's Bluff or burrowed through the haymows in a game of hide-and-seek. Though she and Alice were nearly the same age, twelve, and Eleanor was the taller, they had little else in common. Alice was radiantly pretty with her golden hair, fine features, and white, even teeth, merry, athletic (now that the hated brace for an early leg weakness was no longer necessary), serenely confident, even a bit arrogant. Eleanor was plain if not exactly homely, awkward, unsure of herself, obviously feeling herself an "outsider." Edith could sympathize with her. How often in childhood she had felt the same way, unable to share herself with others, emotions locked tight inside of her!

A real ugly duckling. Edith shook her head sadly. Not at all attractive. Her mouth and teeth don't seem to have any future. But who can tell? The ugly duckling may turn yet into a swan!

The contrast between Eleanor and Alice was even more marked some months later when they both attended one of Corinne's famous Christmas parties at Orange. Eleanor's grandmother dressed her like a child. At the evening affair she wore a short white nainsook dress with little blue bows on the shoulders, while Alice, always expensively attired because her Chestnut Hill family insisted on providing her with the best clothes, was wearing her first sophisticated long dress. For the "ugly duckling" the party was a fiasco.

"Something should be done," Edith said worriedly to Conie. "If only the child could be gotten away from her grandmother and sent to some good school, like the one Bamie went to in England!"

"A wonderful idea," Conie agreed, her blue eyes agleam with speculation. "And might not Bamie be just the one to suggest it!"

In due time this very thing would happen, with results which would surprise not only the family but millions of others—the whole world, in fact.

When living in the city Edith was more closely involved in Theodore's strenuous life as police commissioner, and even the children became curious about his crusade, especially his nocturnal activities. Seeing him prepare to leave in street clothes, not dinner dress, in the evening, they bombarded him with questions.

"Where go, Dada?" "Not here for bedtime? No pillow fight? No story?" "Can I go too?" "But you went to work this morning, Father. Why now—again?" This last from Alice, at twelve, in the process hopefully of growing from tomboy into proper adolescence.

Theodore was vague. Yes, he was going to work, and no, they could not come with him. But to make up for the loss of a pillow fight, he would take them for a sleigh ride in Central Park his first free day. He promised.

Edith knew very well where he was going, and, as always, she worried. He was making so many enemies because of his stubborn insistence on enforcing the law for the Sunday closing of saloons, his action deeply resented not only by saloonkeepers but by the general public, who depended on this outlet for celebration on their one day of rest! He was about to make one of his habitual sallies into New York streets, perhaps with his new reform-minded friend Jacob Riis, author of the illuminating exposé of New York's social evils, *How the Other Half Lives.* He would tramp the streets in disguise until midnight and after, perhaps into the early hours of the morning, seeing if his policemen were doing their duty, noting those who were on the job, those who were asleep or dallying with a friendly prostitute, discovering instances of heroism that deserved promotion. Even after a festive dinner or theater party he might drape a black cape over his evening clothes, pull a wide-brimmed hat down over his forehead, and go prowling. At dawn he would probably go into Mike Lyons's restaurant in the Bowery, have a hearty meal of ham and eggs, then sleep for an hour or two on a couch in his office on Mulberry Street before starting his official work for the day. Such measures were bearing fruit. The police force was fast becoming more disciplined, ineffective members weeded out, faithful ones promoted. The New York streets were actually getting safe to travel at all hours of the night.

Edith heard of his exploits, sometimes from him, often from the newspapers, which related them with great glee, occasionally in the shape of cartoons. One of the latter showed two policemen standing before a shop window in which a set of grinning false teeth was displayed in close juxtaposition to a pair of spectacles. They were throwing up their hands in horror, obviously in the act of fleeing.

"Listen to this!" he chortled once, returning from one of these nocturnal adventures. "I found one of my policemen chatting happily with a young lady of the streets, and I stopped to ask them what they were talking about. 'What's that to you?' he retorted, then asked his companion, 'Shall I fan him, Mame?' 'Sure, fan him to death' was her reply. About then I lifted my hat, and they recognized me. You should have seen them run—in both directions. Wasn't that simply bully?"

Edith's laughter was perfunctory. It was amusing, yes, but—oh, so dangerous! She never stopped worrying. The tension was almost worse when they moved to Sagamore in May. At least when living in the city he could come home almost every night.

Sometimes he even seemed to court danger. There was the time the German brewers' societies organized a parade to protest his enforcement of the law closing saloons on Sunday.

"What do you think!" he demanded gleefully. "They have actually invited me to review the parade and sit on the platform!"

"But of course you're not going to!" said Edith in alarm.

"Of course I am. And of course they don't expect me to. What a bully good joke on them to see me there!"

Edith suffered agonies fearing what was happening. A demonstration could turn so easily into a riot! Stones, brickbats, even bullets! But he returned the night of the parade unharmed and apparently well pleased with himself.

"What happened?" she inquired anxiously.

"Nothing of importance. They made their point, and, as a matter of fact, I agree with them. It's a poor law, but as long as it remains the law, it must be enforced."

It was Conie who filled Edith in on details of the event. Occasionally she lunched with her brother down at the old Vienna bakery on the corner of Tenth Street and Broadway, where they enjoyed their favorite squab and *café au lait* and he told her some of his more bizarre, often humorous experiences.

"Oh, yes, he went to the parade, sat on the platform and watched the mass of men marching by with banners and signs saying 'Down with Teddy' and expletives a lot worse. When one company went by, someone shouted, *'Wo ist* Teddy?' *'Hier bin ich!'* he called out in his best German, leaning over the railing and flashing his white teeth in one of his beaming smiles. Wouldn't you know! They couldn't resist him. They hid their hateful banners and began to cheer him, every company as they went past. Wouldn't we like to have been there, you and I!"

By the end of 1896 Theodore was getting restless again. He had campaigned with his usual vigor in the presidential election and seen McKinley, the Republican candidate, elected. He had raised the police force to "a very high point of efficiency," and given the city "the most honest and orderly election it had ever had." He had made bitter enemies, but enforced the law in spite of them. "I have done nearly all I can with the police under the present law," he wrote Bamie, "and now I should rather welcome being legislated out of office." In fact, he was ready to move on. Some of his friends, among them John Hay, Henry Cabot Lodge, and Speaker John Reed, were using their influence to persuade McKinley to give him a government post, but the newly elected President was proving reluctant.

The uncertainty was disastrous both to Theodore's well-being and to Edith's peace of mind. Frustration made him even more strenuously energetic, hence more careless. On one weekend in December he played "bear" so violently with the children that he had one of his old severe attacks of asthma. Then he bruised his arm when chopping wood. After that he cut his forehead bumping his head on the mantelpiece when putting a log on the fire. Next he took a bad tumble when skiing.

But Christmas at Sagamore was as usual, ideal, unclouded by stormy past or nebulous future. On Christmas Eve they all drove down in the farm wagon, fitted with sleds, to Cove Neck School, where Theodore made a speech about good citizenship and they listened to the pupils' songs and recitations, Ted's among them. At nine he had started school there the preceding autumn, an enlightening experience after his years of being tutored by Alice's governess, for his local peers had ridiculed not only his spectacles but his homebred habits of what they termed "sissiness," such as courtesy to girls and kindness to animals. Ted had handled this problem in a manner highly satisfactory to his father, who had written Bamie that his son had "just despatched in single fight a fellow-American citizen named Peter Gallegher."

After the program Theodore played Santa Claus, as he was to

do for years on end, dispensing gifts to all the pupils, substantial items purchased thriftily by Edith at Bloomingdale's. Then, after a six o'clock dinner they drove in the woodsled to the little Episcopal church in Oyster Bay for the Christmas carols, which always included the hymn beginning, "It's Christmas Eve on the river; it's Christmas Eve on the bay."

But it was Christmas Day that the children loved best—waking on an icy morning, crowding into Edith's bedroom where, snuggled into blankets and shawls, they emptied their stockings in front of a roaring fire. Even Archie, though somewhat puzzled, opened his presents with mounting enjoyment. After breakfast they all repaired to the gun room, which, as Edith wrote Bamie, was "like nothing but the North Pole," and opened the bigger presents, skis, books, a "bowie knife" for Kermit, a doll's tea set for Ethel. After lunch they all combatted the unusual cold by playing "pillow-dex," which, as Edith noted, was "very idiotic but very funny."

"Christmas week here was lovely," Theodore wrote his darling Bye, who was still in England. "Heavy snow, bright cold weather and out of door sports from morning to night."

Back to the city with its tutors, its dancing classes, its social obligations, for Edith its futile struggle to make ends meet, for Theodore its bitter frustrations and eternal wranglings—yes, and its torturing uncertainty as to his future.

More months passed before his friends managed to persuade the new President to give a position of influence to a man whom he considered a potential firebrand. It was April 1897 when Theodore was finally appointed Assistant Secretary of the Navy. Though "dee-lighted," he was also astonished, for, as he wrote Bamie, "McKinley rather distrusted me, and Platt [Republican party boss and his sworn enemy] actively hated me; it was Cabot's untiring energy and devotion which put me in."

Though relieved to see Theodore's mood of despondency change to one of elation, Edith secretly regretted the disruption. Another move, another shock of adjustment, aggravated by the recent discovery that she was again pregnant, not an unpleasant discovery, for she and Theodore would welcome the newcomer gladly, even though some family eyebrows, Emily's especially, would be elevated in disapproval. "I know you thought the stork had paid enough visits here," she wrote her dour sister.

At least the appointment had come at an opportune time. They were vacating Bamie's house permanently in preparation for her return in May. Edith would enjoy the summer at Sagamore. Theodore would make his home with the Lodges in Washington, returning home even more infrequently than usual, with his new job demanding every iota of his time and abounding energy. He seemed to be bent on playing as furiously competitive games with the American navy, thought Edith, as had Ted and Alice with their little lead ships.

He was at Sagamore on July 4, of course, along with a horde of other Roosevelts, including one young member of the Hyde Park branch, Franklin Delano, aged fifteen. He had just finished his first year at Groton, where Theodore intended to send his boys. Bamie had asked him to come to this holiday gathering, where he could get acquainted with more vigorous and—yes, rambunctious Roosevelts. "He's sort of a mother's boy," she explained. "She didn't want him to come, and refused my invitation for him. But would you believe it, he wrote back to her, 'Please don't make any more arrangements for my future happiness.' So here he is."

Edith was impressed with the handsome young man. He was well-mannered and genial, though his young cousins considered the F.D. to stand for "featherduster," not rugged or sporting enough to suit them. She suspected that ten-year-old Ted's contempt was due partly to jealousy, for Franklin revealed an ardent admiration for Theodore, whom he had heard speak at Groton on his adventures as police commissioner, a speech which he had thought was "splendid." Indeed, Franklin would always describe "Cousin Theodore" as the greatest man he had ever known. The two spent hours discussing what proved to be remarkably congenial views on politics. The holiday, with Theodore flashing in and out like a meteor, was all too short.

In August Edith was in Washington, trying to settle in their rented house at 1810 N Street, once more fitting the combined pieces of furniture gleaned from her and Theodore's family households into some semblance of homely cheer—not too successfully. As Theodore wrote Cabot Lodge, who was out of the city during the hot season, "Edith is here with me; and fortunately the weather is cool. She is grappling with desperate energy with the new house and the old furniture. The house will have a certain incongruous look next year, being furnished scantily in some directions, and over-abundantly in others, but we are very much pleased with it, nevertheless. It seems very comfortable indeed, much more so than our old one."

It was mid-October when they made the move to Washington. Now that they were finally settled, Edith looked forward with anticipation to the future. They were back in the city she loved best. Though many of their former friends were no longer here—Cecil Spring-Rice was in Persia, John Hay in England—Henry Adams's coterie, though depleted, awaited her participation. Theodore had installed the two older boys in one of the Washington public schools, and they seemed happy. As soon as the new baby was born (and she was in her eighth month) she planned to settle into a comfortable and congenial routine for the foreseeable future. She could not have been more wrong.

Her fifth child and fourth son arrived unexpectedly on November 19. By riding furiously on his bicycle, Theodore was able to get the doctor and nurse just in time. Soon after the birth he noted in a letter, "I have a new small boy just two hours old, whom I have entered for Groton." A month later, on December 22, he was writing to their friend "Fergie" that they would "attend the christening of Quentin" (named for Edith's grandfather, Isaac Quentin Carow) "tomorrow, where Cabot also will come, with gloomy reluctance, as it is against his principles to sanction anything so anti-malthusian as a sixth child."

By Christmas Edith was almost fully recovered from her confinement and ready to enjoy the Washington melee. As Theodore wrote Bamie, "Alice, Ted, and Kermit went with me to the dinner at the Lodges', and all, down even to Kermit, had a seraphic time." Early in January he was noting that "Edith has just been out for her first little walk; and she is beginning to look and feel herself again. When she is well she will enjoy Washington more than ever. How glad I am I am here!"

But he rejoiced too soon. On the seventeenth he was writing

Bamie, "Edith does not seem to get much better; she has very bad neuralgia pains, and is weak. Ted has dreadful headaches each day. The others, thank Heaven, are well. I am not at all easy about Edith." A week later he was more hopeful. "Edith is a *little* better; Ted no better; and this morning Kermit seems sick. Only my positive engagements make me leave at this time. . . . I guess Edith will have to wean the baby."

Her condition did not improve. Doctors failed to diagnose the trouble. Was it typhoid? She maintained a temperature of 101 degrees. Never in her unusually healthy life had she suffered such continuous distress. Worry over Ted added to her malaise, with additional concern about Alice, who at fourteen was becoming unruly. Still a thorough tomboy, she persisted, as Edith wrote Emily, in "running the streets uncontrolled with every boy in town." With Edith too sick to maintain discipline and Theodore too busy, they decided to send her to Bamie in New York.

Edith had other worries. At Sagamore, Theodore's absorption in his work, his obsession in securing for the country what he considered a proper navy, had seemed remote and impersonal. Here she was plunged into a maelstrom of national furor. She had known, of course, that Spain was involved in colonial disturbances in Cuba, that the American press, especially the journals of Hearst and Pulitzer, inclined to sensationalism, were publicizing terrible atrocities which the Spanish army was perpetrating against the native insurgents. Now she discovered that the Administration was being hounded by outraged Americans to intervene and liberate the island, that McKinley was lukewarm about the idea of going to war, that Theodore was one of its most ardent proponents. It was a conversation she overheard unwittingly between him and Cabot Lodge that told her how deeply he was involved.

"I guess I wrote you what I told the President, that if war was declared, of course I would be the first to go. I'd be glad to raise a regiment and lead it."

"And what was it he said?" inquired Lodge tersely. Edith, suddenly tense, listened with bated breath.

"Well—he asked me what Mrs. Roosevelt would think of that. I told him that both you and she would probably regret it but that this was one case where I would consult neither of you."

Edith let out her breath in a long sigh. It was not a conversation that reduced her fever.

She did not improve. Finally, toward the last of February, Theodore decided to call in the eminent Dr. Osler of Baltimore for consultation. He diagnosed an abscess in the psoas muscle and recommended immediate surgery. But for some reason Theodore, listening to other doctors, dallied, hoping such an extreme measure could be avoided. But so critical was her condition that on March 5 a gynecologist was consulted, and he operated on the following day. The surgery was successful, but it would be months before Edith would fully regain her health. On March 21 Theodore was writing, "Mrs. Roosevelt has been very sick all winter; for weeks we could not tell whether she would live or die. Now, very slowly, she is crawling back to life. I hope never to see another such winter. We have had to send all the children away from the house."

Slowly, yes . . . and crawling . . . pretending strength when she felt only excruciating weakness, insisting on walking when she could barely put one foot ahead of the other. Yet if she had ever needed strength and stamina in full measure, it was now. For she was facing not only physical change but mental anguish, and sickness of body seemed almost inconsequential beside the fear and tension aroused by the grim crisis taking shape in the nation. As winter waned, merged into spring, she saw the storm clouds gather, turn black and ominous, erupt into turbulence.

In February of that year, 1898, there was the sinking of the battleship *Maine,* sent to Cuban waters as, according to the President, an "act of friendly courtesy." "An accidental explosion?" hoped the peace-loving President. "An enemy act!" insisted the warmongering journalists. "A Spanish mine! The *Maine* blown up!" Whether the latter supposition was true or not—and it was never proved—war was now inevitable.

As Edith well knew, Theodore had been promoting the cause of the oppressed Cubans for months, hounding his superiors for action, insisting in his role as Assistant Secretary of the Navy on increasing naval power, once at least taking advantage of the absence of the Secretary, John D. Long, to issue orders which would virtually prepare the nation for the war which he felt would surely come. Thanks to the inflamed press, the country went wild. "Remember the *Maine!*" became the battle cry. Still McKinley, and some more moderate leaders like Speaker "Czar" Reed, skeptical of the sensational stories of Spanish atrocities and stressing the fact that Spain had already been instituting reforms in response to the insurgents' desire for independence, held off taking action.

"That McKinley!" fumed Theodore. "He has no more backbone than a chocolate éclair!"

Edith mildly demurred. She liked and admired the President, and he was certainly no coward. Why, he had fought in the Civil War, been made a major. He knew how terrible and cruel war would be. Surely it was not weakness to want to spare his people such suffering and death! "Besides," she continued gently, "do you think it's always wise to push people into actions that may seem right to you but which might in the end cause more harm than good?"

Theodore flushed. "I suppose you're thinking of Ted, but—I can't see what connection that has with a country's defending its honor and, even more important, trying to free an enslaved people!"

During Edith's severe sickness, Ted, still afflicted with headaches, had been shipped off to Bamie to join Alice and to consult with more experienced doctors. His trouble had been diagnosed as nervous prostration, occasioned at least in part by his father's driving him too hard, both mentally and physically.

"I know," he admitted now, reluctantly defensive. "As I've said, I'll never pressure the boy again. I love the little fellow so much! I guess I've wanted him to be all the things I'd like to have been and wasn't, so I pushed him too much. I've learned my lesson."

With or without his urging, the country was rushing headlong toward war, which was declared by Congress on April 14.

When Theodore divulged his plans, Edith felt such a recurrence of weakness that she had no strength to question, much less protest. But Cabot Lodge made the objections for her.

"What's this I hear, Teddy? You're going to resign your office and raise some sort of regiment and go fighting? What an all-fired foolish thing to do!"

Theodore was derisive. "You think I want to chafe my heart out here at a desk instead of being at the front? Shouldn't I practice what I've preached?"

"But think, friend!" Lodge continued more reasonably. "It's so unnecessary, and you're needed here. Aside from your official duties, you have a sick wife, six children, one of them a mere babe! Think what you'd be letting Edith in for!"

Theodore's jaw set stubbornly. "She's no longer sick," he said. "And even if she were—I say, you understand, don't you, Edie?"

Edith hesitated. She knew what he had almost said. *Even if she were, I would go just the same.* Fortunately she would never know what he was to say to a close friend years later. "I would have turned from my wife's deathbed to answer the call." She gave him a long thoughtful look. That fiery gleam in his eyes, like sparks struck from steel—when had she noticed it first? When he had seen the dead seal and started on such a tireless quest for knowledge? When his father had challenged him to "make his body"? And how often she had seen it since! A fight! Always it had presaged a fight, a crusade—against corruption, weakness, ignorance, oppression, anything he despised. What sparked it? Sense of duty—or love of battle—or just a boy's thirst for adventure? No matter. Her probing gaze softened.

"Yes," she said. "I understand."

Others than Lodge tried to dissuade him: Chanler, Adams, his brother-in-law Douglas, his uncles, cousins, even his sisters, who idolized him, thought he could do no wrong. He was jeopardizing his political career. He was mad, duped by the desire for vain glory. He was a fool, hungry for a fight of any kind. He was a cad, deserting a sick wife and all those little children!

Edith used no persuasion, either for or against. She saw little of him in the days following the declaration of war. He was rushing around the country, thumping up enlistments for his regiment, sending telegrams, encountering no difficulty, for volunteers came pouring in, from Westerners who knew his reputation, were "young, good shots and good riders," from Harvard classmates and other Ivy League "gentlemen." There were twenty-three thousand applications within a few days. Though Theodore himself was, at his own insistence, second in command of the regiment under Colonel Leonard Wood, it was his flamboyant self that naturally captured the limelight. The conglomerate of volunteers ran the gamut of "Teddy's Terrors" and "Teddy's Cowboy Contingent" and other such sobriquets to be finally immortalized under the nickname "Roosevelt's Rough Riders."

For the next two weeks, while Theodore was frenziedly assembling the wherewithal to fight a war, Edith was patiently battling physical weakness to perform equally herculean but more mundane tasks—making ready to close the house, store the furniture again, and make what might well be the final move to Sagamore. She admired Teddy in his cavalry lieutenant-colonel's blue cravenette-treated uniform when it arrived in response to his wire to Brooks Brothers in New York, though secretly she was reminded of Ted strutting about proudly in his first long pants. She attended farewell dinners with him, tried to make his few precious hours with the children as happy and carefree as possible. And on May 12 she packed his duffel bags with necessities, including his new uniform and twelve spare sets of spectacles; then, as cheerfully as other wives or mothers similarly about to be bereft, she saw him off for the training camp of his regiment in San Antonio, Texas. Fortunately there was no time then to grieve or wonder if she would ever see him again.

The children, thanks to Theodore's obvious exhilaration over the course of events, saw nothing unusual or threatening in this particular departure. Father might have been faring forth on the trail of more fascinating animal heads. Even Kermit, the sensitive, the thoughtful, took his forthcoming absence in stride. "Father went to war last Thursday," he wrote Aunt Emily. "I sted up untill he left which was at 110."

6

It was a strange anomaly, that summer of 1898—heights and depths, triumph and defeat, intimacy and loneliness. Edith hoped never to see another like it. But, of course, being married to Theodore, she would.

For the children's sake she tried not to show her unrest and terrible foreboding. At least he was safe for the present. His letters were as full of exciting detail as those from his Western ranch but even less descriptive of hair-raising adventure. His motley regiment was training furiously from five in the morning to "Taps" at nine each night. After that he sat in his tent, turned up his lamp, and wrote letters. His men were simply "bully." He had only two complaints, worry that the war might be over before he could get into it, and disgust with the delays of the War Department. *Slow*. Everything was too slow. That his motley assemblage of cowboys, Ivy League grads, and Knickerbocker "gentlemen" should require at least two weeks of rigid discipline to amalgamate and prepare for battle was to him incomprehensible. But at last toward the end of May he cabled that they were leaving for Tampa, Florida, whence they would embark for Cuba.

Edith's only pleasure in the news was his suggestion that she join him in Tampa to spend a few days before they sailed. It was with a lifting of spirits that she prepared for the trip. She would not let her fears for the future mar this brief time together. It would be a second honeymoon.

The train trip was so long and dreary that it revived all her feelings of depression. The country looked barren, all "white sand and low palmetto bushes," as she wrote Emily. Her cab ride through the little town was equally discouraging, suffocatingly hot, through dusty streets crowded with rowdy sailors and soldiers, for the harbor was filled with transport ships, and some thirty thousand soldiers were adrift on the town. Half of them, it seemed, were assembled on the broad porch of the bizarre Tampa Bay Hotel, aptly named a "folly," with its Moorish-style architecture, its exotic domes and minarets. But when she saw Theodore waiting for her in the lobby, teeth gleaming in a huge smile, eyes eager and arms outstretched, depression was swept away.

"Edie, darling!" he greeted her. "Good news! Colonel Wood has given me leave from before dinner to after breakfast all the time you are here!"

They spent a halcyon three days. As Theodore wrote the "bunnies" on June 6, "It has been a real holiday to have darling Mother here." One day he took her to the camp, and she saw the men drilling, the tents in their long company streets, the horses being taken to water, and his little horse Texas. She met the colonel and the majors, saw the company mascots, a mountain lion cub and a jolly little dog named Cuba. On another day she went again to the camp to witness the cavalry regiments in formal mounted drill. Escorted by the journalist Richard Harding Davis, she joined a group of foreign attachés to watch two thousand riders galloping back and forth, conspicuous among them the Rough Riders brandishing Cuban machetes instead of the usual sabers.

"It's amazing how your husband has got his regiment into shape!" Davis marveled. "Such a motley crowd, and such a short time! It's hard to believe."

Three days . . . so long when looked forward to, so short when looked back on. But time bore no relationship to the following weeks. They seemed endless.

Because of the children she tried to make life as normal as possible, encouraging the visits of cousins, planning games, picnics, clambakes. Alice and Ted were caught up in the glamorous furor of war, like the rest of the country. For them Father had just gone on another hunting foray, this time on the trail, not of savage beasts but of evil Spaniards. Avid readers, they scoured the newspapers for reports of their father and his fascinating Rough Riders. Only Kermit sensed his mother's unusual depression, and he followed her about like a shadow. Kermit—and Mame. For the old Irish nurse she was still as much a beloved charge as baby Quentin.

"Now, now, colleen, take it aisy. Don't thry to kape it all inside. I know how it is, ye not aven slapin' for worryin'. Let it out and have a good cry. Ye'll feel better afther."

Letters, of course, were long delayed. Edith knew from newspaper reports that he had finally left Tampa on June 14, that on June 22 he had landed in Cuba near Santiago. Letters began to come, increasing rather than easing her worry. On June 24 they had struck the Spaniards, lost a dozen men, with sixty wounded. One man standing beside a tree with Theodore had been killed. Baggage had been left on the ship. He had been sleeping on the ground in his mackintosh, was so drenched with sweat that he hadn't been dry day or night. One of his two horses had drowned. He had no soap, toothbrush, razor, medicine, socks, or underclothes. Fortunately several pairs of spectacles had been sewn into the lining of his uniform. For four days he never took off his clothes . . . had no chance to boil the water he drank . . . buried the dead after the fight, with vultures wheeling overhead, plucking out the eyes and tearing at the faces of the dead Spaniards. . . .

Edith read on, her head whirling in sickened confusion. Yet there were words which brought her comfort, for when she wrote back with cheering news about Sagamore Hill, she added, "Last night I slept better because I held your dear letters to my heart instead of just having them under my pillow. I felt I was touching you when I pressed against me what your hand had touched."

Letters did little to allay her fears. When one arrived he might well be sick or wounded or dead. Still, she could not help responding to the exultation which surmounted all the grim and gory details. He was where he had wanted all his life to be, in the midst of the worst conflict imaginable, ever since they had sat together on the steps of the old brownstone and he had read to her from his favorite "Saga of King Olaf."

> And King Olaf heard the cry,
> Saw the red light in the sky,
>   Laid his hand upon his sword,
> As he leaned upon the railing,
> And his ships went sailing, sailing . . .

July 1. As she went about her normal routine, did she sense that they were hours of life-and-death struggle, that fifteen hundred miles to the south Theodore was living his own saga . . . leading his Rough Riders in a fierce charge up one of the San Juan hills, first on his pony Texas, then under such devastating fire that he had to desert his horse and continue on foot; still leading the way with a wave of his hat and a flourish of a polka-dot handkerchief tied to its brim; shrapnel screaming about him, one bullet scraping his elbow . . . charging . . . recharging . . . driving the Spaniards over the brow of the chain of hills fronting Santiago? Though he went into the fight with 490 strong, 86 were killed or wounded, a half dozen missing. Nearly 40 had been prostrated by the severe heat. But the day had ended in victory. As he was to write later, it had been "aside from Edith, *the* time of my life."

The next day, Saturday, there were glaring headlines in the *Times*. BIG BATTLE AROUND SANTIAGO. "The American loss is heavy. . . . Estimates place it at 500 killed and wounded." It was a day of soaring heat, yet Edith shivered.

"Was Father in the fight, do you s'pose?" demanded Ted eagerly.

Yes, Edith supposed. The Sunday *Times* confirmed it. ROUGH RIDERS AND CAVALRY START IN. "Col. Wood's command behaved with great bravery, firing steady and deadly volleys with the enemy's shells screeching and bursting over their heads. Our losses serious."

On July 3 the temperature soared to 99 in the shade. What must it be in Cuba! Still, though her heavy-boned corset and tight bodice clung to her like a steaming compress, Edith felt no inner warmth. The next two weeks were an eternity. Each day she scanned the long lists of "officers killed or wounded," often with familiar names of Rough Riders, breathing a sigh of relief when one name was missing. Even when letters arrived, full of details of that furious charge up Kettle Hill, they brought little comfort. He had been safe when writing. But what *now?*

On July 13 she spotted a curious item on a back page. ROOSEVELT FOR GOVERNOR. "Campaign buttons were put in circulation yesterday bearing a portrait of Theodore Roosevelt as a candidate for

Governor . . . military hero. . . ." How amusing! for he had thought his resignation as Assistant Secretary of the Navy had jeopardized any future participation in politics. She clipped it out to include in her next letter.

At last on July 15 it was over. SANTIAGO OURS WITHOUT A FIGHT. Edith drew a long breath, and the irregular beating of her heart seemed at once to steady. Ted acted slightly disappointed. But Archie ran out to the stable and told the coachman to go down to the station to bring back his father.

"Silly!" Ted derided his four-year-old sibling. "You think Cuba's next door to New York? It will be several days, at least, before he can get home."

Several days, yes . . . weeks. Soon Theodore was writing of incredible suffering among his troops. Malaria and dysentery were rampant. Yellow fever had broken out. Of his 400 men left after the fighting, 123 were sick. Those who went to the hospitals were lying in mud, unattended and unfed. His sick men had nothing to eat but bacon, hardtack, and coffee. He had managed to get them some rice, beans, and tomatoes, paying for them himself, toting some of them eight miles on his back up a muddy mountain path. One Rough Rider later claimed that Theodore had spent five thousand dollars of his own money buying supplies. The colonel was cursing the quartermasters and the wretched management of those higher up, though he must not be reported, or he would be court-martialed.

So—the worry was not over. Disease was as much a killer as bullets. Once more Edith opened each newspaper with fear, waited with hope for the postman, dreaded the coming of the blue-coated messenger boy from the Oyster Bay telegraph office, bringing the fateful yellow slip of paper. Her twenty-seventh birthday passed on August 6, and still no good news came, only the report that Theodore had led the men in sending a round-robin letter to General Shafter pleading that the troops be sent north before they were completely decimated—an action that probably jeopardized his chances for the Medal of Honor for which he had been recommended.

Then at last on August 15 the messenger did come, but, thank heaven, not with the yellow slip. There being no telephone at

Sagamore Hill, Theodore had called the office at Oyster Bay. He and his Rough Riders had landed at Montauk, Long Island, and he wanted her to come. The journey seemed endless, five hours on the Long Island Rail Road, west to Jamaica, east in the slow dusty cars along the South Shore to the tip of the Island. Their old friend Jacob Riis, reporter for the New York *Sun,* met her train.

"I carry a picture in my heart always," he was to remember, "of Mrs. Roosevelt hooded and cloaked against a threatening storm, on the board-seat of an army wagon bound for the Montauk hills, to receive her lover-husband back from the war."

But he brought bad news. Yellow fever had broken out at Camp Wickoff, and the troops were under strict quarantine. All that agonizing trip for nothing? But at the Red Cross station she found a young officer who managed under cover of darkness to inveigle Theodore out of quarantine long enough for a secret meeting. They had an hour together, and the long months of worry and separation were swept away. She was surprised and relieved to see how well he looked. Bronzed, husky, though a bit thin, trim in a fresh brown uniform with gaiters and boots, he confessed to feeling "disgracefully well, when I see how badly off some of my brave fellows are." He went back into quarantine as surreptitiously as he had left it—fortunately, for some of his superiors would have liked nothing better than cause to court-martial this insubordinate popular hero.

That he *was* a hero Edith was not long in discovering. His men idolized him. And as days passed, she found herself included in some of their doglike affection. "They follow me about like a bodyguard," she wrote Emily.

She spent four days at the camp sleeping in a grubby boarding-house and managing to enter the camp proper by volunteering to tend the sick and wounded in the makeshift hospital. On August 20 Theodore obtained permission to go home with her for a short leave. And what a welcome—not only from the children, from the whole town of Oyster Bay and, it seemed, the whole city of New York, come to honor their latest hero! As the train pulled into the station, whistle screeching, it was met with thundering cannons, blaring bands, blazing muskets.

"The crowd seemed mad with enthusiasm," reported the New

York *Herald* the next day. "Women and children were brushed aside like feathers. The crush was so great that a little girl, caught in the crowd, was literally stripped of her frock."

The furor continued. During his four days' leave there was no peace. Reporters, politicians, neighbors, relatives—all came swarming. Newsmen bombarded with questions. Cameras clicked. "Are you going to run for governor?" And the children, happily excited yet longing to have the hero to themselves, were not exempt from the bombardment.

"Where is the colonel?" One reporter managed to corner Archie. "I don't know where the colonel is," replied the four-year-old, "but Father is taking a bath."

"The house is besieged with reporters and delegations," Edith wrote Emily. "When we came up from bathing just now, two men were waiting in front of the house, more were on the piazza, more in the library and a crowd of mixed sexes surrounding Quentin at his bench, beside a camera fiend taking snapshots at the house from the fence of Smith's field! It is something horrid but will not last long."

She was wrong. Though Theodore sidestepped all questions of his political future and returned to Montauk, pleading, "My place is with the boys," the furor continued. Even his old enemy, Senator Thomas Platt, the Republican "boss" of New York State, determined to capitalize on the new hero's popularity by using him for his own ends, was supporting the idea of making him governor.

Edith was indifferent to the outcome of such pressures. If Theodore wanted to run for governor, she would support him, of course. But all she wanted was to get him back home, safe and healthy, with time to satisfy the long-suppressed hungers of his wife and children. She took the four oldest to Montauk for a day's visit as a first taste of family reunion. It was a grand success. As she wrote Emily, "Ted and Kermit slept in Theodore's tent, one on his cot, the other on his air mattress, while poor Theodore occupied the table." Alice especially enjoyed the distinction of being "the Colonel's daughter." Her fourteen-year-old budding femininity was already receptive to the buzzing admiration of young males.

On September 17 the Rough Riders were mustered out, and

Theodore returned home, bringing their final tribute, a bronze Bronco Buster, which was to become one of his dearest possessions. Now, thought Edith, it was finally over. At last her heart, proved to have become enlarged during the weeks of nervous tension, was restored to its normal pace. Even the mounting threat of the possible governorship did not disturb her serenity. Though offers for large sums of money by *Scribner's* and other magazines for articles about the Cuban experience aroused the hope that he might be content with a quiet literary life, she was willing to accept what came, even though it might mean a thrusting into prominence which could not help violating her innate yearning for privacy. Whatever happened, they would at least be together.

Theodore refused to attend the Republican state convention. On Sunday, September 25, he tried to conceal his perturbation in normal activity. Reporters from the New York papers found him, dressed in white flannel trousers and a loose sport shirt, coming downstairs with a flock of children at his heels and left him "calmly sauntering over the lawn with his wife, seemingly unconcerned about the doings at the Saratoga convention." But Edith knew he was on tenterhooks. When they all adjourned to the library after dinner, he paced the floor, hands thrust in his pockets, as he regaled the children with anecdotes from his Cuban forays, but with ears obviously cocked for sounds from the outside world. At about eight-thirty they began to come, first the messenger on his bicycle bringing telegrams.

"You are nominated for Governor. Our hearts are with you. Congratulations. Isaac Hunt—William O'Neill." His old cronies in the legislature, bless them!

"Accept my sincere congratulations upon your nomination for Governor. May your march to the capitol be as triumphant as your victorious charge up San Juan Hill."

The official notification came with the arrival of a committee of party dignitaries the following day. While he read his acceptance speech on the west porch, Edith stood leaning against the balustrade, eyes cast down, smiling, tightly clasped hands and downcast eyes the only signs that she was not completely at ease. Later, as she moved among the guests and served lunch to some thirty people, a thoroughly poised and gracious hostess, no one would have guessed that inwardly she was quaking at the prospect of continuing such public self-sharing ad infinitum.

Theodore rose to the challenge with his usual zest. On October 5 Edith attended the campaign's launching when seven thousand rooters packed Carnegie Hall from floor to roof. "The house was jammed," she wrote Emily, "and there was a large overflow meeting outside. I was glad I had gone, for there was so much enthusiasm that I had no opportunity of feeling as nervous as I usually do when I hear Theodore."

She saw little of him during the following weeks. He was touring the state by train, escorted by a bevy of his Rough Riders. His campaign buttons showed his picture attached to a tiny broom, revealing his intention to make a "clean sweep" of New York's corrupt politics, a suggestion which must have dampened the enthusiasm of Boss Platt. One week he made 102 speeches, many of them outdoors in industrial towns filled, Edith feared, with possible anarchists. But the news reports were good. ROOSEVELT MARCHING ON. GREAT OUTPOURING OF PEOPLE. He moved amid excited acclamations. "Teddy!" "Hooray for Teddy!" "Teddy, we're wid yer!"

Teddy! How did he like being called that? Edith wondered. Neither she nor his friends would think of using the nickname now. He had always despised it.

Election night came. Theodore seemed unconcerned. He and Alice sat reading beside a tall oil lamp on a table near the fire. Edith sat by another lamp doing embroidery. The other children were in bed. A little after eight two reporters charged in, with news that the Democratic papers in New York had conceded the election. Theodore was unimpressed. No word yet from Odell, the state chairman.

He went to bed. At one o'clock, in response to a peremptory ringing of the doorbell, he donned his red dressing gown, lighted a kerosene lamp, and padded downstairs. He was still half asleep.

"You're elected by eighteen thousand!" shouted a reporter excitedly.

So . . . Edith drew a long breath and braced herself. Wife of the governor of one of the largest states in the Union! Frightening? Yes, but, fortunately, she need face only each new task as it came. At present it seemed to be superintending Theodore's little secretary, Amy Cheney, daughter of a local editor, in the handling of huge quantities of mail—congratulations, solicitations, questions of policy, and, occasionally, dire criticisms and warnings. She learned to handle them all with surprising expertise. Amy later remarked that, thanks to Edith, life at Sagamore during those hectic days was "one of order and harmony, except when Ted got careless with his pet snakes or toads."

Christmas was as usual—the annual holiday program at Cove School, gifts, recitations (Kermit rattling off "Higglety Pigglety Went to School"), Theodore called on to make his customary speech. "Father," muttered Ted, "don't speak long. Think of the poor children!"

The governor's mansion in Albany was a gingerbready monstrosity—or, as some considered it, the height of architectural beauty. Edith found its towers, cupolas, balconies, innumerable angles and porches odd but unimportant, not much more ornate, in fact, than Sagamore. It was a good solid house, with three stories and eighteen bedrooms, plenty of room for all six "bunnies" and any number of guests. They could easily spend two years—or more—here in comfort. The huge fireplace in the entrance hall and the furnaces (fortunately stoked at state expense) would provide heat for upstate New York's cold winters.

But her emotions on arriving the last day of December were complex and turbulent. Physically she was exhausted, and the influenza which had attacked all the children and their nurses during preceding days was already stirring a fever in her veins. There was another cause for perturbation. Albany! This was where Theodore had lived with his beautiful, adored Alice. Perhaps they passed the house where he had experienced such ecstatic marital bliss. How could he not remember? And the legislators, some of those who had known Alice, must still be here. How could she possibly compete with their memories of that gay, blithe, glowing personality?

"Darling! How wonderful that you're really here!" It was her first guest, her old friend Fanny Smith Dana, now widowed and married to James Russell Parsons, a university regent, whose home was in Albany. "Everybody wants to meet you. You're coming to dinner at our house tonight."

Edith did not attend the dinner. She was too completely exhausted. She did not even know when Theodore arrived home late from the festivities, so late, in fact, that he had been unable to rouse anyone at the house and had had to break a window and climb through, which was reported with glee by the New York *Tribune*. But she managed to drive to the Capitol on Inauguration Day, Monday because January 1 fell on Sunday. Sitting on the dais beside Alice, who looked very grown up in pink silk and sable furs, she saw Theodore sworn in as the thirty-sixth governor of New York and listened to his Inaugural Address. In it he stressed his credo that "it is absolutely impossible for a Republic long to endure if it becomes either corrupt or cowardly."

Later that afternoon in her new home she stood beside him and greeted some five or six thousand people, smiling, gracious, in spite of her fevered discomfort, a much admired governor's lady in her simple but elegant gown of watered white silk. No one seemed to mind, or even notice, that the little bouquets she held, one in either hand, prevented the formal handshakes which had always been considered the vogue. If her manner was slightly reserved, it seemed but a natural foil for the new governor's beaming and effusive style of greeting.

After the two-hour ordeal was over, however, the influenza took its toll. She went to bed and remained there for the next week. But the worst of her initiation into the role of governor's lady was over, and once health was restored she could devote herself to more congenial duties. She tackled the dreary interior of the sadly neglected mansion, making it much more homelike, even creating a gymnasium for Theodore and the children out of a third-floor billiard room.

Theodore was delighted. "Mrs. Roosevelt is really enjoying herself," he wrote Cecil Spring-Rice in February. "We have a great big house which is very comfortable although in appearance and furnishing, painfully suggestive of that kind of elegance one sees in a swell Chicago hotel. . . . The children are perfectly happy and on the whole well."

The children! With them in the house it was far from resembling a hotel. As usual, their already overpowering quota of six was multiplied by an indeterminate bevy of animals. They proceeded to acquire quite a menagerie—guinea pigs, rabbits, squirrels, and a 'coon. One pair of guinea pigs was christened "Bishop and Mrs. Doane" after the city's Episcopal dignitary and his wife. "Father, father," Archie once announced loudly to family and assembled guests, "Bishop Doane has just had twins!" They kept the menagerie in the cellar under the parlor. During the winter when all the windows were shut all was serene, but when spring came, no. One day when receiving important guests Edith noticed a very strong scent in the parlor. Fertilizer on the lawns? No, fertilizer never exuded such an odor. The boys had opened the cellar windows to give the animals air. The parlor had acquired the more unpleasant attributes of a zoo. The denizens of the cellar were hastily removed to remoter quarters.

But the children themselves were well adjusted. Alice and Ethel had a good English governess. Ted and Kermit were enrolled in the Albany Military Academy. Mame, the stern and capable disciplinarian, had charge of Archie and Quentin. Edith had time to fit herself comfortably into her new role. She became a member of the Friday Morning Club, a group of young women who met to read papers on intellectual subjects. To Fanny's satisfaction she was "greatly admired during those years" and "wore the attractive clothes needed by even the prettiest women." They often went on long walks together looking for botanical specimens, for Fanny had become an authority on wildflowers, having published some bestsellers on the subject.

Meanwhile Theodore was pursuing his usual vigorous approach to his new job, until the gymnasium was finished deriving his exercise by rushing each morning to the Capitol and scrambling up the 117 marble steps two at a time to his office. Craftily, he made every effort possible to get Boss Platt and his strongly entrenched machine to go along with his plans for reform. He consulted with Platt openly and treated him with respect at all times. Surprisingly, during his term of office he was able to secure passage of several important reform measures—a new civil service law that struck at the machine's power; a Tenement House Commission Bill, continuing the sweatshops reform which he had taken up as assemblyman; a bill levying taxes on the big corporations which had obtained franchises to use public thoroughfares for street railways and had never shared their profits with the public to whom the thoroughfares rightfully belonged; and he managed to oust a superintendent of insurance who, as he phrased it, was able out of his seven-thousand-dollars-a-year salary to "save enough to enable him to borrow nearly half a million dollars from a trust company, the directors of which are also the directors of an insurance company under his supervision." Also, with the help of Gifford Pinchot, F. H. Newell, and others, who knew the public domain, he was able to formulate New York's conservation policies.

Most of his measures were moderate, too much so to suit his erstwhile reform-minded friends. Better, he felt, to secure only part of the necessary social changes than to so antagonize that he could get none at all. And he showed remarkable tact as well as moderation, both qualities decidedly foreign to his nature. But Boss Platt was not happy. Neither were his corporation cronies who saw their precious profits slightly dwindling because of the new legislation. True, the governor was living up to their agreement, which had been the price of Platt's support. He consulted with Platt about every move he intended to make—appointments, bills to be considered—but without the results the party chief had foreseen. Theodore listened respectfully, conversed reasonably, but—then acted as he pleased.

These conferences often took place in New York, first at Bamie's house, until she moved to Washington to be near her husband who was in the Navy Department, then at Conie's home at 422 Madison Avenue. They often took the form of breakfast parties, to which Theodore invited so many friends that Platt would find himself crowded into a motley group, wedged perhaps between a labor unionist and a Rough Rider—wedged, because Conie's table was small and Theodore invited so many that two were apparently expected to sit on one chair.

Platt found neither of these neighbors congenial to his taste. Thanks to his friend Jacob Riis, Theodore had lost much of his early prejudice toward the labor movement. Remembering his visits to the tenements, he pushed through a law requiring state inspection and licensing of all tenements in which manufacturing was taking place. He supported schoolteachers in their demands for higher salaries and fought for a measure ensuring an eight-hour day for state employees.

And a Rough Rider, Platt discovered, was always turning up. At one breakfast a letter arrived from one of them which aroused great mirth. It contained no name or address. On the front of the envelope was a drawing of a large set of teeth and on the back the notice: "Please let Jack Smith, 211 W. 139th Street, know whether this reaches its destination. It is a bet and a lot of money hangs in the balance."

Theodore chortled. "Good old Jack! He wins his bet, all right."

Another letter aroused even greater merriment. "Dear Colonel," it ran. "Please come right out to Dakota. They ain't treatin' me right out here. The truth is, Colonel, they have put me in jail and I ain't ought to be here at all. They say I shot a lady in the eye, and it ain't true, Colonel, for I was shootin' at my wife at the time. I know you will come and get me out of jail right off, Colonel. Please hurry. J.D."

"Needless to say, gentlemen," Theodore said with mock gravity, "I passed up this opportunity."

As usual, Platt waited impatiently for the breakfast to end. "And now, Governor Roosevelt," he said with some sternness, "I should like to have a private word with you."

"Certainly, Mr. Platt. We will go right up to my sister's library. We shall be quite private there except for my sister. I like to have her present at these conferences."

Platt could hardly protest, though the presence of a lady was not his idea of privacy. It was a typical interview, Theodore listening with great courtesy, agreeing wherever possible, but promising nothing. "Mr. Platt," he might say, "I would rather accept your suggestion of an appointee than that of anyone else *if* you will suggest as good and honorable a man as anyone else. But I must reserve my own power of decision in all matters."

Theodore swept through his first year of office with all the cleansing vigor of the broom which had been his campaign emblem. Action was constant, fast, and furious. The word "rest" was not in his vocabulary. And he was talking of another term to clean up the corruption he had barely touched. At this rate, worried Edith, he was sure to work himself into another attack of asthma. Conie also was concerned.

One day in the spring of 1899 Edith went with him to Conie's house. They found his sister laid up in her room with the grippe. Theodore went bounding up the stairs two at a time to her room, Edith following more slowly.

"Pussie," she heard him call out, "aren't we having fun being governor of New York State?"

While Edith settled herself on the chaise longue, he sat down in a rocking chair and rocked violently back and forth while talking to them about his plans.

"Theodore," Conie said laughingly when he finally stopped for breath, "aren't you going to take a complete rest *sometime* this summer? You certainly need it."

Edith seconded the suggestion heartily and waited hopefully for his answer.

"Yes," he said, "of course you are right. I do mean to take a rest of *one whole month* this summer."

"That's not much," objected Conie, "but it's better than nothing. Now do you really mean that you are going to rest for one whole month?"

Good! thought Edith. That's putting him on record.

"Yes," he answered, as if conferring on her a personal favor, "I really mean to rest one whole month. I don't mean to do one *single* thing during that month—except write a life of Oliver Cromwell."

Edith and Conie exchanged a look of hopeless resignation, then burst out laughing.

He did just that, finishing the manuscript on August 7, his thirteenth book and third biography, sixty-three thousand words of detailed and accurate British history, though without distinctive literary style. One houseguest remembered seeing him engaged in three activities at once—dictating his governor's correspondence to one secretary, his Oliver Cromwell to another, and getting himself shaved by a barber. During the month he also traveled to Washington for consultation with President McKinley and spent three days with Boss Platt attempting to mend their some-what strained relations.

Edith was neither surprised nor disappointed. She had long since despaired of seeing his pattern of action—or, rather, inac-tion—resemble that of a normal human being. Fortunately she could not realize that summer that there were far worse pres-sures soon to come.

7

By the middle of Theodore's two-year term, Boss Platt was be-coming increasingly frustrated. Another two years of this maver-ick governor would upset the whole economy of the state. He was being besieged by corporation heads, railroad magnates in-censed at the idea of having to pay corporate taxes, manufactur-ers shocked by the possibility of restrictions such as an eight-hour day or liability insurance. They had heard rumors that The-odore was bent on more "altruistic" (socialistic!) legislation, fur-ther limitation of trusts and even more careful preservation of the state's natural resources. Yet so popular was he with the com-mon people, who recognized him as their champion, that he was sure to be reelected. What to do? Platt had a bright idea. Why not move him upstairs? President McKinley's Vice President had died in November. The office would be wide open.

"The Vice Presidency?" Theodore scoffed at the suggestion. It was the last thing he wanted. Become a mere figurehead, with no power, no opportunity for action?

"It would be like being shoved into a backwater!" he com-plained to Edith.

She sympathized. Though she would welcome an office which involved him in less tension and responsibility, she had no desire to move. She liked the big rambling house in Albany and appreci-ated the governor's salary, which made them for the first time financially secure. The Vice President's salary would be two thou-sand dollars less. More and more she was enjoying the position of State First Lady with the chance to accompany Theodore on many public occasions, like the trip to New York City to greet the triumphant arrival of Admiral Dewey, hero of Manila Bay. And she was becoming surprisingly comfortable in fulfilling the public duties expected of the governor's wife. That Theodore was "dee-lighted" with her as a helpmeet, even as a political asset, was evident. Witness a paragraph in one of his letters to Arthur Lee, a young British captain, congratulating him on his engagement.

"There is nothing in the world—no possible success, military or political, which is worth weighing in the balance for one moment against that happiness that comes to those fortunate enough to make a real love match—a match in which lover and sweetheart will never be lost in husband or wife. I know what I am writing about, for I am just as much devoted to Mrs. Roosevelt now as ever I was (She has come in at the moment, so I have got to stop the sentence). . . ." Edith was happily conscious of his approval without reading the letter. She had long since ceased to be haunted by the presence of Alice's ghost in Albany.

As a mark of his disapproval Platt stayed away from the governor's New Year's reception. He continued to push the idea of the Vice Presidency even though his close associate, Mark Hanna, Republican Party chairman, was strongly opposed. "Don't you realize," the latter reminded caustically, "that there would be only one life between this madman and the presidency?"

Theodore remained adamant. In February he was writing Lodge, who favored his considering the possibility, "In the Vice Presidency I could do nothing. It would not entertain me to preside in the Senate. . . . I could not *do* anything, and yet I would be seeing continually things I would like to do. . . . So, old man, I am going to declare decisively that I want to be Governor and not Vice President."

Edith was relieved. She could not imagine him fuming in inactivity. Secure in the prospect of no immediate change, she traveled to Cuba in March. Emily had arrived just before Christmas for a visit, and they went together. They were treated royally, met at the dock by Leonard Wood, now the governor-general, and taken to his palace; given tours of the island. Edith reveled in the tropical warmth and glorious vistas. Most of all she exulted in actually climbing Theodore's famous hill, trying to recreate out of the terraced little gardens of vegetables, now so quiet and peaceful, the wild scene of blood and terror when Theodore and his gallant men had stormed their way to the top. As on her visit to his Western paradise, it was a journey into another of his multiplex worlds.

"Edith had a lovely three weeks' trip in Cuba," Theodore wrote. "It did her good to get away from the children, the house and myself, and she came back looking just like a girl."

But even more delightful was a visit to Washington, for Theodore was with her. The pink dogwood, blooming in all the squares, while less flamboyant than Cuba's hibiscus and bougainvillea, was far more in harmony with her mood of well-being. The latter was somewhat threatened when she heard Theodore's name mentioned as a possible vice-presidential candidate. But he seemed adamant in his decision, or—she sometimes wondered shrewdly—was he protesting too loudly? They had busy but happy four days, meeting old friends, the Lodges, the John Hayses, the Elihu Rootses; had dinner twice with Bamie; were entertained by the McKinleys.

"I confess I felt rather puffed up at the White House," she wrote Fanny, "when I realized how very much younger Theodore and I were than any of the other prominent people, but on the other hand, by the time we reach their ages we shall probably have retired into obscurity."

But the crowning excitement of that spring was yet to come. Theodore permitted himself to be chosen a delegate at large to the Republican Convention at Philadelphia, and Edith was going with him. It was her first experience with politics at the fountainhead. The minute they arrived at the Hotel Walton on June 16, 1900, they were plunged into bedlam. Everywhere there were blaring bands, marching delegates. To Edith's dismay the theme song of many of the groups, especially the Western delegates, was, "We want Teddy! We want Teddy!" They roamed the corridors, beating on their drums, storming the hotel room.

"Please," begged Edith, "tell them! Can't you make them understand that you want to remain governor, that under no circumstances would you consider—?"

But she could see that he was wavering. She was sure of it

when he telegraphed to Conie and Douglas, begging them to come—to advise him, or, she hoped, just to stand by him in his decision to remain firm. When Conie arrived she was escorted through the noisy corridors to a room of comparative quiet. Edith was seated sewing. Theodore sat by an open window reading from a huge volume. Tiptoeing to his side, she looked over his shoulder and exclaimed in hearty amusement. But how like him to be studying the *History of Josephus* when his future was hanging in the balance!

The mood of serenity was short-lived. Presently the door burst open and in marched a delegation from Kansas to the raucous accompaniment of fife and drum and bugle. Round and round the room they marched, intoning over and over, "We want Teddy! We want Teddy!" Theodore stood this barrage silently for a while, then he held up his hand for silence and pleaded with them.

"Please—my friends, I wish you would withdraw your desire that I should be a candidate." He went on to explain why. He *wanted* to be governor of New York. Please—let him do what he thought best.

They listened, then began their march again with its monotonous refrain of "We want Teddy!" It echoed back as they left the room and retreated along the corridor. Theodore lifted his hands in despair. "What can I do with such people?" he lamented. Then his eyes gleamed. "But what good fellows they are!"

Edith was in the gallery when the convention convened on June 19. She could see the New York delegation down in front at the left of the center aisle. But—where was Theodore? All rose as a clergyman read the invocation, then sat down. Still he did not come. Then—there was a commotion in the back of the room, and the place erupted into cheers. Delegates stood up on their chairs. Again the shouts resounded, "We want Teddy! We want Teddy!" There he was walking down the aisle, a black version of his Rough Rider's sombrero set squarely on his head, and wearing his Rough Rider suit of khaki.

Sometimes Edith did not understand her husband. This was one of the times. Why, if he was so opposed to being nominated, did he deliberately make himself so conspicuous, enter the hall late, his appearance reminiscent of the reason for his popularity? Was it possible that, in spite of his protestations, he secretly wanted to be forced into acceptance? She knew then what the end would be, even before he gave his seconding speech for President McKinley, followed by another burst of applause from two thousand pairs of hands, before McKinley had sent word that the New York governor would be acceptable to him as candidate for Vice President. The result was inevitable. As Thomas Platt put it with satisfaction, "Roosevelt might as well stand under Niagara Falls and try to spit water back as to stop his nomination."

Going back to the hotel room, Edith found the object of this conjecture placidly sitting by the window reading. Having finished with *Josephus,* he was now deep in the *Histories of Thucidydes.*

His nomination was almost unanimous, 926 for McKinley and 925 for Roosevelt as his running mate. Theodore had cast the only vote against himself.

The enthusiasm was contagious. In spite of her distress, Edith succumbed to the mood of wild spontaneous tumult. As one reporter noted, "The wife of the man who had been the inspiring figure at this great convention was unable to resist the terrific force that was expending itself in shouts and shrieks of exultation. With just a little gasp of regret, Mrs. Roosevelt's face broke into smiles, as she, once for all, accepted the situation with a grace worthy of a true patriot." As usual, she was not revealing her true feelings. Also, as usual, she was accepting with good grace the inevitable. At least there were some advantages in prospect. As governor, Theodore had been working himself to the hilt. He might now get the rest he so badly needed. Though his salary if elected would be less than now, she would have less entertaining to do and would need fewer new clothes. No black cloud without a silver lining!

A week later at Sagamore she donned a China silk dress trimmed with black velvet ribbon and black lace and stood by Theodore's side on the porch as he addressed the notables who had come to apprize him of his nomination; submitted with more grace than he did to the barrage of clicking cameras; then directed Kermit, Archie, and Ethel in their distribution of croquettes, salmon, and other kinds of sandwiches, with tea the sole beverage.

Rest, had she envisioned? McKinley preferred to conduct his campaign comfortably from his porch at Canton, Ohio, tenderly solicitous of his invalid wife, while his vice-presidential nominee rushed about the country making speeches, sometimes seven in a day, 673 in 567 towns in twenty-four states, traveling over twenty thousand miles in four months and speaking an average of twenty thousand words a day to three million people. As the satirist Peter Finley Dunne put it in the words of his quaint philosopher Mr. Dooley, " 'Tis Tiddy alone that's a-runnin, an' he ain't runnin', he's gallopin'."

Meanwhile Edith was managing the Sagamore household, entertaining a continuous stream of relatives, friends, and politicians, tactfully disposing of reporters and photographers, getting Ted ready for his first year at Groton and taking him there, a painful task for both of them, clipping newspaper items of Theodore's travels and pasting them into scrapbooks . . . and worrying. ROOSEVELT IN DANGER. FIERCE FIGHTING IN THE STREETS read one New York headline. While he was thriving on "the strenuous life," fulfilling his boast to Hanna that he was "strong as a bull moose," and suffering no more debilitation than an increasingly shrill and squeaky voice, it was Edith who endured the physical distress of that summer and fall.

"I have grown so thin with the anxiety of this campaign," she wrote Emily, "that the bones in my neck show. If all goes well I hope to gain a few pounds." As for the Vice Presidency, she wrote, "I hate even to think of it, and can't be reconciled at all."

But, attending the mass meeting with Alice and Kermit in Madison Square Garden celebrating the Republican hero's return, she acknowledged that it was "really a triumph." "I bought a new hat for the occasion," she wrote Emily. "Brown velvet with a white plush crown, almost entirely covered with a bird. It tips low over my forehead and, alas, cost sixteen dollars!" The meeting was nothing, however, compared with the ninety thousand men shouting "Teddy! Teddy! Teddy!" as they paraded before Theodore's grandstand seat in a pouring rain the Saturday before election, marching to the theme song which had pursued him across the country and back, "There'll be a hot time in the old town tonight!" Edith's fears that seven hours, bareheaded, in the drenching rain would result in either rheumatism or a cold were unfounded.

"Rheumatism? Cold? Why, I never felt better in my life! I believe the bath did me good. I hope the same was true of those gallant men who showed their mettle by marching."

On November 6 McKinley won over Bryan by the largest majority since the victory of Grant. Theodore had six weeks remaining of his term as governor, but the family did not move again to Albany. Edith often accompanied him there during the week, leaving the children in charge of Mame and Alice's governess, Miss Young. Though his two years as governor had been hampered by necessary compromise with the conservative Platt, Roosevelt was well satisfied with his achievement. He had managed many reforms in response to the progressive mood slowly developing in the country. His own thinking had changed. He was learning to assess society through the eyes of the common man.

With the advent of the new century came two months of marking time. While Theodore went west on a hunting trip in the Rockies, Edith nursed Ted and Quentin through bouts with asthma and surgery for adenoids, rented the Bellamy Storers' house in Washington for $3,000 a year (more than half Theodore's reduced salary!), and made preparations for the family to attend the inaugural ceremonies on the fourth of March. Since they would remain in Washington only two days this time, they would stay at Bamie's newly rented house at 1733 N Street.

With the Robinsons, Uncle James Gracie, Bob Ferguson, Bamie's friend, and all the children, the house was filled to overflowing. Still Bamie planned a celebration breakfast. What was Edith's amazement and dismay to come downstairs the morning of March 4 and find two florists erecting a gigantic floral arrangement in the drawing room, reaching from floor to ceiling, too huge for any other place in the house! It was the anonymous gift of one of Theodore's ardent admirers, explained the head florist. "And it cost $3,500!" he added proudly.

Edith was speechless. A thousand dollars more than their cut in

salary! To say nothing of the inconvenience of appropriating Bamie's drawing room!

But even she found the inaugural proceedings exciting. The
family were given conspicuous seats in the Senate gallery, all
present except Quentin, who had refused to "hear Father pray at
the Senate." All looked presentable except possibly Ted, who,
adjured to bring his best suit from Groton, had complied by appearing in the trousers of one suit, the coat of another, and the
waistcoat of a third.

"Now, Mother," he had replied indignantly to her protests,
"you know you wrote me to come in my best clothes; and these
are the best, the best coat and best trousers and best vest, too."

He was no more confused as to attire than reporters, one of
whom described Edith's costume as a "dark tailor-made suit with
a tight-fitting jacket and a small velvet toque," another as a dress
of "light tan cloth combined with darker brown fur, white lace
and blue panne velvet, with a hat of white chiffon, trimmed with
black velvet and pompoms of chiffon." Alice's seventeen-year-old
dignity was also affronted by conflicting descriptions of her costume of "cadet blue with military trimmings" and a "red dress,
trimmed with black velvet."

Unlike Alice, Edith could not have cared less how her outfit was
described. Her concern was all for Theodore as he entered the
Senate chamber escorted by a senator and a representative, and
for the children, who nearly fell over the balcony rail in their
excitement. And no wonder, she thought. Theodore did look every inch a hero, bronzed by his hunting trip, shoulders thrown
back, muscles bulging under his tightly buttoned frock coat, a red
carnation in his buttonhole.

"A great work lies ready to the hand of this generation," he
proclaimed. "As we do well or ill, so shall mankind in the future
be raised or cast down."

And to Edith's relief, for once his voice was not high and
strained, with that sort of squeaky resonance. "He was very quiet
and dignified," she wrote Emily, "spoke in a low voice and yet so
distinctly that not a word was lost."

It was Alice, not Edith, who felt insulted when their party of
nineteen, in spite of their own assigned policeman, had to wait

for twenty minutes in a pouring rain for conveyances to take them to the White House for the inaugural luncheon. She had been delighted, however, when a similar deluge had descended on the presidential ceremonies, held on the Capitol portico, drenching the participants as well as the guests. It was Father who should be getting the top honors, she thought, not this mild, paunchy, good-natured but obviously ineffectual McKinley.

Quentin had already arrived at the White House, delivered by their faithful servant Pinckney, and was already occupying center stage.

"What do you suppose he just said?" Mrs. Elihu Root reported to Edith. "I asked him if he knew what his father had become because of the morning's ceremonies. 'Just Father,' he replied confidently."

With six children to watch, Edith did not enjoy the luncheon. Ted, to her dismay, drank two glasses of champagne. Probably he thought it was bad fizzy water and was unusually thirsty. Fortunately it seemed to have little effect, which, as she wrote Emily, "speaks volumes either for Ted's head or the President's champagne." She was concerned also for Ida McKinley, who looked pale and drawn, her blue eyes clouded as if with pain. So it was true that she always sat beside the President at dinners and that he watched her closely, ready to cover her face with a large handkerchief if she showed signs of one of her fainting spells, later to be diagnosed as epileptic attacks. His hand strayed to the handkerchief protruding from his waistcoat pocket, and his attention seemed divided between his guests and his wife.

"Please, my dear," the First Lady suggested to Edith after the luncheon, "bring Mrs. Cowles and Mrs. Robinson up to our rooms for a little. I want to get better acquainted with all of you."

"Oh, but are you sure—"

"Yes. Please."

They found her resting on a chaise longue. Close beside her was a table on which stood a little Austrian vase in which bloomed one beautiful red rose. As they sat down, she pointed at the vase and said with a glowing smile, "My dearest love brought me that rose. He always brings me a rose every day. Oh," she continued softly, "my dearest love is very good to me. Every evening he plays eight or ten games of cribbage with me, and I think he sometimes *lets* me win."

Edith marveled. She realized suddenly that she had been pitying the First Lady. But no woman who was the object of such complete and single-minded devotion was to be pitied, rather to be envied.

Sharing the presidential box that night at the inaugural ball in the gallery of the Pension House Office Building, Edith was glad that Ida McKinley in her dress of heavy white satin, its front panel embroidered with pearls, its bodice of rose-point lace, was the object of admiring glances. Her own white dress with its silver and chenille embroidery and modest train, she was sure, attracted far less attention. Since the First Lady was too frail to dance, Edith was almost sorry when she and Theodore were prevailed on to come down from the box and join the revelers. She insisted on their walking just once in stately fashion around the room, though she knew Theodore felt more like prancing in a continuous round.

Three days, and the excitement was over. The next morning, March 5, 1901, she bundled the children into the train and left for Sagamore, much to the disgust of Alice, who was still pouting over the little-girl dress of white point d'ésprit which Edith had bought her to wear to the ball. If she could have stayed with Auntie Bye, she was sure she could have maneuvered herself into an adult role in Washington society. Hadn't she just turned seventeen? Theodore remained to fulfill his official duties, presiding over the Senate for a mere four days, after which Congress would adjourn until December. He arrived at Sagamore charged with the excitement of the inauguration and in high spirits. No problems to solve, not a care in the world. A whole spring and summer to spend frolicking with his "bunnies"!

His euphoria lasted perhaps a week. Picnics, clambakes, point-to-point races, pillow fights—all were snacks, no substitutes for a substantial diet. He became restless, began fuming, complained that the Vice Presidency was a sham and should be abolished. He wrote hundreds of letters, many of them to his Rough Riders, who were always needing help, started another book, but two years as governor, with his fingers in the hot, spicy political pie, had spoiled him for humdrum desk work.

In May Fanny Parsons and her husband Jim came for a weekend. Sagamore was at the peak of loveliness, the orchard in full bloom, the woods aglow with the pink and white magic of dogwood. But it was cold. Fanny was shocked to hear Jim suggest a swim in the bay, a suggestion which Theodore and his sons acted on with gusto, though one of the latter remarked with foreboding, "Mr. Parsons is going to hear from Mother!"

"Jim, how could you be so foolish!" Fanny rebuked him.

"Well," he replied, shivering, "I knew Teddy would make us do it sooner or later and I thought I might as well be the hero of the occasion."

The subsequent dash down Cooper's Bluff probably saved the shivering swimmers from pneumonia. But in spite of Theodore's persistent activity, Fanny noticed a change in him. "As always," she wrote, "Theodore was vital and stimulating, but there was a difference. The spur of combat was absent. It was another atmosphere."

But there was occasional relief from the doldrums. Also in May Theodore took Edith and Alice to perform the official opening of the Pan-American Exposition in Buffalo—to Alice's intense satisfaction. A sign that at last she was considered grown-up! While Edith reveled in the pictures and statuary and the Temple of Music, Alice rode on camels and tapped her foot to the new dance called the "hoochee-koochee."

In spite of Theodore's restlessness, for Edith it was a nearly idyllic summer. For the first time since their honeymoon she had Theodore close at hand. She bought a new brown mare, naming it Yagenka, and every day they took rides together. Even the family's ailments—Alice's abscess in the jaw, Archie's chicken pox, Quentin's infected ear, Theodore's bronchitis after his usual hunting trip—were passing worries.

But for his sake she was glad when he left for a speaking tour late in August that took him from Minnesota to New England. To help the sick children convalesce, she took them all for an outing in the Adirondacks at the Tahawus Club, one of Theodore's pet conservation projects as governor. Theodore planned to join them there in the middle of September. Then they would all enjoy a vacation in the wilds and do some mountain climbing.

Came September 7, when Theodore was expected to join them at a friend's lake camp, meeting them there for lunch. But on the way she was interrupted by a telephone message. Theodore would be unable to join them. President McKinley had been shot. She could not believe it. That mild, good-natured man, so devoted to his wife, inspiring such hatred? It was incredible. It was, she discovered later, as she had suspected, the work of an anarchist, a Pole who had come up to the President at the Buffalo Exposition with a gun concealed beneath his handkerchief. When the President, thinking it a bandage, had reached out toward the man's left hand to shake it, the man had fired two shots. McKinley was not dead but seriously wounded. Theodore was leaving for Buffalo from Vermont at once.

Strangely, the thought did not occur to Edith that the tragedy might affect their own fortunes. She felt only horror and grief, especially for the gentle, ailing Ida McKinley. Suppose her "dearest love" should die! Never again to have a lovely fresh rose by her side each day! And for her, always the lonely evenings when they had once played those happy games of cribbage! Not so Ted and Alice, especially the latter. Though they remained dutifully sober, secretly they exchanged glances of hopeful triumph. The superstitious Alice had long been practising every sort of magic to get her beloved father into the White House, herself beside him.

To Edith's intense relief a telegram arrived the next morning, Sunday. The President was much better. Theodore found it no longer necessary to remain in Buffalo. He would soon join them for the anticipated vacation.

"Theodore arrived," Edith wrote Bamie, "naturally much relieved at the recovery of the President. It has really been a most trying position for him. . . . Rain is pouring, and we are planning to camp out tonight."

That afternoon she and Theodore, with Miss Young, the governess, Kermit and Ethel, two guides, and a group of students, tramped five miles up the trail to Mount Marcy, arriving at two cabins on Colden Lake. Ted and Alice had gone to another camp for an outing with a group of their young friends.

"We had a delightful day," Edith wrote Emily, "for, in spite of the rain, the woods were beautiful and we dried ourselves before blazing fires and enjoyed the good supper the guides cooked for us."

The next morning Theodore and the other men started for the trip to the top of Mount Marcy while Edith, Miss Young, and the children returned to camp on the Upper Works. On the way they were passed by a guide moving swiftly in the direction of the mountain. Edith looked after him, wondering. "I should have asked him where he was going," she called back to Miss Young. "Oh, he told me," the governess answered. "He has a message for one of the party going up the mountain."

Theodore arrived at the Upper Works camp at six that evening, tired and hungry. The message had been for him from Elihu Root. The President was worse. Members of the Cabinet thought he should come to Buffalo. He sent a message to the clubhouse at Lower Works ten miles away, where the nearest telephone was located, to pick up any more recent messages. But there had been none.

"No reason yet to hurry back to Buffalo," he told Edith wearily. "I have been there once and that shows how I feel. I am going to wait here."

At eleven o'clock there was a brisk knock at the door. A guide had brought a sheaf of telegrams from the Lower Works. The President was dying. Theodore must come at once. A special train would be waiting for him at North Creek.

Outwardly calm but inwardly terrified, Edith saw him go. That road! Thirty-five miles in a buckboard over treacherous mountain terrain to North Creek, where the train would be waiting! It would be bad enough by daylight, but at night, rutted and dangerously washed by days of heavy rain, the road would be almost impassable. Archie's wailing did not help. Father was going away to be shot, he howled, like Mr. McKinley! Yet a girl there at the Upper Works remarked later on the calmness of both the Vice President and his wife.

It was the longest night Edith had ever spent. She passed most of it pacing the floor, picturing the buckboard and its occupants at the bottom of some precipice. As soon as it was light she bundled the children into the waiting cart and started down the mountain. At the Lower Works she was handed a telegram.

"President McKinley died at 2:15 this morning. Theodore Roosevelt."

Again her first feelings were grief and pity for the woman who had suffered such irreparable loss. It was only later that it suddenly occurred to her that Ida McKinley was no longer the First Lady.

Herding the children together, she traveled the rest of the way down the mountain to their rented cottage and began hastily to pack. At the same time Theodore was taking his oath as the twenty-sixth President of the United States.

Part Four

FIRST
LADY

Edith's arrival in Washington as First Lady was no occasion for festivity. She came heavily veiled, and, though an object of curiosity, she was by no means the center of attention. The crowds in the station were waiting, not for her train but for the evening special bringing McKinley's body from Buffalo. It was a scene of mourning, not rejoicing. And she went, not to the White House, now her logical home, but to Bamie's at 1733 N Street, where she was joined presently by the nation's new President, who had come with the funeral train. It was their first meeting since the fateful incident which had suddenly thrust them both into such unexpected and untried roles.

She scanned his face anxiously. Was he nervous, a little frightened by the challenge? True, he looked very grave and, yes, older, but nervous? Frightened? Hardly. He might have been looking forward to a Western hunting trip or even to an obstacle race with his "bunnies." It was she who had misgivings. The next morning, when gathered with others of the funeral guests in the White House Red Room, she could not help expressing her fears to their old friend of the early Washington days, Grover Cleveland.

"Oh, Mr. Cleveland," she worried aloud, "my husband is so young!" And, indeed, at not yet forty-three, Theodore was the youngest man ever to accede to the office.

The genial ex-President smiled. "Don't worry, my dear," he said confidently, "he is all right." Nothing could have given her greater relief and assurance than those simple words from a man who had faced the same formidable challenge not once but twice.

The new First Lady had no meeting with the former one during her brief stay in Washington. The grief-stricken widow received no visitors. Had her "dearest love" arranged for the continued delivery of a single lovely red rose, wondered Edith, so that she had one on this bleakest of all days? She hoped so. After Theodore left that evening for the burial services in Canton, Edith prepared to return to Sagamore Hill the following morning for a last week before assuming in fact as well as in name her new role. Just a week—to adjust herself to complete emergence from her precious shell of privacy!

The week was all too short for winterizing the house, sending vans of furniture and other necessary supplies to Washington, getting Ted off to Groton, preparing the other children for the most violent change in their frequently altered lives. That they were already fully aware of the situation was evidenced by the row of dolls she found ranged on a bed in the nursery, each one equipped with a black arm band. "For poor President McKinley," four-year-old Quentin explained gravely.

This time, when she arrived in Washington on September 25, 1901, with Ethel, Kermit, her cook, and two maids, Rose and Mary, plus all the present menagerie which the boys could carry in their arms, she went straight to the White House. Theodore was already installed, having come two days before. Inspecting the place now with the eyes of its mistress, she was appalled. Big, yes, impressive with its long corridors and huge public rooms, but, oh, so dark and gloomy and, if you looked closely, actually shabby! Stuffy! And the section on the second floor reserved for the family—how could eight people and more be crowded into those five bedrooms, with their two outmoded bathrooms, a small guest room, a maid's room, and a sort of library! At least half the floor, all the space over the huge East Room, was taken up by executive offices, separated from the family quarters only by a glass screen. Clearly something radical must be done.

Meanwhile she did as much as possible—flung up the windows to air the place out, shifted furniture, sent some of the horsehair relics to the attic, made the rooms homelike with flowers from the greenhouses, some of their best-loved books, toys, personal treasures, and allotted the limited space to family members. She and Theodore would use the large southwest bedroom overlooking the Washington Monument. Alice would have the second largest room opposite looking out across Lafayette Square, Ethel the tiny room on the southeast corner. The four boys would have to

share rooms, the two youngest together conveniently close to
their parents, Kermit alone while Ted was at Groton. There was
left a small room for the two maids, Rose and Mary. The other
servants would have to room in the basement. Fortunately
Mame, who was suffering from many ailments and becoming
more and more crusty and demanding, was remaining at Sagamore for the present. By the time the rest of the family arrived, all
except Alice, who was pursuing her quest for independence at
Bamie's home in Farmington, Connecticut, reaction from the excitement had set in, and Edith collapsed from weariness, sleeping
some forty-eight hours. "To me the shadow still hangs over the
White House," she wrote Emily soon afterward, "and I am in
constant fear about Theodore. He is well, but I have to consider
him at every turn to make all go smoothly."

Thanks to her calm and capable supervision, however, go
smoothly things did. She enrolled Kermit in a public school, an
action which commended itself to most people in the country,
Ethel in the Cathedral School in Washington, where she would
board five days a week. Alice would also attend the Cathedral
School when she arrived—a possibility which that young lady
heartily opposed. She had had enough of schooling.

By the time Archie and Quentin arrived, the middle of October,
Edith had established a fairly firm routine, which included
breakfasting with the family, then walking with Theodore in the
garden, consulting with the White House steward, chef, and
maids about plans for the day. Edith was determined to be her
own housekeeper rather than hiring one as other First Ladies had
done. However, it was her plan to delegate to specialists the responsibility of preparing food for official dinners, even though
caterers were expensive, charging up to $7.50 for each guest. This
would save her much work and also protect her from public criticism.

One way she devised to lower the expenses of social activities
and control excessive entertaining was to consult with Cabinet
wives in the meetings she held with them each Tuesday in her
personal sitting room (the former library.) They were not gossip
enclaves or sewing circles, but serious discussions, like the ones
their husbands were having with Theodore in another room of

the White House. Tactfully she led them in setting boundaries for entertaining so that competition would be avoided. Though the presidential salary was $50,000, she knew there was need to economize.

Fortunately at present there was a minimum of entertaining, for the city was still in mourning. Even the personal letters she wrote were bordered in black, like the one to Fanny Parsons telling her of the "lovely cluster of Virginia catchfly" she had seen at Tahawus. "You must put it in your next edition. Theodore is very well and of course bears all this responsibility with the utmost ease."

Theodore was deeply appreciative of her own ease in making adjustments. "Edith is too sweet and pretty and dignified and wise as mistress of the White House," he wrote one friend, "and is very happy with it." And to another he boasted, "She is forty, and I do not think I deceive myself when I say that she neither looks nor feels as if she was thirty."

The children, too, were adjusting to the new life with remarkable expertise, especially the three youngest, Ethel, aged ten, Archie, seven, and Quentin, four. On arrival about four one afternoon, they inspected the White House hastily but thoroughly from top to bottom, penetrating corners and crevices probably unexplored except by mice and spiders since the days of the equally adventurous Tad Lincoln. Then they started on the outside.

They arrived at the park across Pennsylvania Avenue about dusk, just as the watchman was climbing his short ladder to light the streetlamps. Ethel's eyes sparkled. What a chance for a new game! As soon as the lamplighter had finished lighting one row of lights and was out of sight, she would shinny up the posts and turn them out, repeating the fascinating procedure to the glee of her younger brothers and the bewilderment of the poor public servant. Just as he had finished with one side of the park, the other would be in darkness. But the sport ended when they were discovered, were made to confess their identity, and were brought home in disgrace. Such exploits with her brothers, Edith told her with an attempt at sternness, must cease. Meekly, but with inward reservations, the child agreed.

Though she adjusted as well as her brothers to the new environment, like them Ethel had no intention of conforming to its rigid standards. Born between two sets of boisterous male siblings, she had acquired few feminine niceties of dress and conduct. She regarded with amazement and disdain the little girls of her age who, as was proper, came to pay their respects to the President's daughter. They were one and all dressed for their formal calls as fussily as their mothers, with silk or satin skirts, little velvet jackets, flowered hats, and, of all things, gloves! They looked like little mannequins in a store window!

One Saturday morning Ethel was summoned to meet one of these young guests. She had been in the stables, and looked it, short hair disheveled, face streaked with dust, simple everyday clothes in disarray. She found her guest sitting primly in the hall, immaculate in her finery, not a ruffle or a hair out of place.

"I'm sorry to keep you waiting," Ethel greeted her breathlessly. "I was down in the stables trying out a new pony."

"Oh!" The other child's face lighted eagerly. "Could I play with you? It sounds exciting. Could we really play with the horses?"

Ethel regarded her with pitying horror. "Play!" she exclaimed. "With you all dressed up like that? Why don't you go home and get on your everyday clothes and come back? Then we can play."

History does not record whether the guest accepted the invitation or not.

Edith was in hearty sympathy with Ethel, even though she knew she could not always condone her hoydenish ways. She believed that clothes for her children, whether boys or girls, should be comfortable and practical, and she had always dressed them accordingly. However, she realized that Mame's stern tutelage had not extended to disciplines preparing a young girl for Washington society. That was why she and Theodore had chosen the Cathedral School for Ethel rather than trusting her education to a governess. Five days a week she not only would be separated from the boys but would enjoy the companionship of girls of her own age and class, while receiving training in manners as well as in French and history and mathematics. After school and on weekends all the children were free to choose their own pursuits.

Both parents believed in imposing as few restrictions as possible. And the children took full advantage of the liberty permitted.

Within days of their arrival they were as much at home in the White House as at Sagamore Hill. It was all theirs (at least most of it and much of the time)—the long halls and corridors, the marble staircases, the huge rooms, public as well as private. They slid merrily down the flights of stairs on trays borrowed from the kitchen. Even the ladylike Alice, when she arrived just before Christmas, deigned to try out that sensation. It was almost as exciting as catapulting down Cooper's Bluff. The halls and corridors with their hardwood floors seemed made for roller-skating and bicycling, or, even more challenging, negotiating on stilts.

As Ike Hoover, the head usher, described it helplessly, "No stairs were too well carpeted or too steep for their climbing, no tree too high to scramble to the top, no furniture too good or chair too elegantly upholstered to be used as a resting-place for the various pets in the household."

Jacob Riis could believe that. One day he was having breakfast with the family. This was a rare treat for any visitor, for it was the only meal the family was sure of enjoying all together, and strangers were seldom invited. As so often in conversation with his best friends, Theodore had been talking about the children's interests, which always included their pets.

"I wish you could have seen Kermit's kangaroo rat," he commented. "It's one of his latest acquisitions, a cute little fellow."

"Oh, but he can," volunteered Kermit eagerly. "I've got him right here in my pocket."

Forthwith he produced the little beast, which hopped daintily across the table, now on two and again on three legs, stopping to sniff at a lump of sugar held out by the President. After it had made its rounds, the little animal was returned to Kermit's pocket, where it undoubtedly snuggled down contentedly. No one seemed surprised or disconcerted, not even the guest, for he had long known the Roosevelts. In fact, Riis had often marveled at the possibilities of a boy's pockets from a study of his own children's. Fishhooks, jack stones, bits of glass, even frogs he was familiar with. But this was a new one, a tame rat!

Of course the children were not completely uninhibited. Edith,

especially, exerted a certain amount of discipline, much more
than Theodore. But even he drew the line at some indignities.
The flower beds in the White House gardens, he told them, were
not to be used as practicing ground for stilts, a prohibition which
elicited an indignant response from Quentin. "I don't see what
good it does for you to be President. You can't do anything here! I
wish I was back home."

Theodore also made the East Room and some other parts used
for official purposes off limits. And they must not be seen in the
downstairs rooms when they were open to sightseers, nor must
they interfere with official guests or be destructive to the furniture. "No?" questioned the poor servants, seeing the younger
ones bouncing on the best sofas, walking on their stilts in the
halls, riding their bicycles in the long corridors, taking their pets
to bed. But even they were so intrigued that they could not help
feeling lenient.

With only a few reservations the White House belonged to the
children, and the children belonged to the people. Not since Wil-
lie and Tad Lincoln had young presidential offspring so captured
the affection and imagination of the country. Tales of their doings
soon were convulsing not only Washington but a much wider
audience.

"Have you heard what Kermit said when a schoolteacher asked
him what his father did for a living? 'Father?' he replied airily. 'Oh,
Father's *it!*' " or "Did you know T.R. has a pillow fight with his
boys every night?" Or, "They say one of that little Quentin's best
friends is Roswell Flower Pinckney, son of the black White House
steward!"

But of all the stories none exceeded for amusement the one
about Archie and his pony. Some months after the family arrived
Archie succumbed to measles. Quentin decided that nothing
would help him get well as fast as the sight of his beloved calico
pony, Algonquin. They decided to take him up in the elevator.
Charlie Lee, the White House coachman, adored the children and
was happy to cooperate. They got the pony into the basement,
thus escaping the attention of ushers and guards in the foyer. Up
Algonquin went in the elevator, and Quentin had his wish. Un-

doubtedly the sight of his cherished pet hastened the patient's recovery.

The two younger boys soon proved too much for the French governess to discipline, and of course Edith was too busy to spend much time with them. One day when she and Theodore were taking their ride in Rock Creek Park, they stopped to chat with the black policeman who was director of the chain gang building one of the park roads. The man remarked that he had a son out of work and that he wished there might be an opening for him in the White House. That was how young James Amos came to be the caretaker of the Roosevelt children. Edith wanted someone who could play with them but who knew when play must stop. Amos suited the job to perfection. One of his duties was to care for them at their meals. When he was having lunch with them one day, Edith and the President entered.

"Where is this wonderful man I have been hearing about?" demanded Theodore. "By George! I hear you have these rascals under command. Bully for you!" "Why can't we have James in our dining room, too?" he asked Edith before he left. "He can help up there after he gets through with the kiddies."

So it was that James Amos became a valued member of the household, serving in many capacities for the next seven years.

If the country found the Roosevelt children intriguing, it was equally enamored with the personality of the new presidential incumbent. The mood of the new century was one of progress, of crusading, and "Teddy" with his youth, his abounding energy, his reputation for reform, suited it to a T. The people, most of them, were "dee-lighted." Not all, however. Now that "that madman" was actually in the White House, Platt, Hanna, and their associates in big business were apprehensive. His first message to Congress, when he spoke of industry being regulated, of its vast wealth being shared more equitably, of all the people being assured of a "square deal," was not reassuring. And one small act of friendliness outraged a whole segment of the population.

Theodore had scheduled some meetings with the eminent black educator Booker T. Washington in October, about a month after he had become President, in order to discuss with him how he could best help not only the blacks but the whole South. Arriving at the house of a friend, Washington found a note from the President inviting him to dinner at the White House. "Dear Mr. President," he wrote back, "I shall be very glad to accept your invitation for dinner this evening at 7:30."

It was a pleasant informal meal, with few other guests. The two men had a profitable discussion about plans for the South. Both Theodore and Edith were amazed at the repercussions. Southern whites were scandalized. WHITE MEN OF THE SOUTH, HOW DO YOU LIKE IT? demanded a New Orleans paper. "When Mr. Roosevelt sits down to dinner with a Negro, he declares that the Negro is the social equal of the white man." A Memphis paper declared that the President had perpetrated "the most damnable outrage ever."

"Bigots!" Theodore blustered. "I shall have Dr. Washington to dine just as often as I please." But Edith knew he was disturbed.

Her own first test as White House hostess came with the advent of 1902. The New Year's reception, beginning an hour before midnight, found her descending the stairs in a white corded silk gown and leading the procession at Theodore's side to the Blue Room, where they received the long parade of distinguished guests according to strict protocol: foreign ambassadors, Supreme Court justices, senators, representatives, army and navy officers; then an endless succession of other dignitaries, culminating with more than five thousand ordinary citizens. It was a repetition of Albany on a much grander scale. As there, Edith discouraged physical contact by holding a bouquet of orchids and lilies of the valley. Two hours and a half of smiling, greeting, chatting, acting as usual as a quiet foil for Theodore's ebullience, and it was over.

"You've done your part," Theodore told her at one-thirty, "and admirably, as usual. I'll stay a bit longer so as not to disappoint the people who have stood outside so long in the cold." In all, 8,110 people passed through the line.

It was only the beginning. The next night Edith was hostess at her first Cabinet dinner, this time attired in pale blue, her favorite color—a more severe test, since it involved leadership in conversation, made more difficult because she and Theodore, facing each other across the center of the hourglass-shaped table, could scarcely see each other through the masses of begonias and maidenhair ferns. But she was surprised at the ease with which she had slipped into the role of First Lady of the land. She was even more surprised, and embarrassed, to read journalist Jake Riis's assessment of her impact on Washington society.

"As mistress of the White House," he wrote in an article published that year, "Mrs. Roosevelt has won the hearts of everybody and the secret of it, I am persuaded, is as much in her love for her husband that grasps his work with level comprehension— seeking to be truly a helpmeet to him—as in her own genuine interest in the duties devolving upon the President's wife. Easy they are not, these duties. I fancy they would tax the energies of many a less even-tempered woman."

She was not the center of the next big event, which occurred the following night. Alice, a few weeks from turning eighteen, was making her debut at the most important ball to be held in the White House since the era of Dolley Madison. But that young lady was less than thrilled. In fact, she had been displeased ever since she had come just before Christmas, relieved that the Cathedral School idea for her education had been given up. She thought the presidential quarters as ugly and dowdy and inconvenient as the mansion in Albany. She considered its furniture and decorations "late General Grant and early Pullman."

And she disapproved of Edith's plans for her coming-out party. Waxed white linen crash over the worn, mustard-colored carpet in the East Room! How could one dance a lively polka or a Strauss waltz, even to the music of the Marine Band, on something like a *sponge!* Such crudity would not be tolerated in the high society of Newport or Boston. Why, the whole East Room was not much more modern in appearance than when Abigail Adams had used it to hang out her wet washing! Alice confessed, however, that her stepmother was not to blame for the room. Edith was doing her best to have the whole house remodeled and had asked Alice to assist her with the plans.

Another grievance was Edith's decision against including a cotillion in the dancing, with its constant switching of partners and the bestowal of favors on all the couples. There was always a cotillion at the fashionable debuts Alice had attended. She would have liked to buy decent gifts for her friends who would be coming from New York and Boston. They were accustomed to really fine favors, like little evening bags studded with pearls or rhine-stones, or little watches or bracelets, or, for the men, cigar light-ers or silver cigarette cases. Her own generous allowance from the Lees would have paid for all sorts of such gifts. But, no! Her stepmother insisted that all must be paid for out of Father's pock-ets. Edith had always been penurious. Bamie would not have objected, Alice was sure, for her aunt had almost always let her have her own way when she wanted something badly.

An even worse disappointment—there was to be only weak fruit punch at her debut instead of champagne. A horrible blow to her pride! But she could not blame her stepmother entirely for that. Father was a prudish stickler for abstinence, especially where young people were involved. So aggrieved did Alice feel that she had to run off to Auntie Bye's to shed a few tears.

However, when the evening arrived, there were mitigating fea-tures. At least she looked grown-up in her white chiffon, the skirt and bodice trimmed with white rosebuds, her arms graced with long white silk gloves and hair piled high in a fashionable pompa-dour. And Edith, who presented her, looked very attractive in her white lace and silk. As Aunt Conie reported afterward, there were "men seven deep around her all the time," and the beautiful conservatories with their flowering plants and palms were entic-ing retreats for the girls in their gay gowns and the youths, many of them college athletes or young soldiers in uniform. The buffet supper, too, arranged in the State Dining Room soon after mid-night, though simple, was tastefully served, and then the dancing continued to the fashionable hour of two, when the marines brought it to an end with "The Blue Danube Waltz."

Though the newspapers reported that "no jollier company was ever assembled in Washington," and Aunt Conie was sure that her niece "had the time of her life," Alice's own appraisal of the affair was only mildly favorable. "I myself enjoyed it moderately," she remarked.

Edith was conscious of her stepdaughter's displeasure and knew that much of it was directed toward herself. She was both hurt and distressed. Her relationship with Alice had always been imbued, on her part, with a feeling of guilt. She had been right, she knew, in insisting that the child be a part of her father's family, yet she suspected that her stepdaughter would have much preferred living with Bamie. The two were much alike in temperament: outgoing, gay-mannered, always on the *qui vive,* easily expressive of their emotions. Edith knew, too, that Alice had needed the discipline she had tried to give her, somewhat in defiance of Theodore's easygoing indulgence. Had she been too strict with her? But certainly no more so than with her own children. Perhaps also, though she hated to admit it, was there a tinge of jealousy in her feeling, a sensing that this child of his first marriage was a reminder to Theodore not only of his beloved first wife but also of his old super-righteous sense of guilt in having taken another?

All the children's exploits, like Alice's debut, were grist for an avid press, but the girl's vivid personality especially captured the delighted attention of the country. Stories about her were rampant. Her looks, her clothes, her tastes, her beaux, her habits—"Did you know that she actually smokes cigarettes? Not in public, of course!" "They say she even has a pet green snake which she carries around with her?"—were all subjects of national interest. One of her favorite colors, a shade of blue-gray christened "Alice-blue," became popular with thousands of doting admirers and was immortalized in a hit song, "Alice Blue Gown." Almost as many babies were named Alice as Theodore. And when in February 1902, Prince Heinrich, brother of the German Kaiser, came to America on an official visit, it was Alice who was chosen to launch the Emperor's new racing schooner.

She acquitted herself with poise and dignity at Shooter's Island off Jersey City, christening the yacht *Meteor* in a firm clear voice, careless of the champagne spattered on her blue velvet gown, and at the state luncheon that followed she graciously accepted a bracelet from the Emperor containing a miniature of himself surrounded by diamonds. It was no wonder that after this regal ceremony she was dubbed throughout the country "Princess Alice."

Theodore was for the most part proud of his daughter, though not for the same reasons as the intrigued public. "She does not stay in the house and fold her hands and do nothing," he remarked with satisfaction to a friend. "She can walk as far as I can and often she walks several miles at the pace I set for her. She can ride, drive, ski, shoot, although she doesn't care much for the shooting."

Thanks to the alert newsmen, the country was equally involved, this time with concern, when Ted became violently ill with pneumonia. Edith rushed to Groton, and two days later Theodore followed, then Alice. The other children, left behind, were for once docile and quiescent. Archie expressed their emotions in a brief letter. "I hop [sic] you are beter." For a week Edith remained constantly at the boy's bedside, while the press unfolded to the public, day after day, the gravity of the boy's condition. DOUBLE PNEUMONIA screamed a headline, later in succession, STILL IN DANGER, CHANCES BETTER, then finally, SAFE. The country could breathe again. Government business, which had seemed momentarily suspended, could resume. Theodore returned to Washington, and a week later Edith brought the patient home to convalesce, "bundled to the eyes in blankets."

Ted, of all the boys, was least adjusted to the new role of President's son. At fourteen he was already conscious of its penalties. He had once thrashed the schoolmate who called him "the first boy of the land." Edith, always perceptive of her children's moods, tried delicately to probe his emotions.

"Why should I enjoy Father's being President?" he blurted. "Don't you see it handicaps a boy to have such a father, especially to have the same name?"

"Yes," Edith sympathized. "I suppose it does."

"Don't you know," he continued, obviously relieved to give voice to his secret feelings, "there can't ever be another Theodore Roosevelt? I'll always be honest and upright, of course, but I'll always be just Theodore Roosevelt's son."

"Oh, my dear!" Edith was dismayed. How long had he been feeling this way? And yet how very natural! What could she say? For a moment she was at a loss. Then—"I understand," she said, smiling. "In fact, that's just the way I have felt myself."

His eyes widened. "You!"

"Yes. Being called First Lady. I knew I could never live up to the name. Think of all the wonderful women who have borne it— Martha Washington, Dolley Madison, Abigail Adams. Then it just came to me that all I have to do is just be myself. Just being the best self possible, I decided, was all that mattered."

Ted's worried frown disappeared. He nodded appreciatively. Mother and son had never been closer than at that moment.

Edith's "best self possible" was proving more than adequate. She ran a well-ordered household: breakfast at eight-fifteen, spending a half hour with the children until time for the older ones to leave for school; at nine going over the morning mail with Belle Hagner, her efficient new secretary, sorting out the hundreds of requests and answering some with her own hand; listing the cards of visitors and deciding which ones she would see (fortunately the First Lady was not expected to make calls!); lunching with Theodore and his special guests at one-thirty; entertaining at afternoon tea with Alice by her side, or, if no tea was planned, a ride with Theodore on their favorite horses, accompanied only by an orderly, changing their route each time to avoid the throngs of sightseers; enjoying until dinner the "children's hour" in her room; dinner, usually with many guests; getting the children to bed, if possible after a rowdy pillow fight with Theodore; evenings usually devoted to the public.

Though not a scintillating hostess like Dolley Madison, she presided over luncheons and dinners with gracious ease, sometimes five or six in a week. While establishing few precedents like Martha Washington, she continued the custom of weekly receptions, her version taking the form of a musicale on Tuesday or Friday, beginning with dinner for twenty or more guests at eight and at ten adjourning to the East Room for programs, sometimes simple songs and chamber music, occasionally that first spring with world-renowned artists like Ignace Paderewski and Pablo Casals. Though Theodore preferred ragtime, he was dutifully attentive, greeting the artists and thanking them. If, as one journalist commented, he got restless and his gaze wandered, teeth baring as he smiled and bowed to some friend in the audience, Edith's reproving glance would bring him back to attention.

Hostess, manager, correspondent, entrepreneur, socialite, mother, wife—yes, and intelligent listener, adviser, sometimes gentle but stern critic for a President beset by political problems. While she hemmed some of the hundreds of linen handkerchiefs requested, made "by her own hands" for charitable sales, she would listen to his arguments, agree, sympathize, and urge moderation, more tact and less of bombast, with her gentle, "Now, Theodore . . ."

That spring of 1902 she was immersed in another major task, the renovation and remodeling of the White House. Even a long reluctant Congress had admitted that something must be done. Plans had been designed, and Congress had appropriated over half a million dollars for the job, some $65,000 of it to be spent "at the President's discretion." A new West Wing would be erected for executive offices, leaving the space over the East Room for enlargement of the cramped living quarters. There would be two extra suites with bedrooms and baths for guests. Alice would rejoice in a new polished floor in the East Room replacing the old mustard-colored carpet. No more dancing on waxed linen crash! The family would have to move out for six months, but that was no problem. Summer was coming, with its welcome exodus to Sagamore.

Edith was anxious to have the house restored as nearly as possible to the original concept of Washington's time, and she was very much involved in the plans. Since the chief architect, Charles McKim, had his headquarters in New York, she could follow the project closely from Sagamore—too closely perhaps from the architect's point of view, for they were soon engaged in correspondence about designs and colors for draperies, wallpaper, furniture (she did not like the writing desk he had chosen for her, it should be rosewood to match the carved bedroom pieces), pictures (she would like to have all the ladies of the White House, including herself, placed in the downstairs corridor near the dressing rooms, also the busts). She did not hesitate to take exception to his choices, and she could be imperious in her demands.

She left with the children on June 9, leaving Theodore in their temporary lodging at 22 Jackson Place, off Lafayette Park. He arrived at Oyster Bay three weeks later, leaving Washington in a flurry of cartoons, one of them depicting a morose Uncle Sam contemplating a bare expanse labeled "White House. Gone to Oyster Bay, Back in the Fall. T.R.," while the latter, perched on the

White House and wielding his "big stick," was dragged off by an elephant into the distance.

As he descended from the train at Oyster Bay, he was greeted by a milling crowd, his assistant secretary William Loeb, some of his children, a drenching rain, and a blast of thunder. Loeb urged him to ride home in the covered surrey in which he had brought Ethel and Kermit, but the President scoffed. "No, no, just get me my overcoat. And no umbrella! Never use one." He would ride in his own uncovered carriage. And he did, Ted and his cousin George Roosevelt riding horseback behind. They all arrived at the house drenched and dripping, to find Edith and Quentin waiting on the porch.

"Upstairs, everyone," she greeted cheerfully. "Get into some dry clothes." She was used to such emergencies. Theodore's arrival meant only that she now had five boys instead of four.

In some ways it was like every previous summer; in others, like none that had ever been. There were the same hikes, picnics, swims, races, tennis matches (with Father still grasping his racket like mad halfway up the handle, yet managing a very good game). But never before had they been accompanied on every exploit by an armed guard. Never before had Father worked each morning at offices in Oyster Bay with his two secretaries to take care of a mountain of mail. Never before had he been closeted with so many important officials. Never before had there been so many guests, tourists, reporters, sightseers.

For Edith only one guest was not welcome. She refused to be present when the Russian Grand Duke Boris, a notorious womanizer, sought an audience. Theodore, too, was a stickler for morality, but he could not deny the request of Cassini, the Russian ambassador. He entertained the two visitors at lunch, while Edith, Theodore explained, was absent because of a previous engagement. She had gone to lunch at their neighbors', the Emlen Roosevelts.

"I regret not to find Mrs. Roosevelt at home," rumbled Cassini with obvious displeasure.

Another guest was not too pleased with his visit. Platt, who came in July, was distressed to find the President of the United States in rough riding clothes instead of the proper frock coat and top hat. Theodore was late to lunch that day, and, since even at Sagamore no one could be seated before the President, Archie was sent to find him. Presently they rushed into the dining room, Theodore in pursuit of the boy. "You abominable little rascal!" he was shouting in apparent rage. "You incorrigible scamp!"

Platt was dumbfounded. When Theodore caught up with the child, he fully expected grim chastisement, but to his amazement and relief the boy was merely hugged. It had all been in fun.

For Platt the shortcomings of the family were not ended. "What will you have to drink, my friend?" Theodore asked him at lunch.

"Whatever you have," responded the guest politely.

"Oh, I always have tea," Theodore said pleasantly, while well aware that the favored response would have been something like a double whiskey. He turned to the servant. "Give the senator a cup of tea."

Another guest that summer, an Englishman named Bullen, was far more appreciative. The luncheon, he reported, had been delightfully informal, with simple food: a cup of bouillon, lamb chops with new peas and potatoes, and watermelon for dessert. "Not the best but the brightest, jolliest meal I had in America. For the President would be the life and soul of any party. His vitality is so amazing, his fun so contagious, his earnestness so convincing."

Surrounded by guards and the familiar environs, Edith was almost free from worry about Theodore's safety that summer. But uneasiness again reared its head when in August he began a speaking tour of New England. When on September 3, his last day on the road, she received word that he had met with an accident, her heart quickened ominously. But the cause was not a crazed assassin. In Massachusetts his carriage had been run into by a trolley car. His Secret Service man had been killed, but Theodore, though thrown thirty feet, had proceeded with his tour and was making his last speech that night in Bridgeport. Taking his secretary Loeb and some of the family, Edith rushed to Bridgeport, Connecticut, by the presidential yacht, the *Sylph,* and Theodore, bruised and bandaged and limping, returned with them. Nothing mattered, he insisted, but the death of his loyal guard, who had been a great friend of all the children, especially Quentin. "How my children will feel!" had been his first regretful reaction.

Worry became even more nagging when on September 15 they opened the estate to neighbors and friends, and eight to ten thousand people came. Theodore's invitation had been general. They came "in special trains and in steamboats and behind their own farm horses, a happy, jostling, county fair crowd." Though Edith knew that the guards, reinforced by the White House chief usher and eight New York detectives, were meticulously alert, screening each newcomer carefully, she was terrified. It was at just such a public reception as this that McKinley had been shot, and there had been guards there too. It was a year ago, almost to a day, that he had died! Yet, seeing her move about, attractive in a gown of cream-colored voile embroidered with point appliqué, her smiling features protected by a wide garden hat, making sure the supplies of ginger snaps and raspberry shrub were kept in constant supply, no one would have guessed that under the serene surface that telltale heart was again skipping about irregularly. Certainly Theodore, shaking the myriad hands, sixty of them, it was reckoned, to a minute, and beaming "dee-lightedly" on each individual, had no thought of danger.

"Tired!" he scoffed in response to one woman's sympathetic query. "No. It takes more than a trolley car to knock me out, and more than a crowd to tire me."

"Crowd" was a mild word for the assemblage. Even "mob" would not have done it justice. The three thousand crystal punch cups engraved with "Theodore Roosevelt, 1902," which were bestowed as favors, were soon exhausted.

Some of the White House staff were doubtless relieved when the family with its appurtenances left for Oyster Bay each summer, though they soon discovered that the house seemed deplorably empty. At least they could wax and polish the beautiful parquet floor in the East Room without finding it grooved and streaked soon after with the marks of roller skates.

Edith was also relieved each time they arrived at Sagamore. The children could run wild here. No more worries about damage to public property. And surely Theodore was safer than shooting across the country making speeches and exploring the wilds—yes, even than riding in Rock Creek Park. Yet even here she was besieged with doubts about his safety. Once he took Ted and the young cousins on an all-night horseback ride to Sayville to visit his uncle, Robert Barnwell Roosevelt, on the South Shore. She worried all the time they were gone. No guard this time to protect him! When they returned, she had paced the porch for what seemed like hours.

"I am glad to see you safely home, Mr. President," she greeted him with apparent calmness.

That Edith's fears were justified was abundantly proved on a later occasion. One summer night she rushed downstairs at the sound of great commotion. There were loud voices outside. Theodore came in and spoke reassuringly. "It's nothing. The Secret Service men have just been having a tussle with a drunken man, that's all."

But, as Seaman, the farm manager, told her, it was far from all. A man had driven up in a buggy, saying he had an appointment with the President. The guards had dismissed him, having had no notice of such an appointment. Fifteen minutes later he had come back, was again turned away, then was back again. Suddenly the President had appeared on the porch, his white shirt front a perfect target. "There he is!" the man had shouted and had urged his horse forward. Only the quick action of the Secret Service men had stopped him by leaping at him and dragging him to the ground. A loaded pistol had been found in his carriage. To Theodore's disgust the incident was reported in the newspapers the next morning. When he read about it, Jacob Riis hurried out to Oyster Bay.

"Promise me," he demanded, "that you will never expose yourself like that again. Standing there on the porch like an invitation for a bullet! Promise, I say!"

Theodore had already turned aside Edith's similar pleas with a light, "Nonsense! The man was just a harmless nut, had some kind of a grievance against the world. His brother was out of a job, it seems, and he got all stirred up. I'm sure he was just bluffing."

He still regarded the incident lightly. "All right, I promise. But what would you have had me do? Hide, when that Secret Service man was fighting my fight? Should I have left him to do it all by himself?"

"That's his business," Riis retorted, "not yours. And you're the President. The whole country is your responsibility."

Theodore was obviously not convinced, and Edith was far from satisfied with his reluctant promise. She began to count the months, almost the days, when his term as President would be over.

2

For Edith life had become a series of Theodore's departures, and each left behind its full measure of worry and responsibilities. Seeing him off September 19 on a trip which would take him to the West, she was doubly concerned. There was always that nagging worry for his safety, but now an additional fear. Surely he was walking with more of a limp, and he seemed to twinge with pain at every step. And no wonder! On September 24 she rushed to Washington from Sagamore on learning that his leg had been operated on in Indianapolis for an inflamed abscess. The Western trip had been abandoned, and he was now laid up in their temporary headquarters in Washington at 22 Jackson Place. Four days later he had further surgery and was confined to a wheelchair.

"They made a gash nearly two inches long," Edith wrote Kermit, who had just enrolled at Groton, "and scraped his shin bone."

The aftermath of the encounter with the trolley car was to cramp his flamboyant style for the rest of his life.

While in Washington Edith had a chance to inspect the progress of the White House renovation. She was delighted. The new white and buff color scheme was a happy reminder of colonial days. The upper hall with its green-burlap-covered walls would make an excellent gallery, central to the house, for her desk and favorite pictures—yes, including the controversial one by George Watts, *Love and Life,* which previous occupants had banished to the Corcoran Gallery. Here it could cause no shock waves in

prudish visitors. Especially was she pleased with the master bedroom with its pink and green drapes and matching upholstery.
Some of the furniture had been used by the Lincolns. Perhaps the
spirit of the Great Emancipator remained to inspire Theodore in
solving problems. He certainly needed it right now, for he had
plunged into stormy and controversial waters.

Soon after taking office he struck out at the Northern Securities
Company, an attempt by the powerful financier J. P. Morgan to
found a huge new railroad monopoly, which was arousing public
outrage. It was Theodore's first application of what was soon to
be termed his "big stick," derived from the old African proverb
"Speak softly and carry a big stick." He brought suit against the
company and demanded its dissolution on the ground that it was
illegal, having violated the Sherman Antitrust Act. Not that he was
opposed to bigness, or to trusts—good trusts, that is. "Bad"
trusts, those which resulted in monopolies, opposing the public
welfare, must be dissolved. "Good" trusts must be merely controlled.

Naturally, leaders of the huge corporations were outraged, but
Theodore was adamant. Though it would take him two years to
get a decision from the courts, he would win the fight for the
federal government, and his reputation as a "trust-buster" would
be made, to the chagrin of the lords of finance and the cheers of
the common people.

Then he became embroiled in another fight against even more
powerful corporate leaders, one that affected the well-being of
the whole country. In the spring of 1902 the United Mine Workers
had called a strike of some fifty thousand anthracite workers after
the operators had refused their demands for a 10 percent raise in
pay, an eight-hour workday, and recognition of their union. Theodore believed they were justified in their demands. Working conditions in the mines were dangerous, wages were low, and the
men worked long hours. But the operators were adamant. One of
their leaders, George Baer, pooh-poohed the workers' claims.
Why, they didn't suffer, he maintained, they couldn't even speak
English! By September of 1902 prices were rising. Winter was
approaching. Without swift action the country would be suffering
from the cold, plus a shutdown of railroads and factories.

The impasse reached a crisis. The price of coal rose to thirty dollars a ton, and soon there would be none at any price. On October 3 Theodore called a conference of important leaders in his temporary residence, for the White House was still in process of reconstruction. In the group were Baer, John Mitchell, the young union leader, Attorney General Knox, and others. Still in his wheelchair, wearing a gray dressing gown, Theodore tried to persuade them to accept the findings of an arbitration committee. Mitchell accepted. Baer not only refused but did so in the most insolent and abusive language.

"We object to being called here to meet a criminal," he snapped, "even by the President of the United States." He demanded that the miners be sent back to work, even if troops had to be sent in to make them.

"Arrogant stupidity!" Theodore fumed to Edith after they had gone. But the meeting had given him an idea. Troops. Yes, he *would* send in troops, if necessary, to seize the mines and have the government operate them. Public opinion would support him. Unconstitutional? Perhaps some people would say so, but what was government for but to serve the needs of the people?

"I tell you," he probed the air with a determined finger, "the Constitution was made for the people, not the people for the Constitution." Edith did not counsel moderation this time. Experience had told her when to keep silent, and, as so often, he was right. When he made his intentions known, the operators, as he had expected, capitulated and agreed to arbitration. Some of the miners' demands were met, not all. But the strike ended. The country would be warm that winter.

During his term of office there were other instances of his stern insistence on justice, even in high places. At one time corruption was discovered in the Post Office Department. Party officials favored a hush-hush treatment of the scandal, fearing it would hurt their chances in the next election. Not Theodore. "I want the truth," he declared, "the whole truth, and I don't care a rap who gets hit." He appointed special counsel to investigate, and cases of fraud, blackmail, and conspiracy soon came to light.

"There can be no greater offense against the government," he wrote his Attorney-General, "than a breach of trust on the part of a public official, and, of course, every effort must be executed to bring such offenders to punishment by the utmost rigor of the law."

Party bosses became angry. They pleaded, stormed, almost resorted to tears to keep prominent Republicans from being indicted. But T.R. was adamant. Let the party lose the next election if its leaders preferred corruption to justice. He and Edith chuckled over a cartoon depicting Theodore standing by a well, marked "Post Office Scandal," and cranking down an "investigation" basket containing the Postmaster General. It bore the following caption: "T.R.: You must go clear to the bottom. P.G.: There doesn't seem to be any bottom."

By mid-October of 1902 Theodore was able to occupy his office in the new Executive Wing west of the restored colonnade. It was a beautiful little structure and provided plenty of space for the President and his thirty-eight assistants. Edith herself had helped plan the decor of his office with its burlap walls and curtains, its divan, comfortable chairs, fireplace, portrait of Lincoln. With satisfaction she watched him, still hobbling on crutches, take possession of his new domain, saw him installed behind the big mahogany desk, heard his familiar roar of laughter as he dictated letters to his capable secretary Loeb, who had been with him since the Albany days.

The family moved into the remodeled house on November 5. Dismayed, she found Theodore planning immediately for a Southern trip. Though he was walking now with only a slight limp, surely it was too soon to subject his injury to the risks involved in travel. Fortunately she did not know that the chief object of the journey was not official business but a bear hunt in the wilds of Mississippi. He left, accompanied by Loeb and the necessary guards, also by a bevy of journalists who haunted his every move. He had his bear hunt, but, as he wrote a friend, it was most unsatisfactory. "There were plenty of bears, and if I had gone alone or with one companion I would have gotten one or two. But my kind hosts, with the best of intentions, insisted on turning the affair into a cross between a hunt and a picnic . . . and I never got a shot. Naturally the comic press jumped at the failure and have done a good job laughing over it."

This was not the whole story. His hosts, determined to supply him with a trophy, managed to capture a bear cub and tie it up near the camp, then led him to it. He must have something to show for his trip. "What!" Theodore was indignant. "Shoot that poor helpless creature? Not on your life! Don't you dare harm it. Take it out into wherever you found it and let it go!"

Reporters got wind of the incident, and it reached the Washington papers. A famous cartoonist, Clifford Berryman, drew a picture of it to illustrate the event, showing Theodore—spectacles, bared teeth, bandanna, cowboy boots, and sombrero complete—seated with a protective arm about a very small brown bear. It caught the attention of a Brooklyn store owner, who had a bright idea. He made a stuffed toy bear and wrote to the President. "Could I use the name 'Teddy's bear' for my toys?" he asked. Theodore shuddered. That horrible name "Teddy"! But he gave his consent. So was born the teddy bear, in time to become a national institution as all-pervasive and far more prolific than the American eagle. Samples of this clever production would soon be visible in nurseries across the country, including that at Sagamore Hill, where they can still be viewed nearly a century later.

Theodore entered his second full year as President with aplomb and Edith with quiet satisfaction.

"Well, I have been President for a year and a quarter," he wrote their friend Mrs. Bellamy Storer, "and whatever the future holds I think I may say during that year and a quarter I have been as successful as I had any right to hope or expect. . . . It has been very wearing, but I have thoroughly enjoyed it, for it is fine to feel one's hand guiding great machinery, with at least the purpose, and I hope the effect, of guiding it for the best interests of the nation as a whole.

"Edith has enjoyed it too. I do not think my eyes are blinded by affection when I say that she has combined to a degree I have never seen in any other woman the power of being the best of wives and mothers, the wisest manager of the household, and at the same time the ideal great lady and mistress of the White House."

Guests at the first big diplomatic reception on January 8, 1903, two thousand of them, were given glimpses of her personal contributions to the remodeled mansion. There was the gallery of First Ladies' busts and portraits in a "warm and spacious corridor" inside the new south entrance, among them her own impressive portrait by Chartrain, recently presented as a gift from the French people. It showed her seated on a bench in the White House garden, wearing a white chiffon dress, a black coat, and black Gainsborough hat. Those invited to dinner, among them Theodore's old college chum Owen Wister and his wife, were served on the new china she had selected, there being not enough left from previous sets to serve the more than a hundred guests which the State Dining Room could now seat. Since American potteries did not yet produce as fine work as the European ones, she had chosen over 1,300 pieces of creamy white English Wedgwood decorated with a two-inch colonial motif and embossed with the Great Seal of the United States.

"Very handsome admirable dining room," wrote Wister, "new furnished; simple, dignified new wainscoting of natural wood; and round about, the solemn heads of moose and elk. . . . No display, everything simple—but dignified—as the President's house ought to be."

Theodore left all arrangements for such banquets to Edith—the menu, prepared with the city's caterer, Rauscher, the list of guests, the seating, his only provision being that there would be no bores in his vicinity. Edith's menu for this particular banquet was typical of her choices for a diplomatic dinner, international in its variety. It included Cape Cod oysters on ice plates, potage consommé, tartalettes à la Moelle, mousse of lobster à la Richelieu, English pheasant roasted, paté de foie gras en Bellevue, cheese, petits fours glacé, marrons glacé, bonbons, and, of course, appropriate wines. Theodore paid for it all out of his own pocket, having a horror of being accused of sponging on the government.

Hostess, yes. She played the part to perfection. But the roles she liked best were wife and mother. In fact, she was disappointed that spring when her hopes of another child were ended, as they had been the spring before, by a miscarriage. Not Theodore. He felt that they had plenty of children already, especially since one of them was Alice.

At nineteen Alice's conduct was fast becoming a headache for her parents. Beautiful, high-spirited, headstrong, she was satisfying her thirst for independence with a vengeance. Theodore was both frustrated and infuriated. She was courageous, yes, he certainly approved of that, and intelligent, if she but indicated some inclination to use her brains. But he did not approve of her friends, most of whom he despised as the "vulgar rich." "The house is lonely with only the two little ones and Alice," he wrote Ted in January 1903, "who generally makes her appearance well after noon having been up until all hours dancing during the night before."

Thanks to her liberal Lee allowance, she was able to purchase a little electric runabout which she drove all over Washington, a veil tied over her cartwheel hat. She was seen driving by herself, unchaperoned, to Newport, her favorite haven of fun, which Theodore considered the "mammon of iniquity." It was reported that she rode with one of her friends in a thunderous racer from Boston to Newport in an incredible six hours. When Edith and Theodore forbade her smoking in the White House, she cheerfully agreed and continued her practice of smoking on top of it, up on the roof. "Frightfully annoying for the poor things," she wrote later, "but they were very good about it, both of them."

Of course her exploits were bruited over the country by the delighted press, and the public absorbed them avidly, as much intrigued as shocked. A cartoonist produced a drawing showing a curious baffled crowd joined in the concerted cry of "Alice, Where Art Thou?"

One day she kept waltzing in and out of T.R.'s office while he was having a serious discussion with Owen Wister, her emerald green snake Emily Spinach (named after her unfortunately thin aunt) twined about her arm. The visitor became annoyed.

"Isn't there anything you can do to control Alice?" he asked.

"My dear man," replied her father, half despairingly, half humorously, "I can do one of two things. I can be President of the United States, or I can control Alice. I cannot possibly do both."

He tried hard, hoped to create new friendships by sending her to New Orleans with Edith Root, Elihu's daughter, to see the Mardi Gras. He sent her on a goodwill visit to Puerto Rico to inspect schools and lay cornerstones, and took her with him on a political trip to Cincinnati.

Alice was present, unwillingly, at a White House family dinner in March when Eleanor, who was visiting Bamie, had been invited. Theodore had always been especially fond of his unfortunate brother Elliott's daughter. Edith marveled at the change wrought by three years at the famous Allenswood School in England. The shy, awkward girl had become a tall, confident, self-assured young woman. She was not beautiful, she could never be that, but she was graceful and exceedingly attractive. And the one fine feature, her eyes, blue and warmly vibrant, made one overlook the too prominent teeth and slightly receding chin.

When Theodore began talking, as he liked to do, of his father and the good times he and Elliott had had as boys, especially of their visits to the Newsboys' Lodging House, Eleanor came glowingly alive. "Oh, yes," she said eagerly. "Once I helped Father serve Thanksgiving dinner to the newsboys. I've driven through those slums since, and, oh, there's so much poverty! I wish I could do something about it, the way Grandfather did."

"And why not?" Theodore regarded her with awakened interest.

"But—how—what? What is there for a woman—"

"I'll see that you meet my friend Jake Riis. He'll tell you plenty you can do."

"Oh, Uncle Ted, *would* you?"

Alice's voice broke in, amused, curious, a bit disdainful. "You sound like some others of our last year's debutantes, so enthused about their Junior League, whatever it is. Next thing we know you'll be working in some lousy settlement house."

Eleanor made no reply, but the glints in her blue eyes sharpened. She obviously did not find the suggestion distasteful. Alice left as soon as decency permitted for the engagement she had been persuaded to postpone. When she saw her father again, it was once more to experience his displeasure.

"Out again until dawn, and sleeping until noon," he commented grimly, "and I can well imagine the company you were in. Empty-headed young women, interested in nothing but pleasure.

Why, I ask you, can't you be serious, be interested in something worthwhile, like—yes, like your cousin Eleanor?"

Alice made a wry face. "Like my little mealymouthed cousin? I should hope not. She's always been a frightful bore, full of duty, never gay, not like you and me." She smiled mischievously. "Don't you know what people say, that I'm a chip off the old block? Don't we both say what we think, do what we want to do or what we think is important, no matter what other people say?"

For once Theodore was at a loss for words.

Spring, it seemed to Edith, should have brought release from hectic social and political pressures. Instead it brought only separation. In April 1903, Theodore started on a two-month trip to the West, combining politics with recreation, making speeches and attending receptions, spending a fortnight in the Yellowstone with John Burroughs, the naturalist, exploring the Yosemite with another nature enthusiast, John Muir, traveling three weeks with Nicholas Murray Butler of Columbia, reliving his halcyon days with old friends at Medora. Edith tried to assuage her loneliness by taking the three youngest children on a cruise in the naval yacht *Mayflower,* but they were back in time for the Easter Monday egg-rolling frolic on the White House lawn, a custom started long ago by Dolley Madison which Edith denounced as "needless destruction of the lovely grass." But at last on June 5 he was back.

"I wish Nannie could have seen my homecoming last night," Theodore wrote Lodge. "Washington, to my utter surprise, turned out and gave me a cordial welcome. Edith, with Alice, Ethel, Archie, and Quentin—all five in their best clothes, and Edith in a dress she knew I like—were waiting for me at the window of the East Room. It is not good taste to speak about one's wife; but in writing to my closest friend I can be allowed to say that though Edith looked frail she looked so pretty that upon my word she seemed to me just as attractive as seventeen years ago when I crossed to England to meet her."

He had returned fired with the urge to push new legislation for conservation. He wanted the Yosemite put under national control. "I want to go just as far in preserving the forests and the wild creatures as I can lead public sentiment," he declared. He had plans, too, for a more ambitious physical program, complaining that he was getting fat and lazy. He needed the stimulus of the "strenuous life," for he was struggling with knotty problems— tariff, currency, chiefly the building of a canal across the isthmus connecting North and South America. With the abrogation of an old agreement with Great Britain, the United States was now free to build the canal by itself. A treaty had almost been concluded with Colombia for an annual payment giving right of way, but the Colombians, hoping for more money, were refusing to sign.

Theodore had brought the children a badger, which was greeted with the wildest enthusiasm and named Josiah. It was a new treasure to supplement the White House menagerie consisting of Tom Quartz, a kitten, Kermit's kangaroo rat, Eli the blue macaw, and Loretta the parrot, plus the pony Algonquin, Bozzy, Kermit's dog, and another dog named Jack. It was soon discovered, as Archie put it, that Josiah "bites legs sometimes but never bites faces."

"A nervous person had no business around the White House in those days," wrote Ike Hoover in his memoirs. "He was sure to be a wreck in a very short time."

Although Edith had long become inured to the grueling schedule of the White House and the mad rush of social and political activities required of the First Lady—yes, even to that constant fear for Theodore's safety—she was still counting the months— weeks—almost the days when they could leave the presidency behind. Then slowly she came to the realization that there might be too many to count. The possibility suddenly became less vague when Fanny Parsons and Jim visited them in the fall of 1903.

"If it should be possible for us to attend the convention," Fanny said at dinner that evening, "when you'll be nominated for President, I do hope we can have tickets. And of course we want to be there when you're inaugurated in 1905."

Theodore shook his head ruefully. "How do we know I could get elected, or even nominated? If people read the papers, they must think me the most despicable cur possible." He grinned widely. "But if I should be nominated and elected you shall certainly have tickets, both for the convention and the inauguration, the best places at the latter to be had."

"Oh, can you really do that?" inquired Fanny.

He smiled, a little grimly. "Well, there is *one* thing a President generally *can* do. He can get tickets!"

Edith smiled also, but it was a forced smile, and her heart under the becoming low-cut bodice of her dinner gown seemed to skip a beat. Five years more instead of one?

Even with the election a year away, suddenly it seemed to be on every mind in Washington, especially Theodore's. She could see that he wanted, desperately, to enjoy another term, this time not by accident but in his own right. He could not possibly finish all the goals he had set for himself in one year's time, though in at least one area he was making a gallant effort. Dirt was going to fly in Panama, he was resolved, long before the election. Unable to effect an agreement with Colombia, of which Panama was a part, he did not hesitate to look benignly, if not to promote, an insurrection among the nationalist Panamanians, nor was he slow in recognizing the new Panamanian government once the revolutionary coup was completed. Work would begin on the new canal long before the year was over.

If Edith felt qualms about the likely continuation of her strenuous duties and personal fears as First Lady, she gave no outward sign. Whether reading stories to the children, presiding at a dinner for fifty noted guests, or, perhaps the same evening receiving five hundred more people at a musicale, she remained serene, always gracious and courteous, in complete command of the situation. That she, like T.R., was often the butt of critical gossip, she was well aware. Some, including her old friend Henry Adams, complained because the White House entertainments were too lavish, resembling royalty. It was unimportant. President Washington and Martha had endured the same criticism. More amusing was the reported comment of Mrs. Stuyvesant Fish, one of New York's "Four Hundred," about her manner of dress: "The wife of the President, it is said, dresses on three hundred dollars a year, and she looks it."

Edith was rather pleased with this printed comment, which she cut out and pasted in her scrapbook. She was not ashamed of being frugal. As one columnist wrote, she was not "a woman who centers her attention on clothes. Her gowns last sometimes three seasons, with the sleeves altered now and then to bring them up to date." She altered her wardrobe in other ways, too. "I have had my black velvet hat done over with black roses very prettily," she boasted once to Emily.

Comments by columnists and publicity hounds did not disturb her. In fact, she was showing far more expertise in dealing with the press than First Ladies before her. Of course, the public demanded information about the President's family and their doings. It would not be wise to bar all reporters from the White House as Frances Cleveland had done. Far better, if one had to appear in print, to supply a certain amount of information, though as little as possible!

She furnished pictures of herself and her children and included photographers and reporters to be briefed on preparations for such special activities as Alice's debut or a musicale or a state dinner. For such events she arranged for Belle Hagner, her secretary, to release pertinent details. In this way she could control most of the publicity about the family and the White House and keep it to a minimum.

"I believe," Alice accused her once laughingly but shrewdly, "that you actually *manage* the news." And to some extent she did, even using occasional guile, as when she would wear the same dress on two successive occasions and tell reporters to describe it as "green" one time and "blue" another. Her methods succeeded, as she intended, not in increasing public fanfare about the family but in lessening it.

In fact, so reticent was she about permitting publicity that few people realized what major influence she exerted on Theodore. Each day she read three or four New York and Washington newspapers and briefed him on items she thought he should read. She often, as one journalist reported, put "a gentle brake upon her husband's 'headlongness'" with her "Now, Theodore," when the President would "become meek" and protest, always in the same words, "Why, Edie, I was only—"

But the same journalist noted that she helped him most through her "infinitely superior insight" into men, since she was a much better judge of character. "Never, when he had his wife's judgment, did he go wrong or suffer disappointment."

She did not succeed, however, in influencing him when his Secretary of War, Elihu Root, resigned that February, and Theodore appointed William Howard Taft in his place. With his huge girth (over three hundred pounds), genial manner, and walrus mustache, he was a friendly, outgoing person, but Edith suspected that he was too much under the thumb of his competent, ambitious wife, hence possessed the weak will of a yes-man. Theodore did not agree with her, to his later sorrow.

Theodore had no suspicion that Edith's desire for a second term was less strong than his own. That was evident in a letter he wrote Ted in May.

"I do not think any two people ever got more enjoyment out of the White House than Mother and I. We love the House itself without and within, for its stateliness and its simplicity. We love the garden. And we like Washington. We almost always take our breakfast on the south portico now, Mother looking very pretty and dainty in her summer dresses. Then we stroll in the garden for fifteen or twenty minutes looking at the flowers and the fountain and admiring the trees. Then I work until between four and five. . . . If Mother wants to ride, we then spend a couple of hours on horseback."

It was true. She did love the White House. She had enjoyed the three and a half years, even with their grueling demands on her time and health. Of course they had brought fear, worry for his safety. But marriage to Theodore would always mean uncertainty. Remember the hunting trips west? Remember San Juan? Martha Washington had called her experience as First Lady her "lost years." For Edith, she realized suddenly, they had been her "found years," when she had discovered resources in herself which in her wildest dreams she could not have imagined. So . . . if what Theodore wanted was another four years of this turbulence, then it was what she wanted, too.

The news came on June 23 that the Republican Convention had nominated him by acclamation. Theodore did no campaigning, made no speeches. It would not have been becoming for a President. He trusted to his achievements to win him the election.

They were many, if not all he would have liked. He had created a Department of Commerce and Labor, established forest

reserves and promoted the irrigation of dry land by the government. He had settled the Alaska boundary, ended the coal strike,
broken the backs of some of the major trusts. The Panama Canal
was under construction, with the scourge of yellow fever controlled by discoveries in the Spanish War and the work of the
eminent William Gorgas, who, through his many experiments as
an officer of sanitation in Havana, had discovered that the disease was transmitted by mosquitoes. It was a pity that a statement of Dr. Benjamin Rush a hundred years before had not been
taken seriously. During the terrible epidemic of 1793, which had
claimed thousands of victims in Philadelphia, one of them the
first husband of Dolley Madison, that eminent physician had
noted that in that fatal autumn "mosquetoes [*sic*] were uncom-
monly numerous."

Theodore's trust was in the people, in their belief in his
"Square Deal," which aimed for fairness in all political and economic relationships, especially those involving capital and labor.
A drawing by the famous cartoonist Homer Davenport expressed
this theme aptly—a broadly smiling Uncle Sam standing with his
hand on Theodore's shoulder, under it the caption: "He's good
enough for me."

Among the guests for the Fourth of July celebration in 1904,
was Eleanor, Theodore's niece, who came for the holiday weekend. She's changed even more, thought Edith, become more confident, more alert. Eleanor had indeed joined the Junior League,
as had been suggested, and had been assigned work at the Riv-
ington Street Settlement in New York. She and Theodore had long
discussions about the conditions she had found, factory girls
working fourteen hours a day for a petty weekly wage of six
dollars, the terrible slum poverty, but also the reforms they were
trying to effect, legislation prohibiting child labor and the cruel
"sweating system." However, there was more to the change in
Eleanor than resulted from this new experience. There was a
radiance about her. "I believe she's in love!" decided Edith.

The weeks of waiting seemed interminable. Life on the surface
was normal—dictation of reams of letters, entertainment of
guests and tourists, long rides through country flaming with sunset colors. But always the Nemesis loomed, that fateful day in

November which would decide their future, in Theodore's eyes the future of the country, perhaps of the world. A cartoonist depicted him throwing the life preserver of his policies to a slowly sinking globe and shouting, "I'll save you!"

It came at last. Theodore left for Oyster Bay to cast his ballot, wishing that Edith and others of his female supporters had a right to vote. He was back on election night. Edith, who had been watching for him at the window, met him at the door.

"What have you learned?" she asked anxiously.

"Nothing yet," he replied, "but it makes no difference how it goes. I had a vision on the train, and it was of you and the children. Nothing matters as long as we are well and content with each other."

Edith smiled appreciatively, if a bit skeptically. For she knew it mattered to him very much.

Ted came running. "Buffalo and Rochester," he announced, "they've sent in their news, and report enormous gains for you." Within twenty minutes reports had come in from Chicago, Connecticut, New York, and Massachusetts, all in his favor. When they sat down to dinner at seven-thirty with Bamie and her family, his election was assured. Archie, bedecked with party badges, kept bringing telegram after telegram of congratulations. The victory was overwhelming. Theodore had received the largest popular vote and electoral majority of any candidate in history.

Cabinet members, reporters, judges, congressmen—all came pouring in, and Theodore in the flush of enthusiasm made a speech which he was to regret all his life.

"On the fourth of March next," he announced, while reporters hastened to record his every word, "I shall have served three and a half years, and this three and a half years constitutes my first term. The wise custom which limits a President to two terms regards the substance and not the form. Under no circumstances will I be a candidate for or accept another nomination."

Edith caught her breath. Why on earth had he said that? If she had known he was going to, she would somehow have stopped him. Not that she wanted a third term! Even now she longed for a return to private life and release from the terrible fear of assassination. But it might well cripple all that he wanted to do. All his enemies need do to defeat his policies was to wait!

Theodore continued to rejoice in his triumph, the greatest he "ever had had or could have." "But I tell you," he wrote Kermit, "it was a comfort to feel, all during the last days when affairs looked doubtful, that no matter how things came out the really important thing was the lovely life I have with mother and you children."

Alice shared Edith's skepticism. One of his "letters for posterity," she was to dub such effusions.

3

It was fortunate that Theodore, as he had assured Fanny Parsons, could secure plenty of tickets for his inauguration on March 4, 1905, for his guests were legion. He was escorted to the Capitol by forty Rough Riders and a company of Civil War veterans, who, as Edith wrote Emily the following day, "looked somewhat shaky on their poor old pins." There were enough Roosevelt relatives to fill several rows of seats, and friends could be numbered by the hundreds. The whole length of the avenue was bedecked with a colorful mass of flags and banners and thronged with crowds of applauding citizens.

Edith and Alice drove to the Capitol an hour later in time for the inauguration ceremonies. After them came another carriage holding Mame, still hale and hearty at eighty, sternly in charge of the four younger children, ranging in age from Quentin, seven, to Kermit, fifteen.

Edith was glad that she had chosen a dark blue suit for the occasion. It was less conspicuous and more in keeping with the dark threatening skies. She was more than glad for Alice, in her white dress and coat and white ostrich-plumed hat, the size of a small cartwheel, to be the center of attention. The latter's pride and dignity, to the amusement of her brothers, were somewhat cramped during the exercises by the effort to keep the cartwheel level, to say nothing of preventing its sailing away in the brisk March wind.

Edith had eyes only for the central figure of the day. It seemed fitting that just as he stepped onto the platform for the inauguration ceremonies, the sun should break through the clouds. As he lifted his hand to take the oath, she was sure she could see the glint of the ring he wore. John Hay had brought it to the house the night before. It contained a small strand of Lincoln's hair. Dr. Taft, Lincoln's physician, had cut it from the President's head after the assassination, and Hay had secured it from the doctor's son. "I want you to wear it," his Secretary of State had told Theodore, "because I believe you are one of the few who most thoroughly understand and appreciate Lincoln." It would be one of Theodore's most precious possessions.

In spite of the high wind Theodore's voice could be heard to the edges of the crowd as he admonished the nation to accept the responsibilities that went with great power. "If we fail," he said, "the cause of free self-government throughout the world will rock to its foundations."

But the excitement had been a little too much. Edith returned to the White House to nurse a headache for a brief interval before greeting about two hundred guests for a buffet lunch, where Bill Sewall and his family from the Maine woods, Rough Riders and Western pioneers rubbed shoulders with scions of New York and Washington society. Then to the reviewing stand, where for some hours they sat and watched the long parade—the Rough Riders and cowboys again, Harvard men in college gowns and caps, miners bearing a banner celebrating the settlement of the coal strike, Indians in war paint brandishing spears and tomahawks—all marching past to the tune of bands blaring the Roosevelt theme song, "A Hot Time in the Old Town Tonight."

Solemnity now behind, Theodore on the reviewing stand was as carefree as the three younger children who were roaming through the crowds snapping pictures with their Brownie cameras. T.R. waved at the bands, tapping time with his feet, cheering when his Rough Riders passed, laughing until the tears ran down his cheeks at the antics of the parade marshals in their top hats and cutaways as they tried to control their prancing horses, and at the cowboys who exhibited their skills by lassoing some members of the crowd as they passed the viewing stand.

An interested Englishman who was in attendance, John Morley, was enthralled by this evidence of contrast in the President. "Mr. Roosevelt," he wrote later, "is an interesting combination of Saint Vitus and Saint Paul. Do you know the two most impressive things I have seen on my tour of your country? Niagara Falls and the President of the United States, both great wonders of nature!"

The day was still far from over. At six there was a reception at the White House for the Rough Riders, then dinner for sixteen family members and close friends, late because there was so much reminiscence of old times with the Rough Riders, to which the children listened with all ears. It was time then to dress for the Inaugural Ball at the Pension Office Building. Both Edith and Alice had new gowns for the occasion. Following the custom of Martha Washington, who had worn only American-made fabrics, Edith had the silk woven for her in Paterson, New Jersey, after which the pattern was destroyed. It was a beautiful creation of robin's egg blue brocade, with a raised gold design of ostrich feathers, interspersed with medallions of gold. The bodice was fashioned of family heirloom lace more than two hundred years old. Tonight, contrary to her custom, she wore resplendent jewels. Adding to its splendor, the costume ended in a court train three yards long. Alice's gown was of gold gauze with a white satin top and a long train decorated with pink roses. Later, Edith's costume would be preserved in the Smithsonian.

Fortunately she was not expected to dance. She and Theodore viewed the scene from the balcony, occasionally moving to its edge to be applauded by the dancers. Unfortunately the railing had just been painted, and it took all her maid's ingenuity to remove the spots on her skirt. Only once were they called on to go down to the floor, and, with Vice President and Mrs. Fairbanks behind them, they walked to the other end of the hall and back, while many of the ten thousand people who had bought tickets cheered. So heavy was the weight of the gown with its many underskirts of silk that the Grand March was to Edith's relief limited to five minutes. She had refused the two powdered youths whom the committee had offered to hire to hold her train. There was already too much of a suggestion of royalty in the splendid function!

Bone-weary, she was able at last to return to the White House where, strangely enough, there came a burst of renewed vigor. Bamie, Conie, and their families all assembled in her and Theodore's bedroom where, in comfortable *déshabillé,* they drank the President's health with wine from a small bottle which she had unearthed, and talked over old times and childhood days. She was almost sorry when it came time to say good night.

Two of the Roosevelt guests that day attracted special attention, for in December Cousins Franklin and Eleanor had announced their engagement. The family had been surprised, especially Alice, who, while writing her cousin, "Oh—dearest Eleanor, it is simply too nice to be true!", had privately expressed annoyance.

"What in heaven's name can he see in that—that mealymouth! Why, Cousin Franklin is one of the handsomest and most popular eligibles, even if he is a featherduster! He could have almost anybody."

"You, for instance?" Ted had posed slyly.

She had rewarded his impudence with a blush, angry, not guilty, but still a blush. "Of course not! How dare you! As if I'd even think—"

Ted had persisted boldly. "But I'd wager, sister dear, you would have enjoyed the pleasure of refusing him."

Alice had bombarded him with the object closest to hand, which fortunately happened to be a sofa pillow. But his barb had hit too accurately for comfort. She was at the age and certainly of the disposition of a young debutante who enjoyed dangling scalps. All Washington was speculating delightedly on possible husbands for her, and one by one possibilities, including the German prince, had been discarded.

In spite of her pleasure over the announcement, Edith was also disturbed. "Remember," she worried to Theodore, "how Sara Roosevelt refused to let her precious son come to Bamie's for that Fourth of July weekend? She has always looked down on us, I suppose because of poor Elliott. And now to have his daughter—"

Theodore chuckled. "Yes, but remember also that he came in spite of her, and came to visit us, too, when she surely disapproved. He shows some backbone in spite of being known as 'Mama's boy.' And he's shown it this time."

Edith was not convinced. Poor little Eleanor, facing life with the tight-lipped, strong-willed Sara Delano Roosevelt for a mother-in-law! Then she remembered. It was not "poor little Eleanor" any longer. The shrinking violet had become a full-blown rose, one, she hoped, with a few thorns.

Eleanor wanted her beloved Uncle Ted to give her away. Surely that was not Sara's idea! When could you possibly come? the President was asked. March the seventeenth, he replied, at the latest. And March seventeenth it was. The family went to New York where the ceremony was to take place in the house of Eleanor's maternal aunt on Seventy-sixth Street. Alice, to her satisfaction, had been asked to be a bridesmaid. She could not help being relieved that Eleanor had refused to be married, as Father and Mother had suggested, in the White House. Theodore might feel "in a father's place" to Eleanor, but *she* was his daughter. That unique privilege should be hers. Already she had set her eyes on a certain prospect, one not so young and handsome as Cousin Franklin, to be sure, but destined to rise far higher in the political world.

It was a beautiful wedding. The house was a bower of lilacs, lilies, and roses. Guests came swarming, and spectators crowded outside the open windows, for the day was balmy for March. The bridesmaids, including Alice, in taffeta, with silver-tipped feathers in their hair, came sedately down the stairs, followed by Eleanor on the President's arm. She looked beautiful, Edith saw with delight, in her satin gown trimmed with her Grandmother Hall's rose-point Brussels lace, which her mother had worn at *her* wedding. March 17, opportunely, was her mother's birthday.

"Well, Franklin," Theodore's high-pitched voice boomed after the ceremony, "there's nothing like keeping the name in the family."

For once, Edith noted with satisfaction, Sara Delano Roosevelt, who boasted that her son was all Delano and not a whit Roosevelt, was completely eclipsed, this time by the young woman whom she had done her best to keep her son from marrying. But, Edith also noted, it was Theodore, cracking jokes, being fed cake by the bride, greeted with shouts of "Hurrah for Teddy!" by a crowd of boys outside, who was the real center of attention. As Alice once observed cannily, he wanted to be the bride at every wedding and the corpse at every funeral, even the baby at every christening.

Always adept at combining business with pleasure, he spoke that night to the Friendly Sons of St. Patrick at Delmonico's, possibly giving voice to his reactions after the day's bout with New York's high society.

"America is not a matter of creed," he thundered, "or birthplace, or descent. That man is the best American who looks beyond the accidents of occupation or social condition, and hails each of his fellow citizens as his brother, asking nothing save that each shall treat the other on his worth as a man, and that they shall join together to do all that in them lies for the uplifting of this mighty and vigorous people."

But Theodore's concerns had long gone beyond the boundaries of country. And this year was to see his most important contribution to a problem of worldwide import. Russia and Japan were at war over conflicting claims in Korea and Manchuria. It seemed vital to United States interests that neither one should win a complete victory and become a dominating power in the Far East. At first it had seemed that Russia would win a crushing victory. Then Japan had begun to win. In his Inaugural Address Theodore had declared that America's attitude toward all nations "must be one of cordial and sincere friendship," and that it must be shown in deeds as well as words. Now he intended to carry that principle into action. He would try to make peace between the two countries. He would be their mediator. Russia, which was suffering defeat, agreed to a conference. Japan, though wearied and weakened by the fighting, was hanging back. Very well. Theodore would use friendly persuasion. He would send Taft, his genial Secretary of War, with a big delegation on a peace mission to the Far East, ostensibly to visit the Philippines, where he had been a popular governor. Among other countries, he would also be visiting Japan.

"How would you like to go with them?" Theodore asked Alice. She was overjoyed, especially since a particular congressman on whom she had her eye was to be one of the party. Edith soon became involved in her preparations, for Alice's personal maid, Anna, was inadequate to the task. It proved stupendous. Alice must take along all the gowns and matching hats and shoes in her extensive wardrobe, much of it purchased with her liberal allowance from the Lees, all the ruffled petticoats and white suits fit for the tropics, riding habits, bathing dresses, even her sidesaddle. By the time they had finished packing there would be four trunks plus numerous bags and valises, two huge hatboxes, and a big box for the saddle.

As the Washington social season dragged to its end, under her mask of calm Edith was engulfed in weariness. An April cruise on the *Sylph* through the back country of Florida did little to restore her strength, but it gave her an idea. If only they had a rural retreat near Washington where she and Theodore could enjoy rest and privacy for brief respites! Well—why not? She heard of a cabin for sale by a family friend down in the foothills of the Blue Ridge Mountains. She went to explore it. With just the sight of it— simple, a mile in from any good road, surrounded by pine forest —tensions were released, her lungs cleared, and she felt renewed. It was paradise. Her friends the Wilmers, on whose land it lay, sold it to her for only $195. She fitted the three rooms—one downstairs, two up—with simple furniture. It was perfect, only 125 miles from Washington by train to the nearest station, a store only a horseback ride away, and her friends close by. In June Theodore came to visit it for the first time. There was only one flaw in her happiness. He refused to bring even one guard along to secure his safety. And of course he pooh-poohed her fears. Danger here in this wilderness! Why, he was as safe here as in his Western cabin!

"Mother and I have just come home from a lovely trip to 'Pine Knot,'" he wrote Kermit on June 11. "It is really a perfectly delightful little place; the nicest little place of its kind you could imagine. Mother is a great deal more pleased with it than any child with any toy I ever saw, and is too cunning and pretty and busy for anything."

It was a real holiday, before one of the most hectic summers Sagamore Hill had ever seen. Arriving there on June 26, Edith rushed to inspect a big new room which had been built on the north end of the house. Entertaining so many distinguished guests and delegations, they had decided, needed space larger and more dignified than the library and drawing room. Theodore had commissioned his old friend Grant LaFarge, son of the artist John LaFarge, to design this "North Room." "The most attractive feature of my house by all odds," Theodore wrote the architect. It was most impressive, yet homelike. Forty feet by thirty, it dominated the house at the end of the hall, opening up vistas of expansive space with its luminous red-brown woods, its high arched ceiling, its sunken floor. Theodore soon had the walls hung with elk and buffalo heads. Bookcases, tables, sculptures—his prized *Bronco Buster* and St. Gaudens's *Puritan*—figurines, comfortable armchairs, all added to the room's comfort and beauty. To satisfy Edith's artistic yearnings and to balance Theodore's lusty appetite, there were some really good pictures, among them Marcius Simons's landscape *Where Light and Shadows Meet.* It was a room to live in, the most comfortable and attractive one in the house. Soon a huge pair of elephant tusks, gifts of the Emperor Menelik of Abyssinia, would make an impressive archway over the entrance.

Sagamore was almost as accustomed to welcoming international visitors as the White House, but never had there been more important ones than in that summer of 1905. The place became the center of the world's attention. Theodore was bent on bringing the two warring nations to the peace table. Many of his advisers tried to dissuade him. When Taft and his party, including Alice, left for the Far East in June, Japan, secure in her victories over Russia, had shown no signs of yielding. "If I were the Japanese," Taft had said dubiously, "and had just destroyed the Russian fleet, I would ask for surrender, not arbitration!"

"Suppose we get drawn into the war," suggested John Hay, the Secretary of State.

"You may be badly burned," warned his old friend Spring-Rice, who was now a British adviser in Russia.

Theodore continued, unperturbed. When to his deep grief

John Hay died in July, he immediately secured Elihu Root to become Secretary of State. "Join me," he assured the able statesman, "and you will not regret it."

On July 29 he was able to greet Root in jubilant triumph. "Japan has agreed to a conference," he announced. "Taft has just cabled from Tokyo."

Sagamore burst into a fury of preparation. The emissaries, two from each country, their representatives in Washington, would be meeting there on August 5. Representing Russia would be Sergei Witte, the president of the Council of Ministers, and Baron Rosen, the ambassador to the United States. Representing Japan would be Baron Komura, minister of foreign affairs, and Ambassador Takahira. They would meet first at Oyster Bay, then, hopefully, go on to further conference at Portsmouth, New Hampshire.

As the fifth of August approached, Theodore was beset with problems, many of them ridiculously small. While the fate of millions of people hung in the balance, the delegates were bickering over trivialities. Witte, a burly giant of a six-footer, let it be known that he would not "suffer a toast to his Emperor after one to the Mikado." Komura asserted that he, not a Russian, must be seated on the President's right.

"The more I see of the Czar, the Kaiser, and the Mikado," fumed Theodore, "the better I am content with democracy, even though I have to include the American newspapers as one of its assets."

Saturday, August 5, dawned clear and cloudless. A portent for success? Or was its heat an omen of seething dissension? The presidential yacht, the *Mayflower,* was anchored offshore in Oyster Bay, from its mastheads the flags of the three nations fluttering in the breeze. It was to be the scene of this first informal meeting. At nine o'clock Edith rode out to the boat to confer with the chef about the luncheon. Bombarded by reporters on her return, she refused to divulge the menu. Before noon she took the children, along with a substantially stocked lunch basket, to the top of Cooper's Bluff, where they could watch proceedings at close range.

For once she had them all around her, except Alice, who was still cavorting about the Far East. It was strange to see them all together and quiet, even Quentin, who at seven was as volatile as quicksilver. She regarded them with pardonable satisfaction— Ted, the image of his father, being tutored this summer to enter Harvard in the fall; Kermit, still her devoted shadow, sensitive, introspective; Ethel, at fourteen very much her mother's daughter, good scholar, stern devotee of duty, dependable; Archie, indifferent student but handsome, affectionate, lovable, so devoted to his animals that he had brought Josiah the badger along with him today; Quentin—but what words could describe him? A handful, his father had once called him, "who may cause more trouble to others and to himself than Archie." But he had also spoken of his youngest son as "an affable and canny young gentleman," a budding philosopher. To Edith, the youngest of her brood of five would always be her "baby."

"Look! There's Father!" The cry burst from five throats at once.

Shortly after noon the *Mayflower's* launch emerged from the dock with Theodore conspicuously in view, accompanied by his young military aide, Lieutenant Douglas MacArthur. He was wearing what he termed his diplomatic dress—frock coat, striped trousers, white waistcoat, and tall hat—nothing to suggest the military. As he mounted the gangway of the *Mayflower,* the *Sylph,* anchored close by, fired a volley of twenty-one guns. Other launches crowding the harbor followed suit while hundreds of private yachts dipped their flags and cheered. A little later an eighteen-gun salute, the tribute due ambassadors, greeted the arrival of the *Tacoma,* bearing the Japanese delegation, and shortly after one o'clock came the *Chattanooga,* displaying the white, blue, and red flag of Imperial Russia. Then, when they were all aboard, came quiet.

For Edith the next hours were torture. While the children emptied the lunch basket, then erupted into games which became more and more violent, resorting finally to squealing descents and ascents of the bluff, she tried to read one of the books she had brought, but the words blurred. What was happening? This was perhaps the most crucial test of Theodore's diplomatic career. How was he handling those delicate problems of protocol on which so much depended? He was not noted for his tact. The tiniest blunder might queer the whole proceeding.

For once, as she learned later, he was showing remarkable tact. Greeting the delegates in his deplorable French, he introduced the stiffly formal antagonists to each other, careful not to give either party preeminence. "Baron Komura, I have the honor to present you to Mr. Witte and Baron Rosen." They shook hands, the little Japanese and the huge Russian, the others followed suit, and while Theodore indulged in cheerful monologue, an atmosphere of relaxation was created. The problem of precedence at luncheon? He took each of the two leading hostile envoys by the arm and propelled them toward the dining salon. The food was laid on a round table in the center of the room. Each could help himself and go to eat where he pleased. There was no question of precedence. Even the toast was arranged to the satisfaction of all. "Gentlemen, I propose a toast to which there will be no answer and which I ask you to drink in silence, standing. I drink," he went on, "to the welfare and prosperity of the sovereigns of the two great nations, whose representatives have met one another on this ship. It is my most earnest hope and prayer, in the interest of not only these great powers but of all mankind, that a just and lasting peace may speedily be concluded among them."

It was a beginning, though nothing was really settled that day. Theodore was only mildly encouraged. "I thought it my plain duty to make the effort," he confessed to Edith that night. "At least they are talking to each other, and they have agreed to meet in Portsmouth for further discussion." The impasse dragged on for weeks, with meeting after meeting and voluminous correspondence on Theodore's part. Finally, for certain concessions Japan was persuaded to give up her demands for costly reparations from Russia. Agreement was reached on August 30, and the Treaty of Portsmouth was signed. The event was graphically portrayed by a cartoonist showing Theodore bedecked with angel's wings, holding by either hand a giant of a Russia and a pygmy of a Japan and adjuring them, "Now, boys, get together in peace and amity." The following year he would become the first American to receive the Nobel Peace Prize.

Fortunately, Edith did not know of another of Theodore's exploits that summer until it was all over. One rainy day he slipped from the house, a raincoat over his knickerbockers and soft shirt, and traveled in the *Sylph* to the tug *Apache,* beside which in the bay lay a huge torpedo-like craft called the *Plunger,* one of the Navy's submarines. How practical was this startling new invention? He intended to find out. To the shock of the commander, he squeezed himself down through the eighteen-inch opening and for three hours studied its maneuvers, most of them beneath the stormy waters of Long Island Sound, even taking the controls himself. The press joined an outraged Edith in scolding "Our Submerged President" for his recklessness. The very idea of a head of state risking his life in "some newfangled, submersible, collapsible or otherwise dangerous device!" Edith agreed with them wholeheartedly.

After these events all else that summer seemed an anticlimax. But not for Alice, traveling in the Orient. For her each day brought increasingly dramatic excitement. Though it was a large party, at least eighty, a "junket" she called it, for the newspapers it might have been her trip and hers alone. ALICE IN WONDERLAND. HOW FIRST MAIDEN OF LAND WILL TRAVEL TO ORIENT her trip was heralded. "To cross Pacific in Floating Palace—Will have her own suite of rooms aboard—Luxuries of travel—Her father will pay her expenses—Reception in Japan—Will she make speech to Empress as Mrs. Grant had to?—Hongkong—Philippines—Representative Longworth to go along—Tropical romance anticipated," etc., etc.

She swam and went surfboating at Waikiki, where Taft begged photographers not to take her picture, fearing that the public would be shocked by her half-sleeved mohair suit and black silk stockings. She slept in a royal palace outside Peking and ate shark fins and antique eggs. She rode in a tasseled yellow chair carried by eight bearers and curtseyed before the Empress on her imperial throne. In the Royal Hawaiian Hotel in Honolulu she was serenaded by her special song, "Alice, Where Art Thou?" She attempted to learn the hula-hula, inspiring a song by the native musicians in her honor. "Alice Roosevelt, she came to Honolulu, And she saw the hula hula hula hai, And I think before she reached the Filipinos, She could dance the hula hula hula hai."

Being Alice, of course she raised eyebrows in the party. Occasionally she pulled out her fat, old-fashioned vanity case, which held her cigarettes, and had a good smoke. One hot day, standing by the canvas pool that had been rigged up on the ship's deck, a companion, Bourke Cochran, remarked, "It looks so comfortable that I'm tempted to go in just as I am." "Come along," she challenged, and, leaving behind her shoes and watch, jumped in fully clothed in linen skirt and shirtwaist. A plunge in the Stock Market could not have sparked more speculative news.

But the trip was not perfect. She was besieged by conflicting doubts and yearnings. One day, standing beside a good friend, Lloyd Griscom, she said impulsively, "Lloyd, do you see that old, bald-headed man scratching his ear over there?"

"Do you mean Nick Longworth?"

"Yes. Can you imagine any young girl marrying a fellow like that?"

"Why, Alice, you couldn't find anybody nicer."

"I know, I know." She sighed. "But—marriage."

Yes, he was bald, fifteen years her senior—and nice. She had long been attracted to him. Yet she was still uncertain. Almost as upsetting was the fact that in spite of their closeness on the trip he had not proposed.

It seemed a short summer. Edith returned to Washington with Theodore on the last day of September. With the joyful and clamorous greetings of the crowds assembled to meet them, the rush of the new season began. She went with him on a Southern trip in October and was surprised to find herself given almost as enthusiastic a welcome as was accorded him. Evidently most Southerners had forgiven him for inviting Booker T. Washington to dinner at the White House.

The high point of their trip was a visit to Roswell, the old home of Theodore's mother and Aunt Annie Gracie. It was almost as exciting for Edith as for Theodore, since they had both listened to the tales of Mittie and Aunt Annie. It was all just as she had pictured it—the beautiful Bulloch mansion with its Doric columns, its surrounding cedars and backdrop of mountains. It was sad to see it occupied by others. In Atlanta, where she held a reception in the governor's mansion, she left Theodore and returned home, while he went on to Florida.

"Mother was too sweet and cunning for the trip," he wrote Ethel. "Of course she was the feature of the occasion everywhere, and it was great fun having her along. I felt melancholy when she went away."

Alice returned home on October 27, 1905, Theodore's forty-seventh birthday, with the multiplicity of baggage she had taken, plus twenty-seven boxes of presents acquired on the trip, and at last, after four months of waiting, the right to wear an engagement ring.

One night she followed Edith into her bathroom and waited until her mother was brushing her teeth, "so that she could have a moment to think before she said anything."

"I—I think I'm going to marry Nick Longworth," she blurted. "Nick is down in the study talking to Father right now. What—what do you think?"

Edith hastily finished her brushing. Poor child, she thought, so that's why she has seemed so nervous since she returned. She's afraid we wouldn't approve. Smiling, she held out her arms. "My dear, how wonderful!"

"You—you really think so?"

"Of course. Nick is a splendid person."

"And—Father?"

"I'm sure he will approve also."

He did, though his enthusiasm was somewhat lukewarm. "A good fellow," he considered Nicholas Longworth, "and the best violinist that ever came from Harvard." Also, he came from a well-to-do Ohio family, and a successful, if not brilliant, career was predicted for him. His additional fifteen years might tend to curb her headstrong ways. In fact, the relationship seemed to have done so already. Yet there was something lacking—perhaps that ecstasy of romance which her father had experienced with the first Alice? But Edith had no such doubts. "Alice is really in love," she wrote Aunt Lizzie, "and it's delightful to see how softened she is." She merely wondered how the mercurial Alice could possibly contend with the practical details of life.

Now, in addition to the usual duties as First Lady, there were preparations for the coming wedding, only two months away. She could not have done it all without Hoover, the head usher, certainly not without her treasured social secretary, Belle Hagner. Statuesque, striking in appearance, Belle reigned over the White

House details of procedure with iron hand in velvet glove, censoring all visitors, managing the voluminous correspondence, even scouting for bargains in Edith's favorite antique shops. The children loved her. One of her duties now was to send out the thousand invitations to the wedding, for, as one paper put it, "everyone who had ever given 'Princess Alice' a cup of tea expected to be asked." Then hundreds of thank-you notes must be sent for the gifts that came pouring in.

For they were legion and came from all over the world. Every nation seemed anxious to honor the daughter of the popular President. From the Empress of China came a chest with eight rolls of gold brocade, rings, jade, coats of ermine and white fox. From the King of England there was a blue and gold enamel snuffbox, and from Kaiser Wilhelm a miniature of himself set in a gold bracelet; from Victor Emanuel of Italy a huge mosaic table; from the Emperor of Japan a length of gold cloth embroidered with chrysanthemums; and from Cuba came a string of sixty-three wonderful matched pearls. Franz Joseph of Austria-Hungary sent a pearl and diamond pendant, Alfonso XIII of Spain sent antique jewelry.

"Unconscionable!" roared Theodore. "You must send them back!"

"And insult the donors?" Alice returned calmly.

He was helpless, stuck on the horns of a dilemma. She was right. He could not insult his royal friends. Yet he knew very well what his enemies would say—and did. More indications of royalty and greed!

"I'll accept anything," Alice was heard to say, "except a red-hot stove. And even that if it doesn't take too long to cool."

Theodore did manage to discourage an attempt of the United Mine Workers to raise eight hundred thousand dollars as a wedding gift by selling ten-cent subscriptions, but was obliged to resign himself to a carload of the best anthracite. Other donations came from all over the nation: turtledoves, a pedigreed Boston terrier, washing machines, brooms, clocks, luggage, and hundreds of other things, ad infinitum.

To Alice's delight, Saturday, February 17, dawned beautiful and springlike. Crowds began swarming early. All was ready in the

East Room, decorated with Easter lilies, banks of azalea, roses and white rhododendrons. A platform had been erected in front of the gold-draped east window and on it an improvised altar. All attractive but simple, Edith noted with satisfaction. She entered just before twelve on Ted's arm and, as she walked up a ribboned aisle to her front-row seat, hundreds of appraising eyes noted that her dress of brown brocade was not especially becoming. It made her look pale and tired, which was not surprising since she was almost at the end of what Theodore called "her tether."

Alice, on her father's arm, made up for all deficiencies. In her dress of white satin trimmed with rose-point lace that her mother Alice Lee and her grandmother had worn on their wedding days, its twelve-foot train arousing surreptitious whispers, a floor-length veil of misty tulle framing her radiant face, blue eyes as luminous as the diamond necklace, Nick's wedding gift, about her neck, she was the epitome of all beautiful brides. It was *her* hour. She had even dispensed with bridesmaids. Nick, immaculately groomed, impressive in his charcoal-gray Prince Albert, white duck vest, pearl-hued gloves, and white carnation, was at best a foil for her bridal radiance. Even Theodore, who, as Alice had bantered, wanted to be "the bride at every wedding," was for once eclipsed. In fact, his voice could hardly be heard as he gave her away.

It was probably the most publicized social event to have occurred in the White House. The ceremony was solemnized by the bishop of Washington, the Right Reverend Henry Yates Satterlee. A buffet lunch was served in the breakfast and dining rooms, carefully conforming to Edith's standards of simplicity—salads, patés, sandwiches, ice cream, and petits fours. The four-tier cake was cut by Alice, not with the knife beside it, which proved too dull and short, but with a dress sword gaily borrowed from a major standing by. "When she brandished it aloft and began slashing with it," one paper reported, "the slices fell right and left, and great was the scramble among her friends for it. It melted away like snow under a hot sun, and within marvelously few minutes after the first stroke of Major McCawley's sabre not a crumb of it was to be had."

She changed into her going-away dress, a beige color that she suddenly decided looked like mud. She and Nick left through the garden in a two-year-old racer, one of four cars arranged to confuse the crowds, sped on their way by rice from the children and an old shoe thrown by Theodore. After a few days at a friend's estate, they would spend their honeymoon in Cuba.

It was over. Edith succumbed with relief, stretched on the chaise longue in her bedroom, too tired to remove her dress or reach for a favorite book. As Alice was to write later in her memoirs, "Mother was dropping with fatigue and I know what a relief it was to her to have the wedding over at last and me off."

But it was a happy weariness. One little moment of the day shone in her memory like a bright jewel. After the ceremony Alice had turned toward her, stretched out her arms, embraced her, whispered some loving words, and kissed her, not once but twice. In that one act she had made up for all the restraint, the disparity of temperaments, the resentment of a stepmother's discipline, the misunderstandings of which Edith had always been conscious. They were at last truly mother and daughter.

4

"Shocking! Scandalous!" Theodore shut his book with a resounding bang and paced the floor of Edith's sitting room like a caged lion. "No wonder this writer called the place 'The Jungle'!"

Edith's busy fingers rested. She looked up from her embroidery. "You mean the conditions in the meat-packing industry, I take it."

"Yes. You should read the book. It's atrocious. Uncleanness, rottenness, disease!"

"I have read it."

"Oh? Well—then you'll agree. Something must be done about it."

"And of course you're the one to do it," she agreed calmly. Her eyes followed him, sympathetic, amused. "You know what you remind me of? Hercules, about to clean out the Augean stables."

He grinned. "Ha! One of the old boy's twelve labors. Well—he did it, didn't he?" He pounded his right fist into his left palm. "And so will I."

It was not the first time Edith had thought of comparing his crusades with the fabulous twelve labors. Surely the battles he fought with the huge conglomerates—railroads, coal magnates, political bosses—were against beasts, wild boars, or something of the kind. And in trying to preserve public lands, wasn't he also protecting the "golden apples" of Mother Earth? But she knew he was feeling the pressures of tasks far from completed. Only two and a half years! Was he already regretting that hasty statement which had so pleased his enemies?

This goal at least he was able to realize, for that year at his insistence Congress passed the Pure Food Law and soon after another permitting government inspection of meat-packing houses. Another act regulated railroad rates so they did not favor the big corporations.

If the eldest of her "brood" reminded her of Hercules, the youngest resembled another segment of Greek myth. Eight-year-old Quentin flitted about the White House like a gay, elusive Pan, minus ugliness and goat's feet. In the public school he attended he found other free congenial spirits, like Charley Taft, the Secretary of War's son. Later one of their number, Earle Looker, would immortalize their exploits in a book called *The White House Gang*. T.R. was their hero, often their accomplice, as when the group formed the habit of riding around Washington in the city streetcars and making faces at all the passersby. One day they passed Theodore riding alone save for his coachman and footman, and, knowing he was their friend, they made the worst faces possible. He retaliated with facial contortions which the occupants of the car found most amazing. However, occasionally even his patience was exhausted.

One day, incited by the inventive Quentin, they managed to secrete themselves in the freight crate beneath the passenger section of the two-storied elevator and found it most amusing to manipulate the buttons. If someone pushed an "up" button, they would immediately reverse it, and vice versa. They continued this fascinating sport for some time, until there came a tremendous thud on the floor of the passenger car.

"I have stood this long enough," a voice roared. "Have done with it *at once!*"

"*Father!*" whispered a shocked Quentin.

He stood motionless while the car slowly rose, this time unimpeded. It stopped at the floor of the family apartments. "Let's get away!" urged the gang. "Back to the basement!" "No." Quentin pushed the "up" button. "We'll go and take our medicine." But when they arrived at the family floor, there was no sign of T.R. He had evidently decided not to prosecute—or, as they suspected, unable to condone their action, he had gone away to laugh heartily at the escapade.

Not that many of their pranks went unpunished! When the gang fired spitballs at the portrait of Andrew Jackson, making him look like "an Arabian desert," they were banished from the downstairs rooms for a week. Worse—when they reflected mirrors on the windows of the State-War-Navy building, a figure appeared on the roof and signaled with flags: YOU . . . UNDER TREES . . . ATTACK ON THIS BUILDING MUST IMMEDIATELLY CEASE HALT STOP . . . REPORT TO ME WITHOUT DELAY FOR YOU KNOW WHAT. THEODORE ROOSEVELT.

But when the President alone was the butt of their pranks, he might have been one of them. Once, when the gang were Quentin's houseguests for the night, they were enjoying a fierce pillow fight when they heard steps approaching. They turned out the light. Presently a vague figure appeared in the door, partly hidden by a screen. Each of the six let a pillow fly. As one of the gang later wrote, "The restored light disclosed T.R. in full evening dress, half on the chair and half on the floor, submerged under pillows and nearly covered by the capsized screen. In the brief abashed silence his characteristic (and most caricatured) grin relieved our doubts, and his laughter as he regained his feet and replaced the screen was joined by our own." When he left he was enshrined more securely than ever in the hearts of six small boys.

They did not spare Edith. In the upper regions of the White House where they liked to roam there was a skylight opening looking down into the main hall of the family's living quarters on the second floor. Once when they looked down, there was Edith serving tea to an Italian diplomat and an army officer. They could tell he was the latter because of the bright yellow cavalry stripes on his blue trousers. The Italian was wearing a monocle. Ha! They also had monocles, crystals they had taken from old watches. They ran to get them; then, peering over the edge of the skylight, they began to copy the Italian's gestures. Quentin softly proceeded to mouth words that he conceived to be Italian. His gibbering penetrated the sudden silence down below.

"Quentin!" Edith called severely. She and her guests looked up to see four boys peering down over the edge, each with one glittering eye. The Italian's eyes opened in such wide astonishment that his own monocle fell in his teacup. Then he threw back his head and laughed. "Mrs. Roosevelt," he said, "I beg of you to command those monkeys to come down to tea." Edith found it a relief to join him in laughter. Sheepishly the boys descended and joined the party.

Edith was just as understanding in her way as Theodore. She knew when it was wise to interfere with gang plans and when to look the other way. Later she was to say of Quentin, "What a *fine* bad little boy he was!" "Part of her wisdom," Looker was to comment, "lay in not expecting, or demanding too much of Quentin, with regard to unimportant details. She knew more about the mind of a child—manifesting her knowledge continually, in a hundred different ways—than any teacher of child psychology I have ever known."

As with Theodore, one of her chief concerns was for the child's safety. They were so much alike—fearless, headstrong, adventurous, independent! And of course as leader of the gang he endangered his friends. He liked to climb to the top branches of the magnolia tree under her window. He conducted his friends through the attic and climbed on the roof, once on the drifted snow, slipping and sliding and dividing them up for snowball battles from one balustrade to the other; dropping large snowballs containing old electric light bulbs, which made such loud pops on the concrete of the areaways that they brought policemen, Secret Service men, and attendants running in alarm. On one Saturday when they were on the roof of the north portico they made an especially large snowball which Quentin decided was "too good to waste." Just below they could see the figure of a policeman. With much rolling and grunting the boys heaved the enormous ball onto the wide shelf and dropped it. It landed on the policeman's helmet, and he sat down suddenly. Their delight was suddenly quelled at the sight of the President emerging from the door and rushing to help the policeman, then looking up with eyes blazing. "Come down off that roof!" He roared. "At once!"

Meekly they descended, but to their surprise he was not furiously angry. "Fortunately," he said, "you didn't break his neck. But you've done something else quite as bad, you hurt his dignity in front of *me*. And, worse yet, he saw that I laughed. I shouldn't have done so, of course, but how could I help it? It was terrible! Now—apologize to him, all of you."

They did, so genuinely that the poor policeman was embarrassed.

"Quentin is a roly-poly, happy-go-lucky personage," Theodore once wrote to a friend, "the brightest of any of the children, but with a strong tendency to pass a very happy life in doing absolutely nothing except swim or loaf about with other little boys."

Edith could not agree with his opinion that her youngest was fat and inert and ate too much and ought to be more active. More active! Heaven forbid! And how could one deplore the mental laziness of a nine-year-old who once compared his sunburned legs to "a Turner sunset"?

She often felt conflict between her roles of wife and mother. In the fall of 1906 she had to choose, for Theodore wanted her to go with him on a trip to Panama. She chose him. They spent over two weeks traveling from port to port on the USS *Louisiana*. It was a voyage into history, with reminders of Columbus, the buccaneers, the Spanish explorers, pestilences, turbulence, the "hot, evil, riotous life of the old planters and slave owners;" and, most important to Theodore, the signs that the war in which he had participated had helped bring better conditions to Cuba and Puerto Rico. But of course his greatest delight was in his inspection of the Panama Canal construction. While he joyously tramped through mud, exulted over steam shovels blasting their way through mountains, inspected workmen's quarters, Edith marveled at the luxuriance of tropical forests, palms and banana trees, gorgeous butterflies and brilliant birds. They were back in Washington in time to receive the amazing news that Theodore had won the Nobel Peace Prize. It presented problems as well as satisfactions.

"What am I to do?" he voiced his perplexity. "They say there is money that comes with it. Of course I hate to refuse money which would sometime come to you and the children but—how can I accept money for making peace between two nations, especially since I was able to do it simply because I was President! It—it would be like being paid for rescuing a man from drowning!"

"Of course," Edith agreed wholeheartedly. "It wouldn't be right to accept it."

"But—what can I do? I can't very well throw it back in their faces!"

"Why not apply it to some public purpose?" she suggested, while relinquishing the possibility of extra money with reluctance. It could have meant so much to the children's future!

The official award was made in Oslo (then Christiania) on December 10, and at the same time the American minister to Norway announced that the money, forty thousand dollars, would be used to establish at Washington a permanent committee for industrial peace, to provide for more equitable relations between labor and management.

Spring was lovely that year of 1907. The most beautiful spot in the world, it seemed, was around the north fountain, with its white magnolia, the pink of the flowering peach, and the yellow of the forsythia. Never had the wildflowers blossomed with such profusion along Rock Creek. But for the country there was no sign of prosperity. Businesses were failing, unemployment rising, and there were rumors of a Stock Market crash. Of course Theodore was blamed for these conditions, especially by his critics who scolded at "Theodore the meddler," and it was dubbed the "Roosevelt Panic." Its chief cause, however, was the failure of the Currency Act of 1900 to establish a stable currency. If his critics hoped that the "panic" might restrain him in his reform of big business, they were disappointed. Federal investigations into improper business practices continued.

During that year also he managed to circumvent an attempt by

Western lumbermen to thwart his efforts at conservation of the country's precious timber resources. When an Oregon senator secured passage of an amendment to the Agricultural Appropriation Bill forbidding the creation of new forest reserves in six Western states, he was baffled. What to do? He could not veto the bill, canceling all funds for the Forest Service. He consulted his friend Gifford Pinchot, and they came up with a happy solution. During the ten days of leeway, he created, by proclamation, twenty-one new forest reserves in the specified states. "The opponents of the Forest Service turned handsprings in their wrath," he recorded gleefully, "and dire were their threats." But they could do nothing. He had succeeded in adding sixteen million acres of precious timberland to the public domain before signing the bill.

These and other problems took their toll, however. Edith noticed that for the first time in her memory he actually looked tired, and when he took to his bed for two days, apparently with a toothache, she was really alarmed. But she could not give him the attention she would have liked to bestow, because he was not her only patient. Ted had become suddenly afflicted with painful boils, and Archie was just recovering from a severe case of diphtheria.

But nothing could keep Theodore down for long, certainly not a toothache. And not even the exigencies of his presidential problems—the economic crisis, trouble in California over the influx of Japanese immigrants, the second peace conference at The Hague, which he hoped would result in a limitation of armaments—could dampen his lust for physical activity. In May he was out jumping rails and stone walls on his horse Roswell with his Secretary of the Navy George Mayer, who proceeded to take his new fine horse over a big brush hurdle.

"I shouldn't have tried," Theodore confessed ruefully. "I could have stood Ted and some of his young cronies getting ahead of me, but not one of my Cabinet. I made poor Roswell take the jump. He managed it, but it was hard, with my weight on top of him. With saddle and all, I'm about 230 pounds for him to carry."

Edith made no comment, merely shook her head in futile resignation.

For Edith the autumn of 1907 brought changes and new anxieties. It was Archie's turn now to leave home for Groton. She could not help fearing for him, he still seemed such a little boy, so sensitive and vulnerable! To add to his grief over separation from his beloved animals, Skip, his favorite little cur and constant companion, died just two days before his departure and was consigned, with proper rites, to the well-populated pet cemetery at Sagamore. Quentin, now almost ten, became the inheritor not only of superior sibling status but of his brother's small zoo, which, as Theodore had discovered the preceding May, was of manifold variety.

"Yesterday evening," he had written Ted, "I met Archie going to his bath, and he cordially invited me in to see the livestock; there were tadpoles in a jar, four wee turtles in the bathtub, and a small alligator in the basin. Mademoiselle told me that he regarded the turtles 'avec beaucoup de tendresse,' but found the alligator 'antipathetique'—I hope spelling is right!"

Quentin already had a respectable menagerie of his own. Before leaving for Washington in late September he had collected two large snakes, but had lost one, which did not turn up until an hour before departure in one of the spare rooms. He let it loose and took the other one with him, creating some incidents on the way when it wriggled out of its box. Arriving in Washington and visiting his friend Schmid in the latter's animal store, he presented his little snake to Schmid in a fit of generosity; whereupon the pet store proprietor gave him three snakes in return: a large friendly king snake and two smaller ones.

Excited, Quentin came rushing back on his roller skates and burst into Theodore's office to show his treasures, dumping them into his father's lap. Since the President was having an important conference with his Attorney General, he suggested that the boy take his menagerie into the adjoining room, where four congressmen were patiently waiting to confer with him. "The snakes might enliven their waiting time," he remarked gleefully.

They did. Discovering that the snakes were not wooden, as first thought, the congressmen displayed marked recoil, and when the king snake disappeared up Quentin's sleeve, all three feet of him, they were both shocked and helpless. "The last I saw of Quentin," T.R. wrote Archie, "one congressman was gingerly helping him off with his jacket, so as to let the snake crawl out of the upper end of his sleeve."

With the return of the family, the White House resumed its normal routine of multiple and, because of Quentin, unpredictable activity. As a result of emergency measures by October 1907, the nation also was restored to near economic normalcy. T.R. departed on a speaking tour of the West and South, plus a short interim of bear hunting in Louisiana. Did she fear for him more, Edith wondered, when he was barging around the country, presumably under armed protection, or when he slipped off with friends, unguarded, to scale fences or lead them on endurance tests through Rock Creek Park? At least, when he was on a trip like this, his letters brought some comfort. One of them especially, written from a hunting camp, contained passages that she read and reread.

"Darling Edie, All your dear, dear letters have come; I love them so. . . . I am very homesick for you; whenever I wake up at night, or stay still waiting to hear the hounds in the day I find myself counting the days before I get back—a little less than thirteen now, my darling sweetheart. . . ."

He returned safely, bearless but having shot a deer, winning, as he said, "undeserved praise from all the party." But his efforts to secure further national reforms were even less successful. In his message to Congress early in 1908 he called for a new employers' liability act, an act compensating government employees for injuries incurred in public service, for restrictions on the use of injunctions in labor cases, and for increased control over railroads and industrial corporations. Only the first two were implemented, but he was not discouraged. The rest, he was sure, would come in time.

"I am well satisfied with the message," he wrote Kermit on February 2, "and I think it was time to send it in. Of course it caused a flutter in the dovecote. . . . All of my advisers were naturally enough against my sending it in, for councils of war never fight; but Mother likes the message and I am sure it is on the right track." He added in longhand, "7:30 now I have just come in from a brisk three hours walk over the frozen snow out to Chevy Chase and back by Rock Creek."

March 1908. Election year. Theodore had said at the beginning of his present term that he would not run again. But—had he really meant it? The country waited—the majority of the people hopefully, his opponents fearfully—wondering if he would change his mind. He did not, though Edith knew that he bitterly regretted having made the statement. She had known he would when he made it. There was no possibility of his finishing all the grandiose tasks he had set himself in a year's time—controlling the trusts, securing the public lands and waterways from exploitation, strengthening the country's defenses so that it would be free from attack by any nation. The latter goal, he felt, had been partially achieved by his sending the fleet on a "peace mission" around the world. A "rattling of sabres," some had called it. No, he had maintained, merely a friendly visit, but if any nation, say Japan, chose to take it as a warning, well and good.

His greatest worry now, Edith knew, was in choosing a successor who would be most likely to continue his crusade. He often discussed the problem with her. Charles Evans Hughes, governor of New York? No. Theodore doubted if he would consider becoming, so to speak, the tool of the present incumbent. Elihu Root, his trusted Secretary of State? But—Elihu was a businessman, too closely associated with the industrial interests.

"Taft," he decided finally. Genial, lovable, popular, always in hearty agreement with the most progressive ideas, he seemed the perfect choice.

"He will be greatly beloved as President," Theodore enthused. "I almost envy a man possessing such a personality. One loves him at first sight. He has nothing to overcome when he meets people." He grinned ruefully. "No one could accuse *me* of having a charming personality."

Edith did not try to dissuade him, though she had misgivings. Always in hearty agreement, yes, she thought, but with whomever he happens to be speaking.

Taft agreed to the proposition, though with reluctance. He would have preferred appointment to the Supreme Court. But his wife Helen had her heart set on becoming First Lady and, as usual, Edith suspected, she had her way.

The convention in June was a triumph far more for Theodore

than for Taft. Lodge was chairman, and he had difficulty controlling the excited cheering for Roosevelt, which sometimes lasted up to three quarters of an hour and savored of rowdiness. His first mention of Theodore's name aroused acclamation hard to quell. Presently someone brought in a large teddy bear, which almost caused a riot. It finally rolled under the feet of a lot of people fighting to possess it. It took police to finally subdue the excitement, and the teddy bear disappeared for good. (Could it possibly be the one sold later at Sotheby's auction house in England for $8,237?) "Four years more, Roosevelt!" the crowd shouted. "Four years more of the Square Deal!" But finally, after a mere twenty minutes of applause for Taft, he was nominated by seven hundred votes.

"It has been a curious contest," Theodore wrote one of his friends, "for I have had to fight tooth and nail against being nominated myself. . . . I could not have prevented it at all unless I had thrown myself heart and soul into the business of nominating Taft and had shown the country that he stood for exactly the same principles and policies that I did."

Life in the White House was eased and brightened that year of 1908 by the presence of a new staff member, Captain Archibald Willingham Butt, who became Theodore's military aide. He played the role to perfection. Inordinately proud of his uniform, when he wore it, which was as often as possible, gorgeous with gold braid and broad yellow stripes, he stood so ramrod straight that his stocky body seemed stretched to giant height. Freckled, redheaded, eyes agleam with boyish anticipation, he took over his new duties on May 8 with gusto and alacrity. Though a scion of old Georgia and Massachusetts families, he was as capable of courteous friendliness with the White House's lowliest servants as with its distinguished guests. Once, as he was hurrying to the White House for an official function, resplendent in full military dress, an old Negro whom he had befriended looked after him and observed to an acquaintance, "He's de highest wid de mighty and de lowest wid de lowly of any man in Washington."

He arrived just in time to assist Edith at a governors' conference with which Theodore was attempting to further implement his conservation plans—successfully, for it resulted in the creation of thirty-six conservation commissions and, on June 8, of the National Conservation Commission. One of his appointees as a delegate to the conference was Sarah Decker, president of the General Federation of Women's Clubs. So favorably impressed was Theodore with Archie Butt's dignified yet friendly demeanor that he came up with an idea.

"I want him to accompany you on these walks you like to take," he said to Edith. "With the assaults going on around the city, many of them on unescorted women, it isn't right for you to be wandering around alone, even with another woman. He's just the man to protect you and will, if I'm not mistaken, prove an intelligent companion."

Edith found him so. The first walk was to call on her friends, the Glovers, which meant several miles each way. Archie Butt, who was an inveterate letter writer, first to his mother, then, after she died that year, to his sister-in-law, wrote of the expedition: "She is a pretty good walker and knew all the out-of-the way paths. When we got to the Glovers' we had iced tea and lemonade. On our way out I stopped at my house and I took my pointer dog Duke with us. She is very fond of animals and fell in love with Duke. Poor Duke does not understand a word of English and I tried to teach her enough Spanish to call him to her. He minds beautifully but not in English."

Archie became a favorite in every enclave of his new life—in the bachelor quarters where he lived on H Street, in the servants' quarters of the White House or its formal sanctums, in the family rooms where the children held sway. He played tennis with Theodore, on a par with what was called the "Tennis Cabinet," the coterie of T.R.'s Cabinet and others who both joined him in slamming balls across the net and, between plays, gave him pointers "on people and things." He scrounged through antique shops with Edith (or *for* her), proving adept at what she called "snooping" in search of bargains. On their long walks he conversed with her, not merely intelligently but learnedly, about the classics, art, music. Visiting Sagamore that summer, he flew kites with Quentin and shared the family dinner of soup, fish, fried chicken, corn on the cob and jelly, only water to drink; he gamely participated in one of the "point to point" races and went to church with them on Sunday, after which they all discussed their favorite hymns.

"Holy, Holy, Holy" was one of Theodore's choices, as well as "Jerusalem the Golden" and "The Son of God Goes Forth to War." For Edith it was "Nearer, My God to Thee."

"Queer," observed Archie, "I don't believe I have any favorite hymn, but—" he pondered, "I think at my funeral I should like to have sung 'Nearer, My God to Thee.' " It was a remark that they were to recall later with poignant vividness.

This last year in the White House rushed on—for Edith with devastating speed. She was facing not merely transition, it seemed, but disruption. For the family was breaking up. Ted, twenty-one in September, had graduated from Harvard and going into business, taking a job in a Connecticut carpet factory. Kermit was entering Harvard that fall. Archie was still at Groton. Even Quentin was leaving home, being enrolled as a boarder in the Episcopal High School in Alexandria. Ethel, seventeen, would be having her coming-out party before the year ended. At least Edith would have the comfort of her dependable, mature support for a while. And she would need it. For Theodore, her love, her very life, was making the disruption complete. He must not stay around, he had decided, to complicate life for his successor. He must leave, not only Washington but the country. He was planning an African safari, a major specimen-collecting expedition through Kenya and Uganda, and he had been preparing for it for months.

Outwardly Edith was resigned. She knew he needed to get away. He must have some compelling interest after these grueling seven years. She could not imagine him contenting himself with grinding out articles on nature or hunting or politics at his desk at Sagamore. He would be like a caged lion. Lions! The very suggestion made her shiver, for that was what he had in mind, hunting lions—and, to compound her fears, he was taking Kermit with him.

One evening they were sitting at dinner with guests, and, as usual, Theodore was keeping the party amused and edified with conversation ranging from tropical fauna to Greek drama to Irish lore to political economy and the persistence of journalists.

"Somebody from the Associated Press has been hounding me to take along a representative on this African jaunt," he said with a chuckle. "Of course I refused, but he persisted. 'Now see here, Mr. President,' he reminded me, 'the yellow journalists are sure to follow you and if anything should happen we couldn't afford to be scooped by the yellow press.' 'What do you mean,' I asked him, 'if anything should happen?' 'Well,' he replied, 'should a lion really do his duty, you must realize it will be the one great news item of the year and we could not afford to get left.' "

Of course the guests laughed, a bit perfunctorily. But Archie Butt, who was present, glancing at Edith, noticed that she was not even smiling, in fact that she had turned pale. For she was terrified at the thought of his going. Yet, though he gamely protested that he hated the prospect, would have preferred staying at home, not for worlds would she have said anything to deter him. For she knew that he was looking forward to the safari with the enthusiasm of a child anticipating his first circus. All during that fall he could scarcely talk of anything else, and long before the year was over he had finished most of his plans for departure. Edith was to meet him in Egypt, and they would travel home together. He was collecting extensive paraphernalia, including a dozen pairs of spectacles (as for Cuba) and what he called his "Pigskin Library." Among the sixty volumes were works by Browning, Carlyle, Cooper, Dante, Dickens, Euripides, Holmes, Homer, Keats, Longfellow, Poe, Swift, Tennyson, Mark Twain, Shakespeare, and, of course, the Bible. Occasionally Edith vetoed certain of his more extravagant ideas.

One evening at dinner he was discussing with Archie Butt the proper dress for the more ceremonial functions he might be attending in Europe on the way home. "Certainly not knickerbockers and black stockings," he mused. "Archie, how about ordering for me a uniform of a colonel of cavalry? Wouldn't that be appropriate?"

"Excellent," agreed the aide. "You have the legal right to wear it, and, I'm telling you, when I was a colonel it was brilliant with yellow plumes and gold lace—" Meeting Edith's disapproving glance, he subsided into uneasy silence.

"Theodore," she said severely, "you should never wear a uniform that you did not wear in the service, and if you insist on doing this I will have a *vivandière*'s costume made and follow you throughout Europe."

The picture of Edith as a Frenchwoman accompanying soldiers into battle to sell provisions or liquor—or render more questionable services—was enough to convulse Theodore as well as the guests.

"Don't you dare order it," she adjured Archie Butt later, "even if he insists. It would make him a laughingstock in this country."

Reluctantly Theodore gave up the idea and agreed to wear an ordinary frock coat.

Edith's fears were hardly allayed when Cecil Spring-Rice sent her a pamphlet on "sleeping sickness," with the jocular explanation that Theodore might not die of that, because (in the event of his not previously being eaten by a lion or crocodile, or killed by an infuriated elephant or buffalo), malarial fever or a tribe of enraged savages might take him off before the sleeping sickness got him! She could not help laughing.

In spite of her fears the expedition had its bright sides. Safer perhaps for him to be a target for lions than for every crank within American shores! Also it would solve their financial problems, at least temporarily. They had been able to save nothing from his presidential salary, which had all been expended on upkeep of the White House and official entertaining. But *Scribner's* would pay well ($50,000) for articles about the trip, and he could expand them into a book on his return. It was also a relief when a doctor of the United States Medical Corps was assigned to accompany him. Another bonus: taxidermists from the Smithsonian Institution were going along to take care of the trophies.

"I would have to move out of the house if he filled it with more stuffed animals, queer antelopes, stuffed elephants, and the like!"

As she well knew, Theodore was not as robustly healthy as his vitality seemed to indicate. He had the old Cuban fever in his blood. Due to his numerous accidents, he was completely blind in one eye and had imperfect sight in the other. His leg still bothered him. He was much overweight. Not that such liabilities inhibited his volcanic activity!

Archie Butt found that out one day in October when Theodore invited him to go for a walk. Since the President was dressed in what looked like a handsome cutaway coat, Archie thought it would be an easy walk, especially since Theodore had been told by his physician, Dr. Rixey, to rest his leg for a while. Arriving at Rock Creek Park, he dismissed the two guards who had followed, and they started, taking a circuitous route through the underbrush and coming out farther up the creek, where there were no paths. After pushing through the brush like an Indian scout and arriving at the water's edge, T.R. began clambering out on the ridges and overhanging rocks, with Archie attempting to follow. Sometimes they passed along the outer faces of rocks with hardly enough room in the crevices for fingers or feet. Finally they reached one cliff that went straight up from the water, made a turn, and the ledge they would have to reach hung over some very jagged projections. Archie watched his companion's ascent with alarm. "Just as he was on the point of reaching the highest point," he wrote later, "imagine my horror when I saw him lose hold, slip, and go tumbling down. I stood paralyzed with fear. However, he managed to miss all sharp projections and fell straight into the water. With a laugh he clambered to the bank and started up once more, making it this time." All in all, the "walk" was for Archie a revelation of a man's character. But to his surprise, it had been one of the most enjoyable experiences of his life.

Jules Jusserand, the genial and popular French ambassador, could have told much the same story. Invited to take a promenade with the President, he arrived at the White House in afternoon suit and silk hat, expecting a stroll in some civilized spot like a park. Theodore appeared in tramping suit, knickers, and thick boots. They started off at a breakneck speed, going pell-mell over fields, coming at last to the bank of a stream, too wide and deep to be forded—or so Jusserand thought. "We had better strip," Theodore advised, "so as not to wet our things in the creek." Feeling the honor of France at stake, the ambassador complied, removing all his clothes except his lavender kid gloves. Seeing the President's questioning glance at them, the ambassador, who had a remarkable sense of humor, said, "With your permission, Mr. President, I will keep these on, otherwise it would be embarrassing if we should meet ladies." So they jumped into the water and swam across.

November. The months of this last year were speeding past. To Theodore's intense joy and largely as a result of his promotion, Taft was elected. Theodore was as happy about it as a boy just released from school, full of jokes and pranks. One of the latter was to send a faked telegram to Edith telling her that her beloved Pine Knot, containing perhaps three acres of land, had gone for Bryan! He could now slough off his most perplexing problems, leaving his successor to solve them as he himself would have done. Ahead were only four months of an unexciting lame-duck presidency, then—the wilds of Africa.

But for Edith the social season, with all its grueling demands, was just beginning. First came the usual diplomatic tea. As she donned a new black velvet gown with silver passementerie work down the front, she calculated shrewdly that this was her last expenditure for clothes for many months. She had seldom bought new gowns even for the most important occasions. In fact, each member of the family had a favorite, which he or she would have liked her to choose for every state function, and there was often a fight as to which it would be. Theodore and Kermit preferred a heavy black silk, ribbed and slashed with white. Ethel liked the steel-blue which she wore often at luncheons and was very soft and becoming. Alice, always more flamboyant in her tastes, favored a rich plum-colored velvet. Today Edith felt indifferent to any impression she might make. She was tired. Was she getting old? Surely not at only forty-seven!

She had been amused by an article in *The Ladies' Home Journal* the preceding month entitled WHY MRS. ROOSEVELT HAS NOT BROKEN DOWN. Her secret for "placid, equable poise," the author decided, lay in following two or three simple rules—keeping out of doors as much as possible, riding, walking, insisting on simple food, being suitably, tastefully dressed yet going to no extremes, always trying to keep out of the public eye. Well—only three months to go. She squared her shoulders, smiled at her reflection in the pier glass, and went down to meet her guests.

If Theodore was convinced that the new Administration would

make no changes in his policies for the country, Edith had no such assurance in regard to the White House. On November 30 she was taking her usual walk with Archie Butt when he told her that Helen Taft had decided to change the ushers.

She stopped suddenly. "All of them?" Her voice quivered.

"Yes. She is going to replace them with colored liveried servants."

"Oh!" Edith's voice broke. She raised her veil and for a while she could not speak. "Oh, it will hurt them so!" she managed finally. Then, controlling her emotion, "Captain Butt, don't think me foolish, but if you knew how those men have served us and how kind and thoughtful they have been in times of illness and trouble, you would understand me now."

He did understand and tried to do all he could to change the decision. He persuaded Mrs. Taft to keep on some of Edith's favorites in charge of the footmen. But he could not influence her intention to replace the police guards at the main entrance with black footmen. Edith was greatly disturbed. Suppose the new plans displaced servants like Charles Loeffler, the assistant doorkeeper, or Captain Pendel! Both of them, so loyal, so dependable! One of them, at least, had been on duty for forty years, serving Abraham Lincoln!

December. More state functions. On the seventeenth, at the Cabinet Dinner, Edith wore her heavy white brocade and carried a corsage, no jewels. "I have never seen her looking lovelier," Archie Butt wrote his sister-in-law Clara. Both Theodore and Edith were glad it was the last one, Theodore because he must sit beside someone who bored him, Edith because she found the formalities of precedence, of marching to the hackneyed strains of "Hail to the Chief," artificial and unimportant. But Christmas, their last in the White House, was all family and intimate friends—the Lodges, the Longworths, Bamie and her husband with their small son Sheffield, fifty-eight in all. The table was decorated with red leaves and ferns, as at Sagamore. At each plate there was a tissue-paper package which popped when opened and contained some sort of paper headgear, from fool's cap to crown. There were turkeys, salads "which a child could eat without fear of cramps,"

and plum puddings with burning brandy. The ices were tiny
Santa Clauses, each holding a little Christmas tree.

Now, after years of quiet, competent, affectionate but undra-
matic roles, it was Ethel's turn to take center stage. Her coming-
out ball on December 28 was just as elaborate but less flamboyant than "Princess" Alice's, in keeping with their diverse personalities. She received the four hundred and forty guests in the Blue
Room, demure in white satin ornamented with crystals, Edith accompanying her in dark blue brocade. Tables for the midnight
supper were set up in the basement, whose long glass colonnade
looked like fairyland, leaving the first floor rooms free for visiting
and dancing. All seemed to enjoy the event except Theodore,
who at such times felt inhibited by the restrictions of his office.

"My Southern nature never comes out so much," he told Archie Butt, "as when I am having a party. My desire is to mingle
freely and introduce everyone and see that the girls all know the
men and vice versa, and to start the ball rolling. But I can't do
that, for the moment I attempt it I am about as foolish as the
donkey who wanted to be a lapdog. Even you tell me that I must
not go to supper, for everybody will promptly rise from the table,
thereby checking the merriment." Edith also had forbidden him
to eat, for food at midnight gave him twinges of the gout.

January . . . February. The days rushed by, Theodore trying
to crowd into them all his unfinished tasks of the last seven years,
Edith adding to her usual duties the hundreds of details involved
in divesting herself of one identity and taking on another.

She ordered an inventory of the White House china, stipulating
that all the chipped pieces be broken and that those of past Administrations be carefully collected and designated for the Smithsonian. Discovering to her dismay that one of the White House's
most precious possessions, the Washington portrait by Stuart that
Dolley Madison had saved when the British were entering Washington, was in deplorable condition, she had it restored and hung
in the Red Room over the fireplace. Meticulously, while superintending the packing, she separated personal possessions from
those that might be considered belonging to the house, leaning
over backward in favor of the latter when there seemed to be
doubt. Only two items did she refuse to leave behind: a pair of

Sèvres figures which had been given to her personally, "with documents to prove it," and a little antique sofa which she had bought with her own money and wanted very much for Sagamore. She knew that the absence of the figurines would be a disappointment to Helen Taft, who had said they were the most beautiful things in the White House; but she was for once ruthless. They were *hers* by right. Yet when she learned that a newspaper article had appeared about the sofa, accusing her of removing furniture from the White House without paying for it (though she had agreed to substitute a duplicate for it at a much higher price), she stated with an anger unusual for her that she no longer wanted the "wretched little sofa."

There were long faces and tears among staff members as they assisted with preparations for moving, for none relished the coming change. Not only was a colorful, exciting era ending, but all had come to love the Roosevelt family, especially the even-tempered, considerate First Lady. There were long faces in the city also, for, though many of her charities had been dispensed anonymously, always unobtrusively, hundreds had benefited from her largesse—impoverished individuals, families threatened with eviction, churches, hospitals, charity patients, friends in trouble. The city would not be the same without her.

Sadness pervaded the atmosphere. Perhaps Quentin expressed the feeling most vividly when he remarked, "There is a little hole in my stomach when I think of leaving the White House." And for the family the mood was devastatingly heightened when on February 21 they returned from church to learn that Stewart, Conie's youngest son, age twenty-one, had fallen by accident from a window in his room at Harvard and been killed. One of the most lighthearted, lovable, and promising of all the children!

It was hard to feel any sense of joy or triumph when Theodore and Edith went the next day to Hampton Roads to welcome the fleet returning from its round-the-world cruise. But it was a triumphant occasion nonetheless. As Theodore appraised it, "I could not ask a finer concluding scene to my Administrations."

It was well that he had this satisfaction in achievement, for in past months he had encountered increasingly bitter opposition from party leaders. Congress had bucked his attempts to obtain legislation on many issues—outlawing child labor, protection of workingmen's right to strike "for just cause," equal employment opportunities for women, a clarification of criminal codes which frequently exacted the maximum punishment allowed from the poor, while businessmen who cheated the public rarely suffered. Recently in his fight against corruption, Congress had denied him the use of Secret Service men to ferret out misdoing for fear he would use them against members of the House and Senate. But he retorted fearlessly, "I have pledged myself to wage war on corruption and graft wherever they can be found, and the higher up the criminal the more necessary it is to strike him down."

His frustration reminded Edith unpleasantly of a conversation which had taken place at one of their more informal dinners. One of the guests regaled the party with a tale about sixteen lions that he had seen filing slowly out of a cave.

"By George," Theodore had exclaimed with sparkling eyes, "I wish I could turn those lions loose in Congress."

"But, Mr. President," a congressman who happened to be present interposed, "aren't you afraid they might make a mistake and choose the wrong targets?"

Theodore's teeth showed in a wide grin. "Not if they stayed long enough."

March. The beginning of the end. They were packed. Numerous gifts had been dispensed. In fact, Theodore had indulged in a frenzy of giving, almost denuding his office. Archie Butt went to the basement to smash the china which he had been gathering, taking out two plates, broken but with pieces intact, for himself, selecting two small broken butter plates for Miss Hagner and some chipped pieces of the Roosevelt china for Edith. Her eyes filled with tears when he gave them to her.

Theodore gave a luncheon for thirty-one friends, his "Tennis Cabinet" and a motley array of other intimates. There was scarcely a dry eye among them. Later Madame Jusserand, whose ambassador husband had sat next to Theodore, remarked, "Is there another man in the world who could have had such a luncheon, or who, having it, could have had on one side of him the Ambassador of a great country and on the other a 'desperado' from Oklahoma?"

On March 3 there were receptions for intimate friends, again with almost no dry eyes, some of them women with whom Edith had had close associations. She wept when, returning to her room, she found lying on her bureau their parting gift, a diamond necklace. The Tafts came to dinner and to spend the night, Helen very gracious in a superb gown of white satin and filmy tulle, Edith looking unusually pale in her more modest black silk and lace. Guests were few, beside the Tafts only Bamie and her husband, Archie Butt, the Longworths, and the Elihu Roots.

When they went upstairs to the library, Alice looked out the window and exclaimed, "It's snowing!" She did not sound at all regretful at the prospect of a wretched day for the inauguration.

When it came time to retire, Edith took Mrs. Taft by the hand and expressed the earnest hope that her first night in the White House would be one of sweet repose.

"Thoughtful and gentle to the last," thought Archie Butt, wondering when the White House would again have such a mistress.

March 4 was indeed a foul day, heavy snow at first, then, when the sun came out, unmanageable slush. There was an icy east wind. Because of the weather the ceremonies would take place in the Senate Chamber instead of on the east portico of the Capitol, to Alice's intense satisfaction. It would be much less impressive indoors, and a smaller crowd could be accommodated. It could not help but compare unfavorably with the inauguration four years before.

After Theodore had departed for the Capitol with Taft, Edith drove with Bamie, Belle Hagner, and Quentin to lunch at the Longworths'. Ethel had already left for Sagamore to get the place ready. Quentin would be the only Roosevelt staying in Washington, to finish his term at school.

After the lunch Edith went directly to the station, where she was joined by Theodore, who had not been invited to ride back to the White House with the new President. Helen Taft, defying precedent, had insisted on that honor for herself. As they entered the train, crowds surrounded them, many weeping as they shouted, "Good-bye! Good luck!"

It was over, that act of their drama. "Mother and I," was Theodore's appraisal of the past seven years, "are in the curious and very pleasant position of having enjoyed the White House more than any other President and his wife whom I recall, yet being entirely willing to leave it, and looking forward to a life of interest and happiness after we leave."

Already for him the Washington scene was becoming blurred, fading into a new and more exotic setting, the jungles of Africa. Edith made no comment. As usual, she was keeping her emotions to herself. Interest and happiness? Perhaps. But not until the next six months had passed.

Part Five

❖

MISTRESS
OF
SAGAMORE

1

One day in June 1909, Archie Butt drove up the long winding road to Sagamore Hill. As he passed the old landmarks, he half-expected to see a familiar figure dash out, teeth bared in a wide grin of welcome, shrill voice yelling, "Archie, old boy!" It made him homesick. But as he passed the tennis court, there, walking across the lawn, wearing a light blue gown and a big white cloth hat, came another familiar figure. He stopped the car, got out, and went to meet her.

"Archie! How wonderful! Thank you for coming."

"The pleasure is mine," he responded. "I would have come even if the President hadn't made me promise to see you. This is the first chance I've had."

Her eyes widened. "The President? You can't mean—"

"He will always be the 'President' to me," Archie confessed with a rueful smile, "and not to me only. The other day when I was riding with Mr. Taft, I spoke of Mr. Roosevelt as 'the President' and apologized. 'Never mind, Archie,' he said, 'he is my President too, and we will have him as our President still, you and I, even if he is nobody else's President.' "

He was relieved, for Edith seemed the same as usual, calm, in complete control of her emotions, though Kermit had confided to him just before he and his father left for Africa that in spite of her self-possession he thought her heart was broken at the prospect of their long dangerous absence.

"Tell me all about what is happening," she demanded as they walked toward the house. "The Tafts—the servants—how are they all?"

She listened eagerly. Mrs. Taft, he told her, had been very ill. She had had a sort of stroke and had become a near invalid.

"Oh!" Edith was distressed. "How tragic!" She went on thoughtfully. "There have been so few happy women in the White House!

I think myself and Mrs. Cleveland were the only two, so far as I remember, who were entirely happy there. And—" she paused, then continued—"I doubt if even I was entirely happy, for there was always that anxiety about the President when he was away from me. I never realized what a strain I was under continuously until it was over."

Archie regarded her shrewdly. Surely there were lines about the clear gray eyes and indomitably smiling lips which he had never noticed before! As if she could be under less strain with Theodore risking jungle dangers instead of assassins' bullets!

"Would you believe," she said gaily as if in answer to his doubts, "that up to this time he has actually killed ten lions and they have shipped over twenty animals to the Smithsonian? As he would say, what a 'bully' time they are having!"

"You should have seen the frenzy over his leaving!" Taking her cue, Archie proceeded in the same light vein. "New York was as excited as over another inauguration. Although he tried to keep his departure quiet, people swarmed to catch a glimpse of him. They literally fought their way to the steamer's side. I wonder— what did you do that day?"

"The children and I spent it in the woods," she said calmly, "just walking about and trying to imagine what he was doing. But —it was a dreadful day. We all crawled into bed about eight that night, and—since then we have been very happy and content."

The children certainly seemed so when they crowded delightedly about Archie and bombarded him with questions and effusions at lunch. How were Major Loeffler and Captain Pendel, the doorkeepers, and Ike Hoover ("Hooie") and all the other servants? Had he seen Charley Taft, and how did he like being the President's son? Were any of Father's ten horses still in the stables? Had he heard that Father had already killed ten lions? And did he know that they were all going to Europe in just eleven days?

"Yes," said Edith. "Ethel, Archie, and Quentin are going with me. It will be an educational tour for them. We will spend about five months traveling, then return home for a few more months before"—there was a slight break in her voice—"before it's time to meet their father—we hope, in Egypt."

Archie nodded approval. "Fine. I have a dream of going to Europe sometime myself. Perhaps when Taft no longer needs me—"

He was relieved. At least, with the excitement of travel the five months would not seem quite so long for his favorite family, especially for the calm, self-possessed woman who for him would always be the First Lady. Later he was to write Theodore of this visit. "Mrs. Roosevelt was looking well when I saw her; and if her eyes were not to see this letter, I would tell you how altogether lovely she was looking. . . . The seven years at the White House without ever having made a mistake will shine like a diamond tiara on her head some day."

As Edith watched him leave, she was overcome once more by loneliness. Then, seeing the long faces on Archie and Quentin, she squared her shoulders and smiled. "Come on, boys," she challenged gaily. "Race you to the house."

"If it were not for the children," she had written Kermit soon after his and Theodore's departure, "I would not have the nervous strength to live through these endless months of separation from Father. When I am alone and let myself think, I am done for, for self-control is a moral muscle which exercise strengthens."

Entering the house, she applied herself once more to the herculean task of acknowledging the more personal of the fifteen to twenty thousand letters which had come pouring in bidding farewell and godspeed to the erstwhile President and his family. In the few days before their departure for Europe her moral muscle would get plenty of exercise.

The last of June she and the three children sailed for Europe on the SS *Crete*. The five months spent abroad were at least a respite from the lonely emptiness of Sagamore Hill, though they seemed but marking time. They spent most of July with Emily in her rented villa outside Porto Maurizio. While the children bicycled and took lessons in French, Italian, and Latin at a nearby Franciscan monastery, Edith passed the time strolling, rowing, swimming in the tranquil azure sea. In August they were in Paris, the children continuing their more or less painless education with trips to museums, cathedrals, and other historic monuments. In September Archie and Quentin returned home with some fellow Americans to begin their new term of school, while Edith and Ethel continued their travels in Switzerland and Italy.

Though her artistic soul reveled anew in blue Mediterranean vistas, sophisticated plays, eminent galleries, venerable cathedrals, only once did she give expression to deep emotion. She was in Rome on November 6 when early in the morning she was roused and given a report, unconfirmed but terrifying, that Theodore had been killed in Africa. Though a cable arriving that afternoon denied the rumor, it brought only uneasy relief. She felt that she would never be quite the same until she actually saw him.

His letters to herself and others of the family were enthusiastic but not always reassuring. He had recently killed six more lions, two rhinos—"both of which charged viciously"—two giraffes, one hippo . . . "Kermit is a pleasure to me, and of course a cause of much concern. Do you remember how timid he used to be? Well, my trouble with him now is that he is altogether too bold, pushing daring into recklessness." His articles for the *Outlook* were being well received. Since he had been out there twelve men had been killed or mauled by lions . . .

But she and Ethel, returning to New York in November, were back at Sagamore when she received one letter which, like that other she had saved, she could never bring herself to destroy. It was like the huge glowing hearthfire in the North Room shedding warmth through all the bleak winter days.

"Oh, sweetest of all sweet girls, last night I dreamed that I was with you, and that our separation was but a dream; and when I waked up it was almost too much to bear. Well, one may pay for everything; you have made the real happiness of my life. . . . Darling, I love you so. In a very little over four months I shall see you, now. . . . How very happy we have been for these twenty-three years . . . !"

But as the time of his return came closer she felt unease as well as anticipation. Political dissension was rife. Taft was not continuing the programs of progressive reform, as Theodore had expected. The more liberal wing of their party was clamoring for Theodore's return. The more conservative wing was hoping he would stay away—forever. But at least before he need face the problem there would be their long interim in Europe. She would not look beyond that. In fact, she had eyes for only one goal—Khartoum. In December he had left British East Africa for the far more dangerous jungles of Uganda, "the land of sleeping sickness and the fever tick." March. She lived for it to come.

It did at last. On March 14, 1910, as the train neared the end of its long dusty journey from Cairo to Khartoum, she sat clutching Ethel's hand, hardly believing that the agony of separation was soon to end. But there was apprehension also. A whole year had passed. How would they find them, husband, son, brother?

The train groaned into the station, and there they were. Edith drew a long breath, the first, it seemed, in months. For Theodore looked well and thriving, less careworn than under the oppressive burdens of the presidency. And Kermit, the sensitive child who had once followed her around like a shadow, the youthful stripling who had shied away from violent activity—could he have turned into this lean, brown, sturdy creature taller and appearing tougher than his father?

No time at first for privacy, because they were surrounded by the army of reporters who had raced up the Nile to intercept the party as soon as it emerged from the jungles. Disappointed because he would speak nothing of politics, only of his hunting experiences—296 specimens shot and shipped to the Smithsonian, bundles of articles sent to *Scribner's* and a book, *African Game Trails,* already in process—they still pursued him relentlessly. But in the sumptuous palace of the British Sirdar, Sir Richard Wingate, where for three days they were lavishly entertained, the long months of separation and loneliness were ended. Surely never again. . . . But, knowing Theodore, Edith was too wise to speculate on the future. Enough that now they were together again.

So began a second honeymoon that surpassed the first as completely as the subsequent developments of their life had surpassed their expectations. On the first they had talked of books, pictures, statues, plans for the future. Now they talked of the children, laughing over Quentin's latest *bon mot,* worrying over Archie's introduction to Groton ("Remember how the hazing had so terrified him at that first boarding school?"), rejoicing over

Ted's engagement to lovely, fair-haired Eleanor Alexander. "I hated so to go off and leave them," Edith confessed, "in these happy days which can never come again."

Only once did Theodore mention politics. "I couldn't believe that Gifford Pinchot had actually been fired," he complained bitterly. "The man who has done more than any other to conserve our national resources! How could Taft have done it! Is it true that he has really surrounded himself with reactionaries, as Pinchot seems to think? But, there! We'll forget all such things now, concentrate on these wonders at Abu Simbel and Luxor and, especially, Karnak. Bully old boys, those Pharaohs, weren't they? I used better language to describe them when I first saw them as a fourteen-year-old, something like 'ineffable, unutterable, stupendous!' "

After the trip down the Nile on the steamer *Ibis* they took another steamer, which Edith designated as "dirty and uncomfortable," for Naples. Then began one of the most surprising, exotic and, at times, embarrassing periods of their whole career, at least for the self-effacing Edith. For in this milieu of kings and queens and titled dignitaries they were treated like royalty. She felt almost apologetic for the size of their party, though it was really very modest—beside the four of them a valet, a maid, and three secretaries.

When they attended the opera *Andrea Chenier* in Rome, unfortunately arriving after it had started, they were greeted by a ten-minute ovation which interrupted the performance, and during the intermission Theodore was surrounded by eager admirers.

"Just like one of my presidential tours," he remarked. "The same courtesies and kindnesses, and the same wearing fatigue and hurry."

They were feted by King Victor Emanuel III and his Queen, who entertained them at a delightful dinner at the palace. Theodore was less fortunate, however, in his request for an audience with the Pope. That dignitary refused to see him unless he refused to meet with a group of American Methodists then in Rome, the leader of which had recently denounced the Holy Father. Theodore fumed. If the Pope reserved the right to see whom he pleased, then he as a free American citizen certainly had the same right. The controversy ended with his seeing neither. A few days later, however, the Papal Nuncio at Vienna greeted Theodore at a reception wearing his official ecclesiastical robes, in obvious defiance of the Pope.

After that came a visit with Emily at Porto Maurizio where, to Edith's secret relief, her sister had purchased the little rented villa, thus ensuring her future residence in Europe. "Villa of Great Quiet," it was named, a delightful little house in a flowery garden on a hillside overlooking the sea. Quiet? Rest? Hardly. Messengers kept coming with communications at all hours of the day and night. Theodore and his secretaries were kept busy answering requests for engagements, opinions on every subject ranging from "Hungarian Emigration to the United States" to "International Peace." When the family took drives, their carriage was bombarded with flowers, filled almost to overflowing. One old peasant woman tossed a bunch of flowers when the carriage passed, a scrap of paper pinned to a large green leaf bearing the scrawled words, "Viva, viva, viva Roosevelt."

Belgium, Holland, Denmark, Norway, Sweden. More kings and queens and banquets, crowds in the streets, receptions, speeches. One of the most important of these was in Christiania, Norway, where they were entertained at the royal palace, and where again they drove through dense throngs of people cheering and shouting.

"I really can't understand it," Theodore confessed to Edith. "Perhaps it's largely because I am a former President of the American Republic, which stands to the average European as a queer attractive dream, sort of a Utopia. They think of me as someone representing democracy, liberty, honesty, and justice. But—oh, how fatiguing and irksome! How wonderful when we can be back at Sagamore Hill again, in our own house, with our own beds, among our own friends!"

In Christiania in the National Theater before the Nobel Prize Committee, the King and Queen, the Cabinet and Parliament, he finally gave his acceptance speech for the Peace Prize awarded him in 1906. Its subject was "International Peace," and it called for a limitation of naval armaments by mutual agreement and for the enforcing of peace by a league of nations acting in concert.

The day was observed as a holiday in Christiania. For Edith the day was marred by worry for Theodore because he was suffering from a bout with sore throat and bronchitis which none of her remedies was able to mitigate. But he got through it creditably, and they went on to Sweden, where they were the guests of the Crown Prince and Princess. Theodore was slightly relieved that the King was away.

"If I met one more monarch," he was heard to remark once, "I should bite him."

Germany. Because of the death of King Edward VII of England, the Kaiser's uncle, they were not housed in the royal palace but with their own ambassador. However, they lunched with His Majesty in the palace at Potsdam, and Edith sat next to him. They talked enthusiastically of art, and, somewhat to Theodore's envy, they departed together to see the palace's famous treasures. The next day in Berlin he was invited to review the field maneuvers of the German troops for five hours, an honor never before conferred on a private citizen. Wearing a simple riding suit of khaki and a black slouch hat, he rode beside the richly caparisoned Kaiser and expressed dutiful admiration of a military display which even then he was beginning to profoundly distrust.

"Medieval, artificial!" he fumed afterward to Edith. Four years later he would be using much stronger and more denunciatory terms.

England. Theodore had been asked by Taft to represent the United States at King Edward's funeral. "With him and the Kaiser present," Archie Butt had remarked caustically, "it will be a wonder if the poor corpse gets a passing thought."

It was almost like being at home again. Just to hear English spoken by the servants, on the streets! They stayed with Whitelaw Reid, the American ambassador. Their old friend Cecil Spring-Rice was in London. To add to the feeling of hominess Alice came over, in mourning over the recent death of Grandfather Lee, who had left her a very respectable legacy. Edith attended the royal funeral in St. George's Chapel, Windsor, sitting in the choir section with Ambassador Reid. She was amazed at the attention Theodore received. All eyes seemed to be on him. She was not the only one who marveled. In America President Taft, in his genial, generous manner, was commenting to Archie Butt, "I don't suppose there was ever such a reception as that given Theodore in Europe now. It does not surprise me that rulers, potentates, and public men should pay him this honor, but what does surprise me is that small villages, which one would hardly think had ever heard of him, should seem to know all about the man. It's the force of his personality, of course, that has passed beyond his own country and the capitals of the world and seeped into the small crevices of the universe."

Edith was graciously received by Queen Mother Alexandra and her sister, the Dowager Empress of Russia, and liked them both, though she was not exactly pleased when they expressed a desire to kiss her. Somehow being touched by anyone except family offended her innate desire for privacy, but she endured it gracefully. In Cambridge Theodore addressed the College Union, and the undergraduates gave him a rousing reception, during which a teddy bear was lowered from the ceiling. But the high point of the English visit was his "Romanes Lecture" at Oxford, which he had spent months preparing. What the lecture lacked in popular appeal, for it was a sober scientific treatise, it atoned for in the buoyant personality of its deliverer. The Archbishop of York commented later, "In the way of grading which we have at Oxford, we agreed to mark the lecture 'Beta Minus' but the lecturer 'Alpha Plus.' "

For Theodore one of his happiest memories of this English visit was a cartoon which appeared in *Punch*. It showed the lions of Trafalgar Square being guarded by a bobby wearing a big placard: "These lions are not to be shot." As Edith well knew, he loved to laugh at himself.

Their arrival in New York on June 18, 1910, was no anticlimax. As the *Kaiserin Augusta Victoria* steamed into the harbor, it was met by whistles, sirens shrieking, a flotilla of destroyers, a battleship, yachts filled with citizens anxious to welcome back "Teddy." Congressmen, Cabinet members, Archie Butt, the White House military aide, came swarming up the ladder. Archie brought letters from the President for Theodore and one for Edith from Mrs. Taft.

But for her only one thing was important, the children.

"Come," she said to Archie, "let's see if we can see the children in any of the boats." Going to the railing, they saw far below Belle Hagner, Conie Robinson, Bamie Cowles, Archie, Quentin, Ted with his fiancée Eleanor Alexander. "Look, Archie!" Edith exulted. "There they all are. Think! For the first time in nearly two years I have them within reach!" Running back to the cabin, she called, "Come here, Theodore, and see your children. They are of far more importance than politics or anything else." When he arrived on the bridge a shout went up from the shore, as Archie Butt described it, such as to "waken the stones."

But, as usual, for Theodore family had to wait. There was the official welcome by Cornelius Vanderbilt, who headed a Committee of One Hundred that had organized a review of the fleet and a street parade, a welcoming speech by the mayor, a long parade up Fifth Avenue past thousands who had assembled. Edith fortunately was already united with family and had come with them to the town house of Eleanor's mother, Mrs. Alexander, at 433 Fifth Avenue, where they all watched the parade. She had written officials from Europe that she refused to ride in any welcoming procession. There were gifts of welcome there, including a beautiful pitcher from the Tafts. After the parade Theodore arrived for one of his favorite luncheons of creamed chicken and rice.

"They must have some Georgia blood in their veins," he exulted, "or else Mrs. Alexander knew she would have a goodly contingent of Georgians as her guests."

Later in the day a frightful storm arose, the worst New York had seen in years. Seventeen persons were killed. It had rained also the night before. Only the morning hours had been clear. Roosevelt luck, people called it. Perhaps the storm was symbolic of the political tempest already boiling in the teapot. For the dismissal of Pinchot had been only the first indication that Taft was not following his predecessor's policies. The reform movement was dead. The party was in a shambles.

But, as Edith had said, the family was all-important. Action, if he was to take any, must wait. First, two days after their return, came Ted's wedding at the Fifth Avenue Presbyterian Church. It was filled to the doors. At the last minute it was discovered that five hundred Rough Riders who had come to welcome Theodore were still in the city, and a block of seats in the gallery was reserved for them. It was one of the hottest days of the season, and as Edith made her way through the crowds in the street, she pitied the poor policemen in their heavy blue woolen uniforms and gray helmets. She was glad she had chosen a cool dress in a pretty soft shade of lilac, one of her favorite colors. The wedding reception afterward was held in the house belonging to Eleanor's aunt and uncle at 4 West Fifty-eighth Street. The five hundred Rough Riders consumed most of the wedding cake.

Ted had hoped to avoid publicity, but his plan backfired. Though they dashed uptown at full speed in a car while the police kept others from following, and went to Philadelphia, then on to Chicago, where they registered as "Mr. and Mrs. Winthrop Rogers," the ruse was detected, and they were besieged by newsmen. To Ted's disgust publicity pursued them to San Francisco, where he was to work at the office of the Hartford Carpet Company.

"Poor Ted," said Edith ruefully. "He has always so hated being the son and namesake of such a famous man!"

"Fame!" scoffed Theodore. "What is it? Cheers today may, probably will, turn into hoots of derision tomorrow. I've found that out."

He reached over and took her hand. They were sitting on the western porch side by side at Sagamore Hill, haven from all their travels, watching the glories of the sunset, listening to the songs of the wood thrushes, the warbles of the vireos and tanagers, and, down in the woods at the base of the grassy slope, the flight song of an oven bird. All seemed to be at peace. They were at home again. He was busy writing his *Autobiography,* which dealt with activities all in the past. For once he was rocking gently, not violently. But Edith was not deceived. She knew that it was only an interim of peace.

She was not mistaken. Party leaders kept coming to Sagamore. Extremists on both sides were urging him to take action, the insurgents *against* Taft, the "standpatters," alarmed lest party dissension might lose them the coming election, *for* the President. Both groups blamed him, one because it feared he would not take action, the other because it feared he would.

"Poor Theodore is so harassed and worried that I could almost wish him back in Africa," Edith wrote Bamie, "and the worst of it is that he sees no way out of his present problem." One eloquent cartoon showed a huge heavily burdened elephant peering over the top of the wall at Sagamore Hill and labeled: "I've got to see him."

It was an unhappy summer. Kermit and Ethel were away visiting. Archie, having been expelled from Groton for writing a letter ridiculing the headmaster, was with Theodore's sheriff friend, Seth Bullock, in South Dakota. Poor Quentin languished without the companionship of cousins, who were scattered. It was, as Theodore wrote Ted, "the definite end of the old Oyster Bay life that all you children used to lead." But there was no lack of visitors nor of correspondence, for mail came in by the ton. Though Theodore had vowed not to participate in politics, his concern was too great to resist the pressure. He would involve himself in state issues, he decided, steering clear of national ones.

Though both he and Edith had refused the Tafts' invitation to visit the White House, he traveled to the President's summer home in Beverly, Massachusetts, for a conference. All was cordial. National politics were not mentioned. Taft genially agreed to support Governor Charles Evans Hughes's fight for a bill to ensure direct primaries for nomination to state offices in New York. But Theodore sensed that the President's support was lukewarm.

"Taft is utterly helpless as a leader," he wrote Ted in August. "I fear he has just enough strength to keep with him the people of natural inertia, the good conservative unimaginative people who never do appreciate the need of going forward."

The old Tammany forces, as well as the "standpatters" in his own party, attacked him venomously. He was dubbed "radical," "socialist," "revolutionary." The primary bill did not pass. And in the election that fall the governor was defeated.

"It matters little," was Theodore's reaction. "I have nothing to ask, for I desire nothing personally, and attacks pass just as praise passes."

It mattered more to Edith. Fear for his safety once more reared its head. In August and September he made a long trip west, speaking in sixteen states and expounding his views on the New Nationalism. Now a member of the staff of the *Outlook*, he traveled in a special car which the magazine provided. Edith knew the speeches he had prepared were red flags arousing all the hostility of his enemies. "We are face to face with new conceptions of the relations of property to human welfare. The man who wrongly holds that every human right is secondary to his profit must now give way to the advocate of human welfare. . . . The essence of any struggle for liberty has always been, and must always be to take from some one man or class of men the right to enjoy power, or wealth, or position, or immunity, which has not been earned by service to his or their fellows." And now he had no Secret Service guards to protect him!

Fortunately she did not know of one physical hazard until it was all over. In St. Louis he was invited to take a "hop" in a plane that had just made a record flight. "By George!" he exclaimed. "I believe I will."

It was a flimsy craft, looking a little like a boxed kite, no cockpit, open to the sky. Theodore's two hundred plus pounds were almost too much, but after some lurching it rose and circled the field. The crowd below cheered, then fell into anxious silence; yelled with relief when, after about four minutes, it came down, and "Teddy" climbed out. "By George, it was great!" was his delighted comment.

"There's nothing left for him to try now," one of his friends remarked. "He's been down in a submarine and up in an airplane. That's about the limit."

A quiet winter compensated for the unpleasant summer. Theodore was safely "caged" at home, the children all well accounted for. Ted was happily engaged in business in California. Kermit was at Harvard, Archie at school in Arizona, Quentin, always unpredictable, leading his class at Groton. Ethel, happily, was at home. Finances also were no worry. Theodore was on a regular salary from *Outlook,* and he expected to make up to forty thousand dollars from his African book. To add to Edith's feeling of euphoria, in January Ted wrote that they were expecting a baby in August. A grandchild would make her happiness complete. She still looked back regretfully, as she wrote Archie, "to the days when the old hen could brood you all under her wings."

But Theodore hungered for action. He was soon planning another long trip to tout his doctrines of the New Nationalism, this time to the Southwest. To Edith's relief she was included in the plans. She would meet him in Albuquerque and go on with him. They visited Archie in Arizona, motored from Phoenix to the Roosevelt Dam, which Theodore had been invited to dedicate, went on to California and spent ten days with Ted and Eleanor, returning to New York in April.

That August of 1911 Edith turned fifty. The new grandchild, Grace, Ted's child, was the most precious present, arriving slightly late on the seventeenth. To celebrate the occasion she planted a little grove of pine trees on the Sagamore grounds. "A place for her to play when she comes to visit," she explained delightedly to Theodore. Otherwise it was an uneventful summer, just the sort she liked best. The children were in and out. She coached Archie in French for his Harvard preliminaries, while Theodore prepared him in history and civics. Quentin, enjoying relief from his surprising scholastic efforts, spent the summer in lazy preoccupation with his animals.

But September brought tragedy. On Saturday, September 30, Edith was riding with Theodore and Archie when her horse, Pine Knot, suddenly swerved without warning or cause and threw her on the hard macadam in front of the Cove schoolhouse. She was knocked senseless. Fortunately a delivery wagon was passing, and Theodore brought her home in it, while Archie rode Theodore's horse, Sirdar, and led his own horse and Pine Knot. Theodore was frantic until the doctor came. Though she had broken no bones and the doctor discovered no concussion, she did not regain consciousness for thirty-six hours. Then she suffered an agonizing headache. For nine days she was lucid only at intervals. She remembered nothing of the fall. Theodore consulted a nerve specialist and hired nurses to attend her around the clock. And he scarcely left her side. "Sometimes," he wrote Ted, "I just sat quietly and held her hand and at other times she wants me to repeat poetry, which I do conscientiously but not as successfully as Ethel, for the poetry I know by heart is apt to be of a grandiose and warlike character, not especially fitted for soothing purposes in the sickroom."

It was a long siege, but recovery came finally, all except regaining a sense of smell. No small loss for one who had reveled in the aromas of apple blossoms and wild strawberries, of lavender and wood smoke and new-mown hay! She was feeling almost well by Christmas, though something seemed to be lacking beside the smells of roasting pig and spiced pudding and cedar boughs. It was small children, of course. "Christmas loses some of its fine edge" Theodore wrote Ted, "when the youngest child is a boy a half inch taller than his father."

Even sickness could not mar these months of tranquillity for Edith. Since his African trip Theodore claimed to be "thoroughly happy" to be here with her in their own home, "with our books and pictures and bronzes, and big wood fires, and horses to ride, and the knowledge that our children are doing well." As Owen Wister had once commented, "Mrs. Roosevelt had married the whirlwind, and for a while it was not blowing!" It was well that she had this respite, for once more a hurricane was in the offing.

Early in 1912 Edith came face-to-face with a certainty which had been only the vaguest of possibilities. Theodore wanted to run again for the presidency! She knew, of course, that he had been under constant pressure from friends. Now the tenor of his letters was changing from "not under any circumstances" to "not unless it is by the will of and for the good of the people" and, finally, "yes, if nominated, I would accept." In February he was writing, "My hat is in the ring, and the fight is on!"

Edith was strongly opposed to his decision and did not hesitate to say so. "You can put it out of your mind, Theodore. You will never be President of the United States again." But he had scented the enticing odors of the racetrack and was champing at the bit. Once more he was out on the campaign trail, fearlessly making statements that cheered his friends and shocked his enemies.

"I believe in pure democracy . . . that human rights are supreme over all other rights, that wealth should be the servant, not the master of the people." He endorsed the initiative and referendum, direct primaries, recall of elective officials when provided with adequate safeguards. Some of his friends were shocked too. Though Cabot Lodge felt he had gone too far in his speeches, it did not end their friendship. Nicholas Longworth remained a staunch supporter of Taft, causing a dilemma for Alice, who was always a rabid supporter of her father.

Archie Butt, advised by Alice to leave the Administration before it was too late, firmly refused. "My devotion to the Colonel is as strong as it was the day he left, but I won't have it said that another Roosevelt man reads the handwriting on the wall and gets out of the sinking ship, or some other mixed metaphor." So torn by loyalty to his two presidents that he sickened and needed a physical rest, Archie sailed for Europe in March, recuperating so well that he started back home in April from England—on a vessel called the *Titanic*.

He did not leave the sinking ship. Though Edith scanned the list of survivors with an almost frantic hope, his name was not listed. "Do you remember," she asked Theodore tearfully, "how he said he wished he could hear his favorite hymn sung when he was dying? I wish—"

Her wish had come true. For it was later reported by the survivors that Archie had taken charge of the passengers during the sinking and had directed them in bravely singing "Nearer My God to Thee" as the ship was going down.

2

Edith went with Theodore to Chicago in June, 1912, for the Republican Convention. He was in high spirits. Enthusiasm for his nomination had swept the country. According to the primaries his victory was assured. He had received over a million votes to Taft's seven hundred thousand. But he was also as taut as a strumming wire. The National Committee, chosen with his approval four years before, was questioning the status of many of the delegates, deciding in favor of those committed to Taft. Two days before the start of the convention he found himself seventy delegates short of the nomination.

"Theft!" he exclaimed bitterly. He was furious. Immediately he began writing a speech to deliver the following evening to a rally of his supporters. It blazed with vindictive language. When he read it to Edith her response was, as so often, restraining. How much better, she observed, if he eliminated some of the more vindictive passages! "You know some of those hot utterances make it so difficult for your friends to defend you."

"Edie—" He looked wounded, like one of the children being corrected. "You know I was only—" But as so often, he took her advice, and the speech when delivered was a model of reasonable and dignified protest.

When Elihu Root, once his Secretary of State and loyal supporter but now a Taft man, was elected chairman of the convention, he knew his fate was sealed. The shouts of "Teddy! We want Teddy!" that started a ten-minute ovation when he entered the hall were but echoes of false hopes.

Back in their hotel room, Theodore was for once helpless, gloomy, undecided. What should he do? Fight? Try to find a compromise candidate? Let such dishonesty rule, this action which was "dangerously near to being treason to the spirit of free democratic government?" Edith gave him no advice. This must be his choice. "Fight, of course!" urged Alice with her usual decisive vigor.

Taft was nominated, while Theodore's ardent supporters walked off the floor. That evening they held a "rump" convention in Orchestra Hall, and Theodore agreed to consider nomination as presidential candidate for a new Progressive Party that would hold its official convention later in the summer.

So the siege began. But before he finally committed himself there was a brief respite. It was almost like one of the old summers, the family again together, with additions, in fact, for Ted, Eleanor, and little Gracie were there, Ted having given up his business with the carpet company for a position on Wall Street. For Theodore as well as Edith it was a blessed interlude. In spite of feverish plans and organization, constant visitors, conferences at the *Outlook* office, thousands of letters and telegrams, "Theodore bears all these worries and hurts marvelously," Edith wrote Bamie, adding a paean of praise to baby Gracie. "He runs in half a dozen times a day and picks her up in his arms."

Edith reveled in the normal family bustle and pandemonium. Not so, Ted's wife Eleanor. "Before twenty-four hours passed," she wrote later, "I realized that nothing in my bringing up as an only child had in any way prepared me for the frenzied activity into which I was plunged." At first she thought everyone would be tired when the day was over and she could go to bed early, but no. The family could not waste time sleeping. They stayed downstairs until midnight, then, talking at the top of their voices, they trooped up the wide uncarpeted stairs and went to their rooms. Surely no one would wake up before eight! No? By six she was the only one not joyously beginning the day.

Then came a picnic. Good, thought Eleanor. She liked picnic food—dainty sandwiches in waxed paper, maybe a nice salad. Lunch outdoors perhaps under a cool tree. No. Friends and cousins began gathering by the dozen. They walked a half mile through the woods as fast as they could put one foot before the other. Why so fast? She found out. When she slowed down, trying to keep cool, mosquitoes came in swarms, and she was soon running. On the beach they piled into five uncomfortable rowboats and rowed and rowed under the blazing sun. Two hours later they landed on a beach, seemingly just like the one they had started from. Provisions were spread out—not dainty sandwiches but thick ham sandwiches, not salads but huge clams! No shade of trees for fear of poison ivy! A roaring fire was built to cook the clams. When they were done Ted's father opened one, sprinkled it with salt and pepper, and handed it to her. Big, with a long black neck! It burned her mouth when she thrust it in. Although gritty, it tasted delicious at first, but soon turned into a piece of old rubber hose. She slipped it under a log, hoping to escape observation, but Theodore's eyes were keen.

"You aren't as persistent as Archie," he said kindly. "The first time he was old enough to eat a clam he chewed for a time, then ate three sandwiches, some cookies and an orange. Later he asked what he should do with the poor little dead clam. It was still in his mouth."

They rowed in a head wind and it took four hours instead of two to get home. They were sunburned and blistered. "One of the best picnics we ever had," was the delighted verdict.

For Edith the beatific interlude ended in late July when Kermit, now twenty-two, sailed for Brazil for a management position with the Brazil Railroad Company. Knowing the sensitive, dreamy nature of this son who was so like herself, she feared for his future. Could he really find happiness in business? His leaving was only the beginning of change, for the next week she was off again with Theodore for the Progressive Party Convention in Chicago. Hopefully, loyally, she listened to his opening address, his "Confession of Faith," while knowing well the disruption, perhaps the tragedy, it would create in their lives.

"The new party," he said, "will put forth a platform which shall be a contract with the people and we shall hold ourselves under honorable obligations to fulfill every promise it contains."

The platform included many of the reforms he had advocated, measures which a few generations later would be considered commonplace, but which at the time seemed revolutionary— woman suffrage, social welfare legislation for women and children, workmen's compensation, limited injunction in labor disputes, farm relief, health insurance in industry, inheritance and income taxes. Many represented wishful thinking, impossible of attainment.

Now the campaign was on in earnest. September found him rushing about the country making fiery speeches in behalf of his new National Progressive, or, as it was soon dubbed, "Bull Moose" Party, a term derived from his own self-appraisal, "I feel as fit as a bull moose!"

Alone again after the summer's exodus, Edith was assailed by the old fears. Where was he? What madman might be waiting in the crowds? In October, after he had departed on another tour, this time of the Great Lakes states, she could stand the loneliness of Sagamore no longer. She moved to New York to the home of Cousin Laura Roosevelt. It was October 14, and they had gone to the theater together to hear Johann Strauss's operetta *Die Fledermaus*. They were sitting on the aisle, Edith on the inside with an empty seat beside her. They hoped Laura's son, Oliver, who worked at the Progressive headquarters in the city, would join them. He came and slipped into the seat beside Edith. When she leaned over and put her hand on his knee, she found he was shaking violently.

"What is it?" she whispered, feeling a strange presentiment.

Cousin Theodore had been shot at but not hit, he told her. Edith gasped, then said quietly, "You say he wasn't hurt, Oliver? But— please go back and—and make sure." After an eternity he returned. More details had come in. He had been "scratched," Oliver told her, but he had gone on with his speech. So—what she had feared for years had actually happened. But surely, if he had gone on with his speech, he couldn't have been hurt too badly. Refusing to leave the theater, she sat through the performance in numb misery. Reporters had already assembled outside, but she and her party escaped by a side door and went directly to Progressive headquarters. Here she learned more details.

Theodore was in Milwaukee. As he left the Gilpatrick Hotel to go to the hall for his speech, he found a huge cheering crowd outside. Then, as he walked to his car, lifting his top hat, smiling, all but mouthing his favorite "Dee-lighted," a pistol shot rang out. He fell back, clutching at his chest. The crowds fell on the assassin, intent on tearing him to pieces, but Theodore pulled himself to his feet and shouted, "Stand back! Don't hurt him!" A physician appeared. "You've had a severe shock, Colonel," he said. "You must be taken to a hospital."

"No, no, nonsense. I can't disappoint all those people who came to hear me." He climbed into the car. "Go to the hall," he ordered the driver. "I will make this speech or die," he vowed. "It is one thing or the other."

Even when he reached the hall and it was found that the bullet had passed through his coat, suit coat, spectacle case, and even the thick manuscript of his speech, he still insisted on speaking. To an audience tense with apprehension, for they had heard the news, he began in a low voice, unlike his usual strident staccato style.

"Please excuse me from making a long speech. I'll do the best I can, but there is a bullet in my body. I am not hurt badly. It takes more than a little bullet to kill a bull moose. I have a message to deliver and will deliver it as long as there is life in my body." Pulling the mutilated, blood-stained manuscript form his pocket, he spoke for almost an hour. Then, and only then, did he permit himself to be taken to the hospital.

"How can you be so calm and cool?" demanded Laura when they had returned to the house.

Edith did not feel calm and cool. She felt like a boiling stream under a thin coating of ice. Not until after midnight, when a telegram arrived from Theodore saying that he was "in excellent shape" and the wound was "trivial," did she draw a long breath. He was at the Emergency Hospital and expected to go right on with his engagements. Still, she was not really relieved. He always made light of his accidents.

The morning papers were full of the misfortune, even though most were his political opponents. INSISTS ON SPEAKING. NO THOUGHT OF SELF. SMILES THROUGH IT ALL. "We are against his policies, but we like his grit."

Returning to Progressive headquarters, Edith learned that he was in the Mercy Hospital in Chicago. The bullet was still lodged in his chest. Hearing that doctors were worried because he was insisting on going on with his campaigning, she made her decision. She could handle him if the doctors couldn't. That afternoon, with Ethel and Ted she left for Chicago on the Twentieth Century Limited. She also took Alec Lambert, their beloved family doctor.

They found Alice already there when they arrived at the hospital. Trust her to be on hand when anything of importance happened to her father! Edith was infinitely relieved. Theodore looked comparatively well and his whole condition seemed good. But he must not be moved. Without fanfare, in her firm but gentle way, she saw to that. Soon, reported the Chicago *Tribune,* "she was practically managing the hospital, as far as the Colonel was concerned."

Theodore was a surprisingly docile patient. Indeed, he seemed to be enjoying himself. "Dearest Bye," he wrote his sister, "I am dictating this in bed, and it will have to be signed for me by Edith. It is just a line to tell you I am in great shape. Really the time in the hospital, with Edith and the children on here, has been a positive spree, and I have enjoyed it. . . ."

Even after their return to Sagamore a week later he was more or less docile, submitting to the watchful attention of his beloved servant James Amos and the stern insistence of Edith on keeping visitors away form the house. The docility lasted for three whole days. Then he was up and out of doors, looking for Edith. He found her in the garden picking flowers. Though she was not pleased, she let him walk as far as the tennis court. The next day, his fifty-fourth birthday, he declared that he would make his scheduled speech in Madison Square Garden three days hence. Though both Taft and the democratic candidate Woodrow Wilson had gallantly refused to campaign until he was well again, he had no intention of lengthening the hiatus. Edith resigned herself to the inevitable.

When seven o'clock arrived the streets around the Garden were thronged with thirty thousand people, some sixteen thousand having pushed through to seats inside. When his limousine arrived, as the *Sun* reported, the people "yelled their immortal souls out, went through a battery of photographers, tried to sweep the cops off their feet, tangled, jammed and shoved. . . ." Only by a miracle did the police manage to hold them back while Theodore entered the building.

Edith sat in a box with Ethel, Ted, Eleanor, and Quentin and listened to one of the greatest speeches of his career. The roar that greeted his appearance on the platform lasted forty-one minutes and would have gone on longer if he had not quelled it with a stern "Quiet, down there!" He spoke nobly, outlining his credo of political faith, this time without a hint of malice or bitterness, his voice never once breaking into that characteristic falsetto, making no attacks on his competitors. It was a plea for human rights, for equal justice and liberty for all.

"Our people work hard and faithfully. They do not wish to shirk their work. They must feel pride in the work for the work's sake. But there must be bread for the work. There must be time for play. . . . When they grow old there must be certainty of rest under conditions free from the haunting terror of poverty."

Edith's eyes were misted. Never had she been so proud of him. If experience of near death had had such a purifying, chastening effect, perhaps it had been worth all the horror and suffering.

Chastened or not, he was hard on the campaign trail again, fighting with all his terrific lust for battle. A cartoon described the situation well. It depicted a huge elephant and a small donkey looking with dismay at an opening in the woods from which a thundering bull moose came charging. The two were exclaiming, "Here he comes again!"

Because of the Progressive movement, which divided the Republican Party, Woodrow Wilson was elected, but not by a popular majority, for he received only 6,286,124 votes to Roosevelt's 4,126,020 and Taft's 3,483,922.

The night following the election reporters crowded to Sagamore Hill, avid to find out how the Progressive candidate reacted to his defeat. They found him sitting beside a lamp in his library reading one of his favorite books, while a log fire glowed in the huge fireplace. "He was all buoyant and good-humored," reported the *Times* the next morning, chatting "in the most cheerful manner imaginable."

The battle had not been entirely lost, as future events would reveal. His crusade against privilege and exploitation, which had stirred the conscience of the country, would compel action on many of the social issues during the next and subsequent administrations. Before Wilson's term had ended most of the principles the Bull Moose Party had so vigorously espoused would be written into law.

Edith knew the cheerfulness was only a pose. "Theodore is rather blue," she confessed to Bamie. "Many things that he had no time to think of during the campaign come to him now." Yet even she could not fully gauge the depths of his emotions. He was neither disappointed nor bitter. He had expected defeat. And he had fought a good fight. But he felt like a race horse suddenly turned out to pasture. His political life was ended. No African wilderness to conquer in the months ahead! No lions to hunt!

It was a strange winter. Reporters no longer flocked to Sagamore. The telephone was for the most part silent. For days at a time the new macadamized road put in the previous year remained empty of visitors on horseback, in carriages, in chugging motorcars—the politicians, office seekers, sightseers who for the last fifteen years had come thronging to this cynosure of national attraction. Now that he was a loser, even many of the once attentive neighbors had become suspicious of the doctrines he had so vigorously espoused, fearing lest such "wild" and "revolutionary" ideas might threaten their comfortable security. With all the children gone the big house seemed like an echoing void.

If Edith worried about Theodore's secret frustration, he was equally concerned about her. "Mother is not well," he wrote Kermit in December. "She never has been well since she was thrown off that horse a year ago. I anticipate, however, that after a little while she will begin to recover the tone of her nerves and body."

Christmas came, an antidote for frustration, illness, loneliness. "Christmas was great fun," Theodore wrote Emily Carow. "All the children acted as if it were fifteen years ago. They hung up their stockings and came in and opened them on the bed next morning, and after breakfast trooped in to see their presents in Edith's drawing room." And in January he was writing, "Edith is now distinctly better than she was, and I am delighted to say that has put upon Ethel a good many tasks which Ethel can do, and which Edith ought not to do. Edith is able to get down to lunch and to dinner and to take little walks. She and I have just returned from a stroll to Cooper's Bluff."

Frustration—defeat—inactivity—they were not words in Theodore's vocabulary. While the logs "roared and crackled" during the long winter evenings in the huge fireplaces he sat at his desk and ground out articles for the *Outlook,* later to be compiled into his *Autobiography,* worked on a two-volume opus to be titled *Histories of African Game Animals,* and prepared a lecture for the American Historical Society, of which he was president, entitled "History as Literature." This he delivered in Boston at the end of December. He came back restored in energy and optimism, for the Bostonians, stuffy as he had often thought them, had responded to his masterful portrayal of past cultures as enthusiastically as had the crowds to his political diatribes. As always, Edith was amazed at his versatility. He could declaim as eloquently and intelligently on the "kings of Nineveh where they drink from ivory and gold" as on the domestic habits of the African lion or the virtues of clean politics.

The doldrums of winter passed, and once more Sagamore sprang into activity. Edith was surprised one day in February when Ethel came into her room and announced with her usual forthright matter-of-factness, "Mother, I have decided to marry Dick."

Edith accepted her announcement with pleasure but equal lack of fanfare. "My dear, I am so happy for you."

"Dick" was Richard Derby, a New York doctor whom Ethel had met at Roosevelt Hospital. Though ten years older than Ethel, who was now twenty-one, he was eminently suitable, of a fine Massachusetts family, with independent means above his adequate salary as a surgeon. Theodore was "dee-lighted." "He's the best young fellow I know," he told Bamie. The wedding, it was decided, would be in April.

The household burst into springtime life along with the maples, white birches, and poplars. While the orange-liveried orioles wove their gray nests in the drooping branches of the weeping elm at the corner of the house, Edith happily prepared the family nest for the assemblage of her own offspring. Except for Kermit, all would be together again. The two months before the wedding were, as she wrote Bamie, "among the happiest times" of her life, with Ethel, "so sweet and unselfish, but living in a rose-colored cloud quite alone with Dick."

The event itself early in April was a simple affair compared with that earlier White House wedding, as different from it as the quiet, reserved Ethel, so like her mother, was different from the flamboyant Alice. The ceremony was in Christ Church at Oyster Bay, where the family had worshiped for twenty-five years. "The day was beautiful and warm with the air of spring," wrote Owen Wister, one of the guests. "As one looked about, familiar faces were smiling everywhere." Other guests were Henry Cabot Lodge and Winthrop Chanler. Theodore had not invited Taft or Root or others of his former political friends. "I shall never forgive the men who were the leaders in that swindling," he confessed.

Alice came, of course, but her presence added little verve to the occasion. Nicholas did not come with her. The split in the Republican Party had lost him his seat in Congress, and they had moved to his home in Cincinnati. He obviously blamed Theodore for his defeat. Alice also had been torn between her intense loyalty to her father and her husband's more conservative stance, and the impasse had almost caused a rift between them. She was now sullen and resentful, unadjusted to the move from Washington and separation from its brilliant society. Edith was distressed when she revealed her intention to wear a dark blue and ugly yellow dress to the wedding and insisted that she go into New York and buy something more appropriate. Nick's absence and failure to send even a note of congratulation were the only flaws in Ethel's radiant enjoyment.

"We did not really care," Edith confessed, "but poor Sister was deeply hurt."

When it was over and they were all gone, Edith succumbed to exhaustion and spent most of the next day in bed, then renewed her well-being by a long walk in the woods with an understanding relative and friend, Margaret Roosevelt, the daughter of Theodore's cousin Emlen. Again life at Sagamore resumed a welcome but unnatural tranquillity.

As usual, it was only a lull, for presently Edith had new nagging worries. Theodore had accepted invitations from the governments of Brazil, Argentina, and Chile to deliver a series of addresses in the three capitals. He planned to leave in October and hoped that Edith would accompany him. That was fine. She looked forward with anticipation to the holiday, for it would mean visiting Kermit and exploring countries that offered fascinating knowledge of new cultures. But Theodore's plans included exposure to more than foreign cultures. He wanted to head an expedition into the Brazilian wilderness. Already he had approached the American Museum of Natural History in New York with a request for naturalists to accompany him and made arrangements with his publishers for a profitable series of articles.

Edith was not the only one who feared the hazards of such a trip. Many friends tried to dissuade him. Not only was it far more dangerous than his African excursion, but he was too old, lame, half blind, less inured to strenuous activity. He laughed good-naturedly. He was going, anyway. It was his "last chance to be a boy."

When they left for South America in October, Edith had resigned herself to the inevitable. Theodore was his old ebullient self again. Waving good-bye to a throng of well-wishers at the dock, wearing a gray suit and soft gray hat, tie with a stickpin and a boutonniere in his lapel, he looked as jauntily jubilant as when starting off on the campaign trail years before.

"I think he feels like Christian in 'Pilgrim's Progress,'" Edith wrote Bamie from the SS *Vandyck*, "when the bundle fell from his back. In this case it was not made of sins but of the Progressive Party."

During the voyage he was the most popular man on the steamer. He danced the sailor's hornpipe at an evening entertainment. His 220 pounds were the deciding factor in a "tug of war" contest. Edith was glad Margaret Roosevelt, Emlen's daughter, had agreed to come along as her companion, for she saw little of her husband.

At Bahia, Brazil, Kermit, who had been working as a supervisor for the Anglo-Brazilian Iron Company, joined their party and went on with them to Rio de Janeiro, where Theodore's reception had "all the wild enthusiasm of a national holiday." It was not a restful trip. Traveling through Brazil, Uruguay, Argentina, across the Andes and into Chile, Edith was involved in almost as constant social and official events as in the White House days. Margaret proved an ideal companion, even providing romantic interest to the tour, for a young man met on the ship, Henry Hunt, had fallen in love with her and began sending her bouquets of white roses every day. Kermit added even more of an aura to the atmosphere of romance when on November 13 he received a cable from Belle Willard, whom he had been courting, saying that she would marry him.

Belle, who was a friend of Ethel, was the daughter of the American ambassador to Spain. Theodore heartily approved of the match. Edith was not so sure. Would the lovely blonde Belle, a gay young socialite who had reminded her of the lighthearted heroine of a fairy tale, really satisfy all the needs of her introspective and sensitive Kermit? But perhaps she would have questioned the fitness of any possible mate for this son who was so like herself.

On November 26 the dreaded separation came. Edith and Margaret left to sail home by way of Panama, Theodore and Kermit to head up the Paraguay River, the "River of Doubt," under the guidance of Colonel Rondon, a Brazilian army officer of Indian blood, an expedition sponsored by the government of Brazil.

For Edith the next six months were an endless, monotonous wasteland, with only occasional heights and depressions of emotion. The latter began to come quickly—the sudden death of her congenial companion Margaret from typhoid, contracted somehow on their journey, though how she could not have guessed, for they had both drunk only bottled water and eaten no fresh produce; the death of Grandma Lee up in Boston, which concerned Alice more than herself. The heights were few indeed—the birth of Ethel's son, another Richard, on March 7; an occasional reassuring letter from Theodore, like the one written on Christmas Eve.

"Darling Edie. I never felt in better health—in spite of being covered with prickly heat—so if you do not hear from me to the contrary you can safely assume that this condition is permanent." (Of course she could do no such thing!) "Kermit is his own mother's son! He is to me a delightful companion; he always has books with him, and he is a tireless worker. . . . We are now in a hot little sidewheel steamer jammed with men, dogs, bags and belongings, partially cured and rather bad-smelling skins. . . . In ten days we shall be at the last post office . . . and then we shall go into the real wilderness. . . ."

It was his articles which began appearing in *Scribner's* in April that created a last long month of depression. They were full of catastrophes—canoes overturning, one of the party drowning, fever, shortage of food, dugouts jammed between rocks, a bruising of Theodore's bad leg against a boulder, with resulting inflammation. . . . Edith read them with racing heart and compressed lips. Had she known the extent of the horrors encountered, how more than once they had not expected Theodore to live until morning, how, unable to walk, struggling through mazes of jungle with the temperature at 105 degrees, he had begged the company to go ahead for he was only a burden to the party; how they had eaten the tops of palms to keep from starving, how they had been surrounded by hostile Indians, she would have found those last weeks intolerable.

But they were over at last, and he returned on May 19, thirty-five pounds lighter than when he went away, leaning hard on a cane, hobbling down the gangplank. This time there were only a few friends and family to greet him, no welcoming boats, no gun salute, no parade up Broadway and Fifth Avenue. But he was triumphantly satisfied. He had accomplished his purpose, explored a thousand-mile uncharted river that would be renamed Rio Teodoro in his honor, taken full advantage of this last chance "to be a boy." Newspaper men were chagrined to see how thin and old the Bull Moose hero looked.

"Roosevelt returns 35 pounds lighter," the New York *Times* reported. "There was something lacking in the power of his voice. His face had a hearty color, but there were lines that were not there before." Yet he was still able to joke with them. Calling attention to the cane he was leaning on so heavily, he bantered, "You see I still have the big stick."

Less than a week later he was in Washington, calling on the President, giving a lecture on the expedition to the National Geographic Society. Then, a few days later he left with Alice for Madrid to attend the wedding of Kermit and Belle Willard. It was Edith who felt unequal to taking the trip, though she felt sad about absence from her favorite son on this occasion. "It was just not possible," she wrote him. Characteristically, it was she, not Theodore, who had suffered the most emotional strain from his last and most perilously devastating adventure.

"Darling Edie," he wrote her. "Wednesday was the Civil Marriage; simple and rather impressive. Belle and Kermit were so dear! I believe she will be his almost, but not entirely, as you are mine . . . *Your* lover! T.R."

The wedding was on June 11, 1914. The same month, on June 28 Austrian Archduke Francis Ferdinand was murdered at Sarajevo. It was an event which was to set all of Europe aflame and change life for Theodore and Edith, as well as for the rest of the world.

3

"If I had been President," Theodore was to observe later to a friend, "there would have been no war."

The friend looked startled. "You mean—"

He repeated. "There would have been no war."

"But—how—"

It was in a letter to Cecil Spring-Rice that he explained how in detail. "If I had been President, I should have acted on the thirtieth or thirty-first of July, as head of a signatory power of The Hague treaties, calling attention to the guaranty of Belgium's neutrality and saying that I accepted the treaties as imposing a serious obligation which I expected not only the United Sates but all the other neutral nations to join in enforcing. Of course I would not have made such a statement unless I was willing to back it up. I believe that if I had been President the American people would have followed me."

Whatever the possible validity of this idle boast, Theodore was not President when on August 4 Germany, having declared war on Russia and France, invaded Belgium and, though he fumed helplessly at the silence of the present Administration, there was nothing he could do about the international situation. However, he could continue to fight for the abatement of social and industrial evils which his Progressive Party had stood for. He resigned his official connection with the *Outlook* in order to devote himself to politics.

Edith was almost glad that recurrent attacks of jungle fever causing a severe infection of the larynx made it impossible for him to go on the campaign trail, forcing him to give up the idea of running again for governor of New York. Dr. Lambert ordered him to rest for four months. The "rest," as she had expected, was of short duration.

When a New York throat specialist told him that he could make public speeches after only six weeks of rest, he was out on the stump again. But his efforts were useless. In November the Progressive Party suffered a thorough defeat, and he knew that the movement was dead. Edith was glad the fight was over—she hoped. He was at home again, seemingly contented to work off his frustrations in writing letters and magazine articles. He signed a contract with the *Metropolitan Magazine* for an annual salary of twenty-five thousand dollars, which relieved her financial worries. But if she had believed—hoped—that the era of battle was over, she was sadly mistaken. For Theodore was already engaged in the bitterest and fiercest fight of his career.

At first he had given token approval to Wilson's policy of neutrality. "I am an ex-President," he wrote his British friend Arthur Lee, "and my public attitude must be one of entire impartiality." But as he read stories of German atrocities in Belgium in the British press and Edith translated them for him from the French papers, he fumed in helpless frustration. Rocking on the porch, his chair traveling all over the floor as it had a way of doing, then when the weather grew cold leaving his seat by the roaring fire in the North Room to pace up and down, he pondered the situation, and at last took action.

"It's no use," he said finally to Edith. "I'm utterly sick of the spiritless 'neutrality' of the Administration. I can't keep quiet any longer."

He didn't. He began to write articles for the *Metropolitan* condemning Germany for the Belgian tragedy. And immediately he became the butt of furious criticism from all sides—from German-Americans who, to his disgust and amazement, were more loyal to the Fatherland than to the country they had adopted as their own; from pacifists who, like himself, recognized the folly and waste of war yet did not understand the world in which they were living; from Irish immigrants, who were flamingly anti-British. In fact, it seemed, he had become suddenly estranged from the American people, whose hero he had once been. Then on May 7, 1915, the British luxury liner the *Lusitania* was sunk by a German U-boat, resulting in the loss of a thousand American lives.

"Murder!" he raged, and this time many Americans agreed with him. "Not merely piracy but piracy on a vaster scale of murder than the old-time pirates ever practiced. Warfare against innocent men, women and children, and our own fellow-countrymen are among the sufferers. Inconceivable that we can refrain from taking action!"

A few weeks later Alice, who was visiting Sagamore, remarked that the President had sent another polite note to the German government deploring this latest outrage.

"Did you notice what the serial number was?" fumed Theodore. "I fear I have lost trace myself, but I am inclined to think it is Number 11,765, Series B." It seemed inconceivable to him that a man of such high moral caliber as President Wilson could be satisfied with merely mild protest of such action. He became even more outspoken, publicly recommended seizure of all of Germany's interned ships and an edict against all commerce with her.

It was Edith who suggested the title of a book that combined Theodore's articles in the *Metropolitan* on the necessity for preparedness: *Fear God and Take Your Own Part*. When General Wood established a military training camp for volunteers at Plattsburgh, New York, Ted, Archie, and Quentin enrolled for the summer session. Once more Sagamore Hill was invaded by an army of reporters, remnants of the old Progressive movement, even some of his old Rough Riders, urging him to form another battalion, as in 1898, independently if need be, to go to Europe. "I would be able to bring it over in ninety days," he wrote Arthur Lee, "if given a chance."

"He likes the house full of Tom, Dick and Harry," Edith wrote Kermit, who was still working in South America, "and I can't quite keep up with the pace."

In 1916 there was another election. Edith was dismayed when Theodore's supporters began suggesting that he run again for President on a Progressive ticket and was relieved when he proved skeptical. Not that again! It could result only in a fiasco, like the last time. But in spite of his apparent unwillingness to be considered a candidate, there was a movement in the Republican Convention in June to nominate Theodore. However, there was too much opposition. Party leaders were reluctant to make any move suggesting that they were less peaceloving than the Democrats. He was nominated by a withered remnant of Progressives meeting on the same day, but to Edith's unbounded relief, he declined by telegram. He would support the Republican candidate, Charles Evans Hughes.

After Hughes had been nominated, Theodore's friend Dean Lewis found him and Edith sitting on the porch at Sagamore Hill. "I have never seen him more serene," reported Lewis. "There was not a trace of disappointment. We had not been with him ten minutes before our own overstrained nerves were relaxed." If he was secretly harboring disappointment, not so Edith. So little had she ever wanted to return to the White House that back in 1912 she had almost found it in her heart to wish him back in Africa!

One pleasant task that summer was the distribution of the Nobel Peace Prize money of over forty-five thousand dollars among various charities, for Theodore's original industrial peace foundation had never materialized. Theodore chose twenty-eight different organizations and individuals to receive varied amounts, among them the Red Cross, the Y.M.C.A., families of wounded soldiers in countries around the world, and many other welfare groups. It was a happy interlude.

But in spite of his and others' efforts, Wilson was reelected, riding to victory on the slogan "He Kept Us Out of War."

The spring of 1917, with more U-boat attacks on American ships, brought a revulsion of feeling. A German announcement of unrestricted submarine warfare was the final compelling force swaying public opinion. War was declared on April 6.

Jubilantly, Theodore sprang into action. Already he had applied to Secretary of War Baker for permission to raise a division of infantry to take to Europe. Now, visiting Alice, who was triumphantly back in Washington, Nick having been returned to Congress in the November election, Theodore wanted to approach the Secretary of War personally. His nephew Franklin, now in his uncle's old job of Assistant Secretary of the Navy, arranged the meeting. Secretary Baker was noncommittal. Theodore managed an interview with the President. Their meeting was cordial. Wilson remarked afterward, "He is a great big boy. I was charmed by his personality. There is a sweetness about him that is very compelling. You can't resist the man."

But the President was adamant. Theodore's offer was refused. His experience, the White House felt, was too brief and too dated.

Even a request from Clemenceau, the French premier, for his services failed to sway the decision. Theodore, of course, was not only furious but heartbroken. Though not for worlds would Edith have acknowledged her secret relief, she could not help feeling that the rejection was a blessing. In spite of his still unflagging energy, he was lame, half deaf, blind in one eye, subject to recurrences of jungle fever. However great the service he might have rendered in France, it would have meant his death warrant.

Unable to go himself, Theodore did the next best thing. He used all his influence to get his four sons into active service. He persuaded General Pershing to accept Ted and Archie as privates, if they could not win commissions. He was able to get Quentin into the flying squadron. He asked his British friend Arthur Lee to use his influence in getting Kermit, who was untrained, a position in the British army. He would much rather have gone himself, as Edith well knew, and they suffered over the wrenching separation together. As Theodore wrote Ted, "The big bear was not, down at the bottom of his heart, any too happy at striving to get the two little bears where the danger is; elderly bears whose teeth and claws are blunted by age can far better be spared; but . . . I do not sympathize with the proverb: 'God keep you from the werewolf and from your heart's desire!' "

On April 14 the family all went to Boston to celebrate the wedding of Archie to Grace Lockwood. Quentin was best man, Ted and Kermit were ushers. Though they could not know it, this was the last time the family would all be together. As Alice noted in her memoirs, "We were all as cheerful as might be; but there was little of the gaiety of the other family weddings."

Edith remained outwardly calm, as usual, while the world seemed to fall apart around her. On June 20 she saw Ted and Archie sail together on the drab troopship *Chicago*. Kermit was the next to leave, having volunteered to fight with the British in Mesopotamia. In July Quentin came to Sagamore, bringing his fiancée Flora Payne Whitney, slender, dark-haired, lovely, daughter of wealthy Harry and Gertrude Vanderbilt Whitney. Edith was surprised and delighted to find that Flora, "Foufie," as Quentin called her, fitted into the simple Sagamore life as easily as if she had not been born into what Theodore called the "wealthy, kindly, self-absorbed members of the out-door-sport wing of the smart set."

Now there was just one left—Quentin, her "baby." He had passed his tests for combat aviator with flying colors (having concealed the fact of his poor eyesight by memorizing the optician's chart in advance!). The last Sunday before he was to sail he went with Edith to communion at Christ Church. His last night at home she went upstairs and tucked him into bed, as she had done a thousand times. She and Theodore went to New York on the day he sailed, a swelteringly hot day, but they left the ship early, leaving him and his "Foufie" together. Edith could not have borne it to see this last ship sail.

"It was hard when Quentin went," she said to a friend later. "But you can't bring up boys to be eagles and expect them to turn out sparrows."

It was Alice who best described the sorrow and bitterness Theodore felt that day in seeing his last son go, yet being unable to go himself. " 'The old lion perisheth for lack of prey,' " she quoted from the Book of Job, " 'and the stout lion's whelps are scattered abroad.' " Never had the house seemed so empty.

As the months crawled by they lived in two worlds—the daily routine of life at Sagamore, enlivened by visits of daughters and grandchildren or by Theodore's sallies into the boondocks to spur the war effort, and the equally tangible milieu created by letters and news from the war zones.

That summer of 1917 seemed to Edith bereft of life and color. Even the roses and other blooms had lost their brightness and fragrance. Once the day's tasks were finished, she found her hands empty. She compensated by trying to learn how to type, it would make letter writing to the boys so much easier. But her efforts were not successful. When she brought Theodore her first attempt, a letter to enclose with one of his to Archie, he chortled with glee.

"I laughed until I cried over it," he wrote, "and have persuaded her not to make a correction; it contains any amount of news, and the spelling, the repetition of letters, the use of capitals, the telescoping of words, and a genial aspect of exhilaration make it a document of priceless worth."

But summer passed, and with the fall came grandchildren. Eleanor, Ted's wife, was in Europe, having sailed in July to do volunteer work in France under the Y.M.C.A., leaving the three children with her mother. Her desire to be near Ted, her husband, had superseded every other loyalty. In the fall the children came to Sagamore, and Edith's hands were full. With Gracie, five, Ted, three, and baby Cornelius, a year and a half, it was almost like having her own back again. Theodore was equally enthralled. The first evening he read to Gracie about Peter Rabbit and Benjamin Bunny, while Edith read her "Little Black Mingo."

"Ted's memory was much clearer about Peter and Benjamin than about me," Theodore wrote his own Ted. "He greeted me affably but then inquired of a delighted bystander, 'What is that man's name?' "

Ethel's two were there also, Richard and little Edie, for Ethel was away with her husband, waiting for him to sail. But she was with them for Thanksgiving, as were Alice and Nick. For a while the house seemed almost full again.

It was a relief to know that Eleanor was in France, where the boys came in occasional contact with her, and she proved an effective channel for news. Letters from the front were few and severely censored. For a while nothing at all was heard from Quentin, and they were in agony. Theodore wrote him a stern letter berating him for silence, pleading with him to at least write Flora—"interesting letters and love letters. Write no matter how tired you are, no matter how inconvenient it is; write if you're smashed up in a hospital; write when you are doing your most dangerous stunts; write all the time! If you wish to lose her, continue to be an infrequent correspondent."

Then they discovered that he had been recovering from a bout with pneumonia. Eleanor had gone from her post in Paris to Issoudon, where he was training, found him in a bed in a long narrow barracks, poorly heated by a stove at one end, a room bitterly cold and damp! She had taken him back to Paris, and he had been with her for Christmas. In fact, since her arrival in Europe she had had a procession of family visitors, Ted, Archie, Richard Derby, Ted's cousins George, Philip, Nicholas.

"Really, Eleanor has been the kind of comfort to those boys!"

Theodore wrote Belle, Kermit's wife. "But poor Quentin felt too dismal over the Christmas away from home to be really cheered up." He was not the only one who found Christmas a dismal occasion. There was a meager crowd at Sagamore compared with former years. The Longworths were there and Ethel, with her children. It would have seemed even bleaker without the latter, who were an unceasing delight.

"Richard is the manliest, busiest little fellow imaginable," Theodore wrote Dick Derby. "I am of course of second-rate importance in his life, my chief useful function being to give him a lump of sugar as soon as we come down to breakfast, and then to have him hold the strainer while I pour the hot milk into my coffee. As for Edie she is such a darling that I want to take her up and cuddle her all the time. She smiles and laughs and crows and waves her little arms and legs, and is most alluring."

It was a bleak, bitterly cold winter. The roaring fires in the fireplaces kept only the fringes of the rooms comfortable. But they made no complaints. Huddled in shawls and blankets, Edith only kept wondering what it was like in the trenches. And the weather was only a minor cause of its bleakness. In February, Edith spent three weeks in New York while Theodore endured surgery in Roosevelt Hospital for abscesses on his buttock and in his ears, more relics of his many accidents and jungle heroics. She scarcely left his side.

There was sadness too with news of the death of two old friends, Cecil Spring-Rice and Henry Adams, once Edith's fond admirer and literary confrere. But the winter brought life, too, for on January 16 Belle had given birth to a second child, Joseph Willard Roosevelt. Kermit, somewhere in Mesopotamia, might or might not have received the cable that he had once more become a father. And in February Archie's wife Grace gave birth to their first child, little Archie. What a pity, Edith agonized, for the two young fathers to be a world away at such a happy time!

Somehow she could not rejoice over their heroism as Theodore did. In fact, she felt more anxiety than pride when in March they learned that Archie had been given the Croix de Guerre for heroism, for soon afterward the War Department notified them that he had been wounded, and Ted cabled them that his brother had been hit in the leg by shrapnel and had had his arm broken. Poor Archie! He had learned from a notice in the Paris *Herald* that his son had been born! None of the cables had reached him. "Well," Theodore wrote him, "we know what it is to have a hero in the family. You don't know how proud we are of you and how our hearts go out to you."

The weather continued so cold and gray in April that it was hard to realize it was spring. Yet the woods were awash in green. The lawns glowed with the gay yellow of forsythia. Across the wet hollow by the frog spring the brown dead leaves on the hillside were spangled with the brilliant white of bloodroot. And far from Sagamore but close to its outreaching tentacles there were undoubtedly poppies blowing on a field in Flanders.

Of all her fighting sons Edith felt most concern for Quentin. If only he could be united somehow with the girl he loved! She had written him suggesting that before he left his training camp he ask Flora to come over and marry him. In April he wrote back, "Dearest Mother, I followed your advice, wrote Fouf telling her to come over if she possibly could. I know her family will kick, but I really don't think they've got any right to. Heaven knows we'll never know our minds any better than we do now."

Flora was delighted and immediately applied for a passport. Edith even rhapsodized over the idea of going with her, but to her sorrow both she and Flora were refused permission to leave the country. When Theodore left on a speaking tour of the Midwest in May, she felt deserted. All her birds had flown, leaving her in the empty nest alone. But she rejoiced over one outcome of this trip of Theodore's.

He was dining alone on a Sunday in the Blackstone Hotel in Chicago when a familiar figure, a large man with a walrus mustache, came into the room. Theodore suddenly found himself looking up into the face of the man whom he had once loved but with whom in 1912 he had exchanged such bitter and vituperative epithets. Instantly he sprang to his feet and held out his hand. Taft took it and shook it firmly. They sat down together. Other diners in the restaurant cheered. The news spread through the hall and corridors. "Taft and Roosevelt have got together!" They beamed at each other, began talking, found themselves in agreement about how America should be conducting the war. Once more the enemies had become friends. When he returned home, "happy as the proverbial lark," Edith also felt an old burden lifted from her shoulders.

When he went away again in June, she refused to be left behind and went with him on a speaking tour of Illinois, Missouri, and Indiana. Everywhere she heard him blaze away at the weakness of the Administration. "Unless we knock out Germany now," he stormed, "we will have to fight again, probably within the lifetime of men now old, certainly within the lifetime of those now young." And everywhere he was cheered, acclaimed, almost with the old fervor of presidential days, for the country had veered largely to his sense of urgency. Once more he was the idol of the American people.

"Just wait a couple of years," one ardent rooter boasted. "In 1920 we'll make Teddy President again!"

Oh, no, not that! Edith's answering smile was tight and strained. But she had more immediate concerns. Theodore was physically suffering. Going to a meeting in St. Louis, he was attacked by erysipelas in his right foot. In Chicago he had such a fever that he was urged to cancel his appointments. But he would not stop.

Arriving home on June 16, they found a cable from Quentin reporting jubilantly that he had finished his training at Issoudon and would soon be in active service.

"No wonder he's dee-lighted," said Theodore. "He couldn't bear it to let his brothers get ahead of him!" For all three of them had displayed distinguished bravery. Kermit, who had won the British Military Cross for service in Mesopotamia, was on his way to France to become a captain of artillery in the American army. Ted, a lieutenant colonel, in spite of being gassed in lungs and eyes, had led his battalion in a bold raid which would later win him the Silver Star and the Croix de Guerre.

Again Edith's smile was dutiful but joyless. Four now to worry about instead of three, and one of them her "baby." The house now seemed desolate indeed, for on July 1 Ethel left with her little brood for Islesboro, Maine, where they were to spend the summer. The absence of the little ones made a void which put the finishing touch on the emptiness. "They have all gone away from the house on the hill," Edith kept quoting silently, words from one of her favorite poets, Edwin Arlington Robinson.

Most guests only accentuated the emptiness, but two Republican politicians who came early in July, filled it with fresh worries. Perhaps anticipating the importance of their visit, Theodore received them with more formality than usual, even donning a stiff white shirt and dinner coat for the evening meal. They stated their business abruptly. Was he prepared to run for the presidency in 1920? Edith's heart almost stopped beating. She lifted her napkin to hide the trembling of her lips.

"Yes," said Theodore. "I will run if the people want me, but only if they want me. I will not lift a finger for the nomination."

"Colonel," said one of the guests with satisfaction, "it will be yours, without strings and on your own terms."

Edith lowered her napkin and forced a steady smile . . . it was starting all over again.

4

Quentin was indeed in active service. On July 4 the New York *Times* reported that American planes had been engaged in twenty combats and had brought down seven enemy aircraft. Among the airmen had been Quentin Roosevelt. On July 8 it reported that Quentin had brought down his first German airplane.

It was less than a week later that Phil Thompson, the Associated Press reporter assigned to cover Sagamore Hill, came to the house in the afternoon. He found Theodore alone in the library. "Have you any idea what this means, Colonel?" he asked, holding out a censored telegram.

Theodore read it. "Watch Sagamore Hill for ———"

He went and shut the library door. All the usual ruddiness was drained from his face. "Something has happened to one of the boys," he said. "It can't be Ted or Archie, for both are recovering from wounds. It's not Kermit, since he's not at the moment in the danger zone. So it must be Quentin. His mother must not be told until there is no hope left."

He escorted the reporter to the door, went upstairs and dressed for dinner. That evening he and Edith, as usual, read to each other in the Trophy Room. She had no suspicion that anything unusual had happened.

Thompson came again before breakfast the next morning. Theodore had only to look at his face to know that his suspicions were verified. He took his guest out to the piazza to learn the news. Quentin's plane had been attacked by German fighters and shot down inside the German lines. He began pacing the floor in helpless agitation. "How—how am I going to break it to her?" he muttered brokenly.

He went into the house. Presently the reporter saw him walking, his arm about his wife, down a path which led into the woods. A half hour later he came back and handed a brief message to Thompson.

"Quentin's mother and I," he had written, "are very glad that he got to the front and had a chance to render some service to his country, and show the stuff that was in him before his fate befell him."

Theodore was at his office at the *Metropolitan* the next morning. Here an old friend, Hermann Hagedorn, later his biographer, found him and noted that the "old side of him is gone, that old exuberance." In other words, "the boy in him had died."

Two days later Theodore was in Saratoga giving the keynote address at the Republican State Convention. It was "more than ever my duty to be there." He was greeted by deafening applause, which ceased only when he raised his hand for silence. After an unnaturally restrained beginning, he spoke with his old vigorous verve, but Isaac Hunt, his old friend who knew him well, had seen the agony in his face as he mounted the platform.

The news of Quentin's death was soon officially confirmed, ending all hope that he might be missing or a prisoner of war. A letter of sympathy came from the President and a cable from King George of England. The German government confirmed that he had been killed in action and buried by German aviators with full military honors in Chaméry, the place where he had been shot down.

Edith did not weep. It was not her way. Theodore's grief was able to find expression. As he dictated to his secretary, Josephine Stricker, his voice was often choked with emotion and the tears would run down his face. He would break down if the name of Quentin was mentioned, and once he was found weeping in the stable with his arms around the pony's neck. But Edith's grief remained hard and frozen within. In fact, her acknowledged concern was chiefly for her husband. As she had said to Thompson the day the news had come, "We must do everything we can to help him. The burden must not rest entirely on his shoulders."

Knowing that for him, as well as for herself, every object at Sagamore, like the pony, was a reminder of their youngest, the brightest, merriest, most mischievous, most adventurous, yes, and most promising of them all, she urged acceptance of Ethel's invitation to visit her summer place in Dark Harbor, Maine, and they spent two weeks there in late July and early August. There was healing in the homeliness of the "dear little house," the peaceful beauty of the seacoast, and especially the children.

"It has been everything for poor Mother—and also for myself," Theodore wrote Dick Derby, "to be here with Ethel and the two blessed babies. Quentin was to the day he left Mother's 'baby' . . . Little Richard was so glad to see his grandmother and so affectionate with her that it almost seemed as if he knew there was some trouble; and his love was a great comfort to her aching heart."

When they returned to Sagamore they found Alice there, a lively, invigorating presence in the otherwise empty house. Never had Edith appreciated her so much. It was "everything to have her here," she confessed. Then one day came Nicholas Roosevelt, the boys' cousin and close friend. He was in uniform, about to leave for France, and for a moment Edith almost lost control. Years later, in paying tribute to her, Nicholas remembered that moment.

She "stands out in my memory as a great and gracious lady, self-possessed but not egotistical, with a warm heart under a cool exterior. She personified order, duty and discipline. Only once did I see her upset, and then only for a moment. I had gone to Sagamore to say good-bye before sailing overseas with the 81st Division. When she saw me in uniform her eyes filled with tears and she turned away. Then she put her hand on my arm and said, 'I'm all right, Nick, I'm all right.' And she was."

Yes. She was. With the coming of autumn her spirits lifted. Her senses quickened once more to beauty, to the lavish crimsons of maples and sunsets, the ever-changing blues of the Sound, the soaring grace of a fish hawk mounting up into sunlit clouds. And, once, symbol of hope, after a violent thunderstorm there was a rainbow.

In October, Archie was back home, left leg stiff and arm paralyzed, but alive and happy at last to enfold his baby son, though with only one good arm to do it. Their old friend Owen Wister came to visit, and conversation around the dinner table was once more refreshingly stimulating.

They discussed the war, which seemed to be drawing to a close. But Theodore was far from satisfied. The President, he felt, with his "Fourteen Points" and his visionary League of Nations which was to end all wars, was conceding too much to a ruthless foe which sometime their children might have to fight all over again. He feared the prospect of a "negotiated peace" instead of forcing the enemy to accept unconditional surrender. They discussed the fate of the Women's Suffrage Amendment, which was still short of passage, though New York had just in the past year become one of the fifteen states already granting voting rights to women in state elections. Theodore was in favor of the amendment, had been for years a supporter of women's suffrage, though he feared it would do little of the good the militant women anticipated. And they discussed postwar politics and his own plans for running for President again in 1920.

"Oh!"—Edith found herself blurting out, almost against her will —"if we should ever go back to the White House—which heaven forbid!"

Theodore laughed uproariously, then subsided into his toothy, beaming smile. "It doesn't matter what the rest is going to be," he said at last soberly. "I have had fun the whole time."

In his memoirs of Theodore, Owen Wister was to include his final memory of that visit. "They stood at their hall door as I drove off, stood watching, after their words bidding me to come

again soon, she quiet beside him, he waving his hand; Quentin's
father and mother carrying on."

It was becoming a chore to Theodore, that carrying on. Still he
managed to speak at New York City's Carnegie Hall on October 28
to a huge audience, decrying the President's plans for peace with
Germany without unconditional surrender. Edith, listening, knew
how he was suffering physically, for his old rheumatism had suddenly attacked him full force. But he kept on for ninety minutes,
then yielded valiantly to the shouts of "Go on, go on!"

November with its chill dampness accentuated his discomfort.
His feet became so swollen that he could not wear shoes. In spite
of doctors' stern orders to remain in bed, he insisted on donning
loose cumbersome footwear and driving to the polls. When he
entered his car he was surprised when Edith, who had accompanied him from the house, got in with him.

"Why, Edie, I don't need a nursemaid! I'm coming right back.
Why are you coming?"

"I'm going to vote, of course, Theodore," she said equably.

He drove to the Cove in silence. He was dumbfounded at his
own reaction to this very natural outgrowth of his liberal credo.
Female suffrage was of course a just principle. He had supported
it even back in that term paper at Harvard. But somehow the
sight of his own wife casting a ballot took his breath away. What
was the matter with him? Was he perhaps at heart just a throw-
back to his old-fashioned, conventional heritage? Perhaps he had
some rethinking to do.

The Armistice was signed on November 11, but it brought little
celebration to Sagamore. While bells were ringing, bands blaring,
and a wildly cheering populace was snake-dancing through the
streets of New York as well as other cities across the country,
Theodore was being rushed to Roosevelt Hospital for treatment
of his inflammatory rheumatism, a result of his Brazilian fevers
and abscesses, coupled with severe sciatica. Edith remained with
him, staying in a room next to his, with an adjoining bath between them. She tried to keep him cheered by reporting things
she had done in the city, friends seen, plays and operas attended.
In spite of his intense pain he managed to dictate voluminous
letters, at least twenty of them, to friends and acquaintances,

including Henry Cabot Lodge, William Allen White, Arthur Lee, James Bryce, Rider Haggard, Rudyard Kipling, and, of course, to his boys still in Europe. He also came up with a long manuscript detailing his plans for a proposed presidential campaign, with a platform which included an eight-hour day for the working man, social insurance, and an old-age pension scheme.

Finally the doctors were obliged to confess that there was nothing more they could do for his continuous pain and increasing weakness, and that he would probably have to spend the rest of his life in a wheelchair. "All right," he returned with his usual blustering vigor, "I can work and live that way, too." Edith, though shocked at the prospect, was confident that he could indeed. It was a fate that Bamie, crippled with arthritis, had grimly but cheerfully accepted, and it had left her soaring spirit unscathed. They were sprung from the same tough resilient stock, both born fighters.

He had many guests in the hospital. Henry Cabot Lodge came, spending two days in New York. They discussed the League of Nations proposed by the President, and, while Lodge expressed dissatisfaction with the idea, Theodore was in favor of such a league, as he had always been, provided it left the United States with power to defend itself. William Allen White came, rousing Theodore to fresh energy with news that Leonard Wood was thinking of running for President.

"I shall have to get into action on this thing in June," Theodore promised, hands tightening on the arms of his wheelchair.

And of course Conie came many times, and always on the days that he was well enough to see visitors she found lines of people waiting in the corridors for a few words with him. One day, in fact the last she was to visit him in the hospital, he seemed well on the road to recovery. Though his left arm was still in bandages, his right was free to make his usual wide gesticulations.

"Be sure and bring your little grandson, Douglas, to Sagamore during the holidays," he urged. "I'll show him every trophy in the North Room. I must know every one of the children intimately."

"Well, anyway," he remarked, referring to his birthday not long before, "I have kept the promise that I made to myself when I was twenty-one."

"What promise, Theodore?" she asked curiously.

"I promised myself," he said, bringing his right fist down hard on the arm of his chair, "that I would work *up to the hilt* until I was sixty, and I have done it. Even if I should be an invalid, or if I should die"—he snapped his fingers—"what difference would it make?"

Best of all Eleanor, Ted's wife, having returned from Europe, came to the hospital even before going to her mother's. She was "pretty and dainty and happy," Theodore wrote Ted, "but dreadfully homesick for you. Well, next Christmas I hope we shall have the whole family, for three generations, gathered at Sagamore Hill!"

But not this Christmas, though the doctors said he could go home on December 25 for the family celebration. He was still suffering acutely from sciatica, weak with fever and anemia, and afflicted with vertigo resulting from inflammation in the middle ear. Though his balance was poor, he refused help when the doctor tried to take his arm as they left the elevator. "Don't do that," he snapped. "I am not sick, and I don't want people to think I am." He managed to walk fairly steadily toward the waiting car, Edith beside him.

It was a triumphant homecoming. All the children and grandchildren in the country were there—Alice, Ethel and her children, Archie and his wife and baby, Ted's three. The Christmas table was set, all as usual except that there was roast turkey instead of the young roast pig. Because it was not known whether Theodore could come or when, the slaying of the desired porker had been delayed too long. He could play Santa Claus for little Richard, Edie and the other children, but for the first time in years he could not fill the role at Cove School. Archie, though still disabled, went in his place.

In spite of his delight over the holiday excitement, Edith knew he was tired, and she was almost glad when one after the other the families took their departure. Though on December 29 and 30 he seemed better and was able to go driving with her, on the last day of the year he was not as well. Once more he suffered severe pain in his leg and hand. Instead of coming downstairs each day, he spent most of the time lying on the sofa in the old upstairs nursery. Worried, Edith was with him constantly, though she acceded to the doctor's recommendation that she call in a practical nurse to help her. While not unduly alarmed, she hoped desperately that he would not have to go back to the hospital.

Theodore did not enjoy having a nurse fussing about him. "I wish," he said on Saturday morning, January 4, "that James were here. I always felt better when he was with me."

"But—he might not be able to come," Edith objected. "He has a job, you know, with the detective agency. Perhaps he could not leave it."

"He would come," Theodore returned confidently, "if he knew I needed him."

Edith went to the telephone and called James Amos's home in New York. His wife answered. No, he was not there, he was working. But when he came home she would give him the message.

Edith was reading to Theodore that evening when he looked up to see the familiar black features of his former valet outlined in the dimly lighted doorway. "There!" he exclaimed with a big welcoming smile. "He's here. What did I tell you, Edie darling?"

That night she slept more peacefully than at any time since they had left the hospital. James would stay, he assured her, as long as he was needed. He had given Theodore a bath and put him to bed, handling him so gently that the patient had remarked appreciatively, "By George, James, you never hurt me a little bit." And he was staying by his side all night.

Sunday she was still more relieved. Theodore dictated a letter to Kermit. He corrected the proof of an article for the *Metropolitan* and finished a column for a newspaper. But he was still unable to see guests other than family members. The few who came, among them Alfred Noyes, the famous English poet, she entertained downstairs, but she was always glad when they left so she could return to the old nursery and be with Theodore again.

It was the happiest day they had spent since the children left. They luxuriated in their companionship, reading together, Theodore writing while she sewed or played a game of solitaire. "Everything had been adjusted," she was to write Ted about it later. "I had a good nurse and James Amos. He had a happy day. People came in and I went down to see them. Father was in your old nursery and loved the view, of which he spoke, and as it got dusk he watched the dancing flames and spoke of the happiness of being home, and made little plans for me. I think he had made up his mind that he would have to suffer for some time and with his high courage had adjusted himself to bear it. He was very sweet all day. Since Quentin was killed he has been sad, only Ethel's little girl had the power to make him merry."

When James Amos came in to put him to bed along toward midnight, Edith completed her solitaire and was preparing to leave when Theodore looked up from the book he was reading and said, "I wonder if you will ever know how I love Sagamore Hill."

She returned a half hour later just to see that all was well. James had put out the small lamp on the dresser and the room was lit only by the firelight glow. He was sitting in a chair where he could see the bed. Theodore was lying on his side, quietly sleeping.

"Don't worry," James whispered. "You need your rest. I shall be watching."

Another peaceful night, for she knew Theodore was asleep, well cared for, released for a few hours from his suffering. In the master bedroom she turned down the ornate bedspread with its Chinese silk embroidery of peacocks and flowers, a gift from the Dowager Empress of China, blew out the lamp, crawled under the blankets, and sank gratefully against the pillows. But, wearied though she was, she did not sleep at once but lay with wide-open eyes, letting the fingers of wavering firelight stir chords of memory. They wove patterns of light and shadow in the floral carvings of the towering gothic headboard of the bed, so huge and lonely for just one person. She had looked up on it hundreds of times in the last thirty and more years, during ecstasy of fulfillment and agony of birth pangs. They brushed across the photographs of her sister Emily and of the children on the mantel, threw the intricate flowered design of the fireplace into bold relief. When she fell asleep at last, she dreamed it was Christmas Eve and as always she was filling the children's stockings hung on each side of that same fireplace, six of them, stuffing each one with the little gifts so carefully and lovingly chosen.

She struggled up out of sleep to feel a hand shaking her shoulders. The room was dark except for light streaming through the door from the hall. Of course. It was Christmas morning, early, before daylight, and one of the children, Quentin probably, was in the vanguard trying to wake her. Presently they would all be piling in, seizing their stockings, sprawling over the bed, exclaiming over their treasures.

"Mrs. Roosevelt—please! Wake up! Come! You must hurry!"

"Who—what—!"

"That black man—he said—come and get you, quick!"

Fully awake now, Edith sprang up, donned slippers and robe, and followed the nurse to the sickroom. James Amos was standing over the bed, looking down.

"What is it, James? Is he in worse pain, or—" As she saw his ravaged face, her voice trailed off. She leaned over the quiet figure in the bed. "Theodore—darling—" There was no answer, and suddenly her own heart seemed to stop beating.

"I—I heard him breathing hard. I got up from my chair, went to him, placed my hand on his head. He—he seemed to be asleep—peacefully, as when he dropped off. Then—his breath seemed to stop—came again—paused. I waited and waited, but—no breath came."

Edith stood looking down into the still, peaceful face. Somehow, after what seemed an eternity and certainly without her volition, she felt her heart resume its normal beating. "Come, James," she said calmly. "There are many things we must do."

The doctor was called and rendered his verdict. Death from an embolism, was his decision, probably the coronary artery. Innumerable messages were sent. The undertaker came. After he had left, Edith summoned Lee, the coachman, and James Amos to go with her to the quiet bedroom. They all three knelt by the bed and recited the Lord's Prayer. As James noted later, her voice was the steadiest and bravest of the three.

At six o'clock that morning, January 6, 1919, Edith called Conie and told her the news, in a voice, according to her sister-in-law, "gentle and controlled but vibrating with grief." She spent most of the day telephoning, writing, sending telegrams, notices to the newspapers, attending to all the hundreds of necessary details.

She did not weep. Her eyes remained as dry as after Quentin's death a few months before. She moved automatically, as if body were a thing apart from mind or spirit, bereft of emotion.

It was Archie who sent the cable to his brothers who were now with their victorious companies in Germany: "The old lion is dead."

When Josephine Stricker arrived on Monday morning she was faced not only with the usual voluminous correspondence but with continuously arriving telegrams and cables. Relatives and guests began coming. One of the latter commented that, though Edith greeted him with a brave smile, he knew that "her heart was torn out by the roots." That afternoon Conie came, and they walked together "far and fast" along the shore and through the woodlands he had so loved. Side by side they walked, as once they had been wheeled together in their prams in Union Square Park. As they returned in the twilight, they became suddenly aware of airplanes flying low above the house.

"Look!" Edith exclaimed, her voice breaking. "They must be from the camp where Quentin trained. They have been sent as a guard of honor for his father."

"Eagles to guard the eagle," Conie responded softly.

Though his death caused waves and ripples that spread around the world, his burial was as simple as he would have wished it to be. On Wednesday morning, January 8, members of the family gathered about the oak coffin in the North Room and held a little service. Quentin's favorite prayer was read. "O Lord, protect us all the day long of this troublous life, until the shadows lengthen and the evening comes, and the busy world is hushed, the fever of life over, and our work done. Then Lord in Thy mercy grant us a safe lodging and peace at the last, through Jesus Christ, our Lord."

Then the coffin, draped with the Rough Riders' flags he had loved, was borne to the little Oyster Bay church where he had worshiped through the years, and about five hundred villagers and dignitaries gathered for another simple service. No music, no eulogy, only words of prayer and consolation. Edith, according to the local custom for widows, did not attend the funeral. While the family was gone, she sat by a west window and read the service from the prayer book.

Others found relief in weeping, many who had far less reason to mourn. As the taxicab driver was taking two reporters back to the station after the church service and the one at the grave, one said to the other, "Brace up, Phil! We'll soon be in town. Pull yourself together."

"Shut up, you fool!" blubbered the other. "You're crying just as hard as I am."

And on the knoll overlooking the calm blue waters of the Sound, the quiet spot which he and Edith had chosen for their last resting place, after all the others had gone, one man stood alone looking down at the newly turned grave. He was a large man, with a walrus mustache, and he had once been Theodore's closest friend, then bitterest enemy. When Edith heard that Taft had stood there, weeping, the icy core of unexpressed grief seemed to melt within her, and at last she found relief in tears.

5

She could not stay at Sagamore. Perhaps sometime again, but not yet. It was a haunted house. Still feeling and acting like an automaton, she made arrangements to leave the estate for the winter, did her necessary packing, and, taking only her personal maid, Clara, and Lee, her chauffeur, she left the house without looking back.

She went first to Bamie's in Farmington, Connecticut, the home to which her sister-in-law and her husband, William Sheffield Cowles, had moved after leaving his navy post in Washington. Here, as with Conie on their walk through the woods, there was a sharing of grief in which, to Edith's relief, words were unnecessary. Here, however, for the first time she felt thankfulness mingled with her sense of dull resignation. Seeing Bamie bent and old, crippled in her wheelchair, deaf to the world except when addressed through an ear trumpet, completely dependent for motion on her faithful butler, Hopkinson, was a revelation. Gallant though Bamie still was and buoyant in spirit, insisting on being dressed in one of her beautiful gowns each morning, standing on a special stool for it while she gripped the two carved handles at either side, she was a pitiful reminder of the liveliness which had been so much like Theodore's.

Oh! Edith thought. What a blessing that he went when he did! To be chained to a wheelchair? It would have been like caging an eagle!

She stayed only a few days at Bamie's. They had been cordial but never close. There had long been a slight constraint between them, Bamie, as Edith suspected, secretly resenting her deprivation of baby Alice, she herself guiltily sensitive in the knowledge that Alice would have preferred life with Bamie.

After a few days Edith went on to New York and made arrangements for a trip to Europe, prompted partly by a sense of duty, but more from a desire to separate herself as far as possible from memories of Theodore. She had long felt guilty for her neglect of Emily, and two of the boys were still in the war zone. Ted, Kermit, and Belle met her ship at Le Havre, and they went on to Paris, where Emily came to join them. But if Edith had hoped to assuage grief by leaving memories behind, she was soon disillusioned. As if any place, any human relationship, could be divorced from the impact of his indomitable spirit! Wherever she went she was hailed, lauded as the widow of the renowned and revered "Teddy." As Bob Bacon, Theodore's Harvard classmate who was now in Paris, commented, "The whole French nation would do anything for Mrs. Roosevelt, because they worshiped her husband."

One day they went to Chaméry, and she carried great armfuls of flowers to deck Quentin's grave. She and Theodore had long ago decided that he should not be brought home. Tearless as usual but racked with inward emotion, she knelt beside the mound on the country hillside and again, as on that bleak January day a few weeks before beside another last resting place, she repeated the Lord's Prayer.

"How could you!" Emily wondered almost chidingly. "You never shed a tear! But you were always like that. I never could understand how you could be so—so—"

So "cold," so "unfeeling"? Was that what she had wanted to say? Edith had no words to reply. Quietly, efficiently, she arranged for a memorial to be erected at Chaméry, a fountain which would be beautiful but also serviceable, with seats at each side welcoming passers-by to rest.

The weeks spent with Emily at her Villa Magna Quies in Italy were a concession to her feelings of guilt. The rift between the two sisters had been growing wider with the years. During the war Emily had worked as a nurse for the Italian Red Cross, was still doing so but had interrupted her service to be with Edith. But she was more querulous than ever, and the two had little in common. Edith tried to be congenial, took long walks with her sister, played rummy with her, listened sympathetically to her complaints, tried unsuccessfully to interest her in the books she was reading, writings of Anatole France and Edmund Gosse, especially of some of her favorite Italian poets. She was glad when Emily exhibited restlessness, a desire to be back at work, for to her surprise she herself was suddenly homesick, not just for her own country but for the beloved world of Sagamore. Not for herself, it could never be really home for her again, but for the children. She must think of the living instead of the dead.

"I am dead, but no one but you must know that, dearest Corinne," she was writing her sister-in-law in March, "and I am fighting hard to pull myself together and do for the family not only my part but Theodore's."

So—back to Sagamore and the children. The first summer of loneliness was almost more than she could bear. But slowly time, the beauty of changing seasons, especially the prattle and clinging arms of grandchildren, brought healing. The years assumed a pattern, summers at Sagamore, travel somewhere to a warmer clime each winter, growing involvement not only in the lives of her children but in the social and political sphere where she had once played a subordinate role. It was almost a process of rebirth, a struggle to create a new identity as an individual.

Fresh winds of change swept in as her horizons widened. In the winter of 1920 she was in Rio de Janeiro with Kermit, who was working in South America as representative of the American Ship and Commerce Corporation, staying at a little villa halfway up a mountain, spending her days exploring the city or "digging into the shelves of the English library and asking impossible books from the librarian." In 1921, "full of aches and pains," she boarded a little ship of the Trinidad Line and visited lovely Grenada, Port of Spain and, with a party of seven, traveled into the wilderness to see the Kaieteur Falls in Demerara, spending long days of peace and sunshine in a "very primitive boat manned by ten paddlers of various shades," then, after a long perpendicular scramble up an incline known as "fat man's misery," reaching the great fall of water that she had longed for years to see. The adventure did not heal her "bow-knot of aches and pains," for she returned in a "double bow-knot." But she had lost what was far harder to bear than physical pain. "I had found," she expressed it, "the peace that is within the starry sky, the rest that lies upon the lonely hills."

But there was more to the process of healing, she was discovering, than merely to find peace. There were things that needed to be said in these years of the nineteen-twenties, and Theodore was no longer here to say them. Indeed, in this new day of women's suffrage perhaps the simple words and actions of a woman would be more effective than the more blatant speechmaking of a man. Already before the last election she had plunged briefly into politics, writing a few paragraphs for publication in the *Woman-Republican.*

"The time appeals most strongly to the manhood and the womanhood of America. To woman more than ever before because to her has come the perfected opportunity to make her influence weighty in behalf of the nation. . . . Steadiness and staunchness of American purpose are obligatory if we would first bring back our country to its stable place and then by strong endurance do all that can be done for peace and general welfare in all lands."

As Theodore's wife she would never have expressed herself publicly. Not like Alice, who always said just what she thought and during the campaign of 1912 had boldly supported her father instead of her husband!

But it was still as Theodore's widow that she thought and acted, not as Edith Carow Roosevelt. When she gathered friends to pay a memorial visit to his grave on the anniversary of his death in

1922, then led the pilgrims back to the North Room for fellowship, it was Theodore's writings that were read and discussed, memories of his activities and dominant personality that were shared. And there was nostalgia even in the adventurous travels she undertook during those years of the twenties, for they either retraced paths they had taken together in the past or penetrated far places that they had dreamed of exploring in the future.

In January of 1922 she was with Archie in Paris, where he was engrossed in important business. She was glad to spend days alone, wandering through the gray streets, an umbrella in hand, stopping at bookstalls, visiting all her old haunts, once more reveling in the gorgeous glass of the Sainte Chapelle, glowing in its beauty. In Berlin she enjoyed the Alte Schloss and the picture galleries. Then, after a day in London she traveled on an uncertain little ship to Capetown, exulting in the white beaches, the jade green ocean, the exquisite flowers, returning home "fitter to face the world than I have been for a long time."

And she needed to feel fit, for it was a depressing summer. The presence of Emily, who was visiting Sagamore, did nothing to dispel its gloom. One redeeming feature was the proximity of Ethel and her children, for her husband, Dick Derby, had taken a position as physician at the Long Island Insane Asylum, so that they now lived only four miles from Sagamore. Another was a visit from Ted, who was following in his father's footsteps, first as New York assemblyman, then as Assistant Secretary of the Navy. Edith's only regret at this promotion was his greater distance from New York, with less chances for her to see his children. The youngest, little Quentin, now almost two, was a source of both pleasure and pain. "If only Theodore could have seen him!" she thought each time she held the chubby, smiling mite. Or, "How Quentin would love his little namesake!"

There had been a contest between Eleanor and Belle, both of whom were pregnant, as to which offspring would arrive first, hopefully a son, for it was agreed that the first male born in the family would be named Quentin. Somewhat to Belle's disgust, Eleanor had won, her child arriving two months prematurely, just four days ahead of Belle's. Edith remembered the day well, the one when Ted was up for election for the State Assembly, his first public office. The baby had arrived so unexpectedly that there had been no clothes for him, and she had gone down from Sagamore with a little frock that Theodore had worn as a baby. Eleanor had been assured of victory, anyway, for Belle's baby, arriving four days later, had been a girl, named Clochette.

One day a great package came from England, seemingly containing a picture. She waited, hands clenched tightly at her sides, while a servant who had been at Sagamore for many years removed the voluminous wrappings. Would the sight of it revive the pain, start the grieving all over again? Or—

"It—it's him!" exclaimed the old servant, tears streaming down his cheeks.

Yes, it was indeed. There he was, just as he had looked in his most vital, active years, ready to step out of the frame, don the gloves that he held in his hand, and take bold issue with some enemy of the public good. He looked so vivid, so alive that Edith could almost imagine he was there in the flesh.

It was the portrait by the famous Hungarian artist Laszlo which their friend Arthur Lee had had copied for her as a gift in Theodore's memory. Edith had it hung at the far end of the North Room, where it dominated the exotic decor as he himself had dominated it in life, looking out on his magnificent buffalo and elk heads, on the horns of one of them the hat and sword he had worn in his Rough Rider days; on the rich-hued rug, present of the Shah of Persia, the gigantic elephant tusks given him by King Menelik of Abyssinia, the suit of Japanese armor given him by Admiral Togo.

To Edith's surprise the sight of it brought pleasure rather than pain. She enjoyed being in the room with it, sometimes even went in at the end of the day to bid it good-night.

When eight-year-old Richard, Ethel's oldest child, died that fall, Edith found herself not only relieved but actually glad that Theodore was not alive to share her grief. He had loved in a very special way the gay, frail little fellow, suffering asthma as he himself had done in childhood.

Somehow her travels now took on a new zest. She was no longer trying to run away from reminders of the past but seeking fresh knowledge and experience for herself. In South America that winter of 1922 she reveled in exploring a dank jungle where the hideous head of a manatee reared its head from a muddy pool; in attending a masked ball at carnival time; in scrambling through green moss-grown forests in the country near Rio.

In 1924 she was traveling around the world with Kermit, being shaken by an earthquake in her Tokyo hotel, witnessing the fascinating Noh dramas in a Japanese temple, dining at the Maple Club with smiling little geishas crouched at her elbows. Then— Siberia, a "leap from a worn-out civilization to none at all," but all along the way Chinese and Russians "kind beyond words and helpful in many deeds." Once, without a word of Russian at her command, she found herself guarding a pile of luggage in cold so fierce that a kindly peasant woman drew her to her side in the shelter of a wall and wrapped her scarf closer. Then at last— Moscow, lying in cold moonlight in "strange, barbaric beauty" . . . Leningrad . . . the Winter Palace . . . the treasures of the Hermitage. Twenty-five nights in hotels of varying comfort and as many on railroads, all from New York on December 24 to Paris on February 26.

In 1925 she was visiting islands, Sicily and Malta, the true "Garden of Hesperides," and in 1926 she was in Yucatán. In 1927 she was fulfilling a longtime dream of exploring the great falls of the Iguazú in South America.

Fortunately, she was able to satisfy this innate wanderlust without financial worry, for Theodore had left her with a fair income and there was a Carnegie trust that paid five thousand dollars a year to Presidents' widows. Also Congress had recently voted a similar widow's pension of the same amount. Edith's first reaction was to refuse this because she felt it unnecessary. Then she decided it might embarrass other Presidents' widows who might be in dire need. She remembered how Dolley Madison, for instance, had lived in abject poverty until on her eightieth birthday Congress had voted to buy her husband's Constitutional Convention papers, and how Mary Lincoln had been forced to live abroad, where expenses were less. At least, she decided, she could use her pension for charitable purposes, and did so. She met the needs of many of Theodore's Rough Riders, encouraged struggling poets and artists by holding classes and exhibitions, sometimes extended help to total strangers. But all these acts of largesse were nothing new. She had always been almost prodigally generous.

"You're getting to be such a world traveler," Kermit suggested, "you really should write a book about your adventures."

She laughed. Of course he was joking! "Nonsense! Why, I wouldn't have enough to fill more than a chapter! It's you boys who have had the real adventures. All your hunting experiences in Korea and Tibet and Africa!"

Kermit's eyes kindled. "Well, why not? You could write your chapter, and we all could add our bit. I'll wager it would make a good-sized book."

To her amazement the project developed. She wrote her chapter, calling it "The Odyssey of a Grandmother." There were other chapters, four by Kermit, two by Richard Derby, one by Kermit's wife Belle entitled "From the Land Where the Elephants Are." The book, called *Cleared for Strange Ports,* was published in 1927 by Scribner's and was well received.

This was only a beginning, for already Edith was embarked on a far more ambitious literary project. On a visit to Bamie in Connecticut she had on an impulse stopped at Norwich, where her mother Gertrude Tyler had once lived and where she herself had been born. She visited the grave of her great-great-grandfather, Daniel Tyler II, who had had three wives, twenty-one children, fifty grandchildren, and 120 great-grandchildren.

For years she had been delving into her own family history, and in 1928 she published the result of her research, a book called *American Backlogs,* containing through letters the story of both Tylers and Carows from the time of their arrival in the New World to the death of her grandfather, Daniel Tyler IV, in 1882. It mattered not a whit to her that in spite of a favorable review in the *Times* it did not sell and that her royalties amounted to no more than one hundred dollars. It was her final liberating act in the process of rebirth, the creation of an identity all her own.

Not that Theodore was ever far from her thoughts or that memories had not constantly been recurring to make the past as vividly real as the present. It was so especially in 1923 when she first stepped inside the old Roosevelt house on Twentieth Street, Theodore's birthplace, which had been in process of rebuilding and restoration by the Women's Roosevelt Memorial Association. Though of course she had been less involved in the project than Bamie and Conie, she had followed its progress with both anticipation and foreboding. How could a completely new building, for the original had been torn down in 1916, be made to resemble the old storehouse of so many memories?

But miraculously it did. Even the new steps might have been the ones where she and Teedie had sat reading to each other. Inside there was much of the same furniture, and even the fabrics and trimmings for draperies and upholsteries, wallpapers and carpets, might well have been the ones she remembered when visiting as a child back in 1865. Upstairs there was recreated the old nursery where she and Conie and Teedie had played "house," the window which had once opened on the porch where Theodore had built his puny body into such amazing strength. In the adjoining museum, once a part of Theodore's uncle's house, there were ranch relics from Elkhorn, including Theodore's rifle, shotgun, roundup hat, his "chaps" compass, drinking cup, and— yes, his spectacles. It was a journey back into the past so poignantly nostalgic that Edith did not know whether to laugh or cry.

January 6, 1929. Ten years since the world had seemed to fall apart. They had brought changes to others than herself in the family. Ted had left his post with the navy to run for governor of New York, again hoping to follow in his father's steps, but an unjust smear in the Teapot Dome scandal had lost him the race. Alice would always blame Eleanor, Cousin Franklin's wife, for touring the state for the Democratic candidate in a truck shaped like a huge teapot. Edith's chief reaction was wonder that the bashful, awkward little wallflower could have turned into a political activist.

Alice had surprised the family even more than Franklin's wife by giving birth, at age forty-one, to a daughter whom she named, not Alice, as Edith had hoped, but Paulina. It happened on Valentine's Day, 1925, oddly enough the anniversary of the day when Alice's own mother and grandmother had died. Edith had gone to Chicago for Alice's confinement and had pronounced the new arrival "a pretty little baby and a real Roosevelt."

Birth . . . marriage . . . death. The ten years had seen them all, the wedding of Bami's son, Sheffield Cowles, in 1921, the funeral of her husband in 1923. Edith and Corinne both came to Farmington to be with Bamie. The three of them shared a new bond now, for all of them were widows, Conie having lost her husband, Douglas Robinson, in 1918. Edith felt almost apologetic for her comparative good health, with Bamie helpless in her wheelchair and Conie suffering from all sorts of ailments, asthma, skin troubles, partial blindness, yet as gallantly witty and ebullient as ever.

The years of the thirties found the country plunged into economic chaos. In spite of the market crash of 1929 Edith's income did not suffer depletion like that of many others. In January 1930 she was able to visit Ted, who had been appointed governor of Puerto Rico by President Hoover, luxuriating in the sixteenth-century palace, La Forteleza, basking in the sunlit beauty of the lush tropical gardens, swimming in the ocean, taking enormous pride in Ted's efforts to correct the nutrition and health problems of the poverty-stricken island. She had such a good time that she returned the following December. Then, unable to face the loneliness of Sagamore Hill during the bleak weeks of winter, she took a boat for Jamaica, returning on April 2, 1931, in time to attend the funeral of Nick Longworth, who had died suddenly from an attack of pneumonia.

As Edith knew, this tragedy was the climax of a series of frustrations and disappointments for Alice. In 1928 she had hoped that Nick, the popular Speaker of the House, would be nominated for President. Instead Hoover had been the Republican choice. Then, when discontent with Hoover demolished the Republican majority in the House, a new Speaker had been elected. For years Edith had known also that Alice was playing a maverick role in Washington society, flouting custom in every way possible, making slurring remarks about anyone she chose (like saying, it was reported, that President Coolidge looked "as if had been weaned on a pickle"), pioneering in wearing trousers of black satin, in bobbing her hair even though refusing to have Paulina's cut, carrying about with her a huge handbag which had become her trademark, containing a motley accumulation of objects including a jade ring to ward off evil spirits and an ugly figurine designed to work black magic on her enemies. In spite of—or perhaps because of—such eccentricities Alice continued, even after Nick's death, to be one of the capital's most popular society leaders.

In 1932 Edith was seventy. The economy had continued to plunge, and it was an election year. To her amazement and that of all the Oyster Bay Roosevelts, Cousin Franklin was nominated for President at the Democratic Convention in June, promising a New Deal that would end the economic crisis. To her further dismay it was assumed that she was his mother or his grandmother, or even his wife, and she received three hundred telegrams of congratulation.

Immediately she took action. The public must not think that she, Theodore's widow, was in support of a Democrat, even one named Roosevelt. She planned a birthday lunch for Hoover at Sagamore Hill with three hundred Republican women invited and made a welcoming speech which was headlined on the front page of the New York *Times*. Then she flew to Washington on a government plane to stand beside the Hoovers in the Blue Room, where she herself had once received so often as First Lady. It was not a happy experience, even though the White House had been so lavishly redecorated that it looked almost unfamiliar.

She was criticized soundly, scored in anonymous letters, for opposing a Roosevelt relative. But, as she wrote Ted, her wastebasket was "capacious." She had never been one to turn her back on what she considered her duty. On October 31, she made a speech for the Republican ticket in Madison Square Garden before a larger audience even than the one Theodore had addressed on an October night just twenty years before. This rally, too, failed to achieve its purpose, for on November 8 Franklin Delano Roosevelt was elected the thirty-second President of the United States.

"And how are you related to the President-elect?" someone asked Ted.

"Fifth cousin, about to be removed," replied Ted with a wry grin.

He was now governor-general of the Philippines, having been promoted to that office in January of 1932 by President Hoover.

Of course the change of party in the new Administration put his job in jeopardy.

She must hurry, Edith decided, if she was going to visit Manila while Ted was still in office. She arrived there on January 2 and received a red carpet welcome, the Filipinos, as she recorded, treating her like visiting royalty. Of course they were a people who venerated age, and they remarked over and over about her charm, dignity, and grace. Ted arranged a big evening reception for her. Though he had placed an armchair between himself and Eleanor so she could sit with a bouquet of flowers in her hands and merely smile at the passing guests, she insisted on standing and shaking hands for nearly two hours. It might have been years before in the governor's mansion or the White House!

While she was there it was reported in the newspapers that Kermit was off on a cruise with Franklin and his wife in a yacht belonging to the Astors. People were surprised. Could Kermit be trying to cultivate the President-elect so he would leave Ted in the Philippines? Reporters besieged Ted. Why was his brother going yachting with the new President? Before Ted could answer, Edith put in quietly, "Because his mother is not there."

She returned home February 1, saddened by the news that in her absence Corinne had died with pneumonia. Such friends they had been, she and Conie, from the time they had been wheeled side by side in their perambulators! So many memories they had shared! Now the immediate family of Theodore's generation were all gone. But Roosevelts were still superabundant. And in March one of them ascended to the highest position in the land.

Though Edith was too partisan to accept the bold innovations of the new Administration as possible equations with the liberal ideas that Theodore in his Bull Moose campaign had expounded, she could not be as outspoken and vitriolic in opposition as Alice, who, she could not help feeling, was activated in part at least by jealousy. Franklin, the playboy, the "featherduster," was in the position she had coveted first for Nick, then for Ted. And Eleanor, the plain, gawky "ugly duckling," had become not only First Lady but an influential and respected activist in social reform. Edith could not help remembering how Franklin had admired Theodore and wanted to mold his career in the same political pattern, yes, and how he had done so. Certainly this man who had emerged crippled but undaunted from a severe bout with polio was no weakling, no "featherduster."

"As to public affairs," she wrote Arthur Lee, "I am hopeful, for I believe Franklin is a shrewd statesman."

She was even more sympathetic with Eleanor, whose problems as First Lady she could well appreciate, and she was delighted when Theodore's beloved niece wrote her a letter full of news about conditions in the White House.

The years of the Depression were doldrums not only for the country but for the family. Though Edith's own finances depreciated, she suffered far less loss than the children. Ted returned from the Philippines jobless, but with the help of friends he secured a position with the American Express Company. Archie helped solve his financial problems by starting a school in the garage of his house at Cold Spring Harbor, installing excellent teachers who taught classical subjects. Even Alice, possessor of two inheritances, felt the squeeze, and she wrote a book of memoirs called *Crowded Hours,* which was published with great success in 1933. She made public appearances after it came out, though she was petrified by public speaking. Her histrionic gifts ran to mimicking, which she could do to perfection, especially if the production was an embarrassment to an object of her dislike.

Edith helped all of the children financially as they needed assistance, and later she did the same for her grandchildren.

The latter were her great joy during these years of loneliness and depression. They all visited Sagamore during the summers. She swam with them in her voluminous black bathing dress, as one grandchild described it, with small bodies gathered about "playing impudent minnows to her indifferent whale." Sitting enthroned on the piazza in the evenings, knitting and telling stories about her childhood, she would keep them as enthralled as her own children had once been. And on Sundays she would always take them to church, keeping stern order and making sure each child followed the service on the proper page. But she also provided inducements by dispensing candy surreptitiously from a little silver box.

"Grandma was an awesome chatelaine," Archibald Junior was

to remember. "She ruled the house and its unruly visitors in her soft and precise voice, an iron hand scarcely hidden in the velvet glove. Only when we were older did we realize she was small and frail. To us she seemed ten feet tall, and although she never raised that quiet voice, it could take on an icy tone that made even the largest and strongest tremble."

But it was the presence of the "ghost" that Archie remembered most vividly, a "kindly one who kept a jolly and benevolent eye on all of us. He just had too much vitality to die and leave all those grandchildren deprived of his companionship."

Little Archie was sure he was with them at the table, where they consumed mounds of good food, running to rich homemade soups and succulent roasts and always a delicious dessert. And of course he was always present in the fascinating gun room, where he did not seem to mind if they played with his wonderful old weapons. Archie was sure that Grandfather "haunted" two of the rooms, the bedroom where he died, with its bedspread designed as an American flag, and the adjoining dressing room. In the bedroom he even talked to the "ghost" once, asking him to "help me be worthy of him." Though he hadn't answered, Archie thought he might have been listening.

"What a merry, vital, and energetic ghost he was," Archie was to conclude an article he wrote many years later about his visits, "and how much encouragement and strength he left behind to help us face the terrible half century that has passed since his death."

If his presence was so real to a grandchild who had never seen him, no wonder that for Edith the intervals she spent at Sagamore were intermixtures of both joy and pain!

As years passed she was increasingly conscious of that troublesome "thumping heart." In spite of her bodily weakness she continued to take refuge from the cold winters in warmer climes, Greece in 1934, and South America in January 1935. Visiting the old familiar Canal Zone, she was thrilled to find that Theodore was still the people's hero and she wrote Kermit, " 'Dear old Teddy,' the man in the street says. He has become a conglomerate of Santa Claus and a tribal deity."

But it was she, not Teddy, who received the people's acclaim when in the fall of 1935, the one hundred and forty-eighth anniversary of the signing of the Constitution, she made a speech at the National Convention of Republican Women that was broadcast all over the country and would survive in a recording that could be heard on the two hundredth anniversary fifty-two years later. In her high clear voice naturally attuned to public speaking, she pleaded for the American people to be loyal to the ideals of Washington and the nation's founders. It was almost as if Theodore had found his voice again.

" 'The basis of our political system,' " she quoted from Washington, " 'is the right of the people to make and alter their government, but the Constitution, until changed by the explicit and authentic act of the whole people, is sacredly obligatory on all.' "

"To them in this crisis," she continued in her own words, "we dedicate our lives, never to fall back in our purpose to leave to our children, and to our children's children, the freedom of life and thought which has been ours. For if we fall, we fall like Lucifer, never to hope again."

But both public appearance and travel ended abruptly when in November 1935, moving in the dark of night to open a window, she stumbled and fell, breaking her right hip. She was in the North County Community Hospital for the next five months; then, fitted with a heavy brace, she adjusted herself slowly to a new life of stiff bones and aching muscles. Still, with the help of her three servants, her cook Bridget and her two maids, Mary Sweeny and Clara Lee (who was the widow of her old White House coachman Charlie), she was able to convalesce in the warmth of Florida.

To her delight in 1937 Ted decided to build a house for his family on the Sagamore grounds. Though Elihu Root had come to her in 1920 suggesting that she turn over Sagamore Hill to the Roosevelt Memorial Association, she had refused, saying that it must be kept for Ted. She would have been glad to move out at any time and let him have it. But both he and Eleanor shied from the prospect of running such a large establishment. It had been built when domestic help was no problem. So they built a house more suited to their needs in the old apple orchard behind Sagamore Hill and named it "Old Orchard."

But the thirties still had not exacted their full toll of misfortune.

Edith suffered agonies over the increasing dependence of her beloved Kermit on alcohol. It was the story of his Uncle Elliott all over again. Yet she could understand the compulsion that drove him. He was so like herself—sensitive, poetic, idealistic, yet without her stern sense of duty and self-control. Yes, and he was so like his father—brilliant, adventurous, loving the strenuous life and the hunt, yet without his fierce drive and ambition. He hated the business world he was forced to endure to support his family, and the social world which enthralled his lighthearted, fun-loving Belle. Edith suffered with him, hoped, prayed, and loved him even more for his weakness. Had she perhaps failed him in some way?

In 1939, she was besieged once more by guilt when Emily died so suddenly that she was unable to take a ship in time to reach her. Poor Emily, she had been so alone, fifty years in a strange land, never loved deeply by her family but saying to a friend when she was dying, "God bless my sister, nephews and nieces."

But these personal sorrows paled in significance beside the horror which in that same year of 1939 burst on the world. In September German troops crashed into Poland. England and France declared war on Germany. World War II, long dreaded and once foretold by Theodore, had begun.

On August 6, 1941, Edith was eighty. She was surprised and dismayed to find herself subject of an editorial in the New York *Times*.

"The general regard, or should we say affection, that the public has had for her so many years will deprive of any air of intrusion a congratulation on this anniversary. To the elder among us the mention of her name calls back the years when the White House rang with the shouts and laughter of children. Never has it been, nor is it likely to be again, so noisy and happy. And it was through her good offices that the White House was restored according to the plans of its architect. A well-stored mind, a gracious presence and nature, kindness as well as dignity are hers"—she smiled wryly at the further listed qualities—"easy gaiety at the proper time . . . sense of humor . . . in the house of sorrow a tranquil courage."

Courage. She needed it now, but it was not tranquil. Kermit, having distinguished himself in the British army in Norway and Egypt, where he had contracted malaria, been invalided out of the army, was now home, drinking more heavily than ever to drown his frustrations. Ted was already in training, his youngest son Quentin, now twenty-one, also enlisted. Soon, she knew, Archie would be going. The nightmare was starting all over again.

It continued. "The last news has been so bad," she was writing Ted in February of 1942, "that I cannot write of it and it is all I can do to hold myself together. Today I walked down the back road and turned toward the tennis court and stopped and looked at this dear house where we have had such happiness. It is better to live in the past for old ladies like me."

However, she had to face the present, her own physical and mental frailty so increased that her constant letter writing was becoming a chore and she was finding it hard even to balance her accounts. But her own condition was unimportant. She saw Kermit take the "cure," unsuccessfully, in various hospitals, then, thanks to Cousin Franklin, receive a major's commission in the army, and, coming to bid her good-bye just twenty-four years to the day since Quentin had been killed, leave for a post in Alaska. A year later she said good-bye to him again when, invalided home on furlough, he came once more to Sagamore, looking older than his fifty-three years and bereft of all the old vivacity and verve, then left once more for Alaska. Not long after, in May 1943, she received the news that this much loved son had at last found peace. He had died of heart failure, her granddaughter Gracie told her gently, a little too glibly. Later she learned that, having ended up again in hospital and knowing that his usefulness to his country was ended, he had lifted a .45 revolver and shot himself through the head.

The next year she received the happier news that Ted, now a brigadier general, had been awarded the French Legion of Honor. Then, though limping with a cane because of an arthritic hip, he was in England preparing for "the great venture of the war," the D-Day invasion of Normandy. The oldest man in the first invasion wave, he conducted himself with such bravery that he was recommended for the Congressional Medal of Honor, an award that his father had so coveted but been denied. Though exhausted, warned by a doctor that he was taxing his overstrained heart, he continued to direct operations and prepare for further attacks. On July 11 he died of sudden heart failure. Once more it was a Roosevelt son who sent old familiar words flying across the ocean.

"The Lion is dead," wrote young Quentin to his mother, the already grieving Eleanor. "You've heard, of course. . . . To me he was much more than simply a father, he was an amazing combination of father, brother, friend and comrade in battle."

This time Edith wept, silently, all through the burial service in the church. She confessed to Ethel that "Ted's death did something to me from which I shall never recover."

At least Archie, the only one of the four boys remaining, was still alive, a lieutenant colonel with a Silver Star for gallantry, though suffering from a grenade wound, strangely enough in the same knee that had been shattered by shrapnel in World War I, and from malaria acquired in the South Pacific. He was now on sick leave somewhere on the West Coast.

Strange, that they should all be dead or wounded when here she was, old and gray and useless, yet stubbornly persisting in life, like a withered leaf clinging to a bare tree! For a second time —or was it a third?—she gave thanks that Theodore was no longer alive. Perhaps he could have stood it to live in a wheelchair, as he had vowed, yes, even with a fierce dogged cheerfulness. And he would have been proud of these two sons as he had been of Quentin. But to have him live now and know such grief as she was feeling . . . !

Grief, too, was mingled with shock when in April, just when she was waking suddenly to the beauty of purple lilacs and of roses just coming into bloom, harbingers of the hope that the war on all fronts would soon be over, news came that the Commander-in-Chief was dead. Edith felt genuine sorrow. It was almost as if she had lost another son. She had come to admire Cousin Franklin and respect the achievements of his Administration. In many ways he had fulfilled his dream of following in the steps of Theodore, not only occupying some of the same high offices but bringing many of the latter's aims to fruition. As New York assemblyman he had led a revolt against the political bosses who dominated the state government, just as Theodore had done. As President he had urged Congress to pass social security measures to provide old age pensions, unemployment insurance, aid to dependent children, and health services.

Nor could Edith feel sympathy with Alice's deep-rooted contempt of the First Lady, and, though amused, she listened uneasily to her stepdaughter's famous imitation of Eleanor, prominent teeth and all, which convulsed her Washington socialite friends. Alice would have done well, Edith thought, to imitate her despised cousin in more pertinent ways. For, as the years passed, Eleanor Roosevelt was becoming not only a national but a world figure, author, lecturer, pioneer in humanitarian service, representing her country in the new United Nations. No longer First Lady of America, she was rapidly becoming First Lady of the world! How proud Theodore would be, thought Edith, of his beloved little niece! An "ugly duckling" turned—not even into a swan but—yes, an eagle!

As the years passed. They seemed now to have no beginning and no end, one season merging into another. Trees and flowers budded, burst into bloom, waxed into lushness, faded. Leaves turned gold and crimson, drifted off and were buried in snow, then spring came again. Edith now had to hire a secretary to write her letters and keep her accounts. Grandchildren came, great-grandchildren. She loved them, read them stories, took them on short walks, but had hard work remembering all their names. Friends came, among them Fanny Parsons.

"I'm writing a little book of memoirs," she told Edith. "I think I'll call it *Perchance Some Day.*"

"Fine," Edith commended. "You have had a really exciting life, you and James." But she smiled to herself. She could imagine that James Parsons might not be the central male figure in such memoirs. Fanny, she knew, had always cast rather yearning eyes toward Theodore.

One day another visitor came to Sagamore Hill. He was the noted journalist and biographer Stefan Lorant. He wanted to write an illustrated biography of Theodore. Good. Edith liked the looks of him, a charming, gallant man of about forty-five, a little more than half her age. The admiration was mutual, and later he would speak of her "sparkling blue eyes" and the "steel rod in her spine." She thought she could trust him to write a decent biography, not like some she had read, that early one by Henry Pringle, for instance, which had tried to turn Theodore into a warmonger with some of the more unpleasant qualities of a clown.

He showed her a picture and asked her if it brought back any memories. Was it possible that those two little figures in the window of the big house, looking out on what was apparently the funeral procession of President Lincoln—?

Memories! That great giant of a house with the frothy trees of the park beyond. The crowds in the street . . . black . . . something high, towering . . . death . . . a child crying, herself . . . a locked door. Suddenly she felt like crying again, but instead she was laughing. For it had been so long ago.

"Yes," she said, "Oh, yes! I am sure that is my husband, and next to him is his brother." Her thin aging face lighted up with tender memory as she told him the rest of the story.

After he had gone she sat thinking. That was when it had all begun. More than eighty years ago! Yet she remembered it as if it had been yesterday. Strange! All the memories connected with Theodore were sharp and vivid. It was only the years alone that had become vague, like a landscape painting that has no focal point. And yet perhaps not so strange. For since a day in January nearly thirty years ago, life had had no real focal point.

On August 6, 1948, Edith was eighty-seven. Well-wishers came, but for the first time the mistress of Sagamore welcomed them neither on the porch nor in the downstairs rooms. She was confined to her bedroom and spent most of the day on her chaise longue with her faithful maid, Mary Sweeny, hovering anxiously to see that she did not become overtired. There followed days of increased weakness, shortness of breath, pain in arms and legs, finally toward the last of September, lapse into a coma. At six-thirty in the morning of a new day, September 30, she died as she had lived, quietly, unostentatiously, with dignity, as naturally as the ripened leaves drifting off the maples and birches.

Everything had been prearranged methodically, as was her custom, whether for a small family dinner or a White House reception or a trip around the world. Her will had been signed, carefully making provision for servants as well as children, the grandchildren having already been provided with generous gifts to avoid inheritance taxes. She had even given explicit handwritten directions for her funeral service and burial beside Theodore —no embalming, the simplest possible coffin, nothing on it but bunches of pink and blue flowers from the children, two hymns, "The Son of God" (sung not in slow tempo) and "Love Divine," the anthem from Beethoven's Ninth Symphony, service in the prayer book. She did not want her wedding ring removed.

Though she would have preferred no publicity for the event, the "Death of a Lady," as *Time* magazine referred to it, was recorded as an event of national importance. Perhaps the shortest but most pertinent appraisal of the qualities that caused her to be listed among "Some Great Americans" appeared in *Life*.

"One of the strongest minded and strongest willed presidential wives who ever lived. . . . Downright persistence that precluded Gallup Poll thinking, insistence on personal excellence; a refusal to pursue either the dollar or political power for their own sakes; a tart humor, an idealism that never ran off into wishful thinking or futility, and, finally, a willingness to take the momentarily unpopular course."

Bibliography

BOOKS

Abbott, Lawrence F. *Impressions of Theodore Roosevelt.* Garden City, N.Y.: Doubleday, Page and Company, 1920.
———— *The Letters of Archie Butt.* Garden City, N.Y.: Doubleday, Page and Company, 1925.
Amos, James E. *Theodore Roosevelt, Hero to His Valet.* New York: John Day Company, 1927.
Anderson, Isabel. *Presidents and Pies. Life in Washington.* Boston and New York: Houghton Mifflin Company, 1920.
Boller, Paul F., Jr. *Presidential Anecdotes.* New York: Penguin Books, 1981.
Brough, James. *Princess Alice.* Boston: Little, Brown and Company, 1975.
Bishop, Joseph Bucklin. *Theodore Roosevelt and His Time.* (Two Volumes.) New York: Charles Scribner's Sons, 1920.
Busch, Noel F. *T.R.: The Story of Theodore Roosevelt and His Influence on Our Times.* New York: Reynal and Company, 1963.
Chanler, Mrs. Winthrop. *Roman Spring.* Boston: Little, Brown and Company, 1934.
Charnwood, Lord. *Theodore Roosevelt.* Boston: Atlantic Monthly Press, 1923.
Churchill, Allen. *The Roosevelts: American Aristocrats.* New York and London: Evanstone and Harper & Row, 1965.
Colman, Edna M. *White House Gossip.* Garden City, N.Y.: Doubleday, Page and Company, 1927.
Daniels, Jonathan. *Washington Quadrille: The Dance Beside the Documents.* Garden City, N.Y.: Doubleday and Company, Inc., 1968.
Furman, Bess. *White House Profile: A Social History of the White House, Its Occupants and Its Festivities.* Indianapolis: Bobbs-Merrill Company, Inc., 1951.
Gardner, Joseph L. "T.R.'s Last Adventure." From *Departing Glory.* New York: Scribner's, 1913.
Garrity, John A. *Theodore Roosevelt: The Strenuous Life.* New York: Harper & Row, American Heritage Publishing Company, 1967.

Gerson, Noel. *T.R.: A Biographical Novel.* Garden City, N.Y.: Doubleday and Company, Inc., 1970.

Gilman, Bradley. *Roosevelt: The Happy Warrior.* Boston: Little, Brown and Company, 1921.

Goettel, Elinor. *America's Wars—Why?* New York: Julian Messner, 1972.

Green, Constance McLaughlin. *Washington, Capital City, 1879–1950.* Princeton: Princeton University Press, 1963.

Hagedorn, Hermann. *The Boy's Life of Theodore Roosevelt.* New York: Harper & Brothers, 1918.

——— *The Roosevelt Family of Sagamore Hill.* New York: Macmillan Company, 1955.

Harbaugh, William Henry. *Power and Responsibility: The Life and Times of Theodore Roosevelt.* New York: Farrar, Strauss and Cudahy, 1961.

——— *The Life and Times of Theodore Roosevelt.* New York: Collier Books, 1961, 1966.

Hay, Peter. *All the Presidents' Ladies: Anecdotes of the Women Behind the Men in the White House.*

Hoover, Chief Usher Irwin (Ike). *Forty-two Years in the White House.* Boston and New York: Houghton Mifflin Company, 1934.

Howland, Harold. *Theodore Roosevelt and His Times: A Chronicle of the Progressive Movement.* New Haven: Yale University Press, 1921.

Lash, Joseph P. *Eleanor and Franklin.* New York: W. W. Norton and Company, Inc., 1971

——— *Eleanor: The Years Alone.* New York: W. W. Norton and Company, Inc., 1972.

Lewis, William Draper. *The Life of Theodore Roosevelt.* United States and Canada: United Publishers, 1919.

Longworth, Alice Roosevelt. *Crowded Hours.* New York: Charles Scribner's Sons, 1933.

Looker, Earle. *The White House Gang.* New York: Fleming H. Revell Company, 1929.

Miller, Nathan. *The Roosevelt Chronicles.* Garden City, N.Y.: Doubleday and Company, Inc., 1979.

Morison, Elton E. *The Letters of Theodore Roosevelt.* (Several Volumes.) Cambridge, Mass.: Harvard University Press, 1951.

Morris, Edmund. *The Rise of Theodore Roosevelt.* New York: Coward, McCann and Geoghegan, 1979.

Morris, Sylvia Jukes. *Edith Kermit Roosevelt: Portrait of a First Lady.* New York: Coward, McCann and Geoghegan, 1980.

Muzzey, David S., and Arthur S. Link. *Our American Republic.* New York: Ginn and Company, 1963.

Parsons, Frances Theodora. *Perchance Some Day.* Privately printed, 1951.

Pringle, Henry F. *Theodore Roosevelt.* San Diego, New York, London: Harcourt, Brace Jovanovitch, 1931, 1956, 1984.

Bibliography

Putnam, Carleton. *Theodore Roosevelt. Volume One: The Formative Years.* New York: Charles Scribner's Sons, 1958.

Randolph, Mary. *Presidents and First Ladies.* New York: D. Appleton Company, 1936.

Riis, Jacob A. *Theodore Roosevelt the Citizen.* New York: Outlook Company, 1903, 1904.

Robinson, Corinne Roosevelt. *My Brother, Theodore Roosevelt.* New York: Charles Scribner's Sons, 1921.

Roosevelt, Edith Kermit. *Cleared for Strange Ports.* New York: Charles Scribner's Sons, 1927.

———— *American Backlogs: The Story of Gertrude Tyler and Her Family, 1660–1860.* New York: Charles Scribner's Sons, 1928.

Roosevelt, Nicholas. *Theodore Roosevelt: The Man as I Knew Him.* New York: Dodd, Mead and Company, 1967.

Roosevelt, Theodore. *An Autobiography.* New Introduction by Elton Morison. New York: Da Capo Press, Inc., 1985. Copyright 1913 by Charles Scribner's Sons. Renewed 1941 by Edith Carow Roosevelt.

———— *Diaries of Boyhood and Youth.* New York: Charles Scribner's Sons, 1928.

———— *The Foes of Our Own Household.* New York: George H. Doran Company, 1917.

———— *Letters to His Children.* Edited by Joseph Bucklin Bishop. New York: Charles Scribner's Sons, 1919.

———— *Letters of Theodore Roosevelt to Anna Roosevelt Cowles.* New York: Charles Scribner's Sons, 1924.

Roosevelt, Mrs. Theodore, Jr. *Day Before Yesterday.* Garden City, N.Y.: Doubleday and Company, Inc., 1959.

Roosevelt, Theodore Jr. *All in the Family.* New York, London: G. P. Putnam's Sons, Knickerbocker Press, 1929.

Shaw, Albert. *A Cartoon History of Roosevelt's Career.* New York: Review of Reviews Company, 1910.

Slayden, Ellen Maury. *Washington Wife: Journal of E.M.S. from 1897– 1919.* New York: Harper & Row, 1962.

Teague, Michael. *Mrs. L.: Conversations with Alice Roosevelt Longworth.* Garden City, N.Y.: Doubleday and Company, Inc., 1981.

Teichmann, Howard. *Alice: The Life and Times of Alice Roosevelt Longworth.* Englewood Cliffs, N.J.: Prentice-Hall, Inc. 1979.

Thayer, William Roscoe. *Theodore Roosevelt: An Intimate Biography.* Boston and New York: Houghton Mifflin Company, 1919.

Wagenknecht, Edward. *The Seven Worlds of Theodore Roosevelt.* New York: Longmans, Green and Company, 1958.

Whitney, David C. *The American Presidents.* Garden City, N.Y.: Doubleday and Company, Inc. 1967, 1978.

Wilhelm, Donald. *Theodore Roosevelt as an Undergraduate.* Boston: John W. Luce and Company, 1910.

Willets, Gilson. *Inside History of the White House.* New York: Christian Herald, 1908.

Wister, Owen. *Roosevelt: The Story of a Friendship.* New York: Macmillan Company, 1930.

Wood, Frederick S. *Roosevelt as We Knew Him: The Personal Recollections of One Hundred and Fifty of His Friends and Associates.* Philadelphia and Chicago: John C. Winston Company, 1927.

PERIODICALS

Blackford, Reverend Ambler M. "Quentin Roosevelt: Some Reminiscences Recorded by One of His Teachers." *Outlook* 120: 211–13. October 9, 1918.

Burroughs, John. "With Roosevelt at Pine Knot." *Outlook* 128: 170–71. May 25, 1921.

Cross, Helen Reeder. "Theodore Roosevelt, Father Extraordinary." *American Mercury* 80: 27–39. May 1955.

Daggett, Mabel Potter. "Mrs. Roosevelt, the Woman in the Background." *Delineator.* March 1909. Pgs. 393–96.

Eliot, John L. "T.R.'s Wilderness Legacy." *National Geographic* 162: 340–63. September 1982.

Fraser, James Earle. "Sculpting T.R." *American Heritage* 23: 97–99. April 1972.

Freidel. *"Theodore Roosevelt, Twenty-sixth President."* *National Geographic* 128: 540–47. October 1965.

Halliday. "Theodore Roosevelt, Feminist." *American Heritage* 30: 106–7.

Harper's Weekly 46: 1430. October 4, 1902. "The Humor of Roosevelt."

Heuvel, Jean Vanden. "The Sharpest Wit in Washington. Interview with Alice Roosevelt Longworth." *Saturday Evening Post,* December 4, 1965.

Kahn, D. M. "Theodore Roosevelt's Birthplace." *Antiques* 116: 176–81, July 1979.

Ladies' Home Journal, V. 18, March 1901. Pgs. 9, 10. "The Anecdotal Side of Theodore Roosevelt." (Contributed by his closest friends.)

Life magazine 25: 48. December 13, 1948. "Some Great Americans." (Paragraph about Edith as a widow.)

Literary Digest 65: 83–84. May 29, 1920. "Roosevelt's Home to Be Restored as a National Monument."

Literary Digest 67: 44–48. October 16, 1920. "T.R. in Some Anecdotes and Incidents."

Literary Digest 102: 36–41. September 28, 1929. "How Theodore Roosevelt Stacked Up as a Father."

Literary Digest 124: 28. November 13, 1937. "Reshingling a Roof."

Literary Digest 62: 55–58. August 23, 1919. "Theodore Roosevelt's Grave Is the Mecca of Thousands of Pilgrims."

Bibliography

Literary Digest 60: 46–48. "Personal Glimpses." Contains following articles: "Closing Scenes in Roosevelt's Career," "How President Roosevelt Made the Kaiser Back Down," "The Roosevelt Magic of Winning His Enemies," "Roosevelt's Life at Sagamore Hill," "Roosevelt as a Bird Lover and Naturalist," "Roosevelt's Attack on Sunday Drinking," "Traits Developed by Roosevelt's Ranch Life," "Gentler Side of Roosevelt's Nature," "When Roosevelt Entered Politics," "Colonel Roosevelt a 'True Sport,'" "Roosevelt No Aristocrat."

Literary Digest, September 28, 1935. "Constitutionalists on the March." (Tells of Edith's keynote address for Republican Women's Club on the Constitution.)

Laughlin, J. Laurence. "Roosevelt at Harvard." *Review of Reviews,* October 1924. Pgs. 391–98.

Low, A. Maurice. "A Day at the White House." *Harper's Weekly* 48: 21–22. January 2, 1904.

Manners, William. "There Was a Storm Outside and a Bit of Frost Within." *American Heritage* 21: 42–3. 75–80. December 1969.

Marvinney, Sandy. "Theodore Roosevelt, Conservationist." *The Conservationist* 26: 18–21 plus. June–July 1972.

McCarthy, Helena. "Why Mrs. Roosevelt Has Not Broken Down." *Ladies' Home Journal* 25. October 1908.

McDowell, Bart. "Theodore Roosevelt." *National Geographic* 114: 572–90.

Morris, Edmund. "The Saga of Teddy." *Newsweek* 94: 46–47. August 6, 1979.

Morris, Edmund. "The Cyclone Assemblyman." *American Heritage* 30: 34–43. February–March 1979.

New York Times. April 26, 1865. (Story of Abraham Lincoln's funeral procession in New York City.)

Pringle, Henry. "Especially Pretty Alice." *American Heritage* 9:62–64 plus. February 1958.

Ralph, Julian. "Theodore Roosevelt: A Character Sketch." *Review of Reviews* 12: 159–71. August 1895.

Review of Reviews 62: 314. September 1920. "Cuba's Debt to Theodore Roosevelt."

Riis, Jacob A. "Mrs. Roosevelt and Her Children." *Ladies' Home Journal* 19: 5–6. August 1902.

Roosevelt, Archibald, Jr. "The Ghost of Sagamore Hill." *American Heritage* 22: 60–65. April 1970.

Roosevelt, Theodore. "Utopia or Hell." (Plan for the League of Nations.) *Independent* 97: 364. March 15, 1919.

Roosevelt, Theodore. "American Internationalism." (Address delivered in Rio de Janeiro.) *Outlook* 105: 473–76. November 1, 1913.

Roosevelt, Theodore. "Women's Rights; and the Duties of Both Men and Women." *Outlook* 100: 262–66. February 1912.

Sewall, B. "As I Knew Roosevelt." *The Forum* 61: 537–51. May 19, 1923.

Selden, Charles A. "Six White House Wives and Widows." *Ladies' Home Journal* 44: 18–19. June 1927.

Shapiro, Harriet. "Ethel Roosevelt Derby, T.R.'s Other Daughter." *MS.* 5: 14, 15. August 1976.

Straus, Oscar S. "The Religion of Roosevelt." *Forum* 69: 191–97. February 1923.

Roosevelt, Theodore. "My Life as a Naturalist." *Natural History* 89: 84–87. May 1918.

Viereck, Louis. "Roosevelt's German Days." *Success Magazine,* October 1905.

Welling, Richard. "My Classmate, Theodore Roosevelt." *American Legion Monthly,* January 1929.

Wells, Amos R. "Theodore Roosevelt" (Poem). *Independent* 14: 313. February 27, 1902.

CHRISTIAN HERALD
People Making a Difference

Christian Herald is a family of dedicated, Christ-centered ministries that reaches out to deprived children in need, and to homeless men who are lost in alcoholism and drug addiction. Christian Herald also offers the finest in family and evangelical literature through its book club and publishes a popular, dynamic magazine for today's Christians.

Our Ministries

Christian Herald Children. The door of God's grace opens wide to give impoverished youngsters a breath of fresh air, away from the evils of the streets. Every summer, hundreds of youngsters are welcomed at the Christian Herald Mont Lawn Camp located in the Poconos at Bushkill, Pennsylvania. Year-round assistance is also provided, including teen programs, tutoring in reading and writing, family counseling, career guidance and college scholarship programs.

The Bowery Mission. Located in New York City, the Bowery Mission offers hope and Gospel strength to the downtrodden and homeless. Here, the men of Skid Row are fed, clothed, ministered to. Many voluntarily enter a 6-month discipleship program of spiritual guidance, nutrition therapy and Bible study.

Our Father's House. Our Father's House is a discipleship program located in a rural setting in Lancaster County, Pennsylvania, which enables addicts to take the last steps on the road to a useful Christian life.

Paradise Lake Retreat Center. During the spring, fall and winter months, our children's camp at Bushkill, Pennsylvania, becomes a lovely retreat for religious gatherings of up to 200. Excellent accommodations include an on-site chapel, heated cabins, large meeting areas, recreational facilities, and delicious country-style meals. Write to: Paradise Lake Retreat Center, Box 252, Bushkill, PA 18234, or call: (717) 588-6067.

Christian Herald Magazine is contemporary—a dynamic publication that addresses the vital concerns of today's Christian. Each issue contains a sharing of true personal stories written by people who have found in Christ the strength to make a difference in the world around them.

Family Bookshelf provides a wide selection of wholesome, inspirational reading and Christian literature written by best-selling authors. All books are recommended by an Advisory Board of distinguished writers and editors.

* * *

Christian Herald ministries, founded in 1878, are supported by the voluntary contributions of individuals and by legacies and bequests. Contributions are tax deductible. Checks should be made out to: Christian Herald Children, Bowery Mission, or Christian Herald Association.

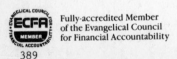

Fully-accredited Member
of the Evangelical Council
for Financial Accountability

389

Administrative Office:
40 Overlook Drive
Chappaqua, New York 10514
Telephone: (914) 769-9000